Shelby Tucker

is an American who read law at Oxford and practised for many years. He has addressed the US National Security Council on Burma and lectured on the Kachins and the Burmese Civil War at the School of Oriental and African Studies, the Royal Scottish Geographical Society and elsewhere. He has also acted as General Counsel for the National Coalition of the Union of Burma.

SHELBY TUCKER

Among Insurgents

Walking Through Burma

Flamingo
An Imprint of HarperCollins*Publishers*

Flamingo
An Imprint of HarperCollins*Publishers*
77–85 Fulham Palace Road,
Hammersmith, London W6 8JB

www.fireandwater.com

Published by Flamingo 2001
9 8 7 6 5 4 3 2 1

The original hardcover edition of this book was
published by IB Tauris & Co Ltd

ISBN 0 00 7127057

Set in Sabon

Printed and bound in Great Britain by
Clays Ltd, St Ives plc

To my companion,

Mats Larsson (despite our quarrels);

our valiant escort,

Seng Hpung, Awng Hkawng, San Awng, Wana Yaw Htung (Peter), Dau Gyung (Timothy), Naw Lawn (Paul), Hkyen Naw (Philip), Tu Lum (John), Brang Shawng, La Awng (Alex), N'Lam Awng, Yaw Htung (Ma Htung), La Seng, Tu Lum, Lahkawng (Mimo), Hkaw Ying and Maran Naw;

and

Ray Lamontagne and Carole,

who rescued us.

With a few simple precautions, cross-country travel is absolutely safe. The jungle covers you like a mist, and you disappear from human knowledge.

Bernard Fergusson
The Wild Green Earth

After a time I knew why I had awoken. It was night in Burma. The quality of the night, of the silence, was different from anything I had known, and it was that which had touched my senses and called me out of sleep. The moon, a little past full, hung a deep orange colour among the high leaf canopies. In the long aisles of our cathedral a pale grey-violet mist seemed to move slowly up the slope, in absolute silence. The edges of the trees round the moon had an unreal quality as though they were not leaves and boughs but the brush-work of a painter, using some technique not yet explored before this, for I was watching the painting grow and change under his hand as the night advanced.

John Masters
The Road Past Mandalay

Contents

Acronyms and Abbreviations *ix*
Glossary *xi*
Itinerary: Dali–Oxford *xviii*
Dramatis Personae *xx*
Acknowledgements *xxv*

1. Fading Red Star 1
2. The General's House Guests 33
3. The Sons of Wahkyet Wa 66
4. The Triangle 103
5. Kumawng 155
6. The Rivers 198
7. Hidden Valley 226
8. Arrest House 269

Epilogue 329

An Appreciation by Dr Stephen Morse 337
Cartographer's Note by John C. Bartholomew 342
Chronological Guide to the Burmese Civil War 346
Bibliography 359
Note to the Author from Ronald Kaulback 367

Index 371

Acronyms and Abbreviations

ABSDF	All Burma Students Democratic Front
ADC	Assistant Deputy Commissioner
AFPFL	Anti-Fascist People's Freedom League
ASEAN	Association of Southeast Asian Nations
BIA	Burma Independence Army
BNA	Burma National Army
BSPP	Burma Socialist Programme Party
CIA	Central Intelligence Agency
CNF	Chin National Front
CPB	Communist Party of Burma
CPC	Communist Party of China
DAB	Democratic Alliance of Burma
DC	Deputy Commissioner
DEA	Drug Enforcement Administration
FACE	Frontier Areas Committee of Enquiry
GHQ	General Headquarters
HMG	His Majesty's Government
HQ	headquarters
IB	inspection bungalow
KIA	Kachin Independence Army
KIO	Kachin Independence Organization
KNDO	Karen National Defence Organization
KNLA	Karen National Liberation Army
KNPP	Karenni National Progressive Party
KNU	Karen National Union
LNO	Lahu National Organization
MNDO	Mon National Defence Organization

MTA	Möng Tai Army
NCGUB	National Coalition Government of the Union of Burma
NDF	National Democratic Front
NLD	National League for Democracy
NMSP	New Mon State Party
NNC	National Naga Council
NSC	National Security Council
NSCN	National Socialist Council of Nagaland
NUF	National United Front
NUFA	National United Front of Arakan
OC	Officer Commanding
OSS	Office of Strategic Services
PBF	Patriotic Burmese Forces
PLA	People's Liberation Army
PNO	Pao National Organization
PSLP	Palaung State Liberation Party
PVO	People's Volunteer Organization
PWD	Public Works Department
SLORC	State Law and Order Restoration Committee
SOE	Special Operations Executive
SP	Superintendent of Police
SPDC	State Peace and Development Council
SSA	Shan State Army
SSPP	Shan State Progress Party
ULFA	United Liberation Front of Ahom
WNO	Wa National Organization

Glossary

of Burmese (B), Chin (C), Chinese (Ch), Hindustani (H), Jinghpaw (J), Karen (K), Lisu (L), Pali (P), Sanskrit (Skt) and Shan (S) words

accha	good (H)
Adeu	Second Son (L)
agyi	headman (J)
ahimsa	non-violence (H)
ahteu	tree fern; its processed pith is consumed as a carbohydrate staple (L)
amen	amen (J)
anda	egg (H)
apka	your (H)
Asoya	Raj/British government (B)
aste	slowly (H)
asura	demon (H)
Azi/Szi	Kachin hill group/their language
babu	clerk/bureaucrat (literally father) (H)
bandh	strike (literally closed) (H)
bara sahib	rich/important (literally big) man (H)
barfi	fudge/milk and sugar sweetmeat (H)
bas	only/sufficient/enough (H)
basha	campsite hut/lean-to (Assamese/Bengali)
baw	head (J)
Baw Hpraw Gam	Hoary-headed First Son (J)
bawi	chief (C)
bawmung	alderman (J)
bawng bam	turban (J)
bum	hill/mountain (J)

bunglat hka	blood feud lasting until a fine for culpable homicide is paid (J)
byuha kyei-ywa	tactical rural village built by Burma Army to isolate local population from insurgents. Much like protected villages British used in Malaya and Americans in Vietnam (B)
chai	tea (H)
chapatti	unleavened wheat flour bread (H)
chaprassi	peon/messenger/delivery boy (H)
chinlon	game in which players compete to keep woven cane ball aloft without using their hands (B)
chitthi	letter/note/chit (H)
chowkidar	warden/caretaker/sentry/guard (H)
chying hkrang pu	mustard flower (J)
dah	short broad-bladed sword/machete (B)
dap	fire/hearth (J)
dawng hkun	intricately woven, embroidered Hkahku shoulder bag (J)
dediye	give me (H)
dep sai	they have caught up/all present (J)
dep sai i?	have they caught up? (J)
dhobi	laundry man (H)
dhoti	loin cloth (H)
Dobama Asiayone	Our Burma Association (B)
dohnwe	fibrous creeper (*Entada scandens*) (B)
du jum	captain (J)
du kaba	great chief/colonel (J)
dukandar	shopkeeper/dukawallah (H)
dum	granary/small barn (J)
dumsa	priest/shaman/bard (J)
duwa	chief (J)
gumhpraw palawng	silver ceremonial women's necklace often made with Imperial Indian coins (J)
hai	is; also used as an auxiliary verb (H)
hath	hand (H)
hathi	elephant (H)
hka	river/stream/water (J)
hka hkawng	ditch (J)

hka kinji — waxy plant that grows on sand banks (J)
hka nhtung — bamboo tube holding water (J)
Hkahku — headwaters/upriver (J)
hkam hkam — koel/Indian cuckoo (J)
hkam htawng — twisted bamboo ring looped round elephant's tail (J)
hkung-rang — hornbill (J)
hkyet — mountain pass (J)
hpa kawp — saddlecloth (J)
hpraw — white (J)
hpun — tree (J)
hting-ga — loosely woven bamboo basket carried as a backpack (J)
i — interrogative auxiliary (*Ndai kaw yup na i?* This place sleep, do we?) (J)
jahkya hpun — plum tree (J)
jahtung nat — wood spirit (J)
jaldi — quickly (H)
ji — yes/prefix or suffix denoting respect (H)
jing cha — police (pronounced 'jin tscha') (Ch)
Jinghpaw — largest Kachin hill group/their language
jumdwi — sugar (J)
ka kwe yei — minority group irregular force allied to and supported by Burma Army (literally you are defending) (B)
kaba — great/big/important/a lot (J)
kadung hpun — silk cotton tree/kapok (J)
kaing — tall grass (*Saccharum spontaneum*), often found on swampy ground (B)
kaja i? — how are you? (literally good is it?) (J)
karap — cane screen/loosely woven cane canopy above a fireplace (J)
kawa hpaw — bamboo suitable for making string (J)
kawa wara — bamboo suitable for making small bowls (J)
Kawthoolei — Karenland (*kaw* country; *thoolei* plant resembling green orchid/alternatively, *kaw*; *thoo* black; *lei* bare) (K)
kia karega? — what can be done? (H)

koonki	senior trained elephant used for capturing wild elephants or in training junior elephants (literally schoolmaster) (H)
la mai tang	bamboo used for weaving matted walls (J)
labu	skirt/sarong (J)
lagat hpun	Indian fig tree/banyan (*Ficus religiosa*) (J)
lahpaw lap	broad leaf used in wrapping food (J)
lam	way/path/route/road (J)
langda	vulture (J)
langu hpun	banana tree (J)
lap	leaf (J)
lasa nat	demon spirit that causes accidents (J)
Lashi or Lahkyik	one of the hill groups collectively comprising the Kachins; also their language
latsut hku	black ink (J)
lau hku	white spirit distilled from *tsa pi* (J)
le-bat	yoke (B)
le-gwin	wet rice paddy field or vegetable patch (B)
Lisu/Yawyin	hill people of Lolo family whom Kachins claim as one of their tribes; their language
longyi	tubular, waist-high, ankle-length skirt (B)
magwi	elephant (J)
manau	festive, ceremonial dance/celebration (J)
mandir	temple (H)
Maru	one of the hill groups collectively comprising the Kachins; also their language
mashaw lap	leaf, probably from a species of *Euonymus*, esteemed for its curative powers; first found in village of Mashaw (J)
matut mahkai jak	walkie-talkie (literally interconnected machines) (J)
mawdaw lam	motor road (from English) (J)
mei	no/not (literally do not have) (Ch)
meugeu	elephant (L)
Mian Dian	Burma (Ch)
möng	place/town/village/country (S)
mu nat	sky spirit (J)
munshi	teacher (H)
myihtoi	oracle of the spirit world/medium (J)

myng	name (J)
n	prefix used to negate meaning of a word (literally not good) (J)
n dep shi ai	they have not caught up (J)
nam dum	lavatory (literally forest store) (J)
nam kahtawng	jungle village built by Burma Army to isolate Kachin communities from KIA (J)
nat	spirit/god (B and J)
naw chying	long drum for ceremonial occasions (J)
nbat	scarf or shawl in which baby is carried (J)
ndai	here (J)
ndai kaw yup na i?	do we sleep here? (J)
ndum	small bamboo tube (J)
nhpye	cotton shoulder bag (pronounced 'm-p-ay') (J)
nhtu	short, broad-bladed sword/machete (J)
ntsa palawng	tight-fitting jacket (literally top shirt) (J)
Nung	Rawang subgroup; also their dialect
oozy	mahout/elephant keeper (*oo* head; *zi* ride upon) (B)
palawng	shirt/blouse (J)
pali	string made from bamboo shavings (J)
pan	flower of an inedible plant (J and B)
pasi tum u	tiny black and white songbird (J)
peimu	alpine medicinal herb (*fritillaria*) (L)
plastik	polyurethene sheet (from English) (J)
preekop	break (from English break up) (J)
pu	flower of an edible plant (J)
puri	coarse, unleavened wheat bread (H)
pyithu sit	people's militia; minority group irregular force allied to Burma Army (B)
Rakhine	Arakanese people
rasta	road/track/path (H)
Rawang	one of the hill groups collectively comprising Kachins; also their language
re	yes (J)
Rohingya	Arakanese Muslim
sahib	master/sir (H)
sai hkaw	rope looped around neck of elephant (J)

salang kaba — revered elder/civilian title (J)
sanaphka — whitish-yellow paste of ground bark; cooling cosmetic smeared on face and body (J)
sangha — Buddhist monastery (Skt)
Sangha Mahanikaya — Council of Buddhist Monks (Skt)
saohpa — prince (S)
sara kaba — headmaster (literally great teacher) (J)
sara ni — Europeans (literally teacher people) (J)
sawn nat — spirit that torments women during labour (J)
shagawng — mountain range (J)
shan hpraw — Caucasian (literally white skin) (J)
shat khat — short cut (from English) (J)
shataw hpaw — bamboo used for splitting into battens (J)
shawa nang kachyi — pendant of strands of minerals women wear on ceremonial occasions (J)
shingnoi — bamboo basket carried on back (J)
si chyee — medicinal root (L)
si nat — death demon (J)
Sinyetha Parti — Poor Man's Party (B)
sumbwi — thorny cane (J)
sutta — sacred aphorism (P)
swaraj — self-rule/independence (H)
taikpung palawng — black silk or satin jacket worn on ceremonial and festive occasions (J)
tat hkang — koel/Indian cuckoo (J)
Tatmadaw — Burma Army (B)
thakin — master/sir (B)
theke — type of tall grass, but shorter than *kaing* (B)
Tripitaka — canon of Buddhist scripture (literally three baskets) (Skt)
tsa — rice mash (J)
tsa pi — rice beer (J)
tsumu — brown mushroom with meat flavour (L)
tuo la ji — three-wheeled motorized cart (Ch)
u kataw — tailless bulbul with red dorsal spot whose song resembles a sequence of hiccups (J)
u tawng — peacock/peahen (J)
u tu — tiny bird with call like croaking insect (J)
ulug ulug — separately/discreetly/distinct (H)

u ra	green dove or pigeon (J)
ura hpaw	large bamboo used to make ground sheets (J)
wa hpaw	bamboo used for splitting into battens (J)
wara hpaw	large bamboo used for *hka nhtungs* (J)
waw	twisted bamboo pannier on elephant's back for carrying passengers or baggage (J)
wawt	leech (J)
Wu Bana	opium cultivators who fled from Yunnan to Kachinland in 1958 (literally Fifty-Eighters) (Ch)
wuhan	yonder/over there (H)
wum bat	interlaced bamboo elephant's girth (J)
Wunpawng	Kachins/Kachin nation (literally centre or core) (J)
Wunpawng Mungdan	Kachinland (the country, not the people) (J)
Yesu	Jesus (J)
yi	dry rice or vegetable patch (J)
Ying Guo	England (Ch)
yup	sleep (J)
Zau	proper name denoting chiefly ancestry (J)
Zhong Guo	China (literally Middle Kingdom) (Ch)
zup	confluence (J)
zup hpawng	gather yourselves together (summons to public meeting) (J)

Itinerary: Dali–Oxford

January 1989	*Depart*	*Sleep*
11 Wednesday	Dali	roadside house
12 Thursday	roadside house	Camp Yunnan border
13 Friday	Camp Yunnan border	Hkai-lekko
14 Saturday	Hkai-lekko	Möng Ko
28 Saturday	Möng Ko	*en route* to KIA GHQ
February 1989		
7 Tuesday	Pajau Bum	Sha It Yang
8 Wednesday	Sha It Yang	Hpundu
9 Thursday	Hpundu	Ting Rawng
10 Friday	Ting Rawng	Lawk Hpyu
11 Saturday	Lawk Hpyu	Shalawt Kawng
13 Monday	Shalawt Kawng	Jum Yang
14 Tuesday	Jum Yang	Camp Hong Kong
15 Wednesday	Camp Hong Kong	Camp Seng Leng Bum
16 Thursday	Camp Seng Leng Bum	Camp End-of-Toil
17 Friday	Camp End-of-Toil	Aura Yang
18 Saturday	Aura Yang	Gaw Nam Yang
19 Sunday	Gaw Nam Yang	Jubeli Yang
20 Monday	Jubeli Yang	Gang Dau Yang
21 Tuesday	Gang Dau Yang	Camp Hpaw Lam Hpya Bum
22 Wednesday	Camp Hpaw Lam Hpya Bum	Hpung Gan Yang
23 Thursday	Hpung Gan Yang	Jing Ma Yang
24 Friday	Jing Ma Yang	KIA 4 Battalion HQ
25 Saturday	KIA 4 Battalion HQ	Pang Sau Yang
26 Sunday	Pang Sau Yang	Shau Kawng
27 Monday	Shau Kawng	KIA First Brigade HQ
March 1989		
1 Wednesday	KIA First Brigade HQ	N'Gum La
3 Friday	N'Gum La	Pan Lawng Yang Mare
4 Saturday	Pan Lawng Yang Mare	Shing Rai Ga
5 Sunday	Shing Rai Ga	Camp Too-Many-Snow

Itinerary: Dali–Oxford

6 Monday	Camp Too-Many-Snow	Hka Mai Yang
7 Tuesday	Hka Mai Yang	Ga Pra
8 Wednesday	Ga Pra	Camp Daru Hka
9 Thursday	Camp Daru Hka	Camp Nhku
10 Friday	Camp Nhku	Sut Awng Yang
11 Saturday	Sut Awng Yang	KIA Second Brigade HQ
16 Thursday	KIA Second Brigade HQ	Tanai Len Mare
17 Friday	Tanai Len Mare	Awng Lawt
18 Saturday	Awng Lawt	Camp Sleep Alone
19 Sunday	Camp Sleep Alone	Camp Dark Night
20 Monday	Camp Dark Night	Camp Tabyi Hka
21 Tuesday	Camp Tabyi Hka	Camp Lawt Hka Lawng
22 Wednesday	Camp Lawt Hka Lawng	Camp Tawang Zup
23 Thursday	Camp Tawang Zup (Tawang Hka 1)	Camp Storm
24 Friday	Camp Storm (Tawang Hka 2)	Camp Rest
25 Saturday	Camp Rest (Tawang Hka 3)	Camp Reunion
26 Sunday	Camp Reunion (Tawang Hka 4)	Camp Torch Taken
27 Monday	Camp Torch Taken (Tawang Hka 5)	Camp Torch Return
28 Tuesday	Camp Torch Return (Tawang Hka 6)	Camp Discussion
29 Wednesday	Camp Discussion	Camp Tarung Hka
30 Thursday	Camp Tarung Hka	Camp Pinawng Zup
April 1989		
1 Saturday	Camp Pinawng Zup	Camp Rain Last Night
2 Sunday	Camp Rain Last Night	Camp Hideout
5 Wednesday	Camp Hideout	Mound of Blessings
6 Thursday	Mound of Blessings	Camp Barn
7 Friday	Camp Barn	Geu Sadi
8 Saturday	Geu Sadi	Camp Muhpa Lo
9 Sunday	Camp Muhpa Lo	Camp Elephant
10 Monday	Camp Elephant	Camp Eat Gibbon
11 Tuesday	Camp Eat Gibbon	Camp Final Night
12 Wednesday	Camp Final Night	Camp Mile 61
13 Thursday	Camp Mile 61	Bulldozer Camp
14 Friday	Bulldozer Camp	IB, Mile 39
16 Sunday	IB, Mile 39	Miau
17 Monday	Miau	Changlang
June 1989		
21 Wednesday	Changlang	*en route*
22 Thursday	*en route*	Itanagar
23 Friday	Itanagar	Gauhati
24 Saturday	Gauhati	*en route*
25 Sunday	*en route*	New Delhi
July 1989		
3 Monday	New Delhi	*en route*
4 Tuesday	Moscow	Oxford

Dramatis Personae

(in alphabetical order by first name)

From Oxford to Dali	
Carole	Author's wife
Carsten	Danish traveller on No. 4 train, Moscow–Peking
Chang	Chinaman in Dali who advised about route
Dany	Swede who travelled with Mats around China
Søren	Danish traveller on No. 4 train, Moscow–Peking
At Möng Ko	
Aung Gyi (Ohn Kyi)	Chief of Staff, People's Army, CPB, Northern Bureau
Kol Liang	Commander, First Brigade, People's Army, CPB, Northern Bureau
Kyaw Nyunt	CPB Northern Bureau translator
Kyi Myint	Burmese name of Jiang Zhi Ming, Vice-Chief of Staff, People's Army, CPB, Northern Bureau
Sai Lek	SSPP Chairman and SSA Chief of Staff
San Awng	Seng Hpung's personal assistant and quartermaster
Seng Hpung	Member, KIO ruling council, and KIO Deputy Foreign Secretary
Suu Aung	CPB Northern Bureau translator
At Pajau Bum	
Awng Seng La	Orderly, KIA GHQ guesthouse
Castro	Our nickname for ULFA chairman
First Son of Sut Lut	English equivalent of Sut Lut Gam, Commander of Liaison Camp, KIA GHQ
Hpau Yan Gam	Orderly, KIA GHQ guesthouse
Kam Htoi	Member, KIO ruling council
La Ring	Baptist pastor
Malizup Zau Mai	See Zau Mai
N Chyaw Tang	Retired KIA officer; formerly served with Northern Kachin Levies; now KIA's official biographer
Tu Jai	Director of Administration, KIO; formerly Chief of Staff, KIA
Zau Mai	Vice-Chairman, KIO, and Chief of Staff, KIA
Zau Seng	Warden of guesthouse, KIA GHQ
Zawng Hra	General Secretary, KIO

Dramatis Personae

KIA column accompanying us from Pajau Bum to Hidden Valley

Awng Hkawng (Du Jum)	Captain, second-in-command of the column
Brang Shawng	Wireless operator
Dau Gyung (Timothy)	Seng Hpung's senior batman
Hkaw Ying	Seng Hpung's junior batman; youngest member of column
Hkyen Naw (Philip)	Our orderly; ex-student; one of 'the lads'
La Awng (Alex)	Ex-student; one of 'the lads'
Ma Htung (Yaw Htung)	Seng Hpung's batman
Maran Naw	Awng Hkawng's batman
Mimo Lahkawng	Seng Hpung's gunbearer
Naw Lawn (Paul)	Ex-student; one of 'the lads'
N'Lam Awng	Ex-student; one of 'the lads'
San Awng	Seng Hpung's personal assistant and column quartermaster
Seng Hpung (Du Kaba)	Deputy Foreign Secretary, KIO; column commander
Tu Lum (John)	Ex-student; one of 'the lads'
Tu Lum	Awng Hkawng's batman
Wana Yaw Htung (Peter)	Ex-student; one of 'the lads'

From Pajau Bum to First Brigade HQ

Gyung Zang	Division Special Organizer, KIA 1 Brigade
Kumhtat Gam	Acting Commander, KIA 1 Brigade
La Nan	Acting Commander, KIA 4 Battalion
Latut Shawng	Assistant Administrative Division Officer, KIA 1 Brigade
N'Gawk Sinwa	Division Committee Secretary, KIA 1 Brigade
Nlum Zau Awng	Owner of house where students in our column were billeted at Hpun Gan Yang
Zau Chang	Commander, KIA 3 Battalion and 253 Mobile Battalion

From First Brigade HQ to Second Brigade HQ

Brang Wa	Villager in N'Gum La once employed by 'Major Collins'
Chyahkyi Hting Nan	Old soldier of Jinghpaw Rangers and Kachin Rifles
Hkawn Shawng	Female soldier at KIA 2 Brigade HQ
Hpauwung Tanggun	Schoolmaster at Awng Lawt whose brother was killed defending Bertil Lintner from Burma Army
La Roi	Civilian Administrator, KIA 2 Brigade HQ
Lahpai Zau Awng	Elder at N'Gum La who represented N'Gum La at Manhkring Conference
Maji	Female soldier at KIA 2 Brigade HQ
Sin Wa	Commander of section that escorted our column from the Mali Hka to KIA 2 Brigade HQ

From Second Brigade HQ to the Vijayanagar track

Adi	Lisu guide
Anna	One of a trio of Lisu met on the Tawang Hka
Ata	One of a trio of Lisu met on the Tawang Hka
Ati	Leader of a trio of Lisu met on the Tawang Hka
Adeu Guide	Our Lisu guide from Geu Sadi to Vijayanagar track

Dramatis Personae

Adeu Hkasher	Hindustani-speaking Lisu who accompanied us from Hkasher to Geu Sadi, then on to Vijayanagar track
Adeu Hunter	Lisu who accompanied us from barn west of Hkasher to Vijayanagar track
Adeu Nephew	John's nephew who accompanied us from Geu Sadi to Vijayanagar track
Afoi	Lisu who fetched Adeu Guide from Midi
John	Lisu elder who accompanied us from Hkalue to Geu Sadi
Noah	Lisu who dissuaded the author from giving himself up to the authorities in Vijayanagar

From Bulldozer camp at Mile 51½ to Miau

Chaunday Saur	Bihari who offered to carry rucksacks from Bulldozer Camp to IB at Mile 39
Devi Singh	Junior engineer, Changlang District PWD, who evacuated us in jeep
Mukerji	Doctor at Miau
Som Bahadur	Nepali in charge of Bulldozer Camp
Zaua Mizo	Zo who offered to carry rucksacks from Bulldozer Camp to IB at Mile 39

At Miau, Changlang and New Delhi

Annika Svahnström	Swedish Vice-Consul, New Delhi
Arun Goyal	Succeeded Kum Arora Archana as DC, Changlang District
Banhot	Major, Indian Army
Battacharjee	ADC, Miau
Bora	Clerk of Court, Magistrate's Court, Changlang
Capo, the	Name we used for an unidentified investigator we suspected of racketeering connections
Chandra	Pseudonym used by official who appeared to be in charge of the people who interrogated us in New Delhi
Deori	Sub-Inspector of Police, Changlang
Gogoi	Transport officer, Changlang
Gupta	One of the Capo's subordinates
Haynes	Assistant US Consul, Calcutta
H. P. Singh (HP Sauce)	Police sergeant in charge of our guards at Changlang
Khan	Pseudonym used by investigator at Changlang purporting to represent Ministry of Home Affairs Emigration Department
Kum Archana Arora	DC, Changlang
Lama	Pseudonym used by investigator at Changlang purporting to represent Ministry of Home Affairs Immigration Department
Mamio	Inspector of Police, Miau
Mansai	SP, Changlang District
Mej	Warden and cook at IB, Changlang
Narayan S. Meyan	ADC, Changlang
Nath	One of the Capo's subordinates
Pradip	State employee lodged at IB, Changlang; Sanjay's roommate
Prem Bahadur	Mej's assistant

Dramatis Personae

Ravi	Inspector, Special Branch, Arunachal Pradesh Police, Miau
Rennie Smith	State Department officer in Delhi
Sanjay	Health officer who lodged at IB, Changlang; Pradip's roommate
Sapru	Lieutenant colonel, Indian Army; Sharma's commanding officer
Sharma	Indian Army lieutenant ordered to intercept us
Sikiani	Sub-Inspector of Police, Changlang
Sinha	Major, Indian Army
Sinha	Indian nuclear physicist suspected of colluding with me in espionage

Those who assisted in rescuing us

Ann Bode	Carole's childhood friend; campaigner for Senator Lott
Berit Larsson	Mats' mother
Bill Cohen	Republican senator from Maine, later Secretary of Defense
Bob Pelletreau	US Ambassador, Tunis, later Assistant Secretary of State for Middle East; author's Andover classmate and Yale roommate
Boudin	American expert on India
Chris Cohen	Bill Cohen's son
Darawalla	Assistant to Indian High Commissioner, London
John Hubbard	US Ambassador, New Delhi
Kaul	Indian Ambassador, Washington
Kit Molloy	Author's Oxford college contemporary
Leo Wollemburg	US Consul General, Delhi
Michael Brock	Author's tutor at Oxford
Moynihan	Democratic senator from New York
Nancy Gentry	Author's cousin
Nanu Mitchell	Daughter of Indian journalist who interceded on our behalf with the Indian High Commissioner in London
Peter Wilson	Republican senator from California, later Governor of California
Ranjit Banerji	Bengali friend in Oxford
Rasgotra	Indian High Commissioner, London
Ray Lamontagne	Author's Andover classmate and Yale roommate
Robert Dole	Republican senator from Kansas, later Republican presidential nominee
Sara Banerji	Friend in Oxford; Ranjit Banerji's wife
Tony Lopez	Member of President Bush's staff; author's Andover classmate
Trent Lott	Republican senator from Mississippi

Others

Angami Zapu Phizo	Late leader of the NNC
Aung San	Burman political leader during transition from British rule
Aung San Suu Kyi	Aung San's daughter; leader of National League for Democracy
Bertil Lintner	Swedish journalist who crossed Kachinland by different route
Betty Morse	Robert Morse's widow; Joni, Stephen, Bobby, Dee Dee, Camille and Genevieve's mother
Bob Tanner	Company commander, Northern Kachin Levies
Bobby Morse	Robert and Betty Morse's youngest son; missionary in Chiang Mai
Brang Seng	KIO Chairman
David Morse	Son of Eugene and Helen Morse; missionary in Chiang Mai

Dramatis Personae

Drema Esther	Russell and Gertrude Morse's adopted daughter; wife of Jesse Yangmi
Edith Mirante	Civil rights activist; author of *Burmese Looking Glass*
Eugene Morse	Russell and Gertrude Morse's son; Helen's husband; David, Tom, Ron, Margaret, Marilyn and Jeanette's father; misssionary in Chiang Mai
Gauri Zau Seng	See Zau Seng
Genevieve Morse	Youngest daughter of Robert and Betty Morse
Geoffrey Rowland	Quartermaster, Northern Kachin Levies, later Anglican missionary to Kachins of Hukawng Valley
Gertrude Morse	Russell Morse's wife
Helen Morse	Eugene Morse's wife; mother of David, Tom, Ron, Margaret, Marilyn and Jeanette
Hpauwung Yaw Htung	Hpauwung Tanggun's brother who was killed defending Bertil Lintner from Burma Army
Ian Fellowes-Gordon	Company commander, Northern Kachin Levies; author of *Amiable Assassins* and *Naw Seng's Kingdom*
Ian Scott	Company commander, Burma Regiment; author of *All the Fours*
Jesse Yangmi	Russell Morse's son-in-law; husband of Drema Esther; missionary in Chiang Mai
Jo Farrell	Mother of late Irish novelist, J. G. Farrell
Joni Morse	Eldest son of Robert and Betty; missionary in Chiang Mai
Khun Sa (Chan Shee-fu)	Leader of MTA
LaVerne Morse	Russell and Gertrude Morse's youngest son
Margaret Morse	Eldest daughter of Eugene and Helen Morse
Marilyn Morse	Daughter of Eugene and Helen; married to Lisu evangelist
Michael Aris	Husband of Aung San Suu Kyi
Naw Seng	Second World War Kachin hero, later rebel leader
Ne Win	Burman dictator
Peter Carey	Oxford don
Robert Morse	Russell and Gertrude Morse's son; Betty's late husband; father of Joni, Stephen, Bobby, Dee Dee, Camille and Genevieve
Robin Jellicoe	Company commander, Burma Regiment; later commander Chyahkyi Hting Nan's company in Northern Kachin Rifles
Russell Morse	Church of Christ missionary who with his family and Lisu congregation settled in Hidden Valley
Sama *Duwa* Sin Wa Nawng	Kachin chief and first Governor of Kachin State
Stephen Morse	Russell Morse's grandson; missionary in Chiang Mai
Webster	Chief of CIA in 1989
Yoshida Toshihiro	Japanese adventurer into the Kachin Hills, 1985–88
Zau Seng	KIO Foreign Secretary (also called Gauri Zau Seng)

Acknowledgements

Besides those mentioned in this book, my thanks are due to John Bartholomew for the excellent maps he supplied, having deduced from my diary notes and existing cartography our most likely route across the Kachin Hills; to Janan Bawmwang, La Raw, Geoffrey Rowland, Evelyn Broughton-Smart, Elsie Ratcliffe, Neville Hogan, Nanu Mitchell, Chunbai Zhang and John Whitehead for help with place names and with the Jinghpaw, Lisu, Shan, Karen, Hindustani, Chinese and Chin words used in the text; to Anna Allott, to whose patience is owed whatever consistency I have managed in the rendering of Burmese words; to Professor Sir Richard Southwood, Dr Alison McDonald and Serena Marner for helping me identify the birds and plants I saw; to Ian Scott and Denis ('Fish') Herring and the late Bill Nimmo, Ronald Kaulback and Frank Ansell for lending me books and maps from their libraries and sharing with me their memories of soldiering with the Kachins; to Nyunt Aung, Bertil Lintner and Martin Smith, who generously allowed me to draw on their unrivalled knowledge of the Burmese Civil War; to Helen Lane, Margaret Hodson, Sara Banerji, Walter Coppedge and Roger Cash, who were kind enough to read and criticize parts of the typescript; to Helen Brock, Elizabeth Scarratt and John Bray, who read it in its entirety, not once, but many times with the greatest care and attention and offered many valuable suggestions; to Hugh Barnes, who insisted on certain revisions, which transformed the book fundamentally and were, I am certain, critical to its publication; to Justin Wintle, who, for no apparent reason other than zeal for travel writing, read all of the text on the eve of its submission and suggested more than fifty improvements; and to Selina Cohen who edited the typescript and set the proofs with meticulous professionalism.

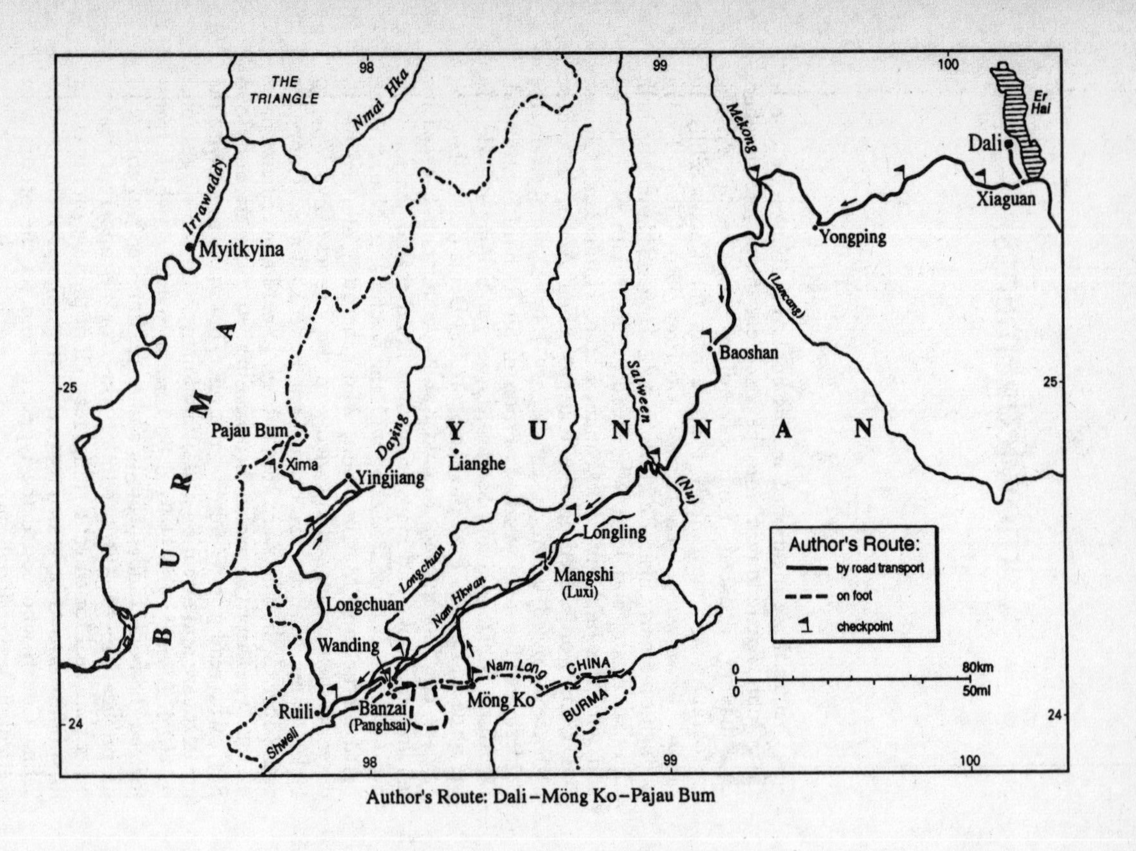

Author's Route: Dali – Möng Ko – Pajau Bum

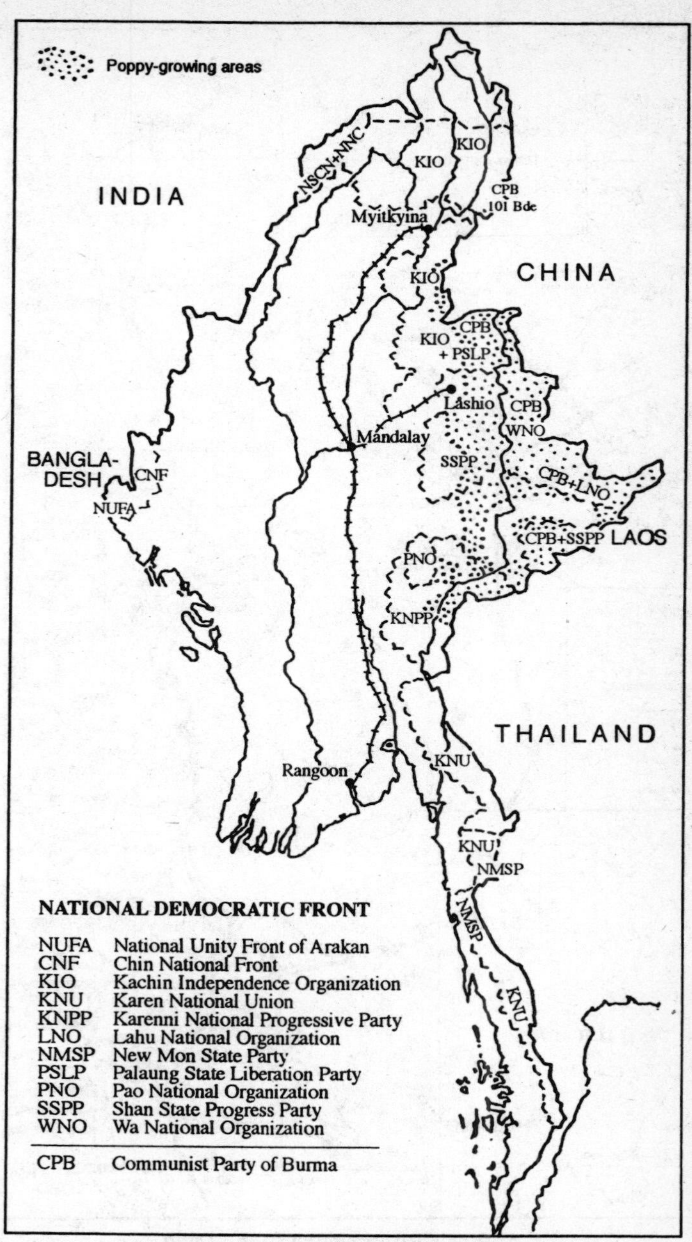

Operational Areas of Principal Insurgent Groups, 1989

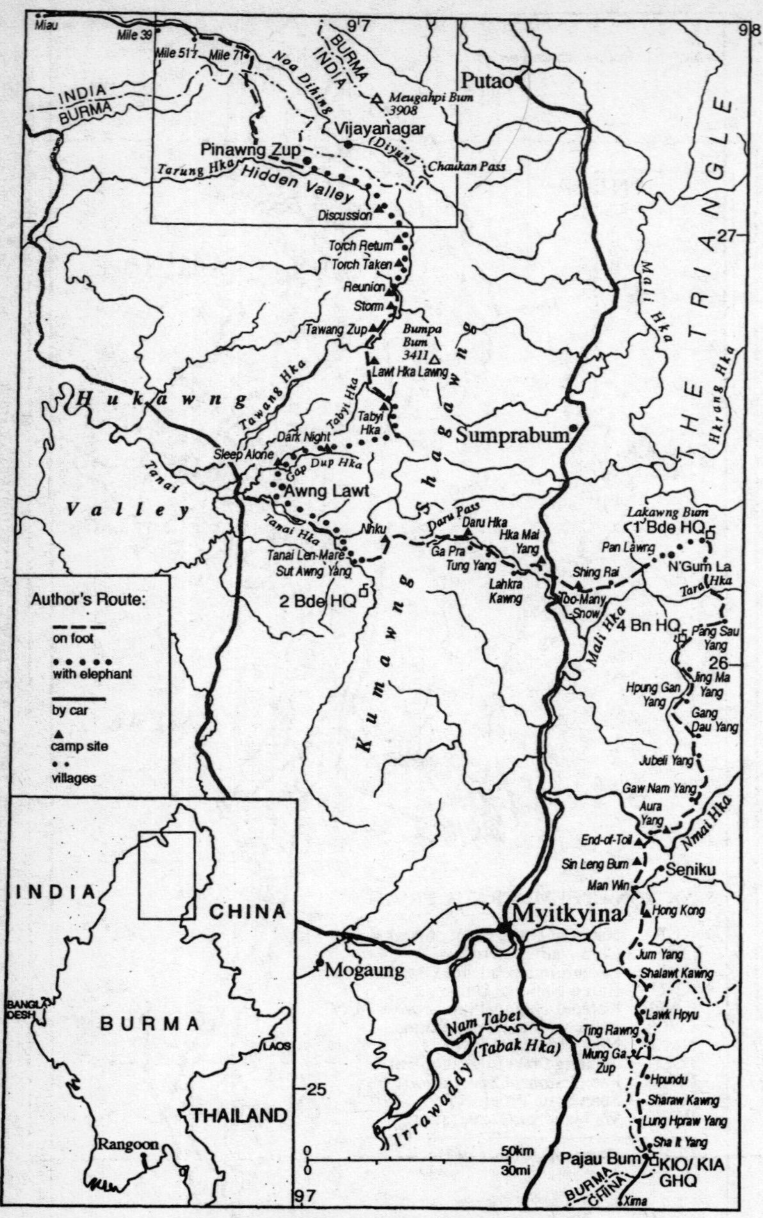

Author's Route: Pajau Bum - Miau

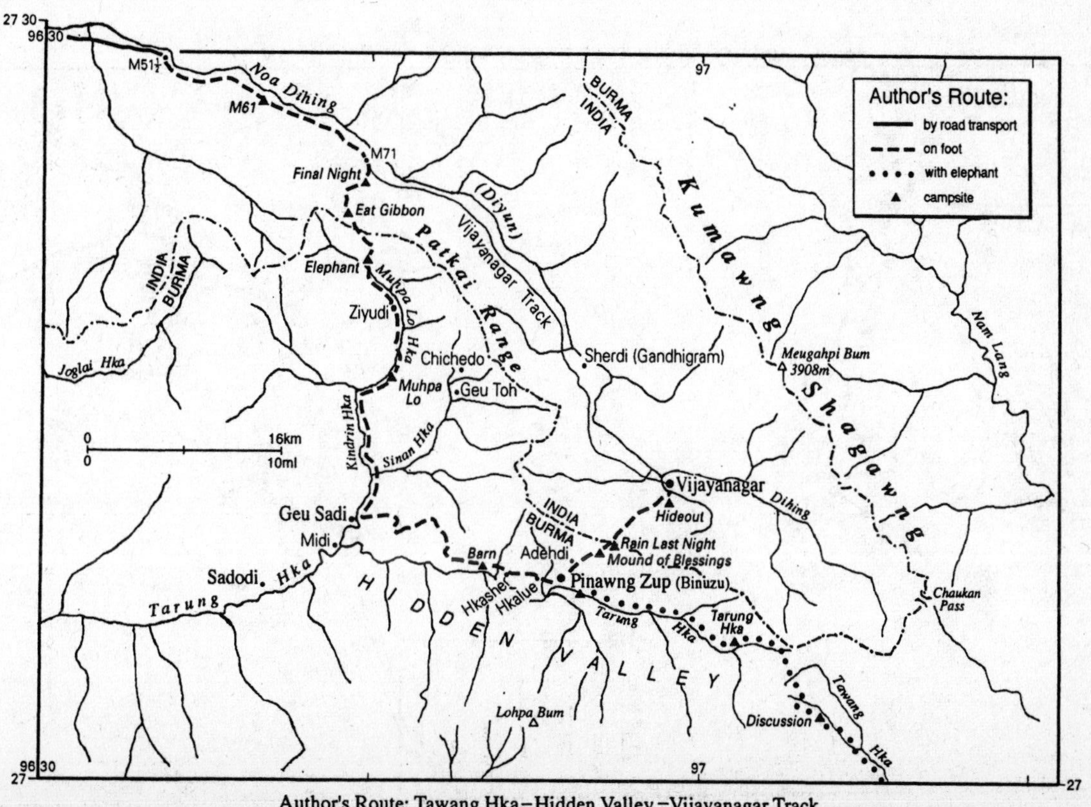

Author's Route: Tawang Hka–Hidden Valley–Vijayanagar Track

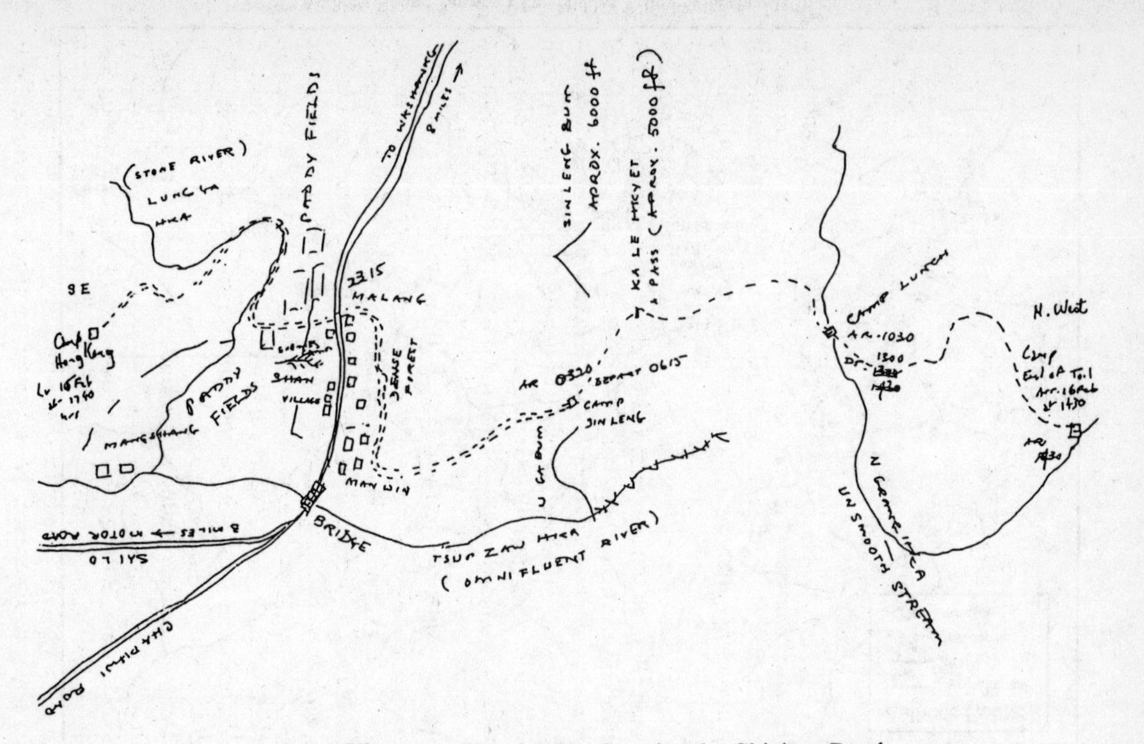

Awng Hkawng's Sketch Map: Crossing the Chiphwe Road

1
Fading Red Star

Some years ago, in the company of a young Swede and units of two armies at war with the military junta that rules Burma, I walked from China, through the Kachin hill country of northern Burma, to India. Our route led through places that had never been surveyed on the ground, but we were not cartographers. They harboured rich and varied plant life, much of it uncatalogued, but we were not botanists. No study of the tribes inhabiting them has been made since E. R. Leach's *The Political Systems of Highland Burma* (1954), but we were not anthropologists. We had no thesis to argue to a public already weary with explanations for the killing and atrocities in Burma. After our trek ended, and as a kind of coda to it, we were arrested and detained by Indian police on suspicion of having 'links with an international espionage network' and being 'part of the CIA's network', but we were not spies. Nor was our interest in the international drugs trade more than the curiosity of two travellers who had never seen an opium poppy in bloom before. Our motive in walking across Burma was only adventure. No one backed us financially, and neither of us intended to write a book about it. Indeed, to have walked across Burma for the purpose of writing a book about it would have spoiled both the adventure and the book.

Until the recent opening of the land route via Tachilek to Kengtung, the land routes into and out of Burma were closed to foreigners and Burmese visas restricted foreigners to entering and leaving Burma by air and travelling to specified areas the Burma Army controlled. These considerations may have contributed to our sense of adventure. Were we out to prove something? Was

Burmese law a taunt to our conceit? Did I really believe, as I used to boast, that all travel restrictions are repugnant to 'real travellers' and that 'real travellers' may be forgiven for ignoring them? 'Can you live with yourself if you do *not* walk across Burma?' I asked Mats when he was undecided as to whether he should accompany me.

I conceived the idea in my youth, but did not act on it until I was 53 years old. Then I resolved to read up on Burma, investigate various routes into and out of the country and obtain a *Teach Yourself Burmese* and master the rudiments of the language. In the event, I did nothing except pay a cursory visit to the Map Room of the Bodleian and obtain from a librarian there some photocopies of obsolete charts. Thus it was an almost complete innocent who, on Thursday 24 November 1988, boarded the Oxford-Link X70 coach for Gatwick and Flight DA 3430 to Berlin–Tegel — *en route* for Burma.

A week later I was on a train towed by a locomotive with an obsolescent red star on its nose. My wife had exacted a pledge from me that I would seek a companion who, she had prudently stipulated, must be young and strong and, most importantly, another male. The train was full of excellent candidates at the peak of their powers, and I talked up the subject at every visit to the dining car, but, curiously, none showed any enthusiasm for the venture. One told me cynically that anyone who professed an intention to walk across Burma was boasting. Another said coldly that anyone who *tried* to walk across Burma was deranged.

Even my wife, who supported me in all else, suspected my sanity on this issue, my 'Burma idea' as she called it. I 'reasoned' with her. She was deeply mistaken, I said. There was no danger, or, if there was, she greatly exaggerated it. She paid too much heed to rumour. Rumour was misleading, nearly always wrong, the common currency of gossips, the mendacity we lived in: it did not deter travellers. Nevertheless, should unforeseen danger arise, I would incur only 'acceptable' risk. But she was not convinced. 'And nothing that you can say *will* convince me!'

In truth, we both knew that reason had played no role in my decision. It was a decision implicit in a way of life begun in the summer before my final year at school, when I left a note for my father informing him that I was off to Mexico. It seemed to me insufficient reason not to go that I had only $1.42 in my pocket: there was a road; it led to Mexico; food and shelter would take care of themselves – *Consider the lilies*... Ten months later I was on a tanker bound for Venezuela, and two summers after that I tramped through Algeria, my first experience of a country at war. In 1957, while a student at Oxford, I went to Peking, then under the quarantine of a ban imposed by the State Department on travel to 'those portions of China under Communist control', and on returning to Moscow was met by the 'eyes and ears of the free world' who reported in equal measure that I was a 'traitor to [my] country' and 'another Paul Revere'. I was on another train in Siberia when the Soviet Union tested the first intercontinental missile, and in India, high on temple music and living on the then equivalent of a shilling a day, when the United States propelled the first monkey into space. I signed on a freighter bound for New Zealand; went on to Australia and hitchhiked across the Nullabor; then, in the winter of 1962, boarded another ship bound for Djakarta. By the spring I had crossed the Mekong with one Hermann from Cologne, and we were travelling through Laos, *avionstop*ing lifts at landing zones and ammunition dumps. I carried on travelling. 'There is *no* land route into Panama!' proclaimed the consul in Bogotá, and everyone else – yet there was, the paths that Indians had cut through the jungle and travelled for millennia. In 1972, when the government of Ethiopia closed its land border with the Sudan, I rode into Metemma on a camel; and when at last I married, it was in Zanzibar in a cathedral that stood on the site of the slave market, placed there by Bishop Steere to mark the abolition of the slave trade. The priest who heard our vows was the son of the man who was Stanley's cook when the Welsh explorer found Livingstone at Ujjiji. He sealed our marriage certificate with his thumbprint. We returned to Europe via the Nile. A notice that my mother posted in the social columns of the *Memphis Commercial Appeal* stated: 'The happy couple are honeymooning in Juba.'

The idea of walking across Burma went back to that spring of 1962 with Hermann. We were hiking through the Kra Isthmus of southern Thailand. Burma lay just over the misty blue hills to the west, enticing by its proximity and mystery. As Hermann the German and I tramped along talking and dreaming in the way tramps do, we planned a kind of mythical journey, assisted by wild but genial hill people who would smuggle us from village to village.

I do not know if Hermann ever got to Burma. He may have died on one of his adventures. I left him in Japan and did not hear from him again, and, by the summer of 1988, I knew that if I did not attempt our fantasy among the hill people then, I never would.

As the train rolled on at a steady 20 miles an hour through the Russian snow, first northeast through snow-laden larch pines, then due east through snow-laden silver birch, then southeast through more snow, I had little to do but eat, sleep, stare out of the window and think. I did not know then that Burma would absorb a decade of my life or more. Then it was only a void that I filled with pictures: terraced hillsides instead of terraced houses; towering trees instead of tower blocks; creeper-tangled forests instead of tangled lawsuits; a garden land reeking with the heady perfume of the moon-flower and the frangipani far from a Europe soon to succumb to another winter. The Russian rivers were already frozen hard and covered in snow. Empty trucks waited forlornly on icy roads by level crossings. The rare villages were clusters of snow-bound bungalows centred on nickel statues of Lenin, always with one prophetic stiff arm laden with icicles pointing towards a metaphorical future that no sensible person could possibly want.

The short, bleak days merged almost imperceptibly with the long, black nights, confusing to my regime of hunger and repose. I was asleep when we passed Yaroslavl and at breakfast when we reached Shar'ya (Nizhni Novgorod), which the waiters in the dining car were able to identify only after debating among themselves. One of them once mistook our location for a place that we had passed the previous day, a margin of error of about 1100 miles; he might have been a sailor navigating through an ocean by the colour of the waves. Once during the night I awoke to find a full moon struggling to disentangle itself from a rag of black clouds, and next morning the sun rose reluctantly, as though encumbered with ice.

At Kirov, an adventurous Swede led a Gadarene crowd of revellers up a pedestrian overpass, only to return a minute or so later to announce that they had found nothing.

'Nothing?' I repeated.

'It's Russia, man!'

I asked him if he wanted to walk across Burma with me.

'Burma?' he replied, puzzled. 'I don't know where Burma is, man, but I'll think about it.'

Two or three thousand miles to the south of us, through the extinct khanates of Turkestan, ran the old 'silk road' to the east, where a century and a half before the clandestine politics of the 'Great Game' were played out. Many died in the enterprise (Alexander Burnes, hacked to death in Kabul by a mob of cuckolds; Charles Stoddart and Arthur Conolly, beheaded in Bokhara). All risked their lives: Conolly drew strength from religious certainties, but I do not believe that any of them acted out of duty to Queen or Country. They were in it for the adventure, and because they loved the outdoors – and might have wanted to test their courage, for in those now remote times the attributes of manhood were still valued.

I got down, strolled around an icy platform and enquired of a railway worker with a woollen scarf over his face, '*Gdye zdyes?*' – Where is here? It was, proudly, my first grammatically correct sentence in Russian. 'Balezino,' he replied into the blowing night snow and passed into obscurity. Some hours later I asked a soldier in a bulky uniform and a fur hat the same question. 'Please!' he cried out in English, imploring me not to speak with him. We were at Perm, where the corpses of two members of the Russian imperial family were found, presumably shot. It was called Molotov from 1940 to 1957, when Khrushchev denounced its eponymous hero and it reverted to Perm overnight. I could not imagine those tired, pale, potato-faced, disillusioned, docile people huddled around the iron stove in its great station waiting room minding greatly what it was called.

After Sverdlovsk (Ekaterinburg, where Nicholas II and his family were murdered) we were in Asia – an Asia, however, on the edge of the Barabinsk Steppe, 3° south of the taiga, where the temperature fell to –56°F – and Burma still seemed remote.

At Nizhneudinsk, more adventurous Swedes stripped to their underwear, rushed onto the platform wrapped in sheets and took up poses that varied from acrobatic to lewd. They joined hands and danced around a circle; ran up stairs and, yelling diabolically, into the waiting room, where a mute, sombre, sober crowd was encamped for the night. One of the revellers put his naked arm around a Russian in the spirit of, 'Forget it, man. It's only a joke. Let's be friends.' But the Russian recoiled, his worst preconceptions about the anarchic West confirmed. His familiar and predictable haven of undisturbed sleep during the bitterly cold nights had been transformed into a hive of demons. Later in India, wondering why we had been arrested and how long our internment would last, Mats and I would remember those empty hours staring out at Russia's frozen infinity. After the guards locked us in our room for the night, we would have the claustrophobia of Siberia for comparison.

Then the sun set over a wind-blasted Mongolian prairie and Burma began finally to assert its pending reality. Next morning we were travelling over a land criss-crossed by rows of tall poplars growing beside irrigation canals and dirt bunds crowded with bicycles and carts with huge, solid wheels. To the north of us was the Great Wall, a pale blue line running along a ridge.[1] Then the great industrial city of Datong hove into sight, a pall of fine black dust. It was 5 December. Carole was due to arrive in Peking on 10 December for a holiday we had planned together. In a few hours we would be in Peking, and, so far, I had nothing to show for my pledge to find someone to walk across Burma with me. Two middle-aged Danes named Carsten and Søren had promised to meet me for a discussion. They now came to my compartment.

With them was Mats. By his own admission, he had come along because he had nothing better to do. He was 23, keen-eyed, about 6 foot 4 inches in height, and he looked very strong. He said that he was a lieutenant in the Swedish Army and that he was bound for Brisbane with a friend named Dany. They had made some kind of arrangement to play rugby for a club there, and, for the past five years, had been saving money for this trip. Apart from a trip to Morocco once to visit his sister and half a dozen weekenders to the Danish coast, he had not been out of Sweden before and knew nothing about Burma save that it was associated with the Golden

1. When President Nixon was asked for his reaction to this monument to Man's distrust of Man, he replied: 'That sure is a great wall!'

Triangle. Did my proposal have anything to do with drugs, he asked? I assured him that I had no interest in drugs and specifically intended to avoid the Golden Triangle. Beyond that, I added, my plans were flexible and subject to many contingencies. I enlarged on them.

'The easiest way into Burma is from Thailand. We proceed to Bangkok and obtain Burmese visas – from the Burmese if possible. Otherwise, we can buy them on the street. There is a flourishing black market for Burmese visas in Bangkok,' I explained.

This evidence of technical mastery of potential difficulties impressed them.

'Isn't that a bit risky?' asked Carsten.

'Not at all,' I said breezily. 'While waiting for our visas, we scour Bangkok for information. I have the name of a travel agent to contact there. Until the riots in Rangoon last summer, he ran tours into Burma. I'm told that he knows the country inside out. Getting *into* or *out of* Burma will be no problem *whatever*,' I continued stoutly. 'The border is porous – people cross at Three Pagodas Pass, Mae Sariang and other places every day. The problems will begin once we're *in* Burma. Three Pagodas Pass is too far south. The further north we go, the shorter the route to India or Bangladesh and the better our mountain cover. Our best bet, therefore, is to attempt the border from Mae Hong Son, northwest of Chiang Mai. From Mae Hong Son there's a road to Ban Sap Mea Sant via Ban Tha Pu Deang and Ban Huai Dua. Ban Sap Mea Sant is about five miles from the border, less than two hours' walk. We follow the river to Wan-Hwe-On. There are bound to be people living along it who speak Thai. They can tell us where we're likely to encounter obstruction. We'll pick up a Thai phrase book and dictionary in Bangkok. The first village of any importance, called Ywathit, is about twenty miles from the border. Ten miles beyond Ywathit is Bawlake, which is on the main road. At the moment I'm leaning towards hitchhiking to Toungoo and hopping a train from there to Mandalay. If the Burmese are anything like other police, they shouldn't challenge us. They'll *assume* that, like all other backpackers, we are tourists. From Mandalay, we take the train to Monywa and hitchhike from there to Ponna and find our way over the Chin Hills to Bangladesh.'

Swept along by the magical force of my own rhetoric, I felt extremely knowledgeable about matters of which I knew nothing. Carsten punctuated the discourse here and there with 'Yeah, man!' and 'Sure, man!' and Søren smiled throughout, willingly. They both gave the impression that their assent was as easily won as lost. One minute they would be high on girls, the next on beer, and the next on walking across Burma. Not so the soldierly young Swede, though that was not apparent to me at the time. I expected never to see them again.

A few days after we parted in Peking, however, I saw Mats by chance in the lobby of a hotel. 'You know, Mr Tucker,' he said in an intense whisper, 'I have been thinking about what you said to me on the train. I do not think that I can live with myself if I don't walk across Burma with you.' But he and Dany had incurred an obligation to two girls they had picked up, and he had not, as yet, made a final decision. We agreed to meet again in Canton at the end of the month. It all seemed to depend rather on how he and Dany got on with the girls.

Carole, full of excitement and expectation, arrived by the overnight Aeroflot flight from Moscow. 'Carole's in China!' I exclaimed, embracing her at the Arrivals' gate. Haunted by the memory of other holidays spent with me, she was dressed in a pair of shiny hiking boots purchased from the Scout Shop in Oxford.

For the next three weeks we were tourists, who, like all the other tourists, praised the food but complained loudly about having to pay in Foreign Exchange Certificates for our hotels and rail fares, and about the crowded buses and the pushy, aggressive Chinese and the clerks who seemed to know only one word in their strangely unpleasant language – *mei* (do not have). We read the same guidebooks, bought the same tickets, stood in the same queues and saw all the same sights. Peking had changed beyond recognition since my visit there in 1957. The walls of the Tartar city had been demolished to make way for China's first underground, and the 16 tower gates with their magnificent semicircular enceintes now were ruthlessly functional tube stations. Temples, pagodas and palaces balustraded and glazed in blue or green tiles, the voluted eaves of their roofs elaborately furnished with mythical creatures to ward off demonic spirits, were no more. The 'city of gardens' had been paved, and over this concrete wasteland now poured a relentless, roaring stream of articulated buses, monochrome trucks, cars and *tuo la ji*s, those ungainly motorized tricycles hauling trailers that are peculiar to China.

We boarded a train, chained our rucksacks to the luggage racks to prevent them from being stolen during the night and went to Xi'an, where we filed inexorably past the ranged columns of terracotta soldiers and climbed wearily to the top of the Big Goose Pagoda. We boarded another train and went to Canton, where sunlit palms alleviated the general drabness. Macau was a comforting concentration of old churches and old cemeteries. A plaque commemorated Camoëns, whose contact with Marco Polo's pagan Cathay inspired him to extol the greatness of Christian Portugal. A ride on the Peak train to Victoria Peak, spending a lot of money on porcelain, faïence ware and silk at the Chinese Arts and Crafts Emporium and Christmas service at St John's was Hong Kong. Then it was back to Canton. And throughout this protracted distraction neither of us spoke of Burma.

Then, suddenly, Carole's holiday was over. When she left me to return to England, hypothesis became reality. Ahead of her were months of anxiety to be endured alone, and, of course, she knew this when she kissed me goodbye. I mocked her fear, but my jauntiness aroused in her no mirth. I promised to be back by 1 March. 'By the first of April at the latest,' I said. But she *knew* that I would not and that the fear would persist through January and February and March and April and May and that she might never know what happened to me; the worst part would be the uncertainty. All those things bought at the Chinese Arts and Crafts Emporium that she had always wanted for the house, that we had not been able to afford before, would arrive from Hong Kong wrapped in brown paper to fill the house with *memento mori*.

On returning to my hotel in Canton, I found Mats in the canteen with Dany and their girlfriends. I wasn't expecting him. They had been to Tibet and were proceeding to Hong Kong to buy cameras and 'see in the New Year'.

'And then?' I asked.

'I have decided to go to Burma with you,' he said. 'Now I will be able to live with myself.' We decided that he was not to waste time in Honkers getting visas for Thailand and India. Depending on eventualities, he could get them elsewhere. I already had my visas. We would defer the plan that I had put to him in the train and first attempt instead a 'China Option'. China *might* not be sealed by a 'bamboo curtain', as I had previously supposed.

* * *

Our objective was to cross Burma, and any route would do, provided that the countries by which we entered and left Burma were not contiguous. The easiest way *into* Burma was from Thailand, but entering via Thailand would mean a much longer trek *across* Burma. We might shorten that distance substantially if we crossed the border where the Burma Road entered China, some 400 kilometres southwest of Dali. Dali was open to foreigners, but not the road between it and the border, and rumour had it that the *jing cha* (police) had shot at a foreigner found there. Nevertheless, we reasoned that ordinary Chinese were unlikely to think our presence there so odd as to report us to the *jing cha* and that the most likely consequence of being caught would be a stiff fine and deportation; that, if thwarted, we would still be free to attempt another route.

Thus the first week in January found us in Dali. It was an ancient city, once the proud capital of the Dai (Shan) people, as seen from its magnificent gates and high brick walls, but little else of its former glory survived. All the restaurants had English names such as Jim's Peace Café and Lisa's and served fruit-centred pancakes, pizzas, brown bread with garlic butter, and muesli. A small army of tailors did a brisk trade in overnight silk suits for reconstituted backpackers; and teachers moonlighting from the state institutions advertised lessons in Chinese. The choice of accommodation allowed Dali No. 1 Hotel (more expensive) and Dali No. 2 Hotel (less expensive). We chose the latter and were assigned to a small, dark, cement room. Outside the room, in a dark, cement corridor, was a spittoon; it was full of sputum and urine. The staff refused to empty it. They despised us and the few other guests for being even poorer than they were and spent their duty hours knitting for their babies. There were notices in the men's lavatory exhorting the guests to abstain from using the cubicle walls as loo paper and to flush 'after making your deposit'.

There was no hot water, and the showers functioned capriciously whenever one braved the cold. Nothing that happened to us afterwards in Kachinland or India, neither wild elephants, nor snakes, nor thorns, nor the Burma Army, nor the Superintendent of Police in Changlang, not even the leeches, quite matched Dali No 2 Hotel for awfulness.

Happily, final preparations for our attempt on the border kept us busy. The plan was simple. We could not travel by buses or taxis, or even by box-body lorries, because the *jing cha*, we surmised, would stop and search them. That left only petrol tankers. Petrol tankers operated a kind of shuttle, the same drivers traversing the same routes back and forth, and there was no place on them to hide suspect cargo. But the *jing cha* would notice us unless we disguised ourselves. So we bought blue cotton Mao jackets, broad-brimmed straw hats and surgical masks. We planned to slump forward at the control points, so that our hats would conceal our white skin, grey eyes and big noses. There would be a brief exchange of banter between old friends through the driver's window, and if the policeman troubled to look beyond the driver what would he see? A pair of Dai tribesmen asleep. Lots of people wore surgical masks to combat pollution. Nothing unusual here, he would conclude. Nothing requiring even a second glance —and, at inspection after inspection, the *jing cha* would wave us through. We would 'sleep' through the control points.

'We need a few provisions for the week or so that we may have to hide in the forest before we make our local contacts,' I suggested. So we bought a dozen packets of dried noodles, some chillies, a plastic water container and a bottle of iodine as a water purifier. We bought a map of Yunnan inscribed with Chinese place names that in seeking directions we could match with those on our *National Geographic* map of China. We found a student and got him to compose for us messages for use in lieu of an interpreter. He detested the *jing cha* and relished the idea of our deceiving them. 'But not let them catch you,' he cautioned. 'They are not nice mans.'

Gleaning information in Dali about the route proved difficult, for no one seemed to have travelled further than Xiaguan, at the southern end of the lake. However, on the eve of our departure, we chanced to meet one Chang, who, during an interlude of

Socialist unemployment, before Dali became a fashionable tourist resort, had tried his luck as a trader. He told us that he had travelled over this route many times. He professed to know it well and spoke about it with great confidence and authority. He liked the idea of our disguising ourselves as Dai and hitchhiking with petrol tankers. Nevertheless, he said, it would do us no good. The restricted area began just beyond Xiaguan, and there were 12 control points between there and the border and another check at the border. All traffic from the border was controlled, and controlled rigorously, the *jing cha*'s dominating obsession being the increasing flow of heroin from refineries in Burma. Inspection of traffic *to* the border, however, was more relaxed, and, if careful – and, he emphasized, *lucky* – we *might* get past ten of the twelve controls. But, he warned, we would almost certainly be detected at either Baoshan or the Nu Jiang bridge, and we should be under no illusion about what would happen to us if we were caught. We would almost certainly go to prison and remain in prison for a very long time: Socialist justice was fair but severe. Even assuming that we somehow got beyond the Nu Jiang bridge, he was not at all optimistic about our chances of reaching the border. In that unlikely event, his advice to us was then to aim for a village about 20 kilometres east of Wanding. He had forgotten its name, but we would find the path leading to it just before we reached Wanding. However, there were many paths from the road, and he did not know how to describe this particular path. We really needed a guide, for he very much doubted we could find the path on our own. If we succeeded in reaching Burma we must be prepared to bribe the Burma Army, which would almost certainly intercept us. Bribes could accomplish anything in Burma, especially if we had dollars. The safest plan, he counselled, would be to wait until spring, when the road as far as Mangshi was to be derestricted.

Armed with this intelligence, I composed and posted to Carole a long letter setting forth our proposed route and exhorting her once more not to worry. Then, next day, after breakfast at Jim's Peace Café, we set out dressed in our disguises. A Frenchman saw us off. He had taken a keen, though amused interest in our plans. He was widely travelled, but he admitted gallantly that he had never walked across Burma. '*Mais pourquoi pas? C'est une excellente idée*,' he said. As we passed Lisa's, a German woman ran out to snap our picture. When, a year later, I happened to run into her at Bangkok airport, she cried, 'Oh, no! It's *you*. I thought you were *dead*.'

The driver who stopped for us outside Xiaguan slapped his dungaree-clad thighs and roared with laughter. In our Mao jackets, Dai hats and surgical masks, we were almost unendurably ridiculous – and imagine not even knowing Chinese! But then everything seemed to amuse him: peasants in baggy blue trousers and conical hats; coolies delicately balancing loads on bamboo equipoises; women harnessed to pink-faced babies; pink pigs wallowing in mud; a goose that waddled onto the road – wasn't life a scream!

At a suspension bridge 30 kilometres on, we came upon our first control post, but the guards, preoccupied with an eastbound bus, waved us through, and our driver was already too deep in another joke to notice that anything unusual had happened.

The tanker made slow progress, labouring up and around hair-pin bends against the grain of the country and disengaging the engine on the downhill runs. About an hour after sundown the light from its headlamps swept over the contours of a woman dressed in black satin trousers and stiletto heels, standing beside some other lorries parked in the camber of the road. She was beckoning us. We stopped, got down and, after a brief but spirited colloquy, followed her into a cane and thatch house, where another woman was stooped over a wood fire, cooking. The only light was that provided by the fire. Half a dozen men were squatting in the shadows. I assumed that we were in a brothel and waited, expectantly; but the woman who had lured us there took no further interest in us. She bent down and kissed a naked baby on the floor, presumably her own, then vanished to resume her decoy role. The men were too tired or hungry or drugged to engage in a conversation. Presently, the woman who was cooking ventured a gesture towards me. Even the baby now seemed to be concentrating on me. 'Because she thinks you have money,' Mats explained cynically. However, the woman was merely trying to ask me if I wanted a pan of hot water for a wash. We all went tamely to bed in an adjacent room after a meal of dried venison, eggs, cabbage and rice, all paid for with petrol siphoned from the tanker, then rose before dawn and drove on.

It was still dark when we passed the next control post, and the soldiers standing guard in wool caps, inert with cold, scarcely looked up.

Dawn came slowly, the sun gradually illuminating the young shoots of soybeans and rice in the paddies and the tile roofs of houses sheltered behind high walls and complicated gates to impede access to evil spirits.

At about 0800 hours we reached Baoshan, its narrow, cobble-stone streets teeming with peasants in padded clothes and noisy, single-cylinder *tuo la jis*. Mindful of Chang's prediction of trouble here, we donned our masks and pulled down our hats, hoping that the driver would not notice. He merely slapped his knees and roared with laughter – these two clowns were at it again! Moments later, however, he stopped at a police station.

He *knew*. Then *why had he not reported us before*? No, I decided on further reflection, he did not know. He suspected and was reporting us now, just in case.

Half a dozen men with Manchu moustaches and wearing plain clothes lolled about outside the police station, smoking – Special Branch, no doubt! The driver got down and went inside. After a few minutes he returned. We studied him for some hint of what was happening. He possessed himself of a length of rubber tube, raised the tanker's bonnet, and began hammering on the engine. One of the policemen seemed to be looking in our direction. Had he seen us? A friend joined the driver under the bonnet. We could hear them chatting gaily above the clanging noises of the hammer. The clanging stopped, the bonnet went down, and the driver emerged, his massive chest again quaking with laughter. The appalling idea now occurred to us that he might introduce us to his friend. We could almost hear him saying, 'Come along, Wu. You really *must* meet this far-out pair of clowns. They are something else!' But he simply got back in the tanker, and we drove on.

We had got past Chang's first big test, Baoshan, and our confidence was running high. Now for the next, the Nu Jiang bridge.

We bade our driver farewell at a road junction and soon caught a lift with a tanker bound for Mangshi. This new driver, however, was no hebephrenic, and we soon sensed that he regretted his impetuous decision to stop for us. What were two rich Big Noses doing here begging lifts, and *why were they dressed like Dai*? He began to question us. We did not understand the words, but we knew what he was asking. We sought to put him off with smiles, but this only exacerbated his suspicions. If we were bona fide there was no need to smile, and, if we were not, what was there to smile about? We considered whether to get down, but decided that leaving him might induce him to report us. Also, there was no plausible place to get down, the hills all around being blanketed in dense forest, except for a patch of brown in the green quilt on a col below, where a thin blue needle of smoke rose from a tiny hamlet. He stopped briefly to inspect our passports; then, still suspicious, drove on. He was travelling at such speed, we calculated, that he would fetch us to Mangshi before sundown. We needed the cover of darkness to slip through Mangshi.

We reached the Nu Jiang[2] bridge at about 1500 hours. A policeman sauntered over. Another truck, another inspection, the same questions, a pair of Dai tribesmen asleep...

Hang on, was that right? The policeman looked again, now with his eyes widening. Disbelief! Then he exploded. Get out! *Get out*! And until now, everything had gone so smoothly. I felt a rush of blood to the brain. Denial, it isn't happening, it can't happen — not to *me*, not to cocky, impetuous, invincible *me*; it isn't in *my stars*; it isn't as I *planned it*. Other policemen swarmed out of buildings to assist their colleague, filling the sleepy, sun-baked compound with their clamour. They clawed at the driver, pulled him from the cabin and began hitting and pushing him.

Keep calm. Mustn't doubt our purpose or its ultimate success. We have made our choice. Now live with it! Don't let them know that you are frightened. And do not excite Mats, lest he give us away. Let them feel our indignation. But I remembered a public convenience in Peking where men squatted in a row over a cement trench. That's what a Chinese prison would be like — and rolled up in Mats's shirtsleeves were the messages the student in Dali had

2. The Chinese call this river the Nu Jiang; the Dai/Shans/Thai the Nam Hkong. In English it is known as the Salween, a corruption of the Burmese name, Than-lween.

prepared for us. *We want to go to Yongping, Baoshan, Longling, Mangshi, Wanding, Ruili. How far is the border? We do not want to go to Burma by the way that everyone else goes. We must avoid Immigration Control, Customs. Do you know anyone who would be willing to act as our guide?'* And, for use only if unavoidably necessary, *On no account must the police learn of our presence.* What could we say? That we had them in case someone else wanted them, and that we intended to report to the police? Chang had warned that we would almost certainly go to prison and remain in prison for a very long time. 'They are not nice mans,' said the student.

For the moment the policemen concentrated on our luggage. They snatched my rucksack and began tearing it open. Just when it looked as though our luck had run out, they turned again on the driver. What would happen to him? He was guilty of nothing save generosity to two European beggars, but Chinese officialdom, reputedly, was even harder on their own than on us. They frog-marched him to a building next to a radio antenna at the other end of the compound, and suddenly Mats and I were alone. 'Just remember,' I said, 'they do not know how *unimportant* we are.'

It seemed a very long time before the police returned to the petrol tanker and our interrogation resumed. Now a young officer accompanied them. We produced our passports for him and, pointing to our tourist visas, made a great show of resentment at the rough way his men had treated us. He studied the passports thoughtfully. 'Visa!' I asserted firmly.

'Visa?'

'*Visa*!' I repeated.

It was a new word to him but he seemed keen to show off his English and did not want to expose his ignorance to his men. He pondered what to do, slowly turning the pages of our passports and intermittently glancing up at us, hoping for some clue as to our guilt or innocence. He studied the visas again, then went back to the building next to the radio antenna, presumably to consult his superiors by wireless. He returned a tense quarter of an hour later and, breaking into a huge grin that shocked us by its suddenness, informed us that we were free to proceed. We surmised that they had concluded that we must be legitimate. How else had we got so far?

By now, of course, we had shredded the incriminating messages and concealed the scraps beneath the seat, where our driver would find them and know for certain what he had really known all along – that we were two bad eggs.

* * *

The *jing cha* had done what policemen unsure of their authority anywhere might do. They had passed on responsibility for arresting us to others further down the road. We knew that their colleagues would be waiting for us – but where? The sky clouded over, threatening rain, and again we remembered Chang's prediction of failure.

We passed Longling, an ugly, muddy place dominated by a sugar refinery, and got down at Mangshi shortly after 1700 hours. As feared, we were put down on a crowded street in the town centre, where we could not disguise ourselves. Somehow we had to get past the town and catch another lift before sunset, after which drivers would be reluctant to stop for us. We hailed a *tuo la ji*. It took us about a mile. We got down and hailed another. Perched on our rucksacks in the open trailers, waving at the people receding through a pergola of banyans behind us, inhaling deeply air redolent of cheap diesel, we suddenly felt majestically superior to more sedentary mortals. 'You are learning me new things,' said Mats. Three months later to the day that same smell would signal the beginning of a motor road in India and the end of a pandemonium of leeches.

As night fell, we caught a lift with another petrol tanker. The driver told us that he was bound for Ruili, which was beyond Wanding, the border town. Burma was now little more than two hours away. We now had to decide how to proceed from Wanding. We had two choices. We could continue beyond it with this driver as far as the Longchuan and follow the river over the border. Or we could get down before Wanding and try to find the path leading east, as Chang had advised. The attraction of the Longchuan route was its simplicity. But we knew there was a checkpoint at the bridge, and if, as we suspected, the Nu Jiang guards had alerted their superiors, the police would be looking out for us and stopping all traffic. We decided, therefore, to look for

Chang's path, reserving the Longchuan option if we failed to find it.

We fixed in relation to the dying sun the positions of several prominent stars to use as a rough navigational guide, and, when Wanding's cradle of lights appeared in a valley below us, we got down. I longed to share our secret with the driver, to tell him that his comfortable lorry might be our last motorized transport for many months and that we were going where there were no roads and only elephants for transport.

Wanding lies on the north bank of the Nam Long (Long River), and where its lights ended, Burma began, an enticing black abyss. Chang's anonymous village was on the Chinese side of the border, about half a day's march east of us. If, therefore, we proceeded to the Nam Long and followed it eastward, we should come to Chang's path. But how to reach the Nam Long? The forest was a riotous tangle of bamboo and thorns, and the only feasible route to the river seemed to lead through the heart of the town. We debated whether one of us should go forward alone to scout it and decided that it would be less risky to chance our luck together.

Wanding proved to be strongly garrisoned. We eluded one lot of soldiers, only to meet another lolling about the approaches to the river. We looked wistfully at the black hole beyond and turned away. 'Whatever happens, we can at least say we got within a hundred yards of it,' I whispered to Mats through my mask.

'Do you think they saw us?' he whispered back.

'I hope not. Let's nip down this street and see where it leads.'

It led to barracks and more soldiers – on a parade square, smoking. We therefore abandoned the plan of reaching the Nam Long by this route and returned to the Mangshi road. 'Exciting.' I said. 'And that is what we are here for, Mats, excitement.'

'It would be just as exciting in the morning, when we could see where we are going.'

'And lose the advantage of our cover? No, we've got to carry on.'

'Shelby, do you realize that we haven't eaten?'

Food was somehow more important to Mats than it was to me. This would not be the last time that the issue would arise between us. But I was hungry too, and there was an inn a few yards beyond the junction with the Ruili road where we had left the lorry. So we climbed back up the hill that we had just descended. A truck was now parked beside the inn, pointed in the direction of Ruili. Its driver was just leaving the inn as we arrived. Had we greater presence of mind, we might have begged a lift with the driver and revived the Longchuan option, but the prospect of a meal momentarily unhinged us – and, in the event, this worked to our advantage, for the Longchuan, we learned later, led inexorably to Burma Army positions.

The innkeeper was an old man, lame in one leg. After eating some cold, oil-soaked cabbage selected from a litter of iron pots in his kitchen, we questioned him about Chang's path, stamping our feet to suggest footpath, splaying our fingers to indicate distances and voicing a resonantly ambivalent phrase, 'Man Guo', to define our destination. In my conversation with Chang, conducted with the aid of our map of Yunnan, I had pointed by chance to Möng Ko, a Shan village east of Wanding on the Burmese side of the Nam Long. Chang had read out to me the name of the *village* instead of pronouncing the *country*, and *Man Guo*, as in *Ying Guo* (England) and *Zhong Guo* (China), thereby entered our Chinese lexicon as the phrase for 'Burma'.

There were two ways to Man Guo, replied the innkeeper, impressed perhaps by our specific knowledge of local place names. One (that which we had just investigated) led south, through the town and over the international bridge to Banzai,[3] and was much the easiest way. It might be the easiest way, we countered stoutly in mime, but, leading him outside and pointing east, wasn't there an alternative route? We indicated that we preferred the greater challenge of a path through the forest. If we really wanted to go by that more arduous route, it was just up the road, he replied. How far up the road? He held up three fingers, which we understood to mean either 300 metres, the distance from the inn to Chang's path, or 30 kilometres, the distance from the road to Chang's village on the Burmese border, which, we somehow managed to convince ourselves, tallied with his '20 kilometres'. Based on this totally haphazard intelligence we set out for 'Man Guo'.

---

3. Möng Ko or Mung Kaw, Banzai or Panghsai and Möng Bo, Möng Paw or Mung Paw are pronounced variously in the different languages spoken in this area, which are Shan, Jinghpaw, Palaung, Yunnanese and Burmese.

We found a path that seemed to comport with the innkeeper's directions. We proceeded without torches until we were well clear of the road. It was a dark night, and I veered off the path and stumbled into a pit, but we met no serious resistance. We followed the path until about midnight, when, exhausted, we chanced a little sleep and lay down on stony ground beside a stack of bricks in a brick-maker's yard. We heard coughing in a house nearby – nothing to worry about but, just in case, I locked my camera in one of the compartments of my rucksack and, chaining the rucksack to a post, took the smaller bag containing my valuables into my sleeping bag with me.

When we awoke three hours later, our sleeping bags were wet with dew and a cold wind was blowing. We quickly remade our packs and resumed the trek. I now felt confident enough to use a torch, but Mats, several paces behind me, preferred to rely on what he called his 'night eyes', developed while soldiering in the Swedish Arctic.

We now sorely regretted the lack of a large-scale map. The constellations had moved and we could no longer rely on the stars we had been using as a navigational aid. From time to time we would come upon a fork in the path and have to decide which of the two routes led east. We came to a T-junction, elected the 'southbound' path and ran into a marsh; reversed and followed the 'northbound' path. It continued 'north' for about half a mile, then turned 'east', then 'south', then 'east' again. We passed a house, the yellow light of a storm lantern seeping through the interstices of its split bamboo walls, and, a few minutes later, although it was not yet 0400 hours, encountered a peasant, who ominously avoided looking at us. He had got up early, anticipating a routine stroll into Wanding, only to meet two giants in facemasks.

We then passed some elderly Shan women carrying wood in baskets strapped to their heads. This ghostly procession was clearly bound for Wanding and, we had to suppose, would report us to the *jing cha*, who we assumed were already wondering what had happened to us. Or, if the women did not report us, their indiscretions about the two giants they had seen on the path that morning would soon reach the *jing cha*. The path was motorable by jeep or *tuo la ji*. How long did we have before they came after us? Two hours? Three hours? We stopped one of the women and enquired if we were on the right path. She confirmed that we were proceeding towards Man Guo.

We carried on. There was no sign of dawn yet. Mountains rose on both sides of us, and the distance between them seemed to be narrowing. We seemed to be approaching a gorge. More wood-carrying women bound for Wanding broke off their chat when they passed us, and a few minutes later we entered a village. The inhabitants were still asleep, but a frightened dog set off a cacophony of barking. Dogs emerged from beneath the houses, becoming braver and bolder until they formed a pack snapping at our heels. I turned my torch on the leader, who bared his teeth and backed off. Outside the village the path degenerated into a muddy trickle.

The path began to climb through scrub forest, but still there was no sign of dawn. We passed some links of steel pipe. A little further on we found ourselves on an escarpment overlooking a shallow stream. Then, suddenly, someone from the far bank turned on a powerful beam of light and directed it at us. We flung ourselves onto the ground and froze. As the searchlight swept the forest around us, Mats whispered to me: 'You know what day is today – Friday, the 13th!'

'Just remember,' I repeated, 'they don't know how *unimportant* we are.'

We decided to wait for dawn, reasoning that whoever operated the alien light would be less inclined to shoot if they could see us.

Dawn found us crawling cautiously but definitively east; parallel to the stream but away from the obscure threat on its south bank. When we felt able to chance it, we resumed walking but soon heard men advancing on us. We hid in some foliage and watched them pass. They seemed innocuous, road workers associated with the steel pipes. In any event, we were confident that they had not seen us. Then, in the distance behind us, we heard the first faint piston thumps of a *tuo la ji* and looked for cover. Whatever the undefined presence on the south bank of the stream, there was a wood there and it was the *only* cover.

The path rose for another 100 yards or so, then wound down to a log bridge. As we hurried forward the sounds of the *tuo la ji* behind us grew ever louder and more menacing. At the bridge we encountered – *coup de foudre*! – a young woman of slim build with full painted lips and lustrous, pellucid, delicately shadowed eyes set wide apart. She made a neat little bow and, clasping her right forearm with her left hand, shook hands. I pointed to the wood and said, 'Man Guo?' Man Guo was east, not south she gestured, puzzled by our confusion and our haste to proceed. The *tuo la ji* was now only a few hundred yards behind us. We left her, reluctantly, entered the wood, and the *tuo la ji* thumped on, steadily less audible.

A few minutes later we came upon a sulphurous spring under a banyan tree, where four young men were bathing. I stripped down and joined them. Then I descried their schoolboy caps emblazoned with plastic red stars and their Kalashnikovs behind some rocks at the far end of the spring. *Chinese border guards.*

* * *

Their weapons were Chinese, and their uniforms were Chinese – but were these naked youths Chinese border guards? They were staring at us in astonishment. I started putting my clothes back on. With luck we could slip away before it occurred to them to detain us. 'Fancy meeting *you* here!' I said with a big, fake grin. 'My Swedish friend and I have travelled all the way from Dali to have a dip in your nice warm spring, and ... this is indeed a surprise!' 'We came here for the excitement,' added Mats.

They giggled shyly. More youths dressed in People's Liberation Army (PLA) uniforms appeared. One scrutinized us coldly and ordered the others to fetch support. They seemed to resent his orders.

We bade them farewell and strode off, glancing back every few seconds to see if they were pursuing us. We trekked hurriedly across rock-hard paddy fields and thrashed about in scrub bush, exploring for a path; climbed a hill and found a path, which led us to a house standing on piles in a field of mustard greens. We climbed to the veranda and knocked on its door and, receiving no response, opened the door and pushed inside. Three enfeebled old men and a young woman nursing a baby were sitting around a fire built on a square of earth at the centre of the floor. They looked up at us incuriously, as though bored numb by Europeans wandering uninvited into their quiet abode. Two of the men were smoking fat, hand-rolled cigarettes; the third was preparing a betel nut and powdered lime concoction that in our innocence we fancied was heroin. Mats offered them some of his chewing tobacco. 'Man Guo?' we enquired. They pointed north, whence we had come.

We protested with various gestures of negation. Surely, Man Guo was south? All right then, if Man Guo was behind us, where, then, was *Zhong Guo*?

Also north.

Impossible! Burma *and* China could not *both* be behind us.

Where exactly did we want to go, they managed to ask after a long silence.

Lashio.

We could reach Lashio by continuing south over the mountains, they indicated. That was the shortest and most direct route. But it was easier to take the motor road from Wanding through Banzai, Möng Yu and Namhpakka. They suggested we return to Wanding.

Something was clearly amiss. How could the Burmese town of Lashio be ahead of us if the Republic of Burma was behind us? Now, for the first time in this hit-and-miss adventure, we consulted our Chinese phrasebook – and, lo, learned that the word for Burma was *Mian Dian*, not Man Guo.

'*Mian Dian*?' we asked, hopefully, and, as one man, they pointed at the ground.

A moment of euphoric self-congratulation ensued. Mats and I shook hands twice, instituting a rite that we would re-enact at the conclusion of each stage of our journey. Phases One and Two already accomplished: we had reached and entered Burma. Now for Phase Three: crossing Burma.

'Plan' is a grotesque caricature of what we proposed to do next, which was to circumvent the border controls and rejoin the motor road between Möng Yu and Namhpakka, then hitchhike down it to Lashio, where we anticipated 'losing ourselves' in a sea of European tourists. Lashio was railhead for the line from Mandalay. We would hop on a train, change trains at Mandalay, proceed to Rangoon and there, with the help of our embassies, regularize our presence; otherwise go on to Thailand by some clandestine route or stow away on a coastal trader bound for Singapore or Calcutta. It all seemed so eminently feasible: we had only to articulate our intentions to reach Rangoon and leave Burma. In fact, there was never the slightest prospect of this 'plan' succeeding. The Lashio road, and particularly its Möng Yu–Namhpakka sector, we learned later, was rigorously patrolled by the Burma Army, who prized foreigners above all other booty. Foreigners unlawfully in Burma to them were proof of that outside interference in their internal affairs without which there would be no rebellion in the Golden Land; and soldiers who captured or shot these abettors of disunity covered themselves in glory. Nor were tourists allowed as far north as Lashio.

Our hosts advised us that the direct route to Lashio was via Möng Bo. They refused to take us there, however. We tried bargaining with them, but they were unyielding. Not at any price, the Burma Army had a bunker at Möng Bo, and the path to Möng Bo was mined, they were probably trying to tell us.

We left them and found another house, inhabited by a woman bundled up in blankets and lying on a bed, stupefied; a man who looked to be about forty and was probably her son; and a youth, probably his son. The skin on the woman's face was shrivelled and had a depressing colour and coarseness, and next to her on the bed was a long pipe, all of which we took to be further evidence of drug abuse. We negotiated a meal from them – but not at arm's length. The man was plainly afraid of us and, while the youth reheated a pot of fermented mustard greens and boiled up some rice, he slipped away, which was disconcerting. Half an hour later he returned with two soldiers in tow. They wore the same uniforms and were armed with the same AK-47s as their comrades at the spring, convincing us that the PLA was operating south of the Chinese border and that we had unearthed unwittingly intelligence of some importance and potential danger to ourselves. Again concealing our concerns with a show of nonchalance, we invited them to share our meal, but they held back. There was an interval of silence while they scrutinized us sullenly and marshalled their observations: we were unarmed and there were only two of us, but who were we? They attempted an interrogation, soon abandoned as hopeless. There was discussion with the man. Then, still sullen, they left. A shot rang out from the forest, but the man hastened to reassure us that it boded nothing sinister. He was probably trying to tell us that it was only a hunter. He seemed quite relaxed now, and when we offered him ten yuan to take us to Möng Bo he eagerly accepted.

We finished our lunch, drank tea and set out. He had not taken us a quarter of a mile, however, before we came upon a section of soldiers asleep on charpoys under a thatch canopy straddling the path. Our sudden intrusion on their siesta seemed rather to please them by its novelty. They wore no insignia of rank, but one, the only one who was not reclining, seemed to have authority over the others. With slight nods and gestures and a few murmured words he roused his men and directed them to search us, which they did with as much energy as they could command. Then he wrote out a chitty, gave it to our guide, who signified understanding, and allowed us to proceed.

The guide now led us off the path and, using a blade that in Burmese is called a *dah* and in Jinghpaw an *nhtu*, hacked a detour through the jungle. (Presumably, this was one of the places where the path was mined.) We descended with difficulty to a stream and proceeded along it for a while, stepping carefully from one slippery rock to the next. The vegetation in this glen was just what we had expected of Burma: waxy, dripping leaves; long, drooping vines and crumbling, perpetually damp deadwood sprouting orchids and yellow mushrooms in a kind of lurid darkness. Then we rejoined the path and began climbing a hill laced with animal paths. Mats, who was very heavily laden, tripped on a root that nearly sent him tumbling down a rock face. Alarmed, the guide offered to carry some of his things, but Mats nobly refused. Here and there the vegetation would thin, and dazzling sprays of sunlight would pierce the dense forest cover, tantalizing us with the thought that we were nearing the top.

Several hours of tedious climbing brought us to a pass. We started down. 'Möng Bo!' suddenly proclaimed the guide, proudly pointing below to a cloud-filled hole in the jungle. A spur of cloud leading west from the main cavity corresponded to a line on our map indicating a road leading to the motor road. Everything seemed to be falling neatly into place, and we were quietly confident that before another 24 hours had elapsed we would be in Lashio or beyond.

Some bamboo houses now hove into view. 'Hkai-lekko,' explained the guide, and, as he spoke, soldiers emerged from the houses, saw us, and came over to us to investigate. They were also wearing PLA uniforms. The guide presented his chitty. They read it and laughed cynically; then began examining our things, and soon were fighting between themselves. 'What's this?' 'No, show it to me!' 'Piss off! I saw it first!' More soldiers, attracted by the fun, appeared and demanded a share of whatever was up for grabs. The guide took offence and marched off; then turned back and peremptorily demanded his fee. We pointed out that we had engaged him to take us to Möng Bo, not Hkai-lekko. The soldiers would escort us to Möng Bo, he said. The soldiers endorsed this plan, so, a little doubtfully, we paid off the guide.

They marched us to a clearing in the forest nearby, where a platoon of soldiers was camped among stacks of guns, crates of ammunition and a wireless apparatus – and for the first time it occurred to us that these jungle warriors might not be Chinese. There was an un-PLA poverty about them; and some of these lads were no older than eight or nine. Two men came out of a tent and looked us over, thoughtfully; they consulted each other and, uncertain about what to do, disappeared into the tent and consulted again. We heard them inside the tent arguing hotly. Then, to help them compose their quarrel and resolve their doubts, they ordered us to be searched. Our possessions were removed from our rucksacks, spread on the ground and again examined, but now in a more or less orderly fashion. An offer of food encouraged in us the delusion that they were treating us as guests. There was an attempt at an interrogation, politely conducted, and, eventually, it was decided to send us with another chitty to a place called Konshua. But we didn't want to go to Konshua, we protested; we wanted to go to Möng Bo, and had already walked excessively for one day. It was no good; their minds were already locked unalterably onto Konshua. No doubt their responsibilities encompassed preventing our capture by the Burma Army soldiers garrisoning Möng Bo.

Three miniature soldiers escorted us to Konshua. We marched behind the eldest and biggest, and the others trailed behind us, the AK-47s strapped over their backs reaching almost to their ankles. None of them wore socks, and their canvas shoes were unlaced. They all had the big ears and bright, wide-apart eyes of fawns, but this fearsome column, we reflected bitterly, might be condemning us to prison. Konshua was a euphemism. They were marching us back to China!

The path divided, and we took the left fork, the right circling back towards Möng Bo. We paused for a moment and looked wistfully back upon what might have been. The path led over another pass and continued along a ridge. Every so often one of the boys behind us would run forward and aim his rifle at a bird. But once the bird was in his sights, he always withheld his fire, like a puppy playing at stalking. The others took a keen interest in these charades and withheld their talk while he aimed at his pretend targets. After a while the little birds would become alarmed by the column's silence and would fly away. Whenever we asked the distance remaining to Konshua (by pointing to our watches), our guards would answer with their fingers, another two to three hours, and urge us to walk faster. We had to keep reminding them not to point their guns at us.

We did not reach Konshua until the next day after noon. Swarms of filthy, ecstatic children greeted us there, and more soldiers inspected our packs. The sedated victim of a land mine, heavily bandaged, bleeding and under a drip, awoke from a deep sleep and looked up at us through dazed eyes, as though glimpsing the first terrible shadows of life after the present. We began to understand that, since our first encounter with these boy soldiers, they had been passing us up a chain of command. They fed us and sent us on with another escort and another chitty to Möng Ko — alias Man Guo.

* * *

The commander of the unit guarding the approaches to Möng Ko read the chitty presented to him and decided upon reflection that, our captive status notwithstanding, we merited respect. He sent us to a plushly furnished, air-conditioned, neon-lit house, where Colonel Kol Liang, a man of relaxed manners with a smiling, oily, round, Chinese face and dressed in a terylene track suit, read the chitty, invited us to sit down and gave us some beer. He made some calls on a wind-up telephone, and Lieutenant-Colonel Seng Hpung arrived about a quarter of an hour later. Möng Ko was the headquarters of the Northern Bureau of the People's Army,

Communist Party of Burma (CPB), and Kol Liang was the commander of its First Brigade. It was their soldiers who had intercepted us. Seng Hpung was our first encounter with the Kachin Independence Organization (KIO).

The KIO and its military arm, the Kachin Independence Army (KIA), controlled all the hills north of the Shweli River and some to the south of it. Seng Hpung was a member of its ruling council and its Deputy Foreign Secretary. He had spent his childhood among Shans, Palaungs and Chinese, spoke their languages, as well as Burmese and Jinghpaw (Kachin) fluently, and had commanded the KIA's Fourth Brigade, which operated in the northwest corner of Shan State (what the KIO calls the Kachin Sub-State). He was therefore the ideal choice of soldier-diplomat for posting to Möng Ko, where he managed the KIO's important and delicate relations with the CPB. The two insurgencies had fought a bitter war but were now close allies.

Seng Hpung was then 53 years old – exactly my age – and wore, disconcertingly in the windowless room, dark glasses. Like all the higher ranks of the Kachin insurgency, Christian missionaries had educated him and had had a Promethean influence on him. The celebrated headmaster of his old school at Nam Hkam, Dr Gordon Seagrave,[4] had died in Nam Hkam about the time Ne Win nationalized the school. Seng Hpung had taught English there before joining the KIO. But little did we realize then, talking to this sun-blackened, incongruously erudite man, what a fascinating organization he represented or how important was his part in it. We knew nothing of the Kachins or their war. Nor was there anything in this luridly plastic place to suggest the jungles that would seal our friendship in the course of the next three months. Seng Hpung then was simply someone who spoke English rather extraordinarily well. 'Tell me frankly, Mr Tucker,' he said, 'what is your purpose?'

'Adventure,' I replied.

He translated for the other important men who were rapidly filling the room to see what all the fuss was about. The plush chairs, the low plastic-covered tables, the beer bottles, the armed

4. Author of a number of books on Burma, for example *Burma Surgeon* (1944); *Burma Surgeon Returns* (1946); and *My Hospital in the Hills* (1957).

soldiers standing guard about the place, the simultaneous playing of a Chinese video and Chinese disco music on a cassette, the strange light and Seng Hpung's shaded glasses produced in me the curiously pleasant sensation that I was among mafiosi. Kol Liang, despite his athletic dress, sat chain-smoking silently, as did the others.

Generals Kyi Myint and Aung Gyi[5] now arrived. Aung Gyi, a genial 56-year-old, puffy-cheeked, bucolic Burman, was the Northern Bureau's titular Chief of Staff – but its real commander was Kyi Myint, who was nearly twenty years younger. The Chinese had ruled the CPB by proxy since its expulsion from the Pegu Yomas in the 1970s. The 'Criticize Liu Shaoqi and Confucius Campaign' was then in full flood, and Kyi Myint, alias Jiang Zhi Ming, had been among the thousands of 'volunteers' who forded the Nam Long and 'assisted' the CPB in seizing 8000 square miles of northern Burma. They had anticipated another Long March leading to another victory of peasants and workers, though Kyi Myint was less zealous than other Red Guards (whom he had restrained from murdering their teachers). In common with millions of other Chinese schoolboys, it had simply been his dream to emulate Mao. Disenchantment had come later: when the CPB's leaders called Deng Xiaoping a 'revisionist renegade', China withdrew its support for their cause, and some elements within the CPB resorted to narcotics to finance the Revolution. But all that, too, remained for us to discover. For the moment, Kyi Myint was just another man wearing a schoolboy cap with a red star, who was curious about who we were and, like Seng Hpung, seemed to have both power and personality.

He now interrogated us through one of his interpreters, a half-Chinese young man named Kyaw Nyunt (pronounced 'Jaw Juan'), a University of Rangoon law student who had fled to the CPB after the student repression that followed the U Thant Riots in central Burma in December 1974. Kyaw Nyunt spoke at great speed with many bursts of enthusiasm, and, like our Falstaffian

5. I have spelled the name as it was spelled for me in Möng Ko and appears in my diary and as others have since confirmed that it should be spelled. Bertil Lintner, whose knowledge of the CPB is immeasurably superior to mine, spells it Ohn Kyi.

tanker driver, everything seemed to strike him as absurd. He announced that Kyi Myint had instructed him to conduct this investigation because it was the sort of nonsense that his unpredictable superiors required of him! He worked for Intelligence – wasn't that ridiculous for somebody with only half a nut for a brain? Requesting our passports and noting the particulars, he asked, 'May I know your profession?' 'Writer,' I said. 'Writer?' he repeated, incredulously. 'Yes, writer.' 'You are journalist?' 'No,' I corrected, 'I write books.' 'May I know who is publishing?' 'No one publishes my books. It is humiliating. However, I am a *real* writer, who writes despite great and constant discouragement.' That, too, was absurd. 'What books might you be making?' 'The book that I was working on when I left home is called *The Last Banana*.' 'Banana?' 'As in banana, B-A-N-A-N-A, the fruit.' 'The Last Banana?' 'Yes, *The Last Banana*.' That was the most absurd of all. But he carefully noted it all down. A stamp in my passport inspired momentary concern. 'Begging your pardon, what is this?' I examined the stamp and replied, 'Botswana.' 'It is like Burmese name.' 'Perhaps it is. But it's African.' 'Have you been to Burma before?' 'Not before yesterday.' This investigation was becoming ever more absurd by the minute.

We would spend more than a fortnight here, during which time many exciting things happened. Apart from Seng Hpung and Kyi Myint, we would meet the great half-Shan, half-Gurkha Sai Lek, Chairman and General Secretary of the Shan State Progress Party (SSPP) and a formidable jungle warrior. We would meet captured Burma Army soldiers, including a major taken in a recent engagement. We would hear the biographies of a lot of revolutionary heroes and learn a great deal about the CPB and other insurgencies and the symbiosis between the war in Burma and the opium trade. I would write a long article distilling my thoughts on these important matters, another trophy of *real* writing, but nothing was so exciting as this first night with our revolutionary hosts.

More beer was fetched – it seemed a great luxury after the worry and strain of our hike from Wanding – and dinner was ordered. More people in caps with red stars arrived. Everyone wanted to see the two exotic Big Noses captured in the forest. And, in response to Seng Hpung's rather gentle prompting, I told our story. I spoke of the clandestine journey southwest from Dali, of our near disaster at the Nu Jiang bridge control point and of groping about Wanding in quest of Chang's hypothetical path. I spoke of the beam of light that sent us hurtling to the ground just before dawn and of our subsequent arrest by their 'boys in the forest'. I put on the full disguise, Mao jacket, straw hat and facemask as a demonstration, provoking gales of laughter. Mats's very size provoked laughter. It was difficult to disguise such an un-Chinese giant, remarked Seng Hpung. Someone went over, picked up Mats's rucksack and paid tribute to its extreme weight and to the strength of the giant able to carry such a burden, and everyone else followed suit. At my insistence and to gasps of amazement, Mats then demonstrated his Swedish Army, arms-through-straps-and-hoist-over-head technique of harnessing his pack. 'Sir Edmund Hilary did not ascend Everest for the view,' I said. 'No,' agreed Seng Hpung, 'he did it simply for the adventure.' I felt that we were gaining ground.

At about 2100 hours – it seemed a late hour – the Northern Bureau's Transport Division, an ancient trap of Chinese make, arrived to fetch us to our billet. Everyone urged me to sit in the front seat. I refused, protesting that this privilege, surely, belonged to the Northern Bureau's distinguished commanders. A young Wa soldier crank-started the vehicle and we drove about two hundred metres to another house. There Kyi Myint directed us with our things to a room furnished with two beds and where about twenty heavy, army-green quilts and a belt with an empty pistol holster hanging from the rafters were stored. This was his house, he announced, and this was where we would stay. But the night was still far from over. Kyi Myint wanted to show us a video film. So more beer was fetched and soon we were viewing a convoy of elephants striding through jungle and listening to Swedish! It was the *Swedish Evening News* broadcast of Bertil Lintner's documentary of his trip across Kachinland and our introduction to this intrepid man, who had entered Burma from Nagaland, was passed on by Nagas to the KIA and by the KIA to the People's Army, which smuggled him across a part of China and then escorted him east until he was too ill to continue, when they smuggled him back into China.

The electricity failed suddenly, abruptly ending the documentary. But listening to Swedish television in the house of the Vice-

Chief of Staff, People's Army, Northern Bureau, was not the least marvellous thing that had happened to us already. If Bertil Lintner could cross Burma, so could we. Before retiring that night Mats and I congratulated ourselves again, and, later in bed, laughed, almost cried ourselves to sleep. Our adventure had begun.

2

The General's House Guests

Our euphoria was premature. Our hosts were gracious, but we were a puzzle to them. It seemed to them implausible that a man of 53, accompanied by a bodyguard (Mats) had no purpose in Burma other than adventure. My attempts to explain the 'Everest principle' (which drives people who have nothing better to do to attempt what is absolutely useless) merely deepened their suspicions. What exactly were we hiding? The guards, they said, were for our own protection.

'What do you want from *me*?' I asked Seng Hpung, after repeating that I was not a journalist.

'We are hidden colonies,' he replied. 'No one ever comes here, and you are here. Everyone ignores us, and you claim that you write books. We want you to *tell the truth*.' It was a metaphor for disaster.[1]

Of Burma, a large basin arched by hills, through which the Chindwin, Irrawaddy, Sittang and lower Salween rivers flow, it could be said (as Peter Fleming decreed of Sinkiang in 1936), 'Her destinies are being worked out by methods and towards ends which their manipulators are the reverse of anxious to advertise.' Burmans, mainly, inhabit the middle, flat land, while people with markedly different languages, customs and traditions inhabit the

1. 'I have been trying to follow and understand the politics of Burma for more than thirty years and fear that I still do not have a real grasp of the intricacies of the players and the goals of some.' (Professor Josef Silverstein in a letter dated 24 October 1989 to the author.) The most comprehensive account of the Burmese Civil War is Martin Smith's *Burma: Insurgency and the Politics of Ethnicity* (1991).

hills.[2] They are (naming only the larger groups as they occur cartologically from the Tenasserim in the southeast to Arakan in the southwest) the Peshus, Salons, Mons, Karens, Karennis, Padaungs, Shans, Lahus, Akhas, Was, Paos, Kokangs, Palaungs, Kachins, Nagas, Chins and Rakhines.[3] Competing religions include Buddhism, Christianity, Hinduism, Islam, Confucianism, Animism and Shamanism. The Kachins and Nagas and many of the Karens, Karennis, Lahus, Akhas, Palaungs and Chins are Christians; the Peshus, Salons and some of the Karens, Mons, Was and Rohingyas are Muslims; the Burmans, Shans and Paos and most Karens, Mons, Karennis and Palaungs are Buddhists.

The Burmans have claimed suzerainty over the hill tracts for centuries, but their hold on them was never secure, the hill peoples as often according nominal tribute to the kings of Siam as to the kings of Burma and sometimes themselves reducing the Burmans to submission. Karens and Mons, who lived in closest proximity to the Burmans, had a particularly parlous relationship with them.

British conquest (1824–85) exacerbated these divisions. Thereafter, Burma Proper (central Burma) was administered directly from Delhi, while British policy towards the hill peoples (the Frontier Areas or hill tracts) was largely to leave them under the governance of their hereditary *saohpa*s, *duwa*s and *bawi*s (rajahs) and village councils. The hill peoples thus perceived the Pax Britannica as deliverance from the Burmans, while the British

---

2. 'Although writers have used the terms Burman and Burmese in a variety of ways, most scholars since World War II use them as follows: Burman is an ethnic term identifying a particular group in Burma. Burmese is a political term including all the inhabitants of the country – Burmans, Karens, Shans, Kachins, Chins, Mons and so on' (Silverstein, 1977: 4).
3. A determined ethnographic assault made on the population of Burma in 1917 disclosed 242 languages and dialects, and, in consequence, the extension of the *Linguistic Survey of India* to Burma was abandoned as 'a thing beyond our present capacity' (Enriquez, 1933: *xiii–xiv*).

found in the hill peoples an abundant source of dependable soldiery with which to control the Burmans.[4]

Christian proselytization was the effect rather than the instrument of British conquest, but proselytization there was, especially among Burma's increasingly Anglicized minorities, and baptism came to assume to the resentful Burmans the significance of a badge of foreign allegiance.

The qualities that endeared the barrel-chested hill peoples to the British *asoya* outraged the Burmans, whose self-styled 'golden land' epitomized for them civilization. This golden land, unlike the wild hills, had roads and irrigation canals, art, architecture, literature and true religion.[5] Every Burman boy learned from the monks how to read, write and chant the beneficial *sutta* (sacred aphorisms) that resounded in the karma-cumulative heavens of the All-Enlightened One. Even the British allowed that the Kachins were 'dirty, ugly and barbarian' (Fytche) and 'robbers who systematically plunder caravans whenever they get the chance' (Davies).[6] Horrific stories reached them, of stacks of sacrificial human skulls in Wa and Naga villages. Kengtung, a valley town near the Was, even boasted a market for human skulls, partly supplied from executed prisoners. Nevertheless, the British used these barbarians and dacoits to hold them in subjection.

Meanwhile, the opening of Burma to the outside world, new

---

4. At least three-quarters of the native levies were Kachin, Karen and Chin. '1st, 2nd, 3rd and 4th Battalions of Burma Rifles each consisted of 4 rifle companies – two Karen and one each, Chin and Kachin. There were no Burmans in the Burma Rifles until just before the war, when one company was tried out in each of the 5th and 6th Battalions. The Burma Military Police and Frontier Force had no Burmans at any time.' (Letter to the author from Lieutenant-Colonel Ian Scott, formerly commander of 4 Burma Regiment and, before that, commander of Burma Frontier Force.) 'A Government reply to a question [in the Rangoon House of Representatives] revealed that [in 1938] there were only 159 Burmans, 3040 other indigenous races, 1423 Indians and 1587 British soldiers in the Burma Army' (Maung Maung, 1959: 42). According to a contemporary recruiting manual (Enriquez, 1933: *xi*, 6), the hill tribes were 'valuable military material' whose martial superiority could be demonstrated anthropometrically in the mean chest sizes of the recruits.
5. There is irony in this conceit. The Mons, not the Burmans, brought Buddhism to Burma.
6. Enriquez, 1933: 32.

legal and commercial institutions and industrial techniques, improved sea transportation and a rising demand for rice overseas were steadily changing the golden land from a subsistence to an exchange economy. Instead of a few trading concessions liberally granted to the East India Company and withdrawn during the seventeenth and eighteenth centuries, foreign companies, such as Steel Brothers, Burmah Oil, the Bombay Burmah Trading Corporation, the Burmah Ruby Mines Company, Patrick Henderson & Company and the Irrawaddy Flotilla Company, now dominated its banking, industry and commerce. Indians flooded into the land in such numbers that nearly half of the population of Rangoon was Indian. Cultivators unfamiliar with the new institutions came to depend on Indian moneylenders, who seized their land when they were unable to repay their debts and sold it to speculators. Increasing numbers of deracinated peasants drifted into the new cities, precipitating from an already potent mixture race riots that the authorities would only be able to contain with difficulty. Most of the conditions for the civil war were thus in place by the first decade of this century. The Burmans felt aggrieved. They were the majority community, yet foreigners made most of the important decisions affecting their lives and economy. An alien religion was spreading among them. English was replacing Burmese as the language of the educated elite. Alien institutions were displacing the influence of the *sangha* and western newspapers and books, the *Tripitaka*. This inversion of the natural order, the Burmans believed, would not have been possible but for the treasonable collaboration with the British invaders of some of the despised minorities — their former subjects.

Professor Silverstein traces the origin of the Burmese independence movement to the Young Men's Buddhist Association, established in 1906 and transformed into the General Council of Burmese Associations in 1920, the year of the first student-fomented strike. A decade later a self-proclaimed messiah named Saya San brought things to a test by convincing his disciples that their tattoos, amulets and magic shirts would repel bullets. Nationalist organizations such as the *Dobama Asiayone* (Our Burma Association) and the *Sinyetha Parti* (Poor Man's Party), which fused messianic notions of Buddhism with the egalitarian concerns of Western democracy, proliferated. Almost all the prominent agitators were students, and the main forum for their grievances was the Rangoon University Students Union. They co-opted an honorific, *thakin* (master), previously reserved for the British. Thakin Nu, who had been elected the Union's president, and Thakin Aung San (Sparkling Victory),[7] who edited the students' magazine, catapulted to national fame when the university backed off from expelling them under pressure of a students' strike.

As war was breaking out in Europe, the CPB was formed, and Aung San, who left Burma clandestinely the following year on a ship bound for Japanese-occupied Amoy, was its first General Secretary. By the time the war reached Burma, Burma Proper was already a diarchy with an elected assembly and cabinet responsible to it in respect of nearly all internal matters – reforms designed to prepare the country for independence but opposed by the more radical agitators among the Burmans (who dismissed them as mere tactics aimed at dividing opposition to British rule); by the minorities (who wanted less, not more 'home rule', which, to them, simply implied a reversion to Burman privilege, corruption, chicanery, intolerance and oppression – fears reinforced by the ever increasing communal tension in the streets); and by their traditional rulers (who saw that democracy must inevitably undermine the aristocratic basis of their own position). The Japanese invasion on 11 December 1941 probably ended whatever prospect remained for a peaceful resolution of these divisions and tensions. Rangoon fell on 7 March and, by the middle of April, all that survived of the hill peoples' protectors were some half-starved, malaria-jaundiced stragglers from the general exodus and the nucleus of a guerrilla force in the Karen Hills under Major Hugh Seagrim.

In the wake of the Japanese Fifteenth Army came Aung San and 29 other *thakin*s (the 'Thirty Comrades') at the head of the Burma Independence Army (BIA). Ian Morrison, in his biography of Seagrim, describes their contribution to the Japanese war effort:

As the British withdrew, thousands of miscreants were

---

7. The father of the leader of the National League for Democracy, Daw Aung San Suu Kyi, detained under house arrest in Rangoon from July 1989 until July 1995.

> released from the gaols. These flocked to the standard of the BIA. The term BIA suggests an army. In reality it was little more than a horde of undisciplined riff-raff. Many Burmese joined the BIA or started to call themselves Thakins because it gave them power, others because they hoped thereby to protect themselves and their property, others because they were out for loot and saw an opportunity of looting under a cloak of legality.[8]

The BIA unit sent to subjugate the Karens in Papun imprisoned, then massacred the elders, looted and incinerated the villages and molested the women. The BIA unit occupying Kadaingti announced that the Japanese had licensed them to kill Christians and required the Christians to pay homage to some Buddhist monks in their party. The Karens responded in kind, and, by the end of May, there was communal war between the Burmans and Karens throughout Salween District. Similarly in the Irrawaddy Delta, where were concentrated most of the Plains Karens. The BIA rabble garrisoning Myaungmya went

> to the Roman Catholic Mission compound ... and ... proceeded to massacre 152 men, women and children in cold blood. ... Father Blasius, the Karen priest in charge, was sick in the clergy-house. The Burmans set fire to the house and burned him and the two men who were looking after him. They then burned down the church, first removing the surplices and chalice. At the orphanage another Karen priest, Father Pascal, came out on to the veranda and said there were only girls inside. The Burmans shot him in the stomach. The girls took refuge upstairs. The Burmans shot up through the ceiling [and w]hen certain [that] there were no armed men upstairs ... went up and cut down the girls with *dah*s. Another Karen priest, Father Gaspar, was killed from behind with an axe. Four Karen lay sisters were killed. The great majority of the girls were cut down inside the mission compound, some on the road outside. The youngest victim was a baby of six months. Only about half

8. Morrison, 1947: 68–9.

> a dozen children escaped. The remaining buildings were then razed to the ground. ... [T]hese hysterical Burmans ... [then] went in a mass to the ... Karen quarter ... on the other side of the town. Here they killed another fifty-two people, all Karens, men, women and children. ... A few days later forty-seven Karen men were taken out [of gaol] and bayoneted to death.[9]

The Thirty Comrades were not entirely to blame for these horrors and Aung San patched up things with the Karen leaders. But, as events proved, the blood-letting had gone too far. The Kachins experienced similar behaviour. The BIA units that preceded the Japanese Army into Myitkyina demanded the villagers' arms, looted them, abducted the women, raped and killed them.[10] The subsequent support given to Aung San by their postwar leaders did not erase these memories in the wider Kachin community.

By the spring of 1945 the Japanese were in full retreat. No one still believed in their Co-Prosperity Sphere, and the opposition was already united in the Anti-Fascist People's Freedom League (AFPFL). The BIA, which had already undergone a permutation of names, now declared for the British as the Burma National Army and was renamed yet again as the Patriotic Burmese Forces (PBF). Aung San controlled both the AFPFL and the PBF. Most of the British soldiers wanted to execute him as a traitor, but others saw in this charming chameleon the only Burman who could rally sufficient support to ensure the stability essential to protect British commercial interests in an independent Burma, and this was the

9. Morrison, 1947: 188–9.
10. The Kachins were also beastly to the Burmans. A correspondent (who has requested anonymity) remembers capturing a Japanese rifle in March 1942, before the BIA units reached Kachinland. 'I examined the rifle with much interest, reaching the conclusion that it was greatly inferior to our Lee Enfield. A Kachin recently arrived in Lower Burma asked me if he could test the weapon. I handed it to him. He loaded and lay down, seeking a target. It happened that a Burman, not armed or in uniform, ran across the fields at a range of about 200 yards, and before I realised what was about to happen, the Kachin fired and felled him. He handed the rifle to me, saying, "An excellent weapon, sir. Very accurate!"' (letter to author).

view that prevailed. When the governor returned in October he announced that representative government would not be revived until order was restored. The AFPFL demanded immediate self-government and organized *bandhs* to promote their demands. Unable to rule without their cooperation, a new governor appointed Aung San as the chief councillor of a representative executive council, and, on 20 December 1946, Attlee advised Parliament that he was inviting Burmese representatives to London to discuss a transfer of power.

The British offered the Frontier Areas the option of a separate independence, but Aung San, liberally promising constitutional guarantees of ethnic autonomy in a federal union of Burma, the right to secede from the Union after ten years, and prestigious posts to the Shan, Kachin and Chin leaders, convinced them at a conference held at Panglong in the Shan States that their 'freedom would be more speedily achieved ... by their immediate cooperation with the Interim Burmese Government'. It is a moot point whether these promises would have been kept had not Aung San and most of his colleagues in the Interim Burmese Government's executive council been assassinated soon afterwards.[11] As the Karens, Karennis and Mons would have nothing to do with any scheme that presupposed Burman hegemony, their only effect was to divide the minorities at a moment that proved fatal to their hopes. The Karens sent a separate mission to Westminster, which abandoned them to their fate without a backward glance, and in the early hours of 4 January 1948, a time selected by astrologers, the Union of Burma was born.

The interim five decades have presented a depressing picture of spiralling hatred and distrust. In March 1948, 12 weeks after independence, the CPB, which had broken with the AFPFL and been outlawed and excluded from government, led an armed uprising

11. The Burmese government has always maintained that the promises made by Aung San to the Shan, Kachin and Chin leaders at Panglong were honoured by the establishment of self-governing political subdivisions corresponding to ethnic demography (Shan State for the Shans, Kachin State for the Kachins, Kayah State for the Karennis, a special division for the Chins). The minorities counter, however, that these were no more than token gestures disguising the paramountcy of the Burman-dominated Union and allowing a process of 'Burmanization' that undermines the vitality of their customs and traditions.

that spread like a bushfire through the country. Irregular forces that had not been integrated into the Army, mutinous Burman battalions and disaffected Muslims in Arakan (Rohingyas) soon joined the Communists. In August, the Union's paramilitary police attacked Karenni National Organization (KNO) headquarters. This provoked the defection to the Karen National Defence Organization (KNDO) of Karen, Padaung and Pao policemen posted to the Shan State and an attack by KNDO and Mon National Defence Organization (MNDO) units on government positions in the Thaton–Moulmein area. Meanwhile, 400,000 Karens demonstrated in Rangoon for an independent *Kawthoolei* (Karenland). On Christmas Eve, Burman territorials under Ne Win's general command hurled grenades into two Karen churches in Tavoy District, killing 80 Karens, which, in turn, triggered the defection to the KNDO of all four Karen battalions of the Karen Rifles and a battalion of the Kachin Rifles. A KNDO/MNDO offensive began, which nearly succeeded in capturing Rangoon.

Nine years later, Shan *saohpa*s and students were demanding the right of secession guaranteed to them at Panglong and under the 1947 Constitution. The AFPFL split into two factions, the 'Cleans' and the 'Stables', U Nu's faction having fallen hostage to a minority of its members who supported Moscow's interests and favoured an accommodation with the minorities, thereby raising fears of the Union's disintegration. U Nu handed over power to General Ne Win,[12] the armed forces' Chief of Staff, who denied the Shans' right to secede, purchased the surrender of the *saohpa*s' hereditary powers and amended the Constitution to end their guaranteed seats in the Chamber of Deputies. The Shans rebelled.

The AFPFL's two factions fought out a general election, and U Nu's Cleans, having promised the Mons and Rakhines (Arakanese) separate states, were returned to power. But the zealous Buddhist U Nu's pledge (later withdrawn) to establish the Doctrine of the Elders as Burma's state religion finally disillusioned the Kachins of the hopes raised at Panglong. Most senior posts in government, schools and universities and all the highest positions in the military had already been awarded to Burmans, and the *sangha mahanikaya* (Buddhist clergy) already enjoyed

12. A *nom de guerre* meaning Bright Sun.

privileges denied to their pastors, priests and teachers. On 5 February 1961 they joined the general rebellion, which now also included the Communists, Karens, Karennis, Shans, Mons, Paos, Chins and Rakhines.

Noting the growing strength of the insurrection, U Nu agreed to a 'federal seminar' proposed by Shan and Kayah leaders, who clung to the belief that parliamentary processes still might achieve a way forward towards the ethnic autonomy Panglong envisaged. But this was too much for Ne Win, whose *Tatmadaw* (Burma Army) had been fighting under the banner of 'One Blood, One Voice, One Command' for over a decade. On 2 and 3 March 1962, exploiting rumours of pending concessions to the minorities, he arrested U Nu, all of the members of his cabinet and the leaders of the minorities' parliamentary representatives, dissolved the parliament and suspended parts of the Constitution. Students agitated for restoration of the elected government. Ne Win answered them with bullets and the destruction of the Rangoon University Students Union building, revered symbol of Aung San's resistance to the British. He nationalized banks, major commercial houses and industrial groups, and demonetized 50 and 100 kyat banknotes. He then established a single party, the Burma Socialist Programme Party (BSPP), and an army of informers to ensure compliance with every eccentric decree that issued from his lips, such as a ban on beauty contests and dance competitions. English was discontinued as a medium of instruction in schools, and missionaries were replaced in their schools and hospitals by Burmans and expelled from the country for alleged sympathies with insurgents and foreign powers. Hundreds of thousands of Indians and Chinese fled his xenophobic demagogy and 'reforms', further undermining the country's industrial and commercial stability, and foreign policy turned markedly introspective, leading eventually to withdrawal even from the non-aligned movement. The coup in effect reinstated Burma's ancestral autocracy,[13] and opposition to

13. 'Within less than a month of the coup, Ne Win had achieved a power over the state machinery that nobody had had since the monarchy was abolished in 1885' (Lintner, 1989: 55). 'Certainly Ne Win will leave a mark on Burma's history as large as Alaunghpaya, Bodawpaya or any of the other all-conquering Burman monarchs. Those close to him confirm his keen regard for history' (Smith, 1991: 199).

the tyrant from Burmans would in time become the main hope for peace for the minorities, who comprise at least a third of the population and inhabit nearly half the land.

Since the coup the killing has intensified and attitudes have hardened. Peace parleys initiated by one side or the other in 1963, 1972, 1980 and 1981 have all shipwrecked on the rock of the junta's insistence on the insurgents' surrendering their weapons as a condition of further talk about peace. In 1966, the *Tatmadaw* instituted its infamous scorched earth policy known as the Four Cuts, designed to isolate the insurgents from the people supporting them with food, money, intelligence and fighting men. This had some success – by 1975 the central plains were more or less 'free' of insurgents – but at a cost of intensifying the hatred between Burmans and the other ethnics. Entire populations living in rebel areas were relocated into *byuha kyei-ywa*, and anyone thereafter found outside these strategic hamlets was liable to be shot, his house and crops burned and his food confiscated. Major General Malizup Zau Mai, Vice-Chairman of the KIO and Chief of Staff of the KIA, had this to say of the Four Cuts as it was enforced in the Kachin Hills and the effect that it had on the Kachins:

> They burned all the villages and crops, and our people were reduced to feeding on yams and the bark of trees. They seized all our rice, then rationed it out to the people in insufficient amounts and without salt. In Sadon District a woman was raped by thirty soldiers, who compounded this outrage by introducing a snake into her vagina. In Kanapa Village in Bhamo District, a slightly demented woman named Hpau Jung Roi died after forty soldiers of the 29th Burma Regiment raped her. They were very cruel. They thought that they would intimidate us, but the more they tortured, the more horrible their atrocities, the more the people supported us. We would keep a section near each [*byuha kyei-ywa*] and create disturbances, and the people would escape and join us in the jungle. Their strategic hamlets are a form of concentration camp.[14]

---

14. Conversation with author, February 1989.

Meanwhile, Burma, once the most prosperous country in Asia, groaned under the stringencies of Ne Win's *Burmese Way to Socialism*, a manifesto of eccentric political and economic theories. Once the world's largest producer of crude oil, it became a net importer of oil. Having rivalled Indo-China as the 'granary of the East', it was now importing rice, and, in 1986, desperate to alleviate interest on foreign obligations amounting to more than half of its hard currency earnings, it applied to the United Nations to accord it 'least developed country' status. Restrictions on private trading were lifted, and traders rushed to empty their bank accounts to buy futures in the pending harvest. Then nine months later, the junta demonetized the three largest banknotes.

If peace ever does return to Burma, historians might trace its origin to the demonetization of 5 September 1987. The war on the borders had not rallied, nor was it ever likely to rally the great mass of Burmans in opposition to the regime. The tyrant's propaganda, which exploited their immemorial prejudice towards the hill peoples, took care of that. No one begrudged his treatment of the rebels, however barbarous and cruel. After all, it was his *duty* to defend the integrity of the Union; the one good thing that could be said of him was that he stood up for Burma. Strikes like those of the oil workers at Chauk, the railway men at Insein and the dockers at Simalaik (1974) might be dressed up by CPB ideologues as manifestations of popular protest, but in reality they expressed nothing more than particular grievances that rarely coincided and were difficult to coordinate. The students were united and organized in opposing the tyrant, but, despite their spirited clamour, it was difficult to take them seriously. If their debating chambers were blown up, so what: who needed a debating chamber? Their parents were rich, and they already had more than almost everyone else had. The cancellation of these banknotes, however, that was going too far. For more than two decades the regime had condoned without legitimating the black economy, and all those who traded in the black economy (almost the entire population) had prudently kept their savings in cash. Now, with a brief announcement over the radio, most of their savings had vanished.

The response was immediate. Hundreds of enraged students stormed the streets of the capital and began smashing and incinerating government property – but now, when the government rusticated them, the enraged folk back home saluted them as heroes. The demonstrations resumed in March 1988, provoking for the first time open dissent within the Army and criticism of the tyrant from one of his former cronies. In July, Ne Win electrified the country by resigning. However, Sein Lwin, known as 'the butcher' for his suppression of past demonstrations, succeeded him, and he in turn was succeeded by Dr Maung Maung, the Party's intellectual and apologist, known as 'the puppet'. The changes, in other words, were perceived as purely cosmetic, and the mass agitation in the streets erupted again. Effigies of Ne Win and Sein Lwin were ceremonially buried in coffins decorated with demonetized banknotes, and enemies of every kind, Karens and Burmans, Buddhists and Muslims, farmers and traders, rightists and leftists, old and young, suddenly found common cause in demanding democracy. Nine of the 11 surviving Thirty Comrades declared their support for the uprising. Soldiers and policemen began to fraternize with the demonstrators. ('Our military skills are not for killing the people.') But the demonstrators also demanded the regimental commanders' heads; and, confronted by these threats, the terrified officers did their duty – hence the massacre of 19 September 1988. The ranks of the *sangha* swelled dramatically as defecting conscripts hurried into holy orders to escape reprisals, and another generation of stunned students fled to the borders to receive training from the insurgents.

This was the condition of the country in January 1989, when Mats and I reached Möng Ko.[15]

* * *

Most of the next two weeks were spent trying to make some sort of plan for the future. We were especially fortunate in that it was in the power of very nearly everyone we met to permit us to traverse territory that his insurgent group controlled.

---

15. This is a very general attempt on a very complex subject, the redaction of a decade of research by one who nevertheless remains a dilettante. I am aware of no alternative presentation of comparable simplicity, but that is perhaps its vindication. See also below, 'Chronological Guide to the Burmese Civil War', and, for citation to weightier authorities, the Bibliography.

Honouring a promise made at our first meeting, Seng Hpung sent a soldier to fetch us to his house and disclosed that the KIA would view sympathetically any plan to travel through the Kachin Hills. He advised us, however, that the shortest route through Burma would be via CPB-controlled areas to Thailand and that permission to proceed by that route would depend on Kyi Myint.

We discussed it with Kyi Myint at the first opportunity. He promised to forward our request to CPB GHQ at Panghsang. He was very encouraging and said we had every reason to anticipate a favourable response. He showed us a map demarcating the operational areas agreed between the KIO, SSPP and CPB. All the hills east and south as far as the Nanding He and hills east of the Salween almost as far as Möng Leng were under CPB control, he claimed. The Salween was two days' march, and we would reach Panghsang a week later. Mules would transport our baggage and a People's Army escort would provide security. At Panghsang his leaders would probably want to meet us. It was therefore important to pace our arrival to suit the heavy demand on their time. It should not take us very long to reach the Thai border from Panghsang; we would travel part of the way by motorcar and part by powerboat along the Mekong. It was simply a matter of coordinating everything through GHQ. While not wishing to pre-empt Seng Hpung's plan to send us through Kachinland, he spoke as though the southern route were a *fait accompli.* He showed us CPB propaganda films depicting the areas through which we would pass – avenues lined with sunny-faced Kokangs, Was, Lahus and Akhas ecstatically cheering the advance of the People's Army, soldiers working alongside hill people, helping them to harvest the golden corn – and next day he informed us that Panghsang had instructed him to give us the fullest possible cooperation. We indicated our preference for this route and waited for Panghsang's final clearance – and waited. We, of course, had only the vaguest notion of the political geography of the options under discussion, but Kyi Myint's zeal, apparent command of the facts and decisiveness convinced us that we had opted wisely. It was a wonderfully comforting picture – and it was to prove a complete mirage.

We welcomed the delay at first and found ways of enriching it. We were learning about Burma, the different insurgent groups and their diverse histories and aims, the war, and the background to the war; while daily intercourse with dignitaries with resonating titles like Deputy Foreign Secretary of the Kachin Independence Organization and Chairman of the Shan State Progress Party lent an air of grave importance to all our activities. I wrote an article entitled 'A Burmese Episode', presuming to analyse the causes and course of the war. We went to a wedding where we received more attention than the bride and groom. We accompanied Kyi Myint on an excursion to a ridge deceptive in its serenity and, between patches of willowy opium poppy, viewed the Burmans' forward positions in the valley below. We interviewed Burma Army prisoners of war captured by the CPB, affecting Red Cross credentials to encourage them to be candid with us about their conditions of custody. They seemed completely at peace and bore their gaolers no malice, as though enjoying a respite from routine soldiering.

Kyi Myint's compound was about an acre in size, bounded by hedge and fence and consisting of the main house and a number of outbuildings, where his Wa orderlies slept and the cooking was done. On its north side it ran down to the shallow, pebbly stream defining the border – here known as the Nam Ko. The Nam Ko flowed westward, became the Nam Long after passing Konshua, and joined the Shweli, which was a tributary of the Irrawaddy; while the watershed three or four miles to the east was towards the Salween. Hills rose on both banks of the Nam Ko and continued range upon range, as far as the eye could see. Shan children in pointed straw hats driving trains of water buffaloes; goats foraging, with bells tinkling from their stiff necks; a scherzo of donkeys braying and pigs squealing; cocks before dawn; fingers of mist lying in the valleys separating hill from hill and range from range in the early mornings; tall orange cannas and floppy-leafed banana palms waving in a gentle breeze against a backdrop of grey hills shimmering through the dusty haze of the late afternoons: these were the sights and sounds from Kyi Myint's compound.

The house was constructed of roughly hewn timbers and soft bricks rendered in a mix of mud and dung. It was crude by Chinese standards but extremely sophisticated by Möng Ko's. Its most technically ambitious feature was an asymetrical pair of glazed windows set in iron-barred wooden casements. A length of bamboo lining the roof overhang sufficed for guttering, and a strip of rattan suspended between wobbly posts fronting the veranda served as a clothes line. The 'old lady who lived in a shoe' inhabited such a place, I thought, when I first saw it.

We shared our host's table. As his wife supervised everything to do with food, most days were spent shirtless in shorts sitting out in the sun relishing memories of the last meal and eagerly anticipating the next. But for the soldiers who came from time to time with worried faces to present messages to our general and the armed men ringing the house, dully standing out their guard duty in blazing sun during the day and bitter cold through the night, we might have been at a holiday resort. The guards were for our 'protection' – but Aung Gyi, the venerable if somewhat ceremonial Chief of Staff, whose compound of pigs, chickens and grandchildren was a few yards from us, required no 'protection'. Nor, we observed, did any of the other rank about the place. We wrote to our families and endlessly in our diaries and waited. Kyi Myint urged us to be patient, and we were.

Although Kyi Myint spoke almost no English, he had a kind of alert urbanity, and everything he turned his mind to seemed easy to him. He exercised considerable power, yet exercised it with a gentleness and generosity that did him great credit. His living room with its television set, a technological wonder in Möng Ko, served as a public recreation hall for his confederates, and evenings, after the starting up of the generator announced that the show was resuming, were always party time. It was not uncommon to see him in earphones listening to a radio in his lap while simultaneously glancing at the television, playing bridge, reading a book *and* participating effortlessly in the conversation around him.

Kyi Myint's father had been a civil engineer employed on the building of the Burma Road, and Kyi Myint was born in Banzai, where his mother had opened a small inn. However, Banzai, a local centre of the drug trade then expanding under the control of the Kuomintang, was not congenial to raising a young family, and the family decided to move to the comparative tranquillity of Mangshi. When Kyi Myint was 16, the Cultural Revolution closed down his school, and he returned to Burma, leading his own company of Red Guards in a successful attack on Möng Bo. Eight years later, he was commanding the Northern Bureau's Second

Brigade. Thus he had been a soldier all his adult life, convinced that he was engaged in an historically mandated and heroic struggle to improve mankind. The scars of wounds in both calves, both thighs and arms, and hair parted by a bullet bore eloquent testimony to the sincerity of his convictions. The workers' ultimate triumph over their oppressors was, to him, inevitable; any attempt at denying its inevitability was as useless as denying gravity.

Although a dedicated communist, nevertheless he was now less passionate than the erstwhile schoolboy Red Guard who had deified Mao. He no longer believed that the pace of the Revolution could be forced. Burma 40 years on demanded political structures that diverged from the model the Great Liberator had laid down for China. Burma must advance with a multiparty system and democratic guarantees of diversity of opinion. Even were the CPB to succeed to power, it would allow others freely to propagate their views, he maintained; and, if genuinely free elections returned a rival for power, it would accept the verdict of the popular mandate. Thus the schools the CPB established in the Northern Bureau taught science, mathematics and grammar – not Marx. 'In our area some families are divided between themselves. One belongs to the CPB, one to the KIO. The children can decide for themselves what they want to believe.' The first necessity was to defeat the junta in Rangoon who oppressed the people and prevented their development. It sounded almost plausible.

Each day followed more or less the same pattern. When Kyi Myint and I got up soon after dawn, the servants were ready with pans of hot water, soap and towels and new toothbrushes already loaded with toothpaste. While we washed and shaved on the veranda, they swept the living room of cigarettes and other droppings, then heated it with braziers filled with lumps of burning charcoal, then brought us tea. At this hour the hills about, an ethereal panorama of smoking precipices, put on their most ravishing show. An hour or so later, Mats struggled sleepily out of bed and onto the veranda to stretch his muscles, sniff the crisp mountain air and speculate what breakfast would bring. Not long thereafter we were sitting about the round table in the living room shovelling down steaming rice with chopsticks, as Kyi Myint's Chinese wife, a visitor from the smoke-filled kitchen, studied us for signs of approval. No one spoke; everyone ate, delicately selecting with the specificity allowed by chopsticks from chicken's offal, pig's offal, fish, fried strips of dried buffalo, cabbage, mustard greens, spinach, watercress, snow peas and bamboo shoots. Some of these succulent things were boiled; some were fried in a wok and flavoured with soyabean sauce, onions, garlic, peppers, ginger and a variety of ingredients inscrutable to culinary illiterates. In brief, the fare was very Chinese.

Kyi Myint tried each morning to converse with us with the help of a dictionary but soon despaired and summoned Kyaw Nyunt (John Juan) or a Burman named Suu Aung to interpret for him. Suu Aung worked in Propaganda – the premier corps in the CPB. He and Kyaw Nyunt were contrasting personalities. Suu Aung was shy and nervous and had the excellent ability to sit in unobtrusive silence while we read or wrote up our diaries. His admiration for my literary status grew steadily as he watched me write. Kyaw Nyunt was confident and garrulous. His supreme ambition was to travel abroad. ('I explain you – leave wife! Delhi, San Francisco, isn't it?') Each was good company in his own right, but as a comic partnership – the Burman with his unlabial, mouth-full-of-mush credulity and the quasi-Chinaman with his jump-up-and-down enthusiasm – they were incomparable. Their routine deserved a wider audience, we told them. We suggested a signature tune, sung by them as a duet to the tune of 'Row, row, row your boat, gently up the stream.'

Aung Gyi would then appear, his big, round face beaming and cheerful. It was the face of a man at one with his convictions, his burgeoning family, his food and his livestock; the face of a man who presides over the activities of others and counts his possessions – the Northern Bureau's token Burman. His arrival was the signal for Kyi Myint to absent himself with the explanation that 'today' (it was one of Kyi Myint's words in English together with 'go', 'know', 'bligade' and 'Langoon govlenment') he must do something that we never quite understood. At first we thought that the monoglottal Aung Gyi came to cadge cigarettes. Then we decided that he visited us because he had nothing better to do and out of general *bonhomie*. Then it occurred to us that the CPB was using his impenetrability to break our spirits. Sometimes the strain of smiling incessantly at us was too great even for him, and he would try communicating in Burmese.

Kyi Myint would return to the compound at about 1500 hours, and we would sit down for our second great meal of the day, lingering at table as the sun set over the western hills. This was the moment most propitious for discussing our prospects. We usually left the initiative to him but sometimes were unable to restrain our curiosity. I remember asking him one evening, 'Have you some crumb of hope for us?' to which, always philosophical, he replied, 'News will come.' After a week of such genial palliatives we presented him with a letter addressed to the Commander, the People's Army, Northern Bureau, Communist Party of Burma. 'We write to ask for formal confirmation of your intentions and [the letter continued], if you are still minded to let us proceed to CPB GHQ, to request from you a safe conduct pass addressed to the commanders of all People's Army units between Möng Ko and Panghsang and that you allow us to purchase or hire from you film, packhorses and spare trousers.' Kyi Myint ridiculed our impatience, repeating his advice that news would come, but promised to transmit the letter to his 'superior', which meant Aung Gyi. Our requests were very modest, he added, and the arrival of the film the following evening seemed a favourable augury.

Eventually the cold would drive us back to the house, where the servants prepared another brazier and the conversation continued about the awfulness of Ne Win and his government or about theoretical versus practical Marxism or about the West or, whenever we could decently persist, our plans. Usually, though, it degenerated into jokeyness centred on Mats's bachelor 'needs'. Then the servants started up the generator and Kyi Myint turned on the television – but rarely to watch it; its noise seemed to compose his thoughts. We retired to our beds between 2130 and 2200 hours, the generator expiring a minute or two later, proving that some lad out there in the cold had nothing to do but wait and observe – like us.

My diary for 24 January reflects our impatience.

> Last night I caught myself listening to a feature programme on the Voice of America about knitting! Our destination, be it Thailand or India, seems more hypothetical now than ten days ago when Mats and I laughed ourselves to sleep rejoicing at our success. Kyi Myint, who was so confidently

reassuring then, now seems strangely troubled. Has something unforeseen happened? Is he embarrassed to tell us? Suu Aung did not come last night or this morning, so opportunities for questioning him were limited, but I did manage to say to Kyi Myint, 'Thailand, today?' and received a negative shake of the head. I impressed on him the need to allow for contingencies and the narrowing margin of time that we had budgeted for our adventure.

We have been here ten days. It is relaxing but perhaps a little unhealthy. I have written to Carole and Mother, finished 'A Burmese Episode', and my diary is up to the minute. So is Mats's, who now has no employment save miscellaneous sewing and has begun to fret. Dressed in *longyi* and straw hat, he dawdles, a caricature of the jungle-bashing hardy of ten days ago. I tried to pepper his spirits with maxims like, 'Idleness is the Devil's workshop' and 'Moaning is infectious', but they only deepened his despair.

Today he found new employment in crafting from the foil capping of a discarded tobacco tin an anti-nose-burner. He, too, feels under pressure to reach Thailand by 15 March, by when his supplies of 'quality chew' [tobacco] will be exhausted. So I conceived an alternative plan for presenting to Kyi Myint. If no response from CPB GHQ is forthcoming by 27 January, could we scrap our plans for Thailand and proceed to India instead?

That afternoon Kyi Myint returned to the compound later than usual. He avoided meeting my eyes and was exceptionally jokey with Mats. Then Kyaw Nyunt appeared. Summoned especially, I wondered? I suspected that Kyi Myint intended to tell us something about our proposed trip that would distress us. Mats's oblique reference to the subject caused him to start and insist, alarmingly, that we defer the discussion until after dinner. After dinner, he unburdened himself. A response *had* been received from GHQ, but, he said gravely, it was *not* the expected response. GHQ had advised that conditions along the Thai border had deteriorated. Fighting had erupted between the People's Army and the narcotics-trafficking Möng Tai Army (MTA), Khun Sa's group. Hence, the CPB could not guarantee our safety beyond Panghsang. This did not entirely rule out the southern route — the fighting at the border might abate, or Sai Lek might let us travel through the Shan State Army's (SSA's) operational area west of the Salween — but it certainly tilted the balance of arguments in favour of the northern route. That route, however, also posed difficulties. The CPB would have to smuggle us by car to the KIA's GHQ at Pajau Bum, and there was a serious risk of interception. Kyi Myint had himself received Panghsang's message about the fighting along the Thai border, and it had greatly saddened him. He had worried how we would respond, but he had already dispatched messages to the SSPP and KIO for clearances in case we elected either of those options. He told us that Seng Hpung was away but that he was due back in Möng Ko the following night.

Allowed now to move about unescorted, we went to Sai Lek's compound first thing the next morning and found his young warrior wife, who looked like Miss Joan Hunter Dunn in her crisply ironed SSA uniform. She informed us that, like Seng Hpung, her husband was away. She said he was 'on manoeuvres'.

Seng Hpung returned to Möng Ko about an hour before sundown. We saw him entering the village at the head of a dusty column of men and ponies, looking older than his 53 years and weighed down with concerns beyond our understanding; we already knew that he had been at the front. We met at his house as soon as he had rested, by which time Kyi Myint had already briefed him. He said that he anticipated no objection from KIO GHQ if we elected the northern route and that, indeed, he had already apprised his Chief of Staff of that possibility.

That evening, after we left Seng Hpung, the KIA proffered a formal invitation to visit their GHQ at Pajau Bum. San Awng, Seng Hpung's personal aide and quartermaster, brought us the message. Still, we hesitated, as Mats hoped to rejoin Dany, who awaited him in Bangkok. Kyi Myint told us to make up our minds one way or another, for he had to make the contingent arrangements. Next day, Sai Lek returned. He received us cordially and without any hint of his troubles, which the serenity of his leafy compound belied. But he refused us permission to cross SSPP territory. That now left us only one option, regardless of the risk:

to accept the KIA's invitation and endeavour to persuade them to let us proceed to India.[16]

* * *

During our infatuation phase, while we still dreamt of boating down the Mekong, one thought alone troubled us. The poppy fields in little patches excised from the forested hills about us were irrefutable evidence of the narcotics trade. Having intended to avoid the Golden Triangle, we now seemed destined to travel through the heart of it. Mats and I would discuss our predicament when we were alone – at night, in whispers, after the others went to bed and we had extinguished the candles in our room. Was the CPB engaged in the trade? If so, how safe would we *really* be in their company? Kyi Myint had accepted us at our word, but would that assessment endure? How disciplined were his subordinates? Anyone in the column escorting us might fancy that we were agents of the Drug Enforcement Agency (DEA). Then what? These were all questions of vital concern to us, but how could we raise them with our captors without seeming too inquisitive?

A chance opening into the subject arose in conversation with Seng Hpung during the first week of our captivity. We were sitting out on the hard, grassless ground of his compound. Everyone else was indoors, and we had retreated beneath an umbrella. It was that static time of day when most of the soldiers garrisoning Möng Ko were playing the local variant of dominoes. Seng Hpung's batman fetched his binoculars, and he trained them on the patches on the hills to the south. 'They bloom between December and March, depending on latitude and altitude,' he said. 'Our people would withdraw their support if we stopped them from growing it.'

'Do they use it themselves?' I asked mildly, trying to conceal my fascination.

He smiled. 'Only if they are addicted.'

'You know,' I said, 'some people in our countries view this business with deep concern,' and turned to Mats for support. He

16. Unbeknown to us, Sai Lek was manoeuvering at that very moment to prevent a palace revolt. A few months later he would be left with a small rump of his once proud army and engaged in a bitter war with his former cronies.

was asleep. 'If he were awake, he would agree,' I said. 'Is the drugs trade an important part of your economy?'

We talked all that afternoon, and I believe that Seng Hpung replied to all my questions truthfully. Later, in Washington, I passed on what he told me to men in the National Security Council (NSC) presented to me as experts on narcotics and Southeast Asia – grey men who, in the belief that they were aiding the 'war on drugs', bore responsibility for Washington's decision to supply the Burma Army with pilots, Thrust aircraft and 2,4-D, a type of herbicide that is banned in the United States. Instead of using the 2,4-D to eradicate all the poppies, said Seng Hpung, the Burma Army confined its spraying to poppies growing in insurgent areas and exempted those grown by its allies, unambivalent traffickers like Khun Sa (Prince Pleasant).[17] Moreover, he said, frontline commanders of the Burma Army were involved in the trade. This was shocking to hear, and in 1989 Washington's experts thought me *very* gullible for believing it, although since then they appear to have changed their minds. Seng Hpung's assertions were the beginning of my knowledge of the trade.

We soon felt sufficiently confident of our status to venture the issue with others. Was the Burma Army involved in the trade? Kyi Myint, who was less tactful than the KIO's Deputy Foreign Secretary, told us bluntly that we were a little simple to ask such naïve questions. The prisoners of war we interviewed also confirmed what Seng Hpung had said. We presented to them written questions and arranged for them to respond in binary mime (right hand for yes, left for no), then interviewed them alone and separately. They had no hard evidence, but two of them had *heard* of instances where Burma Army vehicles had been used for trans-

17. Alias Chan Shee-fu, who merged his Shan United Army in 1986 with Moh Heng's Shan United Revolutionary Army to form the MTA of the Tai Revolutionary Council. The MTA's forces are deployed escorting Khun Sa and Moh Heng's mule caravans and protecting their heroin refineries near the Thai border (see Lintner, 1990a: 108). In an interview with Andrew Drummond published in *Observer Magazine*, 16 July 1989, Khun Sa is reported to have said: 'The Burmese government want me to fight the Communists. As long as I am doing that, it's not to their advantage to attack me.' In December 1995, Khun Sa agreed to surrender the MTA's headquarters at Ho Möng and is now living in opulent retirement in Rangoon.

porting opium. Sai Lek resolved any remaining doubts. For the past two years, he said bitterly, the SSA had been fighting both the Burma Army and Khun Sa.

The trade, a subject of almost intractable complexity in which the players recurrently bump off one another and constantly change their allegiances, has ancient, Mediterranean roots. The anaesthetic properties of *papaver somniferum* were known to both Hippocrates and Galen. However, it was left to modern science to exploit the deleterious potential of extracting morphine from the resin and bonding it with acetic anhydride. In 1898, Bayer Pharmaceutical Company began marketing this synthesis with the trade name Heroin as a wonderful new panacea for common respiratory complaints such as asthma, bronchitis and tuberculosis. The Yale scholar Alfred McCoy in his disturbing book, *The Politics of Heroin in Southeast Asia*,[18] traces the Golden Triangle's important role in the trade to Arabs, who introduced the poppy to India in the seventh century AD. In the sixteenth century, Portuguese traffickers cultivated among indentured Chinese in Java a taste for smoking raw opium blended with tobacco from Brazil, and from there the habit spread to China and flourished. Later, the East India Company asserted a monopoly over poppy grown in Bengal and stole the China trade from the Portuguese. Chinese merchants encouraged hill tribes in Yunnan to grow opium in competition with the British, and, by 1846, poppy cultivation had spread to the adjoining highlands of Burma and Laos. Until 1930, when the Kuomintang restricted its cultivation in China, the Burmese hill tribes grew it mainly for local consumption.

During the Second World War, units of Force 136, the Northern Kachin Levies and Burma Regiment operating behind Japanese lines used opium air-dropped to them from India for small transactions like engaging porters. The Americans used it to finance intelligence-gathering for the Kachin Rangers and Merrill's Marauders, and, a decade later, as McCoy's study shows, the CIA was unwittingly abetting, if not deliberately directing and assisting, the Kuomintang to take over the trade in the Shan State. Early in 1951, 17 years before Kyi Myint and other Red Guards stormed

18. McCoy, 1972: 59 ff. This is essential reading for the innocent at heart.

over the Nam Long, the Burma Army reported the CIA's unmarked C-46s and C-47s making at least five parachute drops a week to KMT forces at Möng Hsat in the Lahu hill country of southern Shan State.[19] In 1961, a combined PLA–Burma Army force found five tonnes of US-supplied ammunition when it attacked the KMT's headquarters at Möng Pa Liao.[20] Heroin was unknown to the hill tribes until the Kuomintang began refining it, said Seng Hpung.

The hill tribes were ignorant of the impact of the trade on American cities and, hence, bewildered by the fuss that we made over it, explained Seng Hpung. Opium had veterinary and medical applications as a remedy for diarrhoea, dysentery and various fevers; it was a soporific, and a balm for porters charged with heavy burdens on long, steep hauls, generally enhancing the user's capacity for hard work. Its only adverse effects were a tendency to emaciation and, when the supply failed, lassitude. Since their conversion to Christianity, the Kachins had reprobated its use for other than medical or veterinary purposes but had condoned its cultivation. Alternative crops like tea and coffee took longer to establish and required venture capital beyond the means of most of their people. If the war could be stopped, said Seng Hpung, the KIO could build motor roads, and these farmers would turn their husbandry to supplying the towns with vegetables. The Karens, Karennis and Mons prohibited its cultivation and punished severely anyone caught trafficking in it, he said.

The raw opium yield from the Shan State rocketed to nearly ten times its former volume while the Kuomintang dominated the trade, and US support for the Burma Army's selective herbicidal spraying had enabled it to take over from the Kuomintang and stimulated still further growth. In January 1989, when Mats and I were in Möng Ko, merchants (according to the merchants themselves) were delivering the opium harvest to Burma Army posts on the Namhpakka–Kutkai sector of the Burma Road for transport to Mandalay or Rangoon, where it fetched a hundred times more than the hill farmers were paid for it. 'The fortunes that their

19. McCoy (1972: 129).
20. The KMT survivors fled across the Mekong into Laos, where the CIA recruited them for fighting the communists there (McCoy, 1972: 134–5).

senior officers are making from narcotics is the main reason why the war continues,' said Seng Hpung.

Only foreign military intervention would eradicate Burma's opium production, I concluded. Without it, the war would continue to stoke the trade, and the trade, the war – they were interdependent. There would have to be, I decided, a Security Council resolution and ultimatum directed at the governments of countries exporting narcotics that tolerated no excuse: desist or suffer intervention. Blue berets would then scamper over the Patkai range and across the Ko, Long, Shweli, Salween and Moi rivers and join forces with the Kachins, Shans, Kokangs, Palaungs, Ahkas, Lahus, Karennis, Karens, Mons, Chins, Nagas and Rakhines to end both the trade *and* the war. The NSC 'experts' mocked me when I presented my ideas to them in Washington.[21] But, in the middle of the night in Möng Ko, it all seemed blindingly obvious.

* * *

Kyi Myint had spoken of smuggling us to KIO GHQ. We were puzzling over exactly what this meant, when Seng Hpung summoned us to his house and announced: 'You have a choice.

---

21. 'On 5 February [1992] US Senator Jesse Helms said that SLORC [State Law and Order Restoration Committee, former name of junta ruling Burma] is using funds earned from the export of heroin to the USA to finance its US$ 1.4 billion arms purchase from China. Senator Helms made the statement while testifying on US foreign policy before the Senate Foreign Relations Committee in Washington, DC. In 1991, Burma produced 247.5 tonnes of heroin, making it the world's largest producer of the drug. According to the US Drug Enforcement Administration, 56 per cent of the heroin in the US came from Burma' (*Burma Alert*, vol. 3, March 1992). On 11 November 1996 the BBC World Service reported that President Clinton stated in a speech at Chulalongkorn University in Bangkok, 'The role of drugs in Burma's economic and political life and the regime's refusal to honour its own pledge to move to multiparty democracy are really two sides of the same coin, for both represent the absence of the rule of law' (*Burma Alert*, vol. 7, December 1996). See also Robert S. Gelbard, US Assistant Secretary of State for International Narcotics and Law Enforcement Affairs, *Far Eastern Economic Review*, 21 November 1996: 35: 'The lawlessness of authoritarian rule ... results in the corruption and criminalization of the state and the entrenchment of the drug trade in Burma's political and economic life'; Jonathan Winer, Deputy Assistant Secretary of State, *Burma Debate*, vol. v, no. 4, 1998: 26.

You can go by car through China, which is quick but risky, or you can walk through our Four and Three Brigade areas, which will take about three weeks and is also risky.'

We elected the China option.

'Then you leave tomorrow night. I have already sent a runner to Mangshi to hire a car. Departure will be after dark; estimated travel time, eight hours. My men and Kyi Myint's will accompany you dressed as civilians.'

'What should we do if we are intercepted?' I asked.

'You talk your way out.'

'We will pretend that we were hitchhiking and that the driver just happened to stop for us.'

A grin spread over his brown leathery face. It was a grin that we would come to know well, his 'Isn't insurgency fun?' grin.

I asked him for directions to KIO GHQ, 'in case we are separated from the car?'

'Don't write this down – use your memory,' he replied. 'Turn right at the police station at the centre of Xima onto a çobblestone road. After about a kilometre, the road crosses a river by a half-finished bridge. Another kilometre further on you will come to a small Chinese village named Cha Huo, beyond which is a small Kachin village named Ying Hpan Paw, which is about forty-five minutes from KIO GHQ.'

I noted in my diary: 'Mats is keen on our prospects: he has a "great feeling". But there is no way of predicting our fate. At this time day after tomorrow we shall be either at KIO GHQ or in gaol.'

That night I slept badly, haunted by round, happy faces and Kyi Myint's irrepressible high spirits and impassioned interest in everything. 'Ah, Lieutenant Larsson,' he would exclaim to Mats whenever an unattached woman appeared. The pawpaw and banana palms and bright, rigid cannas; the tall stands of bamboo rustling in the hollows by the river where the little Shan boys rode their fat buffaloes to water; the pale Shan women in cylindrical white turbans and the Palaung women in their long coats of cotton-velvet; the herons flying in formation overhead ... too soon, I realized, they would be no more than a memory.

Suu Aung came by next morning to bid us farewell. I pretended that he was accompanying us – hadn't he heard? '*Nooo-oo*,' he replied in his mouth-full way, 'I am very busy.'

'Busy at what?' I jeered. 'Propaganda?'

After further reflection, he mused, 'I do not think I will receive such an order. I do not speak Chinese.'

'Chinese isn't the determining factor,' I said and led him to a wooden chest in Kyi Myint's house in which were stored some uniforms. 'You are the only interpreter who is small enough to fit into the chest. If we need your help, we can stop and open it.'

'I hope that you will leave a hole in it,' he said.

Aung Gyi paid us one last uncomprehending and incomprehensible visit; then we repacked our things, reset our watches to Chinese time and donned our disguises. That afternoon, the CPB's derelict jeep took us to Seng Hpung's house, the driver presenting us with two bottles of Chinese spirits. They were sent as farewell gifts from two officers whom we could not recall meeting. We sat with Seng Hpung in his living room into the evening, chatting under an arc lamp from which dead bugs rained down on us, waiting for the driver who was to take us to KIO GHQ. Then we returned to Kyi Myint's, where all the servants who had paraded to bid us sad goodbyes expressed rapture at seeing us again so soon.

Another day passed. Mats's mood darkened. He no longer had a 'great feeling' about our prospects. His gut feeling now was that we would not be going to KIO GHQ at all. The hired car that had not materialized had been a bitter disappointment to him. He plaited a piece of leather for fixing his knife to his belt, visited the market and Kyaw Nyunt's house twice, finished crafting his anti-nose-burner and, finally, retired to a hammock to brood. Kyi Myint, returning for lunch and puzzled to find Mats missing from the chair where he usually sat, asked where he was. I discreetly pointed to a comatose lump suspended between two trees. 'Oh,' Kyi Myint exclaimed, 'in Burma, only children sleep in hammocks.'

Nevertheless, unseen agencies were moving our plans inexorably forward. Another car was found, and the following afternoon, as the sun was setting, the CPB's jeep, the same that had conveyed us to Kyi Myint's house a fortnight earlier, parked outside Seng Hpung's. We got into the back with four men, including Kyaw Nyunt. He had four large empty bags, which he intended to fill with contraband. We sat on the floor. In the front seat by the window on the passenger side was a plump, oily man of inscrutable mien. 'I explain you!' said Kyaw Nyunt. 'He know very well policemen in Meng Hai' — his role was to mediate with the Chinese authorities if trouble arose. His late father, Naw Seng, had been a celebrated warrior who had commanded a Kachin Rifles battalion. After supporting the U Nu government (thereby ensuring its survival), Naw Seng had rebelled and eventually directed the CPB's Northeast Command[22] — hence the cordial relations his son now enjoyed with the Chinese.

Most of the jeep's company were to camouflage our transit through Meng Hai and would return to Möng Ko after transferring us to the hired car. However, Kyaw Nyunt, who spoke Chinese, and a KIA runner, who also spoke Chinese and was familiar with the route, would be accompanying us as far as KIO GHQ.

A large crowd assembled for a final glimpse of us. Kyi Myint's grinning, boyish face appeared over the front seat for final handshakes. I told him that he was the bravest man I had ever known. 'I have known other men who could accept the risks of dying in battle. Had they been wounded in both calves, in both thighs and in both arms, had a bullet parted their hair, as happened to you, they might have fought on. But had they been asked to host for two weeks two strangers who spoke not a word of any language known to them, they could not have done it,' I said. Smooth as cream to the last, he replied that we had afforded him lots of amusement. The anti-nose-burner reminded him, he said, of a picture of a clown that he had seen in a magazine.[23] Seng Hpung

---

22. The Kachins maintain that Naw Seng, Burma Gallantry Medal and Bar, joined the CPB because it was at that time (April 1950) the only insurgent group still operating in the Kachin Hills and he was homesick.
23. I wrote to Kyi Myint after returning home. My letter was six months reaching him, and his reply took another six months to reach me. Following our departure from Möng Ko, the CPB disintegrated and the Northern Bureau now called itself the Brave Nationalist Democratic Alliance. 'At present we are trying to eliminate drug traffickers, but we have met with great difficulties,' the letter states ominously and exhorts me 'to exercise [my] influence [*sic*] to persuade some American, British or even United Nations organizations to assist us in this task.' Bertil Lintner alleges that Kyi Myint has joined the traffickers. (See *Far Eastern Economic Review*, 20 February 1992: 23–4.) However, the evidence proffered for this allegation is 'a source close to' a former CPB confederate of Kyi Myint who, allegedly, is now his partner in the trade.

came round to a side window to wish us good luck. He would be following us in a few days, he whispered. We rehearsed once more our alibis in case of interception, then drove off.

We drove across the Nam Ko and past the police post undetected. A white Subaru Columbus was parked about a hundred yards beyond the police post, with a solitary driver slumped over its steering wheel. We slowed to attract his attention; then drove beyond the village where, in the dim light of dusk, the transfer took place. Then we drove through the night.

The first sector was a dirt logging road, empty save for two or three *tuo la jis* laden with logs. Petrol fumes leaked into the car from a broken exhaust, and the driver amused himself by playing scratchy, squawking Chinese disco music from a cassette. 'He like music too much,' observed Kyaw Nyunt.

At Chefang we passed a checkpoint, inactive, as Seng Hpung had predicted, and turned south onto the tarmacadam from Mangshi. No interference was expected until the Shweli.

There were two bridges across the Shweli, and we were bound for the first, which was supposed to be less rigorously controlled than that further south.

We reached it at about 2100 hours. The driver braked, and our hearts began to thump wildly. We slowed to walking speed. I lifted my eyes above the base of the window and peeked out at the *jing cha* in their wasp-striped caps. Columns of trucks were drawn up on both sides of the bridge. Floodlights illuminated the whole scene. A guard was approaching. He was now within 15 feet of us. I relived the gripping films of my childhood. This was the Jack Hawkins test, those black-faced commandos clipping the barbed wire at midnight within inches of the polished boots of the unsuspecting enemy patrolling the perimeter of the camp. Suddenly, another guard lowered a red flag and raised a green one. He was signalling to a truck behind us, but it was leave enough for our driver, an experienced smuggler who knew exactly the limits of his chances. We lurched forward and swerved, just missing the astonished guard advancing to inspect us; accelerated and, tyres skidding, sped through a gap in the trucks.

Kyaw Nyunt was jubilant. It was now 'eighty per cent certain' that we would reach KIO GHQ. Only half a dozen checkpoints remained, he said.

The next was at Ruili. We drove past it about half an hour later, unheeded, and into a congeries of dark lanes, past a gate and into a walled compound. The driver got out and walked over to a house, through a window of which burned a dim light. He knocked at the door. The light went out, nocturnal visitors evidently being regarded with suspicion. We waited, Mats and I in our facemasks and Shan hats pulled down close to our ears. The driver knocked at the door again, then called out something in what, presumably, was Chinese. Then the door opened a few inches and a whispered conversation followed. Finally, after much whispering, a man appeared. The conversation begun *sotto voce* now flared into a loud altercation. We understood nothing and could see very little, only that there was marked mutual hostility. Both men started making extravagant gestures in our direction. Did their quarrel concern *us*? The driver abruptly broke off the conversation, marched back to the car, opened the door beside me, and fetched some jerrycans from below the seat. There was more loud argument, then a settlement of sorts, and we drove off. Kyaw Nyunt explained that we had stopped at a school to buy petrol on the black market and that we were now looking for a cheaper source. 'Teacher's price too much,' he said.

More black alleys led us to a street lined with dead trucks. We stopped again, another door opened, and there was more messing about with jerrycans.

Finally, we drove to the main street and stopped for food. Kyaw Nyunt urged us to choose anything we wanted, explaining that Ruili abounded in cosmopolitan vendors catering for every taste. 'So many India mans come here to sell everything – jade, rubies, heroin, womans.' He and the others left the car, neglecting, however, to close the front door. Almost at once a thief sprang forth, having waited for just such an opening, but, detecting in the back seat two shadowy Big Noses got up malevolently in weird hats and facemasks, he quickly retreated. Presently, our companions returned with pancakes, muffins and tins of fizzy pop. We drove about 300 metres down the road and stopped again for more food. Mats then did a very silly thing. He lowered his mask to eat his pancakes.

We left Ruili and began another slow ascent over another winding road. Kyaw Nyunt urged us to sit up and relax, promising to alert us before the next checkpoint in time to reinstate our face-masks. Now and then we would stop, and the driver would extract a rag from beneath the seat, get out and clear a small peep-hole in the windscreen, which was caked in dirt. Then he would massage his face with a Noxema-smelling paste to rub out what Kyaw Nyunt called the Sleep Spirit. Sometimes he just jerked his head violently to shake out the Sleep Spirit. The car's somewhat erratic course suggested that his methods might be failing him. Discouraged and frustrated, he would stop and light a cigarette and put on another scratchy cassette for consolation. It was bitterly cold, even in our sweaters and anoraks, yet the exhaust fumes obliged us to keep the windows open.

Gradually the bends ceased, and the cold abated. We were now surrounded by sugarcane. Then Mats, incensed, announced that we had 'yust passed a checkpoint.'

'Sorry,' said Kyaw Nyunt unrepentantly. 'I sleep.'

A few minutes later the floodlit gate and massive wall of the Yingjiang Sugar Refinery hove into sight. We passed the refinery, branched west, crossed a bridge, and soon were in a very large city, which, however, was black and ghostly at this hour.

A few miles beyond Yingjiang the road forked. The driver stopped again and considered, wondering which fork he ought to take. Kyaw Nyunt advised him to take the right fork, remarking that we were 26 kilometres from our destination. 'How do you know that it is 26 kilometres?' I asked peevishly. 'Experience say me,' he replied. We started over another mountain, the driver jerking his head ever more violently in an ever more determined fight to stay awake.

We reached Xima, which consisted of two rows of unlit timber buildings flanking the road leading to Seng Hpung's police station and the junction with his cobblestone road at the town's centre. We turned onto the road and, almost immediately, were con-fronted by the bright headlights of a lorry. But it was only a farm truck.

A few minutes later we reached Seng Hpung's river and his unfinished bridge. It had just been surfaced, and we wondered if the cement had dried sufficiently to take the weight of the car. The KIA runner, our expert on the approaches to KIO GHQ, coun-selled us to cross by the old bridge. Access to the old bridge was by a slender neck of loose earth skirting a pit about four yards deep. The driver reversed the car, drove down an embankment, and braked at the edge of the pit. The runner urged us forward. Further inspection and consultation convinced us that the driver should venture the perilous neck of loose dirt alone. If it held, we would meet him on the other side. If not, we reasoned, then we had limited our losses. We set out walking, leaving him to his fate, when it suddenly occurred to us that he might make off with our things, including the stash of money that Kyaw Nyunt had brought along for his procurements. We hurried back to the car and persuaded him to cross by the new bridge after all.

Beyond the river, we started climbing again, passing Seng Hpung's Chinese and Kachin villages. The surface of the road was now sharp rock alternating with hard, deeply rutted mud, and the gradient was so steep in places that we had to get out and push. Huge, black fir trees rose on one side of us, while, on the other, the ground fell away in tiers of sheer cliff, broken by strips and patches of more fir trees. Mats was in the worst possible mood. Many trying hours had elapsed since the meagre provision of pancakes and muffins from the 'India mans', but, more importantly, water had leaked onto his 'quality chew'.

Seng Hpung's precise briefings had not prepared us for what now happened. Suddenly we came to a barrier drawn across the road. Next to it was a timber kiosk and a small timber house linked by cable to a system of other cables on posts. A uniformed woman emerged from the kiosk and turned on a torch. She trained it on everyone in turn. The light came to rest on my face, then on Mats's. She then returned to the kiosk and picked up a telephone.

3

The Sons of Wakhyet Wa

Ola Hanson, a Promethean figure who devised an orthography for the Kachins adapted from Latin, observed that when they moved to the plains they rapidly degenerated or lost their peculiar characteristics. I cannot affirm or deny this, as I met them only in the thickly forested hills of China, Burma and India, where they have lived for at least three centuries.

The Shans (Tai) and Palaungs (Rumai), who live closest to them, call them *Hkang*, suggesting miscegenation, while the Chinese refer to them as *Shan-C'ou* (hill tribes) and *Yeh-Jen*, *Ye Yen* or *Ye Jein* (wild or jungle man). According to Hanson, the *Hkang* of the Shans and *Jen* of the Chinese may have combined to produce the Burmese word, *Hka Khyen,* or *Ka Khyen*, which English has simplified as Kachin. Henry Felix Hertz, on the other hand, fancies a metaphor flattering to Burman *amour propre.* Combining the Burmese for 'bitter' and 'sour' produces a sound like *Hka Khyen* — pointing up the contrast between the sweetness of cultivated fruit (the Burmans) and the bitterness of uncultivated fruit (their wild neighbours). Hertz was a police superintendent in Kachinland. It has also been noticed that the Burmese and Jinghpaw words for basket, *ka* and *hkyin*, produce a combination of sounds consonant with the unassailable notion that a Kachin is never without a basket. No less implausible is the theory that the term arose when foreigners asked about the name of the people inhabiting the Ga Hkyeng area of Mogaung District and applied a mispronounced variant of that name, *Hka Khyen*, to all Kachins. However the name arose, Kachins share with the Dutch, Welsh and Meo the ignominy of being known by an opprobrious term strangers imposed on them. *Wunpawng* is the name they use for themselves.

Wunpawng is a Jinghpaw word. The *Wunpawng* comprise at least six distinct peoples speaking mutually incomprehensible languages,[1] Azi (or Szi), Jinghpaw, Lashi, Lisu, Maru and Rawang.[2] The Jinghpaws are the largest tribe, and all Kachins use their language as a lingua franca. Indeed, the earlier authorities often use the terms Kachin and Jinghpaw interchangeably. The practice of lumping the Kachins together may have begun as a convenience of British Army recruitment officers to distinguish them from Chins and Karens.

There is no physical record of the Kachins' origin. Oral traditions evoke a prehistoric familiarity with the sources of the Irrawaddy and names designating districts ruled by five progenitors. However, 'prehistoric' here may mean less than two centuries. Nor is a common belief in an aboriginal Majoi Shingra Bum (Mount Naturally Flat) very helpful, as there is no one knoll, butte or plateau distinct from others by which it can be identified in the mountainous borderlands where we know that the Kachins were living in recent times. Hanson suggests that their original home must be sought further north, in eastern Tibet, western Szechuan or even Mongolia. He surmises that the Kachins were part of a protracted migration from China that comprised all the major tribes of Burma. The Paos were already living in the Burmese central plains in the sixth century BC, and the Karens, Mons and Burmans followed them. As the Nagas took possession of the Patkai range and the Chins the Western Yomas, the Karens and Lahus moved gradually down the Salween. Perceived similarities in 'race' and language underlie Hanson's theory, which, for want of evidence and until a more authoritative champion of an alternative theory appears, seems secure. Hanson notes that one-fourth of the roots in Jinghpaw and Burmese are identical.

At any rate, once the Kachins had reached the 'Land of the Four Rivers' (the Mali Hka, Nmai Hka, Noa Dihing and Brahmaputra?), where we first meet them with any certainty, they moved south. Jinghpaws took possession of the country west of the Mali

1. Notwithstanding the claim that Lashi and Azi are dialects of Maru.
2. There is also no uniformity about these classifications, some authorities holding that the Rawangs (Nungs), Hkahkus, Sasans, Dulengs and Gauris (Jinghpaws) are separate tribes. The Lisu are distinct in physiognomy and language, and, though claimed as 'distant relatives' by the other tribes, they 'prefer to regard themselves as an offshoot of the Chinese' (see Hanson, 1913: 13).

Hka and Jinghpaws and Marus the highlands between the Mali Hka and Nmai Hka, known as the Triangle. The steep hills of the Triangle tended to isolate the different Maru communities, and their language ran into brogues and dialects. By contrast, the easier terrain west of the Mali Hka enabled the Jinghpaws there to consolidate their unity against the challenge of a common enemy in the Assamese and Shans. The Jinghpaws were sufficiently strong and organized to attack the Assamese capital, Sadiya, several times during the reigns of the later Ahom kings. They assisted the Burmans in invading Assam in 1813, then expelled the Burmans and Shans from most of the country north of the Mogaung River. They all but exterminated the Shan population of the Hukawng Valley, reducing the survivors to vassals. But the Burmans and Shans blocked their path of westward expansion, so they turned east and south, occupying the hilltops between the Irrawaddy and the Salween. The gentler valley-dwelling Shans there also became their vassals and, but for the advent of the British, might have been exterminated. After Jinghpaws moved south of the Nmai Hka, Marus followed, intermarrying with the strong Lahpai family. From this union developed the Azi, who in turn intermarried with Marans and, probably, Han Chinese to produce the Lashis.[3] Meanwhile, Lisu, Nungs and Rawang migrated behind them into the Triangle and Hkamti Long. Thus today the Kachins are a confederation of various tribes sharing a common way of life and common ancestral and religious traditions.

Few if any people on earth attach so much importance to lineage. They trace their ancestry to an hermaphroditic creator god usually referred to as Shadip or Ga Nat (Earth Spirit). But, as one would expect of traditions preserved by bards relying on memory alone and adapting their *saga* to sweeten the conceits of particular audiences in widely scattered and isolated places, no two versions of their genealogy agree. According to Leach,[4] the story broadly is as follows. One of Shadip's sons, known as *Ka-ang Duwa*, or Lord

3. Hanson (1913: 20ff). Tegenfeldt (1974: 19) follows Hanson in charting the route of Jinghpaw and Maru expansion and imputing it to strong Burman and Shan resistance in the Mogaung area, but Leach (1954: 231) attaches 'no value at all to this kind of speculation'.
4. Leach (1954: 268–71).

of the Middle Earth ('a title with a strongly Chinese flavour'), took upon himself human form and mated with an alligator (= dragon, another Chinese touch), who begat the progenitors of the Rawangs, Chinese, Shans, Marus, Nagas and Jinghpaws. The marriage of a descendant in the Jinghpaw line with Madai Hpraw Nga (Goddess White Buffalo) established the Shingra (Original) Dynasty and was the occasion of the first *manau* (annual feast at which Jinghpaws assemble to hear the recitation of their genealogy). From their progeny eventually sprang Wahkyet Wa, whose sons were the founders of the five clans, Lahpai, Lahtaw, Maran, Marip and Nhkum, comprising not only all Jinghpaws but, by some inscrutable system of cognation, many of the other tribes as well.

Younger brothers rank before older brothers in the Kachin order of inheritance, and, similarly, ultimogeniture governs precedence between clans. Anyone intent upon inciting mischief among Kachins need only ask a member of one clan in the presence of a member of another clan to relate his descent from Wahkyet Wa. The eponymous ancestor of the Marips, although the eldest of Wahkyet Wa's sons, became, according to the Marips, the pre-eminent chief retrospectively by virtue of the fact that the descendants of his younger brothers either died or were absorbed into the Marips. The Lahtaws, on the other hand, maintain that their ancestor (Wahkyet Wa's second son) married a daughter of the sky *nat*, Musheng, and that the descendants of his younger brothers either died or were absorbed into the Lahtaws; that, moreover, modern Marip claims to precedence are bogus, for all true Marips died long ago. Lahpais, Marans, and Nhkums proffer rival versions of this genealogy to defend the superiority of their clans.

Clan denotes consanguinity. Hence marriage between a 'sister' born in the Shan State having the same surname as a 'brother' born in the Hukawng Valley is prohibited as incestuous, although the relationship between them may be likened to that between a Smith born in Wales and a Smith born in Texas. Nor can a female marry into a family from which her brother has taken a wife. These notional relationships are further complicated by the fact that families can carry different names in different places. Thus Labangs of Myitkyina cannot marry Hkahku Dutsans or Jasens of the Hukawng, because they are members of the same family merely answering to different names. Hanson's 1913 list of 'leading families among the commoners' includes 120 names and suggests that only a few of them were able to identify their noble pedigree. Three quarters of a century later it seemed to us that not only all Jinghpaws but many Marus, Lashis, Azis and Lisu as well had adapted these lineages to their own pedigrees and traced their families back to one of the sons of Wahkyet Wa.

Of course, we knew none of this when we encountered the road barrier and uniformed woman that morning (29 January, 0500 hours Chinese time) and waited silently in the freezing taxi while she went through her procedures. Our destiny seemed to depend on Kyaw Nyunt, that great man of words. After putting down the receiver, the woman summoned him into the house. We waited anxiously, thinking it very odd that the Chinese should post a solitary female sentry at this sensitive border. Kyaw Nyunt returned to the car and infuriated us by barking out our names. We told him to be quiet: there was a whisker of a chance that she had not perceived anything unusual. No Chinese soldier would be awake at this hour, he scoffed. '*This woman KIA*!'

We followed him into the house, where we were greeted by Liaison Camp Commander Captain First Son of Sut Lut, who spoke a few words of English, a rare faculty among the Kachins we were to learn. He informed us that we had been expected the previous day. Half asleep and talking errantly, we warmed our hands around a wood fire. The sentry fetched a pot of sweet, hot coffee and plates of sliced bread, which we toasted over the fire on bamboo skewers. Daylight was breaking, and, outside, the ground was blanketed in frost. The empty Subaru parked beside a small cold stone marking the border seemed quite forlorn – but what would happen if the Chinese spotted it and demanded to know who had crossed? 'Never mind,' said Sut Lut Gam reassuringly. 'No need to worry. KIA will take care of you.'

I urged Kyaw Nyunt to rest before returning to Möng Ko, but he replied that he would rest in Zhanfeng. He was keen to make his purchases before the shops closed. 'Work before pleasure,' he proclaimed with a huge farewell grin. The telephone rang. KIO General Secretary *Salang Kaba* (Revered Elder) Zawng Hra was waiting to greet us.

* * *

Pajau Bum, whither the KIA had shifted its GHQ after a sustained siege in 1987 displaced it from a valley beyond a ridge to the west, had a be-quick-about-it, Dettol quality: flagpoles, parade grounds lined with whitewashed stones, a marquee serving as an assembly hall, lined footpaths, cane-edged steps, volleyball courts, whitewashed cane litter baskets, and posts strung with generator and communications wires. A short drive past a training ground for the All Burma Students Democratic Front (ABSDF) and a steep climb took us to the guesthouse, a cane bungalow with a capacious living room and four tiny bedrooms. Outside, at a safe distance, was a pit latrine or *nam dum* (forest store) and a matted enclosure for bathing. All water was fetched by hand in cane hollows called *hka nhtung*. There was no kitchen. Food was prepared outside.

Captain Zau Seng[5] was in charge of the guesthouse. His other duties with the KIA were obscure. Everyone called him Captain, but he had been stripped of this rank for 'firing a weapon without an order and without a target', a crime for which he felt no remorse. He had been overwhelmed by curiosity to test the capabilities of an unfamiliar cannon captured from the Burmans, he said, and were he faced with the same temptation again he would repeat the offence. 'We Kachins are very fond of guns.' He seemed to divide his time between playing with his dog, Rocky, a big fleecy animal like a husky, and flirting with the female soldiers assigned to kitchen duties at the General Secretary's house next door. He was a sensitive and unfailingly delightful host. Under his command were two cheerful young men, Sergeants Awng Seng La and Hpau Yan Gam, who sprang stiffly to attention and saluted when we arrived.

They sprang to attention again at the approach of a balding, bespeckled man in his early fifties, the KIO's General Secretary, who greeted us effusively. 'If you come back after we get our freedom we will give you a bigger house.' We apologized for arriving so

5. No relationship to the KIO's Foreign Secretary, Gauri Zau Seng, or to its former President, Lahtaw Zau Seng, and General Secretary, Pungshwe Zau Seng, who were assassinated in 1975. *Zau* is an honorific used to designate the sons of a chief. Leach suggests (controversially) that it may be a corruption of the Shan title, *saohpa*, meaning 'lord of the paddy fields'.

early in the morning. 'No! No! Everyone at Pajau Bum always get up at 0500 hours,' he protested, and, presenting us with greatcoats and fur hats, he added, 'You must be very cold. With these clozes you will stay warm if you stay near the fire. Anything you want, please inform Captain Zau Seng. KIA take care of everything.'

We settled in, a tailor came and measured us for KIA uniforms, then Zawng Hra took us to a small timber bungalow to meet Major General Malizup Zau Mai, KIO Vice-Chairman and KIA Chief of Staff. A big man, about six feet tall, taller than anyone else we saw in Kachinland, and resembling a marshal of the Red Army in the greatcoat he wore over his barrel chest, he rose to greet us as we entered. Brigadier Tu Jai, formerly KIO Vice-Chairman and KIA Chief of Staff and now the KIA's Vice-Chief of Staff, Lieutenant-Colonel Kam Htoi, the third highest ranking officer on the military side and a member of the KIO's ruling council, and several other very senior aides were with him, all seated in wooden armchairs around his *dap* (fireplace). Mats's nationality provoked extravagant comparisons with Ola Hanson and Bertil Lintner. 'Such people,' said Zau Mai bluffly, 'have given to Kachinland, not robbed it of its treasures,' as had the Burmans. 'Humanly speaking, Kachinland is in Sweden's debt,' he said.

The door remained open to admit the light, and the wind gusting through the tiny house blew the smoke from the *dap* back in our faces to the embarrassment of our hosts, who rose in a body and offered to swap places with us. We huddled in our coats close to the blazing logs. 'This camp is rimmed by mountains,' I remarked. 'Do I understand correctly that the Burma Army is just beyond the ridge, only five miles to the west of us?'

'About a mile from us,' corrected Zau Mai.

'Aren't you concerned that they will renew the attack?'

'They stay in their bunkers,' he replied. 'If they come out, we shoot them.'

'But you are surrounded?'

'They also are surrounded.'

He said that the attack on their former headquarters had been a theatrical stunt to vindicate Rangoon's boast that it was the superior force in Kachin State; indeed, soon after the attack diplomats and journalists had been flown from Rangoon to verify what was presented to them as a significant victory. 'But what is one more mountain in Kachinland, Mr Shelby? If they push us off one mountain we move to the next mountain.'

This was the first of several meetings with the KIO's higher command, under whose patient tuition we would make an earnest attempt to understand the intricacies of Kachin, National Democratic Front (NDF), Democratic Alliance of Burma (DAB) and Burmese politics.[6] But I was too tired from our overnight trip to enter upon much of a conversation then and soon excused myself. They were plainly disappointed. To the stoical Kachins, fatigue betrays a weakness of spirit, and I fear that they perceived my behaviour as lack of enthusiasm for their cause. I might be a writer, but I was no Ola Hanson or Bertil Lintner. We returned to the guesthouse and went immediately to bed. I slept for 12 hours.

When I wake roosters are crowing all over the hills. Soldiers are already exercising, though it is still pitch dark. A drill sergeant shouts at them, belligerently, and they respond in unison, belligerently. Sergeant Awng Seng La enters the living room, lights a storm lantern and revives the fire. Rocky (I can see him through the lattice) rises slowly and, bending back like a contortionist, scratches behind his ear. Zau Seng has tied him to one of the cane struts to prevent him from incinerating himself. There is a snapping of flames and the resinous smell of burning pine, but the fire's warmth does not penetrate through to my room. I reach for my clothes and tuck them into my sleeping bag with me and lie there for a while. It is the moment in the day when I usually confront my failures and make pious resolutions aimed at redressing them, but this morning I was thinking about the Burmese Civil War.

---

6. In 1989 the NDF, a military alliance among the main ethnic insurgent groups opposed to Rangoon, comprised the Chin National Front (CNF), KIO, Karen National Union (KNU), Karenni National Progressive Party (KNPP), Lahu National Organization (LNO), National Unity Front of Arakan (NUFA), New Mon State Party (NMSP), Palaung State Liberation Party (PSLP), Pao National Organization (PNO), SSPP and Wa National Organization (WNO). The DAB, a political alliance of parties opposed to the junta, then comprised all the members of the NDF except the KNPP and ten other groups, including the ABSDF. The CPB belonged to neither the NDF nor the DAB but supported some of their members and other groups opposing the junta with arms. The picture was further complicated by a number of warlord groups, like Khun Sa and Moh Heng's MTA, which professed political aims but were chiefly interested in narcotics.

Who and what were to blame for all this bloodletting? Burman racial arrogance and contempt for the hill peoples? The British who recruited the hill peoples to help subdue the Burmans? The Karens for siding with the British in three wars against the Burmans? The BIA for the atrocities they perpetrated on the minorities before the Japanese interceded? The Director of the Frontier Areas Administration, Henry Noel Stevenson, for failing to persuade the Kachins to continue as a British protectorate until they were able to make wise decisions about their future status? Aung San for sweet-talking them into acceding to the delusive hopes of the Panglong Agreement instead of acting on their gut distrust of the Burmans? Sama *Duwa* Sinwa Nawng for venally heeding Aung San's promise of personal preferment and persuading his people to reject Commissioner Stevenson's offer? U Saw, reputed instigator of Aung San's assassination before the 'Father of Burma's Independence' was able to honour his pledges to the hill peoples? U Nu for excluding the communists from the cabinet that carried through independence? The Buddhist zealots who threw an incendiary bomb into the church full of Karen worshippers at Palaw on Christmas Eve 1948? The insurgents for rebelling? Successive administrations in Rangoon for insensitivity to the minorities? The greed and corruption of the drugs trade? Ne Win for 26 years of purblind, doctrinaire, genocidal, egomaniacal, mendacious dictatorship? The rest of the world for its myopic indifference?[7]

---

7. 'For a few years now, I have been trying to alert people ... in the US to the horrible Southeast Asia tragedy of Burma. I used to tell people over there when I'd sit with them in their bamboo houses, "Burma is like a nice-looking piece of fruit – like a perfect orange – to the outside world. But then if we peel the orange, perhaps inside it's rotten. And perhaps, even though it looks perfect outside, maybe there is a big worm inside." And that worm was Ne Win. Now that the fruit has been ... ripped open, through the courage of the urban revolution in Burma ... [t]he outside world knows ... that Burma has been tortured and plundered by this man, Ne Win, who has the thieving corruption of Marcos, the evil terror tactics of Duvalier, the double-dealing narcotics trafficking of Norriega, and the murderous thirst for blood of Pol Pot. And he has been in power for longer than most of them combined. ... We in the United States now know, so we must care. It's like a miner trapped inside a mine in a cave-in, calling for help. If you don't know that he's down there, trapped inside the mine, and you walk past, that's OK. But if you hear him down there calling "Help me! Help me!", you have to do something about it.' Address made by Edith Mirante at a public rally in New York soon after the 1988 riots. This intrepid lady went to

Light appears through the pores of the outside wall. Dawn is about to break over the hills to the east. A whistle blows. It is time to rise, to make the first great effort of the long and interesting day before us. In a burst of willpower, I lift myself onto a sitting position on the pillow, my legs still within the sleeping bag, and put on my shirt. Golly, it's cold! Then I put on my pullover.

By 0600 hours, when the whistle blows again, I am dressed like a Mongol in padded greatcoat and round, fur-lined hat and in the living room sitting in an armchair of rough-hewn timber writing up my diary. Rocky, released from his bondage, has gone outside on his first recce. In about an hour it will be light enough to open the door and blow out the storm lantern. Zau Seng and Mats are still debating the transition to activity, but, in a few minutes, they will join me around the fire to warm their hands. A new watch has relieved the troops invigilating the enemy in its dark bunkers in the valley to the west of us. I can now hear the new recruits shouting responses in unison while they drill and know that, at least for the moment, we are safe from the Burmans.

After breakfast I climbed up to the ridge above the guesthouse and looked out at Xima, a tiny, inert clump of buildings wrapped in blue haze, and at the road from Möng Ko, a thin, honey-pale trace through the forest, and reflected on the improbability of it all. A month ago I had been waiting for Mats to finish celebrating New Year's Day with a transitory girlfriend without any real belief that he would go to Burma with me, half expecting a telegram announcing that he had changed his mind; nor would I have blamed him. He was 22, with a lot of the world to see. Burma was my enthusiasm, not his, an *idée folle* that I had talked him into. Had we really been to CPB Northern Bureau headquarters and met all those fantastical people? What was I doing here at KIA GHQ, on Mount Pajau, in the Sama hills, in Kachinland? It was really too absurd. Scarcely more than a fortnight ago I had never

---

Khun Sa's headquarters in the Shan State to interview him and was declared *persona non grata* by the Thai authorities, probably for exposing their own involvement with the narcotics trade. Her book, *Burmese Looking Glass* (1993), and her many articles relating to the trade, the devastation of Burma's forests, the spread of AIDS among the hill tribes, and the Burma Army's use of the hill people as slave porters and human mine sweepers are original contributions to our understanding of the Burmese Civil War.

seen a Kachin. Now I wanted nothing more than to learn their curious language and all their strange ways, to send for Carole and share with her my exciting new discovery. I knew as though instinctively that among the Kachins I would be utterly content. Was the Burma Army really poised in bunkers just beyond that ridge behind us? Fancying that Richard Burton, Francis Younghusband, T. E. Lawrence, Richard Halliburton, Peter Fleming and Fitzroy Maclean used similarly to sit on ridges and meditate like absurdities, I studied the terrain and devised a plausible escape route in case the Burmans decided to sally forth from their bunkers.

The ridge path led past Zawng Hra's house, and I decided to call on him. His house was altogether grander than Zau Mai's spartan, untidy quarters, and its ambience of composed domesticity, the picture calendars on the walls, the curtains and pots of cut flowers by the windows, betrayed the fastidious influences of a wife. A table doubled as his secretaire and the KIO's Home Office. He had just concluded a meeting with Mats, who had gone there to thresh out the KIO's intentions for us, but I refrained from asking what had been decided; Mats would tell me later. We talked for a while about the KIA, then about his teachers at Kachin Baptist High School in Myitkyina, where he had spent his early years; then, without any prompting from me, he warned of the dangers of walking across Kachinland. He produced a photocopy of a magazine article by a Colonel James Fletcher, who had commanded a company of Kachin irregulars during what the Kachins call the Japan War (Second World War). It spoke of leeches that would rise from the mud and descend from the overhanging foliage 'moving as though to music'; which would latch onto your skin and, penetrating it with tiny, incisor teeth, inject into your veins a toxic anticoagulant. They had to be removed with a match or cigarette, as pinching them off with the fingers would leave behind their decapitated heads, which often turned septic. 'Only in Second Brigade area are they bad during dry season,' said Zawng Hra reassuringly. Later, I tracked Colonel Fletcher to an address in Georgia and wrote to him to tell him of my own experiences with the celebrated leeches of Kachinland.

Mats's report of his meeting with Zawng Hra was both encouraging and disturbing. While carefully avoiding making any firm commitment to us, the General Secretary had said that, *if* we were allowed to proceed to India, the KIA would escort us and we would not travel by the direct route, as the Burma Army garrisoned the intervening valleys and some of the Shans living there were in its pay. The direct route was ten marches almost due west to Second Brigade headquarters at the edge of the Hukawng Valley, on the Upper Chindwin, then north to the Chaukan Pass. The indirect route, which was north to First Brigade headquarters, then west to Second Brigade headquarters, then north to the Chaukan Pass, was safer, but it was also much longer and led over more difficult terrain. Zawng Hra doubted whether a man of my ripe years could endure the punishing physical strain of such a march. There was another route from Second Brigade headquarters, that taken by Bertil Lintner. It led due west to the hills beyond the Hukawng Valley, where the KIA could hand us over to the Nagas. However, the Nagas had fallen out among themselves since Lintner's trek, and their wrangling had security implications for a KIA unit charged with delivering us to them. 'We do not want that you are cut down in the crossfire,' Zawng Hra had said, obscurely.

* * *

China has since opened the roads south of Dali to Europeans, and *sara ni*, or teacher people as the Kachins call us, are no longer exotic at Pajau Bum, but, in January 1989, our only predecessor was Bertil Lintner. We were acutely conscious of our strangeness. We felt as James Bruce might on reaching Gondar in the eighteenth century, the sensation of numberless eyes mutely studying us, awed and a little horrified. I wrote to Carole:

> Everyone says: 'Do not worry about your journey. We help you!' So don't worry about our journey. The KIA will help us. But as yet no decision has been taken as to whether or when we will be allowed to proceed to India. Please tell Mats's mother that he is well and safe. Hurriedly, because the KIO's car leaves for Xima in a few minutes, and the General Secretary has offered to post letters for us.

As word of our presence spread, visitors began to appear at the guesthouse. The first to call on us was the KIA's oldest serving officer and its official historian, Major N Chyaw Tang, a stout little man with bristly grey hair. Although an Anglocentric note in my diary designates him merely as 'someone who served with the British Army', he had devoted all of his adult life to war. He first trained for it, then practised it, then thought about it in the monasticism of prison, then practised it some more, then thought about it further in the pensive quiet of another prison, then wrote about it. His opinion of it carried weight, and his story, briefly told, bears repeating for the light it sheds on the Kachin insurgency.

In 1941 N Chyaw Tang had been a rifleman with the Myitkyina battalion of the Burma Frontier Force. When the Japanese invaded, his unit retreated to India and assisted in the defence of Imphal. Later, after the Northern Kachin Levies was formed to operate behind enemy lines, N Chyaw Tang volunteered for it and served in C Company under Ian Fellowes-Gordon, whose books described their part in reconquering Burma. Ian Fellowes-Gordon now lived in Scotland, and N Chyaw Tang still corresponded with him.[8]

The Levies' task was to harass the Japanese and prevent them from establishing a base from which their fighters might interdict the C-46s and C-47s of the United States Tenth Army Air Force, then supplying Chiang Kai-shek over 'the hump'. They worked slowly south, down both banks of the Mali Hka, ambushing Japanese columns and forcing their steady retreat, while Chinese and American forces ('Merrill's Marauders') fought through the Hukawng Valley, eventually converging with the Chindits in the siege of Myitkyina. It never occurred to N Chyaw Tang that they would not defeat the Japanese. 'Because of the familiarity with the geographical condition, we had the upper hand,' he said. 'We were used to the hills and jungles, and, also, on account of the hard life, we had the upper hand. We don't know the luxury life.'

Myitkyina was retaken on 3 August 1944, but some of the Japanese escaped through an opening in the Chinese lines. 'In those days, before General Stilwell trained them properly, the Chinese armies were quite useless,' said N Chyaw Tang. 'They had no discipline, and that is everything in an army.'

---

8. Major Fellowes-Gordon, whose mother was American and whose godfather was Franklin Roosevelt, died in 1991 in Scotland. His books about the Levies are *Amiable Assassins* (1957) and *The Battle for Naw Seng's Kingdom* (1971).

Later, the Levies became 1 and 2 Kachin Rifles. The British sent N Chyaw Tang, who by now was his company's quartermaster, for further training at Dehra Dun and Maymyo. First Kachin Rifles supported the government when the communist insurrection broke out in March 1948. 'The Burman soldiers either deserted or joined the rebels.' However, when the Karens revolted the following year, 1 Kachin Rifles joined them, even though it meant the loss of their pensions. Now fighting against their former comrades, they took Maymyo and freed nearly 5000 Karens and were scarcely 50 miles from Rangoon when N Chyaw Tang was wounded in the foot. But the communists and the ethnics wasted their power fighting between themselves and were eventually obliged to retire. Then he and some of the other Kachins left the Karens to fight under Naw Seng in the Kachin Sub-State. He was captured in Kutkai and remained in prison for eight years, until U Nu proclaimed a general amnesty.

Meanwhile, disenchantment with the vanishing promises of Panglong spread among the Kachin community, and they began preparing for their own state. On 5 February 1961, they declared their independence. N Chyaw Tang was indomitably in the thick of it again, in charge of training.

'We had almost no weapons. Lahtaw Zau Tu, our Vice-Chief of Staff, led a raid on the treasury at Lashio for money to buy more weapons, and we soon controlled all of Kachinland.' Hoping to exploit his former contacts in the Indian Army to obtain more arms for the KIA, N Chyaw Tang went to India, where, however, brutish border officials incarcerated him for another two years.

The Kachins had made many mistakes, but their greatest mistake, said N Chyaw Tang, was to gamble their future on the effusions of a youth of 31, Aung San, who was already stained by the blood of hill people. Their other big mistake was to fight the communists in 1948 when the loyalty of the Kachin Rifles was critical to Nu's survival. No Burman leader would ever implement terms such as those agreed at Panglong. Burman arrogance was too great and the hatred between the two communities was too deep, he said.

'Before the Japan War, we saw very little of the Burmans. There was no ill feeling, because there was little contact. They used Aung San's alliance with the Japanese to punish the Karens and Kachins for our sympathies with the British. They burned our villages and raped our women. They cut a *duwa* (chief) into small pieces and salted his wounds. They buried another man up to his neck to die in front of his wife. He told her not to worry, that their youngest son would look after her. The Burmans talk sweet, but they are cruel.' The Burmans 'knew the luxury life', which accounted for their 'cowardice and cruelty.'[9]

I asked N Chyaw Tang how long the war would last and who would win. 'If God gives us the victory, then we will win,' he replied simply. Meanwhile, he kept the manuscript of his official history of the KIA in China to prevent it from falling into the hands of the Burmans.

Next day Zawng Hra took me to meet the new recruits to the ABSDF undergoing training by the KIA. I knew how eager they were to fight the Burma Army, which they perceived as no better than a private army protecting Ne Win's narcokleptocracy. We had seen their comrades at Möng Ko but had exchanged only light pleasantries with them. We found about two dozen youths seated in a circle around a bonfire, behind them some tables spread with plates of biscuits and sticky sweets. Zawng Hra introduced me. Everyone smiled and joined arms, and pictures were snapped. Then I asked for a brief autobiographical statement from each of them, including name, age, where he was studying, what he was studying and his reason for joining the ABSDF. 'That is not possible, Mr Tucker,' admonished Zawng Hra. 'They are afraid you will tell the Burmese government.' (I learned afterwards that some of them had been executed by the ABSDF for spying for Rangoon.)

Zawng Hra abandoned us, cheerfully advising that a car would fetch me when I had completed my investigation. 'You will manage,' he said breezily. 'One of them speaks Hindustani.'

Somehow we managed; partly in a queer vocabulary deduced from their pooled scraps of classroom English, partly in Hindu-

---

9. The human rights abuses the Burma Army routinely practises today may be a legacy of Japanese counter-insurgency tactics. See, for example, Fletcher (1984: 35): 'The Japanese officer in charge of the party returned to where Brown's body lay. He searched the body and ordered one of the Shans to cut a stout bamboo pole on which Brown's head was then mounted. After which they marched back to the Kachin village where the pole was planted in the middle of the village for all the natives to see.'

stani, which I speak very, very badly, and partly in vigorous dumb show. It presently appeared that all of them shared the same aims: 'I am join ABSDF to fight for democracy and human rights.' 'These are laudable aims,' I said, 'but it might help me better to understand your cause if you could provide specific examples of the abuses that you have suffered. If you can give me the names of the victims, age, time, place, names or particulars of the perpetrators, I will relay them to Amnesty International. Has any of you *seen* anyone being beaten or tortured? Do you know *why* he was beaten or tortured?'

A good deal of thoughtful discussion ensued before someone asserted that a policeman had shot one of his mates through the head for demonstrating. However, he cautioned, he had not seen the shooting. He had only heard about this atrocity from someone who saw it.

'*I* was there!' cried one of the others. 'He was killed on 12 August 1988. His name was Zau Nan. He was a Kachin. He was 16 years old, and he was enrolled in the seventh standard at a school in Myitkyina.'

This encouraged others to speak out. They spoke of a Buddhist monk who had been arrested and murdered (though the witness could not recall the exact date). They talked of a monk arrested in Myitkyina on 19 September (but the witness did not know if the Burma Army had also murdered him), and of a Baptist pastor who had been arrested in Myitkyina on 7 July. In August the Burma Army had killed 12,776 people in Rangoon alone.

'How can you be certain of the exact number? I had understood that no more that 5000 died in this particular massacre.' But they were certain; 12,776 was the correct number. 'All Myitkyina march on 8.8.88' – 8 August 1988, when workers, farmers, students, government officers, monks, pastors, priests and mullahs throughout Burma had demonstrated against military rule. 'Six hundred thousand people! No one support government except army, police and government party politicians!'

I asked if the manifestations were spontaneous.

'Spontaneous! Spontaneous!' they cried. 'All students hate Ne Win! Ne Win is monster!' The monster had resigned in form only, was still running everything, and was responsible for the deaths and gaolings of millions of Burmese who wanted only a better government for Burma. Their 701 unit and the KIA's Fifth and Sixth Battalions had attacked a police post at Mohnyin and liberated demonstrators the monster had gaoled, among them a young schoolteacher who had since joined the ABSDF. They indicated a diminutive lady in a *longyi* seated at the far end of the circle. 'Were you gaoled for demonstrating for democracy and human rights?' I asked. She lowered her eyes modestly.

I enquired if they had evidence linking the Burma Army with the drugs trade. The government would not make such a fuss about opium eradication if it were not involved in trafficking, they replied; however, such business was conducted in secret. Then one of them thrust at me a scrap of paper on which had been written some words in Burmese and shouted, 'Proof! Proof!' The others now joined in. 'This letter to Burma Army commander,' they said.

'What does it say?' I asked.

It concerned a consignment of opium transported by a Burma Army convoy. 'Proof! Proof!' they cried in unison.

We linked arms and posed for more photographs. The positives revealed a tired old man in a greatcoat and fur hat amid eager young orientals in smart new uniforms. Anyone might have written on a scrap of paper alleging Burma Army complicity in the drugs trade; but I had not the least doubt of their sincerity. And I learned later that they acquitted themselves with valour in combat against the Burma Army.

The jeep sent to fetch me took me on to meet the Chairman of the United Liberation Front of Ahom (ULFA). Later, Indian Special Branch detectives would show us a rogues' gallery of wanted terrorists and ask us if we could identify any of them — and there he was! He had many pseudonyms, but we knew him only as Castro, owing to his marked likeness to the Cuban autocrat. I knew that the KIO was eager to establish good relations with Delhi. Why, then, was it hosting the leader of an organization that was at war with Delhi? I was also curious to know how he had got to Pajau Bum, presumably by one of the routes Zawng Hra had described to Mats. If so, it would be useful to learn from him what route he had taken, how long it had taken him and how arduous it was.

He and two of his staff officers were waiting for me outside his quarters, dressed in jungle camouflage. I was taken aback, very momentarily, when sentries snapped to and presented arms, a measure of formality for which I was not prepared and eliciting from me by its suddenness a slovenly salute. 'Welcome,' said Castro with a huge, *vache qui rit* grin. 'Welcome,' he said, shaking my hand fervently. 'You are very welcome.' A round of commemorative photographs, more warm words of welcome, then, arm over my shoulder, we went inside and sat together on a bench beside a table where a bowl of seeds had been placed for me to munch on while he spoke of his cause. Even as an undergraduate, he said, he had been planning a better future for his people. 'Like Lenin,' reverently observed one of his aides-de-camp. 'Yes,' concurred Castro with a deep sigh, 'like Lenin.' Although enrolled in the history and economics faculties, his courses had been mere cover for his revolutionary enterprise. Later, he had fronted as a businessman and social worker. The real turning point, though, had come on 7 April 1979, when he and nine other patriots had taken to the jungles and founded ULFA. They had established their headquarters at Dei Kau Reng, and, for more than a decade, under his leadership, their small but determined band of guerrillas had harried and tormented the Indian invader.

'Where is Dei Kau Reng?' I asked.

'It is mobile headquarters.'

'Where is your headquarters now?' I enquired.

'It is here. Where I am is headquarters.'

'So far from Assam?'

'Never mind.'

'How long have you been at Pajau Bum?'

'Two years.'

'Doesn't it blunt your effectiveness being so far from the front line?'

'Not blunt,' he said. 'It is tactical decision. We are regrouping.'

'When will you be returning to Assam?'

'Please, sir,' said the other staff officer, 'Assam is Indian name.'

'Actually, it is Burmese,' corrected the Chairman; 'like *Shan* and *Siam*. We call our country *Ahom*.'

'What is the aim of your movement?' I asked.

'Pardon?'

'Is your revolution nationalist and social, or purely nationalist?'

'We are not Marxists,' interjected his GS1.

'Certainly not!' confirmed the Chairman indignantly. 'Our aims are quite different!'

'What are they?'

'We want to come to final decision with India by armed revolution, not by peaceful means. We can never allow to split our land anymore for any reason by the enemy or by their puppets.'

Suddenly the atmosphere changed. Something was amiss. The Chairman's great round brown eyes flashed; his lips quivered. The two staff officers withdrew, terrified. They returned a moment later and placed a tin mug of black, unsweetened, tepid tea on the bench beside me. All was well again.

It presently appeared that their grievances arose from the imperfect arrangements made after Partition for securing the rights of Indian states whose princes had acceded voluntarily to the suzerainty of the British Crown. The British had ruled Ahom from 1826 to 1947, and, following Partition, Ahom had been a self-governing state until 26 October 1949, when, with the secret connivance of its chief minister, the Indian Army invaded. The chief minister's only authority for this surrender of their sovereignty, said Castro, was the power Nehru conferred on him. 'He is corrupt stooge!' All true Ahomese repined for Ahom's golden age, the sixteenth or seventeenth century, he was not exactly sure, but at any rate when it was governed from Sibsagar. '*Sagar* means sea, and *Sib* commemorates Prince Siba,' a rajah who had excavated a lake next to his palace; hence 'Sibsagar'. 'It is largest man-made lake in world!'

Cultural suppression had followed the loss of their sovereignty. True, Ahomese had remained the language of instruction in schools, but the award of places at university and appointment to government posts now depended on a knowledge of Hindi! Ahomese dance and pantomime, once the envy of the world, were drowning in a flood of Hindi films, Hindi songs and Hindi television and radio programmes. Kalipuja, hateful reminder of the time when an Indian woman betrayed the Ahomese, and Durgapuja, evoking Indian conquest of Ahomese *asura* (demons), were now, outrageously, the state's most important public holidays. There was also economic discrimination. Ahom received only a fifth of the royalties from the oil pumped from Digboi,[10] barely more than Bengal received in transmission taxes. Delhi and private Indian shareholders kept the rest. It was similar with Ahomese tea, timber and coal. Foreigners, mainly Bengalis, Rajasthanis, Madrasis and Punjabis, bribed Indian Administrative Service officers for preferential treatment in the award of contracts and concessions.

But their most pressing grievance, Castro explained, was population infiltration. So many tea labourers and businessmen had migrated to their motherland that the Ahomese were fast becoming a minority there. 'Therefore, we want to overthrow Indian administration and expel from Ahom. India is our enemy. We want our land and we want our peoples to get free from colonial occupation and oppression. Exploitation, either economic or non-economic, in any form by foreign power, cannot tolerate. We are for oppressed and against oppressors.'

'How do you intend to arrange things after your victory?' I asked. 'Do you want a planned economy or one driven by private enterprise?'

'We want democracy.'

We went outside to pose for final photographs.

Mats's agenda had been the converse of mine. 'How were the students?' I asked him.

'One of them said that he wanted freedom and democracy. All the others said that they wanted democracy and freedom. How was your meeting with the Assamese?'

'I wonder why he's here and how he got here? He seemed not to want to tell me. What did you get out of him?'

'We discovered that we have chewing tobacco in common, and I got an idea about the politics of Assam, which, frankly, I hadn't known existed before.'

'Not Assam,' I said. '*Ahom.*'

* * *

---

10. About 70 years ago, so the story goes, a British geologist found oil bubbling up from some marshes and, turning to an Indian colleague, said, 'Dig, boy!' In consequence, *Digboi* became the centre of Assam's oil fields.

Zau Seng had told us not to worry, and, by positing possible routes, Zawng Hra had encouraged us to hope. But after our brief meeting with Zau Mai, the big man had ignored us. Were we in for another Möng Ko of waiting, conjecture, evasion and, ultimately, disappointment? The more we thought about it, the less reason we saw for the KIO to assist us.

News now reached us that Seng Hpung had arrived at Pajau Bum. But he did not send for us; *he* called on *us*, an inversion of protocol that we took to be a bad sign. Obviously, we deduced, we had made a poor impression on his superiors and they had charged him with the task of delivering the *coup de grâce*. We expected an alternative offer: a long stay in Pajau Bum; a visit to the front line; an invitation from the headman of a Kachin village and loads of interviews with dignitaries, coupled, of course, with an offer to return us to Möng Ko at the KIO's expense. He was short of breath and exhausted from climbing the 300 steps to our quarters, but in cheerful spirits. All had not gone smoothly for him. His departure from Möng Ko had been delayed, and his party had not reached Xima until after dawn, where the *jing cha* had intercepted them, seized their maps and detained them for eight hours. Travelling through China with a false passport was always risky, he explained. The PLA and some people in high places in the Party supported the KIO, but, officially, the Kachin insurgents were outlaws. We heard about his harrowing ordeal and his other news and chatted generally. Then he broke the *real* news: we would be accompanying a duty column leaving for Second Brigade headquarters soon after Independence Day. 'I have duties in First and Second Brigade areas and will be commanding the escort column. From now on you are under my orders. You should write all your letters home now, and plan to travel lightly. Take only what you cannot do without, no luxuries. We will cross the Nmai Hka and travel north through the Triangle to First Brigade headquarters, then west across the Mali Hka to Second Brigade headquarters. Then we will turn north – towards India. I will accompany you as far as the border. The trip will take about six weeks. But there is a condition. The condition is that you teach me Indian history. A few briefings will be enough.'

We asked about the possibility of engaging an interpreter.

'*I* will be your interpreter,' said Seng Hpung.

He said that he had already made the decision to take us with him when we were in Möng Ko, but that the delicacy of the KIO's relations with the CPB had prevented him from telling us. We were to disclose these plans to no one.

'MI [Military Intelligence] has its spies everywhere, even at Pajau Bum. If the Burma Army learns of our plans, they will set up an ambush.'

So Zau Mai had ignored us for a reason. Protocol decreed that our escort commander tell us of the KIO's intentions for us. Once that obstacle was removed, we saw a great deal of Zau Mai and his staff. We would meet at his bungalow, and while we talked, muffled in our greatcoats and warming our hands over a blazing *dap*, men drilled in the flag square beyond the volleyball courts. It was bitterly cold, thick cloud occluding the sun. From time to time a soldier would appear at the open door, salute, shout a rapid-fire burst of Jinghpaw at Zau Mai, salute again and go away. Our hosts were hearty, enthusiastic and open. Of course, they must have harboured the same doubts about us that had perplexed the CPB in Möng Ko – a grey-haired man with a 'bodyguard' in tow had to be CIA or DEA – but our secret motives, whatever they might be, precluded nothing. Later, the Indians would venture the possibility of our returning to Mount Pajau as spies. They had no need of spies, we told them; they could go themselves, and the Kachins would protect and honour them, just as they had us, and, indeed, would any Burmans who decided to visit them.

Each of these meetings with Zau Mai and his staff had about it the air of a great occasion. Each morning after breakfast we descended the steps to his earthen-floored bungalow with hearts brimming with anticipation and each afternoon we returned with brains reeling with new, interesting but unassimilated and, for the most part, unverifiable information. As at Möng Ko, there was much to learn in a very short time.

Only N Chyaw Tang, and perhaps the KIO's Chairman, Brang Seng, knew as much about the Kachin insurgency as Zau Mai. At 52, he was the KIA's Chief of Staff and second only in the KIO to Brang Seng. Born in Myitkyina of a princely family of Jinghpaws, he had been educated, like most of the KIO's leaders, at Baptist mission schools. Seng Hpung, who was a year older, had overlapped with him at Nam Hkam Shweli Valley Baptist High School, and Brang Seng, who was three years older, at the American Baptist Missionary High School in Myitkyina.

Before the KIA openly declared its rebellion it existed as small nuclei of students at various institutions of learning and as the Kachin Youth Culture and Literature Uplift Organization in Myitkyina led by Brang Seng. Zau Mai was the secretary of the Kachin University Students Association at Rangoon University. It was a time of great ferment, the interlude between U Nu's two governments. Meeting U Nu merely confirmed Zau Mai in the belief that the Burmans would never honour and probably never had intended to honour their promises.

I asked him if he was not being rather hard on U Nu, who, after all, had convened the Taunggyi Conference specifically with the aim of implementing Panglong. He retorted that the Conference and the coup that ended it were separate stages in a plot agreed with Ne Win in advance to deny the minorities autonomy. A majority in parliament had voted to implement the assurances made to them at Panglong, he said, but as soon as it became plain that the Conference was going to grant them autonomy, all the party leaders, U Nu included, were arrested. But Ne Win released U Nu almost immediately and permitted him to leave the country and later allowed him to return to Burma and even awarded him the First Class Burma Honour Medal. The other party leaders and ethnic MPs remained in the lock-up and were awarded no medals. Sao Shwe Thaike, the first President of Burma, died in prison of remorse after his son was shot. 'U Nu spoke very sweetly,' said Zau Mai, 'but his attitude to minorities was a little crooked, and he maintained that attitude even after Ne Win deposed him. I believe that all the minorities share this impression of him.'

On leaving university in 1960, Zau Mai was instructed to penetrate the Burmese Civil Service. He worked as an assistant subdivisional officer at various posts in Kachin State until Zau Tu, then KIA Vice-Chief of Staff, informed him that he was needed as a soldier. The transition from civil servant to outlaw was swift. The KIA then comprised little more than a small band of enthusiasts led by Lahtaw Zau Seng, a Kachin who had fought with the Karens and Karennis, and his two brothers, Zau Tu and Zau Dan. The seven well-trained and well-equipped battalions of the Kachin Rifles, although sympathizing with their aims, had refused to join them, fearing that they would fail and thus lose their ranks and pensions. They had only 11 weapons, Chinese 79s, Japanese rifles, English rifles and revolvers, left over from the Second World War, some of them broken. 'People were donating their arms, smooth-bore, muzzle-loading, powder-fired, flintlock muskets dating back to 1827, which they had hidden from the Japanese, and our blacksmiths made more cap guns. We didn't have enough lead to make bullets and used metal from broken tools and ploughs and even rocks. But we were strong in military skills and discipline. All our instructors had served under British or American officers or in the Burma Army. And our cause was just.'

They used their few weapons to attack isolated police armouries and to ambush lonely Burma Army convoys for more arms. These captures enabled them to undertake more ambitious operations. The enemy had no target to strike back at, for after each of these operations the KIA units would fade back into the jungle. Their strength was commensurate with the number of their weapons.

By 1963 they were able to form two brigades of 2000 men each, each soldier receiving three months of basic training. Zau Mai was posted as intelligence officer to Model Brigade. Then Ne Win invited all insurgents, including the CPB, to peace talks, and Zau Mai was a delegate at those talks. Five colonels represented the dictator's Revolutionary Council. ('Ne Win did not participate himself, as he did not want to stain his reputation for patriotic purity.') If the KIO wished to discuss peace, said the colonels, they would first have to surrender their weapons. So they returned to the hills and resumed fighting.

A column under Zau Mai's command was sent to the Shwegu Plain between the Kachin and Shan states, inhabited mainly by Burmese-speaking Shans, and stayed there for 13 months with orders to harass the enemy and steal his supplies. The Burma Army retaliated with two offensives, the 'Closed Door' operation to surround them, and the 'Four Cuts' operation to annihilate them, boasting that they would annihilate the column within two months. They established concentration camps called *nam kahtawng* (jungle villages) and herded the people into them to sever their links with the KIA. People died of starvation, from trying to escape from the *nam kahtawng* and from illnesses caught in the *nam kahtawng*. The Four Cuts operation had some success in the Bhamo District, where the KIA was short of ammunition; the people were obliged to feed on yams and the bark of trees. But the more they were tortured, the more barbarous the atrocities done to them, the more they supported the KIA. 'We would keep a section near each *nam kahtawng* and create disturbances, and the people would escape and join us in the jungle.' With insufficient numbers to occupy the country effectively and an ever vanishing enemy always ready to strike at it, the Burma Army, heir to the once proud Burma Rifles battalions and Aung San's Burma National Army, was reduced to garrisoning the few large towns and keeping open the lines of communication between them, a farcical army of bunkers and convoys. It was very galling.

As the KIO widened the areas that it controlled, validating the hopes of the growing number of civilians who supported it, a rival force began snatching bits of its territory and disputing its authority. This was nothing but Burman pretension to hegemony armed with new slogans and cloaked in different uniforms; but it was even more menacing because it had China's support. The remnants of Naw Seng's followers were already fighting under the CPB's colours, and the CPB believed that their ideology entitled them to the support of all Kachins. They wanted, they said, a 'popular front'. 'Communists belong to all of Burma,' they said, meaning that they were entitled to occupy any part of Burma. The KIA was invited to China and promised all the weapons it needed if it would submit to CPB leadership and nothing if it refused. Refusal, said their presumptuous hosts, meant that they were 'running dogs of American capitalists' and 'bourgeois minded'. But the KIA did not quite see it in that light. They replied that they would not submit to anyone.

'The first actual firing was between the Second Battalion of the First Brigade commanded by Lieutenant-Colonel Tu Jai, and the CPB's 303 Force in the Möng Ya area of the Sub-State. This was a most regrettable war, Mr Shelby. Kachins were killing Kachins instead of fighting our common enemy. The Chinese provided modern weapons, military advisers and training to the CPB, while the Burma Army supplied us with weapons to kill them. Rangoon saw this as an opportune moment to renew the offer of peace talks. They thought that we might be in a mood to surrender and become a *ka kwe yei* [force allied to Rangoon]. But we added two brigades and brought up more than 1000 men to oppose the CPB's 202 Force and units of their 303 and 404 Divisions. Our Fourth Brigade commander, Lieutenant-Colonel Zau Dan, Lahtaw Zau Seng's brother, died in action. I took over his command and devised a plan called "Black Cat Storm", involving Palaung and Rakhine units in addition to our forces.'

Five months later, in August 1975, Rangoon agents assassinated Lahtaw Zau Seng and his other brother, Zau Tu, the KIO's Vice-President, and its General Secretary, Pungshwe Zau Seng, near Möng Fang on the Thai border. Disheartening as these killings were, they would prove to be a pivotal moment in the KIO's fortunes. Brang Seng succeeded as the KIO's Chairman and Tu Jai as the KIA's Chief of Staff; Zau Mai became the number two on both the civilian and military sides, Zawng Hra the KIO's General Secretary. Negotiations with the CPB resumed, with the communists renewing their demand for paramountcy and now claiming that the SSPP and other ethnic groups had already accepted their leadership and that the KIO were the only holdouts. Once more, the KIO was offered unlimited weapons, as well as autonomy, and, once more, it refused to yield its independence. Eventually, a purely military alliance was agreed, with mutually accepted lines defining their respective operational areas. 'Both sides have respected them,' said Zau Mai, 'although we both know that they are only temporary lines pending an end to the war. For the time being, relations with the communists are quite good.'

War with the communists had prevented the ethnic insurgencies, some of which had joined the 'popular front', from uniting. They now united in the NDF. The KIO then declared its willingness to join a federation with Burma that guaranteed the Kachins genuine autonomy, effectively reverting to what they had believed they were signing up to at Panglong. Eventually, even the Karens followed suit, marking a radical departure from their previous insistence on full independence. In 1980, talks with Rangoon resumed.

'These talks lasted more than five months and seemed quite promising at first. However, they turned sour when we raised the question of autonomy. Their negotiators said that Kachin State was already autonomous, so we proposed adding the word "Autonomous" to the official name of our state in the Constitution and holding a referendum among the Kachins to approve the change. But they replied that such a change raised a national, not a local issue, and insisted on a referendum to the *whole* of Burma. When we agreed to a national referendum, however, they broke off negotiations.'

Fighting erupted once again and intensified. Rangoon resumed its practice of herding people into *nam kahtawng* and its atrocities, and once again it was the civilian population who suffered the most: 1127 men and 796 women murdered in Western Division (Kachinland west of the Irrawaddy) alone by the end of 1981.

I asked Zau Mai if there was an end in sight, and, if not, how the war might end. He said that he did not know, but one possibility was intervention: one of the great powers might intervene to stop it. Certainly, more bloodshed would not end it. 'The enemy can't defeat us because of the difficulties of the terrain, and we can't defeat them because of their numbers,' he said. 'And', he added, 'as long as the Burmans insist on our surrendering our weapons as a prepayment for *talking* about peace, negotiations will not end it.'

Intervention? My views had shifted since Möng Ko, significantly influenced by a State Department report I had seen in the KIO's archives branding the KIO as narco-terrorists. I knew that, unless this stigma was removed, no one in Washington would risk his name on such an eventuality, and, as Washington's self-appointed envoy to the KIO, I felt it my duty to say so. Poppy cannot be concealed. It grows on hilltops where the jungle has been cut away. It is susceptible to satellite photography of pinpoint accuracy. The journalists the Burma Army brought to advertise the capture of the KIA's former headquarters had seen it. 'You deceive yourselves if you imagine that the Americans will involve themselves on your behalf while poppy grows in areas that you control,' I said.

Zau Mai did not answer immediately. And everyone present was curious to know how he would answer. Then he said:

> In 1964, we banned poppy growing in all our areas except the Southern and Eastern Divisions, where other crops could not be grown. But our people saw this as discriminatory, and we had no completely satisfactory answer to their criticism, since there were also places in the Northern

> and Western Divisions unsuitable for other crops. The farmers there petitioned us, and we granted them an exception, and soon there were so many exceptions that we had to stop enforcing the ban altogether. Opium is like a small hole in a tree. A termite enters the hole, makes more holes, and, before long, the tree dies. But we are not involved in this trade, Mr Shelby. If we were, our people would not support us. Let the DEA come and inspect! How many *Kachins* have there been among the opium merchants captured and put on display as examples of Ne Win's Drug Eradication Programme?

He repeated what Seng Hpung had told us.

> Even if our farmers could manage the capital to grow crops like coffee and tea, the Burma Army would destroy them – just as they cut down the orange trees along the Myitkyina–Bhamo road. I can say this from my own experience. In 1978 the Central Committee sent me to Nam Hkam Pa in Kachin State to supervise an irrigation scheme for paddies costing seven lakhs and involving 300 families. The Burma Army sent a company of soldiers and destroyed the entire scheme.

Seng Hpung had spoken about agent 2,4-D, the herbicide that the United States, in its zeal to combat drug-trafficking, had supplied to Rangoon for spraying on poppy fields. They had also supplied the aeroplanes and trained the pilots used in these crop-dusting operations. But the policy was seriously flawed. The Burma Army quickly discovered that the capabilities of agent 2,4-D, which was banned for use in the United States, greatly exceeded its use as a herbicide. It was so toxic that it killed almost everything it touched. It entered rivers and streams and spread beyond its target areas. People who drank from the rivers or ate food affected by it took violently ill. Its contaminating effects endured in the ground. It could be and was used as a tactical defoliant. It could be and was used to discourage the people from supporting the insurgents and to encourage them to support the Burma Army. It was ideal for ethnic cleansing. Nevertheless, the programme had its advocates in the US Congress and the NSC. It was cheap, no American lives were at risk, and, above all, its proponents were seen to be doing something. Extreme supporters even said that it was effective in reducing the amount of opium produced. Another report I had seen in the KIO's archives claimed that the 2,4-D spraying programme had eradicated 50,000 hectares of opium in NDF-controlled areas. I put this to Zau Mai.

> Good heavens [he cried]! If that were so, no opium would be left in Burma. Very little grows in the areas we control, and the only spraying targeted at poppy fields we have seen has been in a few places in the Sub-State, next to the road between Kutkai and Möng Nye and in the Loi Dau sector, amounting in all to less than forty acres. There has been no spraying in the Karen, Karenni, Pao, Mon, Rakhine and Chin areas, because no opium is grown there, and the opium grown in the CPB areas is protected by anti-aircraft cover. Where does the State Department get these figures, Mr Shelby? From the Burmans, of course. We are quite used to such lies. They pretend that they are America's ally in its 'war on drugs', but the only hill people who support them are those who produce opium, like Khun Sa. Their crops are *not* sprayed, and when their poppy shows up in aerial photographs, Rangoon tells the Americans that it is NDF poppy. 'Join us and save your crops,' the Burma Army says to our people, threatening to destroy our food crops if we refuse. They want to turn us into *ka kwe ye*, like the MTA. The only use that the Burma Army makes of these poisons is to further its war aims!

At the end of January 1987 I was at a place called Man Hpang in the CPB-controlled area of Shan State, on my way to Manerplaw. Some spraying had taken place on the western side of the Salween River, and the farmers living there had come to Man Hpang to ask for CPB anti-aircraft cover. Next to their fields was a plateau controlled by Rangoon. The farmers told me that some of the opium grown on that plateau wasn't sprayed because the farmers had bribed the Burma Army officers concerned, and while we were at Man Hpang we actually watched this selective spraying. What do you imagine we find when we overrun the enemy's positions? Stocks of opium awaiting transport in their convoys. Last March we took a 98 Burma Regiment post at Man Je, about eighteen miles southeast of Bhamo, and captured 180 *viss* [432 kilogrammes] of raw opium and some faked transport documents signed by its quartermaster. We reported this to the DEA, who passed the information to Rangoon, who passed it on to the unit's commander, who arrested and court-martialled his *intelligence officer*. Even the DEA admits that opium production has *increased* since the Burma Army began spraying our food crops.[11] You are a grown man, Mr Shelby. You should know better than to believe everything you read.

All that we saw and heard as we travelled through Kachinland confirmed what we were told at Möng Ko and Pajau Bum. US-supplied poison scattered from US-supplied aeroplanes flown by American-trained pilots had destroyed the Kachins' food crops, killed their livestock, contaminated their water, and prolonged the war with all its bloody consequences. Nevertheless, their faith in us was undiminished. They remembered the *sara kaba ni* (big teachers) who had taught them at Nam Hkam Shweli Valley Baptist High School and American Baptist Missionary High School. They remembered the Columban Fathers in Bhamo, Myitkyina and Kajihtu; the Anglicans in the Hukawng Valley; the Morses in Hkamti Long, and many others of our subspecies who had 'given to Kachinland', and believed that, sooner or later, we would awake to the truth and reverse what was unconscionable.

Two and a half years after Mats and I left the Kachin Hills, the KIO banned the growing of poppy in all areas under its control, and in 1994 Brang Seng died of a stroke, his passing lamented by all of Kachinland. Zau Mai succeeded him as the Chairman of the KIO.

11. The DEA estimated that 2000 tonnes of raw opium was produced in Burma during 1988/9, more than quadrupling the production of the two and a half years in which the spraying programme was operating (December 1985 to August 1988). Most of the product was destined for consumption in Europe and the United States.

* * *

The KIO's *nunc dimittis* hour had arrived – Independence Day, the special day that began without a whistle, without drilling before dawn, without euphonious war cries. Independence Day might have presented ideal conditions for a surprise air attack, but, this year, dense fog provided good cover, and the young warriors were sleeping in to the sound of soft music played over crackly loudspeakers. The General Secretary, who had fretted all week, was at peace. We would not be bombed.

The capacious canvas assembly hall was already well filled when, at 0900 hours, we took up the places reserved for us in the second row next to ULFA's beaming Chairman as the KIO's principal guests of honour. All of the other dignitaries were in uniform. Some even wore neckties. Junior officers were hurrying about putting the finishing touches on the decorations. Ranged along the carpeted, double-tiered earthworks that served as a stage were plastic buckets and pewter pots of cut flowers. Parti-coloured balloons and revolutionary slogans hung from the ceiling and KIO flags (crossed white swords on a red and green background) adorned the walls. Garish oil paintings manifested the twin goals of the Kachin revolution – Defeat of Tyranny (KIA soldiers with raised swords overrunning a Burma Army position) and Peace (a KIA soldier proffering a white dove). A vast red and white banner top centre proclaimed the gala's purpose: '*1989 NING FEBRUARI 5 YA, 28 NING HPRING 29 LANG NA RAWT MALAN N'HTOI MASAT!*' (today marks 28 full years of KIA resistance and the beginning of the 29th year!)

Wives and daughters, curious to see what was happening, peered in at us from the sandbagged gun emplacements outdoors. Major N Chyaw Tang, looking distinctly uncomfortable in a jacket that was too small for him, sat between us. 'I am your official translator,' he announced. First Son of Sut Lut ascended the stage and experimented with a microphone next to a cassette recorder on a table draped in crimson velvet. Something was about to happen.

Now, to a command from crackly speakers all around us, we suddenly rose as a body and saluted Major General Zau Mai, who had entered the tent at the head of his staff. His cortège proceeded to the front row, faced us with granite-like faces, returned the salute, and sat down. Then we sat down again. Then *Salang Kaba*

Zawng Hra mounted the stage and read aloud a long speech in monotone Jinghpaw. Major N Chyaw Tang translated every word. Mats whispered to him that we did not require this service. 'We rise to salute the dead martyrs!' resonated N Chyaw Tang. We rose again, turned at an oblique angle and saluted the KIA colours; then, at another sharp command, bowed our heads, and the General Secretary read aloud a long prayer in which I recognized the words *Yesu* and *amen*. Others succeeded him at the microphone, the audience reverently but restlessly mute throughout except for scattered coughs and throat clearings. There was an awkward moment when N Chyaw Tang's leg erupted into spasm. He had been tapping his foot – a light, staccato, metronomic tapping that had got the better of him. He clasped the wilful thigh firmly in both hands but did not succeed in subduing it until we rose again to sing the national anthem.

An hour or so of prayers and patriotic speeches ended, and we filed out of the assembly hall for a short smokers' break. The ladies, who had not seen a European at close range before, now pranced out of the fog and cold wearing black cotton *palawng* (blouses) over *labu* (sarongs) and *shawa nang kachyi* (multiple-strand pendants of minerals) and *gumhpraw palawng* (necklaces of George V and George VI silver rupees, which are still the main unit of currency in parts of Kachinland). They stared at us in wonder, until one, who was bolder than the others, edged closer and offered us a boiled egg. N Chyaw Tang said helpfully, 'She says this part of Kachinland adopt London climitization!'

'Is she asking if London is as cold as Pajau Bum?'

'Is it so?' asked the ULFA Chairman. 'Is London climate like this?'

I was keen to speak with the ladies and knew that if I let Castro divert the conversation I would lose them.[12] 'London is colder

---

12. Kachin etiquette precludes women from speaking with men while men are engaged in conversation with each other. This custom did not prevent us from conversing with the KIO Chairman's daughter, Janan Brang Seng, and Zawng Hra's wife, but these were exceptional instances probably explained by the fact that we were Europeans. Significantly, they had both lived in Myitkyina. Even the Foreign Secretary's regal mother-in-law kept silence in her own house while we chatted with the men gathered there from her village. It would be a mistake to deduce that the status of women in Kachin society is inferior. Kachin rules of etiquette simply differ from our own.

than Pajau Bum,' I answered firmly and turned back to the ladies, but it was too late. They had already fled.

However, I remember Independence Day chiefly for our auspicious encounter with the Reverend La Ring, a Baptist chaplain dressed in a tartan *bawng bam* (turban), *ntsa palawng* (tight jacket) and *labu*, who led us through the next part of the gala, which was entirely devotional. He prayed for about half an hour, fervently and without break. Then he read out long texts from the Scriptures. Then he regaled us with more fervent prayer. Hymns were sung – bold, full-bodied Baptist hymns resounding with joy and hope, interspersed with more prayers. A lengthy homily followed, and one could see by the tense, almost frightened looks on the faces of those seated even in distant corners of the great tent that he had deeply touched their hearts and shocked their consciences. The Reverend La Ring was renowned for his preaching throughout Kachinland, and, from all that I could understand, his performance this morning did not disappoint his reputation. Indeed, we were all wondering whether there was any limit to his stamina when Major N Chyaw Tang, bless his soul, announced with a deep sigh, 'Finish! Now we can relax!' Relaxation, however, was not in La Ring's nature. For him, this was a heaven-sent opportunity to share fellowship with us and to tell us how the Gospel had come to Kachinland. After the devotions ended he followed us back to the guesthouse.

He showed a monomaniac's grasp of his subject and had a powerful and altogether uplifting story to tell, of which I noted only the highlights. It was a tale of extraordinary courage of European and Karen missionaries in the teeth of sustained and appalling vicissitudes. The funds available for financing their great enterprise were always pitifully inadequate. Everything was lacking except what was most vital; this was the belief common to all who stayed the course that God had called them to convert the Kachins.

It was *the* Lord, said La Ring, and not the British *overlord*, who had transformed the Kachins. Before the missionaries brought the Good News to Kachinland, syphilis and opium addiction were endemic. Society was riven by terrible *bunglat hka* (blood feuds), which often lasted for decades and in which the fighting was done by outlandishly tattooed mercenaries with swords and cap guns.

Neighbours were raided for loot, their women abducted and their men reduced to slavery. Ambushes and assassinations were common. Small wonder that the Burmans treated them as savages who had forfeited their right to survive! But, unlike the Jebusites, said La Ring, God had preserved them.

The first of these courageous men was Eugenio Kincaid, an American Baptist who, in 1837, paddled and poled a small boat 350 miles north of Ava. In small villages where he stopped along the way to distribute New Testaments and religious tracts, he began to hear of the 'Hka Khyens' who had an idea of a Supreme Being and a tradition of lost scripture. He sent out an appeal for other missionaries to proselyte these 'vastly interesting and affecting people'.[13]

Kincaid's efforts were eventually rewarded. In 1877, Bogalay, a Christian from Bassein, began his studies of Jinghpaw, and, a year later, Albert Lyon, the first Baptist missionary to the Kachins from overseas, arrived in Bhamo. To the distraction of the British Resident and the captain of the paddle steamer that had fetched him to Bhamo, however, Albert Lyon died of consumption within a month of his arrival.

He was succeeded by William Henry Roberts, who had served under Robert E. Lee in the Army of Northern Virginia. Roberts petitioned the last King of Burma, Thibaw, for permission to educate the Kachins and asked him for land on which to build a school. Thibaw churlishly conceded land 'the size of a buffalo skin', observing for the entertainment of his courtiers that Roberts might just as well try to teach his dog to read and write as to try to educate the Kachins. Roberts cut the buffalo hide into strips, linked them and measured out the limits of his compound. Sadly, however, both he and his wife soon contracted malaria. She did not survive the attack. Her last words to her husband epitomize the spirit of these early missionaries: 'When I am gone take her [their daughter] to Mother, and when you are well come back again, for there is to be a great ingathering of Kachins. You will be

13. I have supplemented La Ring's account of the history of the Kachin church and changed some of the details to make them conform to the story told in Herman Gustaf Tegenfeldt's (1974) authoritative study of the subject.

permitted to share in it. I go and will await your coming.'[14] Roberts's mission to the Kachins lasted for 34 years.

In 1890 Ola Hanson arrived in Kachinland. He would stay for 38 years. He had brought with him considerable language skills, Swedish, English, German, Greek and Hebrew, to which he now added Burmese and Jinghpaw. There had already been a rudimentary start at modifying the Burmese alphabet to provide a Jinghpaw script. Hanson started anew and devised a new orthography, using the Roman alphabet, and compiled a Jinghpaw spelling manual, a Jinghpaw primer, a Jinghpaw grammar, a Jinghpaw catechism, and a Jinghpaw–English dictionary. He wrote extensively on Kachin ethnography, culminating in his *The Kachins: Their Customs and Traditions* (1913). His translation into Jinghpaw of more than 200 hymns, many of them from Swedish, are the hymns that are sung in Kachinland today. Within two years of his arrival in Kachinland, he completed a translation of St John's Gospel. It was the start of his greatest monument, the Jinghpaw Bible. It was to this man, known to the Kachins simply as 'the Translator', that Mats had been compared at our first meeting with Zau Mai.

George Geis, the last of a trio of pioneer Americans[15] whose mission to the Kachins spanned more than three decades, arrived in Kachinland two years after Hanson. After a risky trip up the Irrawaddy during the rainy season, he determined to found a mission at Myitkyina, where the government planned to locate the northern terminus of the Burma Railway and establish its Kachin District headquarters. The site chosen for the compound was a former *nat* grove. Volunteers from Christian converts in Bhamo assisted in constructing the first buildings, while Geis travelled up and down the river proclaiming the exciting news – another school for the Kachins was rising among them and 'God's book' was being translated into Jinghpaw.

By 1911, three decades after Bogolay and Roberts began their evangelizing, the Kachin Baptist Church had more than 500 communicants, many of them old boys and girls of the mission schools

14. Tegenfeldt, 1974: 103.
15. Hanson was born in Sweden and Geis in Germany, but their parents immigrated to the USA when they were children.

and their families. Karen missionaries gave equally devoted and sustained service to this adventure in evangelism, four staying with the Kachins for more than 40 years and most 'laying their bones among them'. They were better suited than the Americans to work in the hills and asked for no recognition and kept no record of their labours. In 1901, the first Kachin pastors were ordained in Bhamo, and, in 1911, there were further local ordinations. For another half century, the Kachin church would look elsewhere for its leaders, but the numbers of native communicants increased both during the years of Japanese occupation (1942–44) and after Ne Win expelled the missionaries (1962–65). It was steadily finding its own feet.[16]

Meanwhile, work began among Kachins living in the Shan States. Hanson and a Karen missionary worked there from 1911 to 1919, and, in 1938, Gordon Seagrave, born in Burma of missionary parents, began his medical and teaching ministry in Nam Hkam.[17] The Foreign Missions Society of Paris and the Columban Fathers established other missions, and, in 1949, the Morse family, Church of Christ missionaries, settled in Hkamti Long, in the far north of Kachinland. In the KIO's 'archives' was a report by Stephen Morse of a visit to Washington on the Kachins' behalf. Mats and I were to learn a great deal about the Morses, who have worked among the hill peoples of Tibet, Yunnan, Burma and Thailand for more than 70 years, and to see a wonderful legacy of their vocation when we reached the Indian border.

After Ne Win's March 1962 coup, mission schools throughout Burma were nationalized and staffed with Buddhists. BSPP agents began spying on pastors and priests, and children were encouraged to spy on their parents, as Burmanization invaded even the private corners of family life. Nevertheless, La Ring was convinced that human agency could not thwart God's plan for the Kachins, and our own observations confirmed that the great majority of

16. Tegenfeldt states that the numbers of communicants in the Baptist community grew from 11,884 in 1941 to 15,628 in 1947, and from 31,914 in 1965 to 50,956 in 1970.

17. Seagrave died in Nam Hkam half a century later, after being convicted and imprisoned for giving Naw Seng a cup of tea. His son, Sterling, lives incognito, having written a book, *The Soong Dynasty* (1985), alleging that Chiang Kai-shek's in-laws were involved in the heroin trade.

Kachins today are Believers – as Eugenio Kincaid had foreseen nearly a century and a half ago when he wrote: '[I]n the distant highlands are multitudes of Kakhyens, a people who from time immemorial have resisted idolatry. ... All that I know of their traditions, and all that I have seen of their habits, go to convince me that their conversion will be rapid, according as they can be brought into contact with the word of God.'[18]

It was two hours past noon before we sat down for the special lunch. Ladies in uniform, including the KIO Chairman's daughter, Lance Corporal Janan Brang Seng, brought buckets of steamed rice and ladled it onto our tin plates and brought more buckets and served us curried fish, curried beef, curried minced beef and curried cauliflower. 'Eat more meat, less rice,' advised Major N Chyaw Tang with gusto, and, despite his strong Baptist convictions, he urged us to try the *tsa pi*, a milky brew of fermented rice served in large plastic detergent bottles. The final event was that evening: a variety show the KIA Propaganda Team put on, at which was sung in Jinghpaw *What a Friend We Have in Jesus*. Was this one of the 200 hymns Hanson translated, I wondered? Most of the audience knew it by heart and joined in the singing. We had spent a good many hours in prayer that day, as had the ancient Israelites before every important battle. 'With that kind of spirit,' I said afterwards to Zau Mai, 'how *can* you lose?' Although we were still very full of ourselves, dizzy with our success and all the attention we had received, La Ring's little lesson had awakened something in me. It was the beginning of an understanding without which, I submit, there can be *no* understanding of the KIO and its cause. Two days later we left for India.

18. *Baptist Missionary Magazine* (1838: 246); reprinted in Tegenfeldt (1974: 82).

4

The Triangle

The entire War Committee assembled at Flagstaff House to wish us farewell, and we marched off in handsome order, eager to impress them. A section met us at Liaison Camp. They would accompany us as far as the Nmai Hka, where, if all went according to plan, another escort unit would relieve them. Our column comprised 19 men: our *Du Kaba* (Big Leader), Seng Hpung; our *Du Jum* (Captain), Awng Hkawng; our quartermaster, Sergeant San Awng; a signals operator; six lads who had scrapped their degree courses at various universities and technical colleges in central Burma to serve with the KIA; six other soldiers; Mats and myself. Seng Hpung, Awng Hkawng and I were the oldest (53); Seng Hpung's batman, Private Hkaw Ying (16) and Awng Hkawng's batman, Private Maran Naw (15), were the youngest. Seng Hpung, Mats and I were unarmed, but, although we were a duty column, not a fighting column, everyone else carried weapons. Our orders were to avoid, not to engage, the enemy.

We began wonderingly. What was the route like? How arduous? How much up and down? Would we be able to manage our loads? How bad were the leeches? Would the Burma Army lay an ambush for us? Our destination for this first day's half-march was a village called Sha It Yang (Flat Place of Fresh Air) that straddled the Chinese border no more than five miles due north of Pajau Bum.

At first the route skirted the ridge facing that manned by the Burmans, but the guns were silent. They had been silent since we arrived in Pajau Bum. Cold, grey days, mists floating up from the gorge, the soldiers in their bunkers ready and waiting to fire at one another – at least this part of the war, I reflected, was one of set pieces. Leaving the ridge, we climbed a hill and tramped east for about a mile over more or less even terrain, then north, the trail narrowing here and there to squeeze between massive boulders. On all sides of us were poppy fields, less advanced here than in the lower altitudes above Möng Ko, but there was a ghostly feel about them. No one was about, like the invisible armies behind us confronting each other with their silent guns. Were those terraced hills to the east China? Opium in the People's Republic? Surely not.

We now began a long descent. Everyone except Seng Hpung and Awng Hkawng was fully laden, and, after half an hour negotiating drops between stones of two to three feet, my legs began to tremble. Reaching a brook at the end of the descent, we crossed it and immediately scrambled up the opposite bank. That was to be the pattern for the next two months: an arduous climb lasting perhaps 40 minutes; level for a while along a ridge, catching our breath and grateful for the respite; then down, until we heard a rush of water and saw below us the mists rising from the gorge; then more steeply down to the water and up again.

Our escort stopped to wait for the others. Observing these men at close range, it was clear why the Kachins' neighbours had always feared them or thought them uncouth. There was something wild and untamed about them. They wore variegated uniforms and parts of uniforms, some plain olive green, some jungle camouflage, cut from unnatural, machine-made fabric and in a style that was alien to them, dictated by other peoples' dress conventions that did not suit their lean, hard bodies. They wore rubber flip-flops or loose, ill-fitting canvas shoes laced up in different ways, with or without socks. Their hair was long, straight and black, Kung Fu fashion, and they all smoked fat, hand-rolled cheroots made of cheap tobacco obtained from villages along the *mawdaw lam* (motor road). Some had written their names on their weapons, and one had added a fringe of tassels to his jacket. Only one could have been older than 20.

After the break, everyone pressed ahead with renewed vigour. When we came upon the remains of an incinerated house, I asked Awng Hkawng if the Burma Army had torched it. No, he replied and added that such conflagrations were common and were usually caused by cinders floating up into the thatched roofs. Awng Hkawng's father was a Gurhka who had served in the Burma Army. He was more sophisticated than most Kachins, having lived in various cantonments in Burma Proper, and everywhere we went people seemed to know him. Not the least surprising thing about him was an attachment to English poetry — Wordsworth and Yeats in particular, which he often recited from memory. Each morning before we broke camp, he reserved to himself a private time for prayer and reading from a pocket King James edition of the Bible. The Bible, he told me, was a gift from his former 'shepherd', Herman Tegenfeldt, who, though neither of us knew it then, had published his monograph on the Kachin Baptist Church after Ne Win expelled the missionaries from Burma.

We reached a little wood and stopped again to wait for the stragglers, and one of the escort held up his thumb as a sign of respect to me for having kept pace. Then we marched into Sha It Yang. It comprised half a dozen houses at most. A beautiful young woman was squatting on open ground at its centre, engaged in some kind of magic. She had made a small hole in the earth, covered it with parchment from a special kind of bamboo, pierced the parchment in two places and threaded it with a string made of bamboo leaves, which she used as a bow to produce an eerie viola-like sound. She was petitioning the thunder god for rain, said Awng Hkawng. The thunder god was one of the *mu nat*s (sky spirits) descended from the hermaphroditic creator god, Shadip. We were billeted in a house that the woman and her husband shared with his parents. Her husband was a KIA soldier.

The subject of religion arose again after dinner. Two of our column's students, Tu Lum (John) and La Awng (Alex), had already taken Christian names, and the others evinced interest in acquiring them too; so from that evening Hkyen Naw was also called Philip; Wana Yaw Htung, Peter; and Naw Lawn, Paul. Did the thunder god influence rain? Peter thought it might, but the others thought not. We talked about whether the sun god influenced crops, and the hypothetical powers of the *nat*s of the house, love-making, childbirth, the forest, water, mountains. All of these spirits required propitiation by Kachins who still believed in them, they explained. A *dumsa* (shaman) prescribed the sacrifice, which might be a buffalo, pig, chicken, monkey or bird, depending on the favour or protection sought and the supplicant's means. The house spirit required a sacrifice only once every three years, but the fire spirit had to be placated more often, said the woman. Thunder lived in the sky; but only the *dumsa* knew where the other *nat*s lived. In our trek through the Kachin forests Mats and I would find much that affirmed the survival of these gods. We did not meet a *dumsa*, but the evidences of his dark vitality were legion, and it was often difficult to say whether the convert who continued in the old ways did so from conviction or habit, nostalgia or superstition. Certainly, we would hear a great deal about the ubiquitous *nat*s' powers to influence our fortunes, and, occasionally, as at Sha It Yang, come upon villages where there were no Christians.

It was nearly midnight before we dispersed ourselves around the *dap* to sleep, the soldiers without cover of any kind other than their clothes and taking turns at stoking the fire. Next morning I awoke to the sounds of a cock crowing and a pig grunting beneath the house, and, as the first light seeped through the lattice, I heard some of our escort moving about talking in whispers in the adjoining room. Soon afterwards, I found a mug of tea and a pan of hot water beside my sleeping bag, placed there imperceptibly by one of the lads.

For the next two stages a muleteer assisted us. The sun was already high in the sky before the men distributed our baggage among the panniers and loaded them onto his three dwarf animals. We now crossed back into China. Everyone turned his shirt inside out to conceal his KIA arm patch and covered his weapon. Sounds of 88 and 75 mm mortar fire behind us signalled to some of the men the start of the planned offensive to retake Na Hpaw, which had fallen to the Burma Army the previous year. But Seng Hpung stoutly maintained that they were 'just some exchanges between our boys and theirs'.

We walked for a while under open sky through high, waving grasses and between haulms of pale, feathery cane that rustled in the dry breezes. Some young girls working in a field pretended that they had not seen us; but after we passed they stared at our backs with eyes wide as grapefruits. When we stopped for our first *preekop*,[1] Seng Hpung ordered Mats and me to the rear of the column to reduce the risk of capture by Chinese border guards.

Another arduous climb and another descent brought us to Lung

1. From 'break up'. Other words reflecting a legacy of soldiering under British colours include *mawdaw* (motor) and *shat khat* (short cut).

Hpraw Yang (White Stone Flat), where there was further evidence of *nat* worship: scarecrows to ward off malevolent spirits fixed to the houses, a wood carving of a face resembling a Toltec monster painted with blotches of blood dripping from the corners of its mouth. John said that this fiendish totem, mounted on a tripod of fat timbers in an open field, marked a grave, but Seng Hpung maintained that it was the facsimile of a buffalo the villagers used as a burnt offering instead of the more costly sacrifice demanded by the *dumsa*. An old man, a refugee from the war, asked about his son who had served under Seng Hpung's command in the KIA's Fourth Brigade. And a smartly dressed lady who was the widow of a *duwa* (chief) who had died in an engagement in the Sinlum–Loije sector of the KIA's Third Brigade area pressed on us gifts of bottled Chinese beer. We halted in a wood beyond the village. Mats and I removed our boots and soothed our incipient blisters in a pretty stream, while the lads prepared a delicious lunch for us. The same meal of cauliflower, roasted peanuts, chicken and rice would recur without much variation.

The climb to the next pass was so steep that Seng Hpung was sick. 'It was unavoidable,' he said memorably, and, renewed, resumed climbing. The motor road, which the *jing cha* patrolled, was visible from the pass. We planned to stop until dark in Sharaw Kawng (Sharaw Family Hill), a Jinghpaw village near the road, but a scout reported that the *jing cha* were preoccupied with celebrating their New Year and it was safe to proceed. So we continued by a jungle path that the villagers pointed out to us, while the muleteer, who was inconspicuously Chinese, left us to proceed via the road.

Our routes converged about sundown. The muleteer and the rest of the column trekked on, but Seng Hpung and I paused to rest. He drank some of the beer that the smartly dressed widow had given us. When we resumed, the forest was a heap of shadows and the sky moonless, with an overhang of low cloud shutting out the stars. Seng Hpung said half mockingly that not even the *sawn nat*s, which tormented women during childbirth, or the *lasa nat*s, which caused fatal accidents, were as malevolent as the *jahtung nat*s haunting these gloomy recesses of the forest. I noticed that he was now walking erratically and stumbling a lot. He offered me ginseng. 'In my father's time we would have eaten opium as a tonic. Now we have only beer – and ginseng,' he observed. 'The Chinese say that if you are feeling weak, just eat ginseng and you will feel strong. I don't know if it is true.'

A northbound truck overtook us, but we ignored it. The nearest police post was about ten miles behind us, and we were confident that we would reach our destination, a village called Hpundu (Stump), before the driver could report us. At the sound of the approach of a southbound truck, however, we scrambled hastily up an escarpment and flung ourselves on hard ground behind some rocks. To our horror, the truck stopped as its headlights caught our range, and we heard doors opening and men shouting at one another. Had someone already reported us? Seng Hpung whispered: 'It is best not to speak.'

We waited and listened intensely, while the truck inched ominously closer, its brakes squeaking ever more loudly.

Now it was immediately below us, and I could see men – presumably soldiers – alighting from it. Suddenly it occurred to me: they had seized the others and forced them to reveal our presence and soon would start beating the bushes with staves to flush us out. However, the truck was merely braking cautiously around the steep bends in its ponderous progress down the mountain.

On we trudged, now conscious of each shuffling step and wondering how much farther it was to Stump. My shirt and trousers were soggy with perspiration and champed against my shoulders and thighs, and Seng Hpung voiced our common sentiment when he said: 'I have been walking for 24 years, and I have never felt so tired.' Then suddenly, like the bird that landed on the Ark, Paul appeared at our side. Awng Hkawng had sent him to fetch us, lest we lose our way. We did not have much further to go, he said consolingly, and we renewed our efforts. However, an hour later we were still climbing. We left the road to follow Paul down a path that, he announced confidently, led to Hpundu. A few minutes later, however, he admitted that he had erred and led us back to the road. Seng Hpung whispered that just beyond the ridge above us was Sama Pa,[2] which the Burma Army garrisoned.

2. Formerly known as Fort Morton after Captain Boyce-Morton, who died there on 6 January 1893 while trying to rescue a soldier under his command from a combined force of Kachins and Chinese mercenaries (see Hertz, 1960: 60).

We came to another turn-off. *This* was our path, Paul now asserted. 'Are you sure?' I asked. Seng Hpung shambled a few feet along it and peered into the opaque blackness. 'All right,' he said, doubtfully, 'we try this one.' In the distance a dog was barking and a bell was ringing. 'That *must* be Stump,' I ventured hopefully. 'Our men are trying to signal the way,' Paul corrected me. 'Bell is from Chinese village. Kachin village is after.'

The path plunged steeply down, following the loose and slippery bed of a creek. Security concerns precluded using our torches, and I stumbled twice, very nearly losing my balance. Two upward bound, barefoot boys carrying babies in *nbat*s (cloths harnessed to their shoulders) passed us. At the base of the hill was a river. We waded across it, my shoes sinking into the bottom and filling with mud. The Chinese village lay just beyond the river. Pigs and mules picked up our scent and added their sonorities to that of the barking dog. We passed some women with torches, but they were too terrified or incurious to look at us; we then started up another hill. 'Paul,' I said reproachfully, 'you told us that from the Chinese village it would be only another five minutes.' Ahead of us we could now hear other dogs barking. That, Paul affirmed, was Hpundu – and, a few minutes later, I saw with boundless gratitude John and Alex sprinting towards us, shouting, 'We keep lookout! We watch for your torches! We think maybe you lose way! We fear for your safety!'

There was a final agonizing climb up a monkey ladder into a house where we were billeted. Mats took my rucksack from my back and I collapsed exhausted onto the floor. The other men sharing the house must have been almost as tired, but they gallantly brought me tea and asked me if I wanted food; then fetched bread and toasted it over the fire, while others brought me water for washing and, producing cane splints, stuck them in the sand by the fire and fitted my socks over them to dry. They brought more tea and a foul-tasting substance that Alex euphemistically called 'Kachin jam'. Then they laid straw mats next to the fire and, spreading my sleeping bag on them, urged me to sleep. They would wake me at 0200 hours for departure at 0300 hours, they said, and, from here on, they promised jubilantly, everything was downhill. We would be following the road all the way to the border, and the border was a march of only two-and-a-half hours. I voiced concern about the flames from the fire igniting my socks. 'Never mind socks!' they cried. 'Never mind! We will look after socks. Take rest! Take rest!'

I awoke after three hours, my limbs aching, my stomach boiling with undigested 'Kachin jam', and listened to the Dantesque cacophony under the house: the bells tinkling on the mules' necks, the pigs grunting, roosters crowing and dogs barking. All at once mules, pigs, roosters and dogs raged simultaneously. Mats snored and the Chinese muleteer beside me stank. I lay in (having decided that 0300 hours probably meant 0400 hours), until I heard the lads moving about kitting themselves up for departure.

The next stage was downhill, but the promise of an easy descent was a hoax. We plunged down another path so steep and treacherous that we had to reverse onto all fours and ratchet our way down it, hanging onto whatever we could grab. Down and down we went, until we reached a sandy bottom where the vegetation was all bamboo and wild banana palms and, crossing a small stream bridged by loose logs, came to another stream and picked our way across it on stones. And when at last we reached the road, we left it almost at once and plunged down yet another steep mountain.

Toiling endlessly up and down mountains was proving to be decidedly unromantic, and in that moment I confess to entertaining thoughts of turning back. It would be so easy, I mused. My Chinese visa was intact, and, if the *jing cha* intercepted me, I had only to pretend that I had lost my way. Mats and Seng Hpung, sustained by ginseng, could carry on without me, and, in ten days, two weeks perhaps, I would be back at the youth hostel on Shameen Island breakfasting with other backpackers on banana bread from the bakery across the street, boasting that I had been to Burma and congratulating myself on having cut my losses. It was a lovely dream, useful in helping me over the last *shat khat* of what my diary calls 'the Long March'. A *shat khat*, my diary also notes, 'is what the Kachins call a difficult deviation from an easy gradient'. There were more to come.

As dawn began to break above the rim of mountains behind us, we stopped at a house to make enquiries. A Chinese woman appeared at the door, so the muleteer came forward and interpreted. She seemed to mind not at all about being awakened at this hour and gave no hint of fear but chatted with the muleteer as though they were dear friends. Concealed in a deep gorge below us was the river the Shans call the Nam Tabet and the Kachins the Tabak Hka, which flowed north of Sama Pa, past Kasu and into the Irrawaddy. Above us, the road forked, one branch leading south above the line of the gorge and the other zigzagging down to the river. Two *shat khat*s also led down to the river. The muleteer broke off his conversation with the woman and reported to Seng Hpung, who consulted Awng Hkawng, who consulted the men, and a fierce debate ensued about which of the two most difficult routes to take. This could have only one resolution, and Seng Hpung resolved it accordingly by striking out down the steepest route. 'We go by the Kachin way,' he said, implying that easier gradients were for lesser mortals.

No one spoke, and all was silence except for the breathing of our column and the Tabak Hka murmuring invisibly in its tremendous gorge. The exposed roots of huge trees often overtook the path. Some of them you climbed over; others you crawled under. The Tabak Hka came into view, rushing over swirling rapids. We reversed onto our hands and knees again for the final descent, and, a few minutes later, crossed the Tabak Hka by a partly submerged bridge of woven bamboo, the water washing over our feet. Our doubts of reaching Burma at all and the imponderables canvassed in my letter to Carole from Dali now seemed faintly ludicrous. We had crossed its borders thrice in less than a month.

I had expected a *preekop* at the river, but that was not to be. 'We carry on to Munga Zup,' said Seng Hpung. Munga Zup (Gospel Confluence) was an Azi village perched on the lip of the escarpment above us, where the KIA maintained a lookout and a customs gate. Peter and Paul preceded us there and had already prepared a fire when we arrived. 'In here! In here!' they cried, beckoning us into a house. 'Take rest here! You want tea?' they cried excitedly. We dropped our bags and sank gratefully into armchairs, while they made us a breakfast of plovers' eggs and a fiery vegetable curry presented simply as 'Kachin dish'. Seng Hpung's diminutive gunbearer, Mimo, who was still adjusting to our strangeness, stared at us as we ate it. The KIA had provided him with many wonderful adventures but nothing quite so exotic as these disgusting Big Noses.

The Chinese muleteer was leaving us here and now came over to bid us farewell. The return trip to Sha It Yang would be lonely without us, he said feelingly. Terribly lonely. He had not known other Europeans and accounted it a great honour to have known us; he was going to miss us. Mats told him not to repine. 'You have the three mules for company,' he said.

Seng Hpung decreed that we would rest here until after lunch and stay the night at Ting Rawng (Bird Catcher's Lime Rod), which was about an hour's march from Munga Zup. So after breakfast, with time on our hands suddenly, we changed into shorts and revisited the Tabak Hka for a bath. The rugged escarpment that had been so daunting that morning now seemed almost foolishly easy, and, soon, soldiers were bathing and washing their clothes all along the river bank. On the China side the hills were still covered in purple shadow, but everything on our side glowed in the white intensity of the morning sun. Leaves shimmered as kingfishers flew in long questing swoops, stopping now and then to hover in motionless contemplation over the water. Brown dippers flitted from rock to rock, butterflies mated in the tiny coves between silver grey boulders and, crowning all, a column of elephants ridden by KIA *oozie*s (mahouts) in tattered clothes with wild hair came crashing out of the forest and plunged into the water, claiming their reward for having delivered another consignment of jade to China. As each animal reached the deep water, its *oozy* would spring onto its back and administer a good scrubbing with branches snatched from overhanging foliage or *dohnwe* (*Entada scandens*), a fibrous creeper that produces a soapy lather. Each elephant wallowed in the cool water up to its eyes, then reluctantly, at the *oozy*'s command, lumbered heavily out onto the Burma shore. When we returned to the village, a KIA customs officer showed us a book in which was recorded the excise collected on these deliveries, an *ad valorem* of 15 per cent on all China-bound jade and 10 per cent on timber.

After lunch, John and Alex invited us to drink bottled beer with them. It cost almost a quarter of their *annual* pay and tasted no better than the rice beer they made in cane tubes, but it had the romantic stamp of having come from the outside world, the merchants' stalls along the *mawdaw lam*. 'No mind money,' they said when we protested at the expense. 'It is not for money that we join KIA. Money is not important. If we get our human rights, we will not be soldiers. If we get our human rights, no more KIA.'

Then we loaded our bags onto a *tuo la ji*, another welcome respite, and walked on to Ting Rawng, which was another Azi village. It was full of shrines to tutelary deities – small, box-shaped structures like bird cottages supported on X-frames, beneath which the ground was strewn with the blood and feathers of votive sacrifices. Buffalo skulls adorned the entrances of the houses and, on an altar above the *dap* where we slept, there was a necropolis of smoked gibbons' and chickens' skeletons. A ring of keys attached to a woman's waist betrayed a concern for possessions that we would not encounter again until the Indian border. Peter fetched Philip's radio and, that evening, I heard the news for the first time since leaving Canton on the BBC World Service's 'Twenty-Four Hours'. I learned that the Senate was debating President Reagan's nomination of Senator Tower for Secretary of Defense and its approval was in doubt because there was evidence suggesting the senator was addicted to drink. The honourable senators' self-glorifying sonorities seemed to me so wonderfully irrelevant here among the mules, pigs, chickens, dogs and skulls.

* * *

The shrill screeches of a colony of gibbons acrobating in the trees on the hill above us awakened me at 0545 hours. The lads were curled up under olive-green polythene sheets, which they called *plastik*s and would use to cover their *basha*s when we bivouacked. I lay in my sleeping bag thinking, and my thoughts flew to Seng Hpung, who wore a heavy metal crucifix on a pendant and rarely used alcohol. During our long march to Hpundu, he had challenged me: 'Do you believe in God, Shelby? Do you believe in Jesus Christ? Do you accept that Jesus Christ is your Lord and Saviour? Did Jesus die on the cross? Did He die for us?' He told me that his parents were Buddhists who thought that a kind of cosmic bookkeeper kept an exact account of our actions, crediting us for our good deeds and debiting us for our bad, and that the balance would determine our status in the next incarnation. How else could one explain the obvious differences in intelligence between snakes, elephants and people? While some people prayed a lot and remained poor, others who never prayed grew rich. Did not this observable fact also suggest that the Buddhists were right? If he asked God for more money, even if he asked in the name of Christ, would it make him richer? On the other hand, if all we had to do to get what we wanted was pray, then God would be no more than an administrator executing our demands and prayers, a kind of magic. Perhaps our perceptions misled us? Perhaps God redressed these apparent imbalances in other ways, as the Beatitudes suggested? He did not doubt the efficacy of prayer, but its results had to be measured against each individual's potential for evil. For example, he was often disagreeable, but he knew that he would be even more so without prayer. Without prayer he might be a murderer. It was the kind of intense conversation that one had as a schoolboy when every idea was up for grabs – but we were not schoolboys. There was an uncluttered simplicity and purity about the Kachins that allowed adult discussion of such matters.

After breakfast, some women entertained themselves with my rucksack's snap-on plastic buckles, zipped pouches and adjustable straps. They could hardly imagine such a complicated *hting-ga* (basket). I greatly alarmed one of them by inviting her to try it on, which she did to shrieks of laughter from the others. In *The Flame Trees of Thika* about her childhood in Kikuyuland, Elspeth Huxley wrote that the white man's aeroplanes and engines interested the Kikuyu less than our ability to transport fire. What most fascinated the Azi women of Ting Rawng was my Jansport 'Eiger' backpack.

We were waiting for more mules. They finally arrived, and we departed, climbing steeply for the best part of an hour to a ridge, where we turned and looked behind us at China's almost too picturesque mountains receding through ever hazier rafters of blue, wondering if we would see them again. The next sector led along the ridge. I had consigned some of my baggage to the animals and wore extra socks on my feet and, for the first time since leaving Pajau Bum, felt almost comfortable. Crisp, brown leaves carpeted the path beneath our feet, and spears of golden light penetrated the redwoods that towered overhead. Invisible birds tossed their songs at us, while behind us we could hear the

Mats and author in disguise.

Preekop at pass over Seng Leng Bum after night crossing of Man Win *mawdaw lam*.

Philip on the east bank
of the Mali Hka.

Mats and his CPB People's Army guard by the Nam Ko.

tinkling of the mules' bells. Then, as though overcome by rapture at so much natural beauty, the lads sang out boldly in Jinghpaw: *All things bright and beautiful*; *Holy, holy, holy*; and *Amazing Grace*. Even Mats, who was sceptical of religion, was overheard humming one of the hymns. But here and there we would come upon the ominous signs of logging.

We stopped for a long *preekop* beside a brook. While I washed some clothes, some of the lads went downstream to fish. They found a pool of deep water, dropped a grenade there, and scooped up the stunned creatures in their hands as the current bore them wriggling upside down over the shallows.

Our destination, which we reached at about 1430 hours, was Lawk Hpyu (Vale of Hpyu), a village with a mixed Lisu, Chinese and Jinghpaw population. Outside the houses and over the entrances were the same depressing shrines to tutelary deities and sacrificial skulls that we had seen at Lung Hpraw Yang and Ting Rawng. The *agyi* (headman) told us that his one qualification for his office was that he spoke all three of the languages used in the village; that real power was vested in the council of *bawmung* (aldermen), whose decisions he simply enforced. The place swarmed with black blister flies that attacked our legs remorselessly, bringing blood and leaving tiny sores that formed nasty little black scabs. While the Burma Army was not in the immediate vicinity, its patrols had scouted Lawk Hpyu within the past four months. We were waiting for clearance from Third Battalion headquarters and might be stuck here for a couple of days, said Seng Hpung. 'We are quite close to the enemy,' he said. 'The first motto of the soldier is, save yourself so you can kill your enemy.'

But there was a market at Third Battalion headquarters attended by people who might report our presence to the Burma Army, so the next morning we pressed on. We met some coolies bound for the Tabak Hka, Chinese women with cane baskets strapped about their foreheads and dressed incongruously in glamorous black satin trousers. We encountered a mule caravan, and everyone stepped aside to let it pass. The hills to the west cascaded down to the broad ribbon of the Irrawaddy and a faint smudge of grey that was Myitkyina (Near the Big River). About noon we came to a mini-paradise: water frothing among white boulders polished by centuries of erosion, bounding over cataracts into dark green pools patrolled by gyrating dragonflies and widening downstream into diffuse rippling shallows. 'How beautiful is our Kachinland!' John exclaimed. Indeed, the place seemed to epitomize the words of one of the hymns we had been singing, 'All things bright and beautiful. All creatures great and small, all things wise and wonderful, the Lord God made them all.' We stopped there to bath and wash our clothes.

We harboured that night and the next at Shalawt Kawng (Freedom Hill), an untidy cluster of huts inhabited by Chinese opium farmers who called themselves *Wu Bana* (fifty-eighters), after the year in which they fled from Yunnan. They welcomed us with something less than enthusiasm – perhaps because the Burma Army had incinerated their houses twice during the preceding 12 months. We were coming steadily to realize exactly what war meant to these poor farmers and that it had not changed a lot since Genghis Khan. The conqueror arrives in their village, believing that he is defending national unity against the instruments of chaos. At his approach, the villagers fly to the forest, confirming thereby the conqueror's suspicions that they are assisting his invisible enemy, for which imagined offence he punishes anyone who fails to escape. A man's ears are lopped off for allegedly withholding information. A woman's lips are torn from her gums for allegedly acting as an informer. Someone else is tied to a tree; another is buried alive; others are used to spring the mines the enemy has buried on the routes through the forest and as slave porters. Money has been provided for porters, but the conqueror keeps it for himself, perhaps sharing a few kyats with his quartermaster. Why pay it to such scum? Some of the conqueror's soldiers may not like him, but they must obey his orders. Their careers, even their lives depend on it. Mercifully, such visits from the Burma Army were rare.

The *agyi* kindly allowed us to inspect a poppy field. The villagers planted it in October or November, he said, and, as we could see, it was just coming into bloom. As the plants matured, green, golf ball-size seed pods formed, and the milky resin that surfaced when the pods were scarified with a pencil-thin, four-bladed instrument called a *nushtur* was the raw opium. The resin was left overnight to dry on the pods, then scooped into pots attached to the farmer's waist with a crescent-shaped blade called a *seetoah*. After standing for three weeks or so, by when it was the colour and consistency of treacle, it was kneaded into round, grapefruit-size cakes weighing about 1.6 kilogrammes. Each cake sold for about 9600 kyats (approximately $1000 at the then official exchange rate and about $150 at the then free market rate), old opium fetching a higher price than new because it contained less water. Merchants came to Shalawt Kawng, purchased the opium and resold it in Myitkyina; they seldom came from China. A pellet about half the size of the user's thumbnail was enough for sedation, but an habitué needed two or three times that amount up to seven times a day. It was too expensive for the villagers themselves to use.

That evening, John fetched two bottles of Yunnanese wine, and we provided packets of crumbling noodles, stale oat flakes and dehydrated fruit soup — K-rations that Mats had as 'souvenirs' of the Swedish Army — and invited the others to join us. The party was a great success. The soup went down well, despite the difficulties of explaining 'plums', 'apricots' and 'peaches' to our guests, and the day's exertions, sun, fire and wine all had an excellent effect on our spirits. It all ended rather precipitously when the fire leapt its bounds, ignited the cane floor, and sent incendiary sparks flying up to the rafters.

Next morning, a Sunday, Third Battalion headquarters sent a message ordering us to continue at Shalawt Kawng until arrangements were made to strengthen our escort for crossing the Myitkyina–Chiphwe (Seniku) road southwest of the Burma Army's garrison at Man Win. It rained. Awng Hkawng tried (but failed) to procure a pastor to conduct a service. Everyone felt listless. Some of the soldiers resorted to sewing on buttons. Seng Hpung rolled up in blankets and studied *A Book of Great Quotations* (a standard work that accompanied him on all his campaigns, he said). Paul studied a list of English idioms such as 'kill time' and 'pot luck'. John and Philip wrote letters for posting via Third Battalion headquarters, which they would have us believe were last farewells to loved ones.

At about 1030 hours Paul broke off his studies and distributed what remained of the wine. 'Some for you, some for Mats, some for Peter, and some for me,' he said, adding solemnly, 'It is pot luck.' Then, turning to Peter, he observed nonchalantly, 'It is very difficult to kill time.' Then he curled up beneath a *plastik* and went to sleep.

It was important to our companions, a badge of our belonging and an emblem of tribal parity, that we should have Jinghpaw names. The subject had already provoked a great deal of discussion, and that afternoon a meeting was called to settle the matter. Philip was keen to call me 'Gam Shawng' (Eldest Son Forward), which I rejected for sounding too pushy. I suggested instead 'Baw Hpraw Gam', which meant 'hoary-headed eldest son' and seemed to me to combine just the right mix of seniority in age, priority in sequence of children born to my parents, and dash, but everyone rejected the name as ridiculous. Indeed, Philip was indignant. A name was a serious thing, he said. It stamped its character on a man. It was not to be treated frivolously. Awng Hkawng proposed dropping the 'Baw' and calling me simply 'Hoary Eldest Son', but Baw Hpraw Gam (pronounced Bo Pro Gam) stuck for lack of momentum. Mats was to be called 'Naw San', which meant 'Clear Second Son'. 'Clear about what?' I asked him, but, as happened so very often with my obscure witticisms, no one was amused.

We received our clearance from Third Battalion headquarters and departed Shalawt Kawng the following morning. The sun shone, and we moved easily after our rest, except for Mats, whose stomach was on the boil. I had not seen him so unhappy before.

At a village called Zup Ra Yang (Meeting Place Flat), Seng Hpung arranged for new porters. They were Yawyin or Lisu, big men with square flat faces, who wore shapeless blue jackets and skull caps of coarse cotton and carried broader-bladed *nhtu*s. All were barefoot.

From Zup Ra Yang the way was mostly downhill by gentle gradients, and the column, although conscious that every step brought us nearer the enemy, remained in buoyant mood. We seemed to be proceeding through a tunnel of vegetation into which, even during the brightest hours of the day, white light never penetrated. Dense, lush bamboo, wild banana trees and ferns closed in upon us from all sides, and the beauty of the forest now rivalled anything that we had seen so far. Occasionally, the forest would open a little and allow us a glimpse of green quilted hills exhaling a diaphanous vapour of heat, or a blue peak, or a distant ravine. Apart from a solitary, southbound mule caravan, there was no other traffic on the path.

I dropped back to the rear of the column and asked Awng Hkawng about the danger of ambush. He replied that the enemy only laid an ambush when it had advance information. The villagers were loyal to the KIA, he said, but pressure might be brought to bear on them. What kind of pressure? I asked. Sometimes villagers were disloyal or corruptible, but the main cause of leaks was idle talk, he said. Were he in charge we would not tarry so much. Speed was our best protection, he added obscurely. However, he was *not* in charge; nor, in this sector, was Seng Hpung. We were subject to Third Battalion headquarters, while Third Battalion headquarters, in turn, depended on intelligence the villagers supplied. We had to allow for many contingencies. The possibility of erroneous information, a tip-off by a hired informer, careless talk, accidental contact with one of the enemy's patrols, the enemy's capacity for surprise, the enemy's mobility and speed – all played a part in their calculations. Even the best-laid plans could go fearfully wrong. He was far from reassuring.

We came to a decrepit bamboo bridge over a river concealed in a narrow gorge, the N Myen Hka. Seng Hpung announced a break. 'This might be our last opportunity for a bath for several days,' he said. I made for a beach west of the bridge, but, scanning with his binoculars the hills beyond, Seng Hpung summarily called me back and ordered the column upriver, explaining, 'The enemy may approach from that direction.'

We continued up the ever narrowing river, delicately picking our way over the sun-bleached stones along its bank, until, somewhere near its source, we left it for a path that took us to another village.

Jum Yang (Salt Flat) lay in a green meadow blooming with the magnolias that the Jinghpaws call 'bell flowers'. Elements of Third Battalion and 253 Mobile Battalion, who were to escort us through the next sector, had already taken up positions in the surrounding hills. Awng Hkawng introduced us to their commander, a stocky, barrel-chested man in his late forties named Major Zau Chang, who had served with the KIA all his adult life. He was proud that he had no formal education and had risen to his present command through his own merits. The Burma Army had come to Jum Yang many times, and all the usual horrors attended its visits, he told me. During their last visit, he said, they had collected the elders in a house and burned it down and forced the young people to act as porters and human minesweepers. 'We are altogether too familiar with the Burma Army,' he said wearily.

Was there any risk of their attacking us during the night, I asked him?

'Have no fear,' he replied. 'Leave the enemy to me. I will take care of the enemy. It is my duty to protect you. You are our honoured guests.'

The enemy was about 15 miles from us, but, according to Major Zau Chang, it had not been active lately and gave battle only when attacked. Because most of the garrison had been transferred to Rangoon to serve as a praetorian guard for the junta, only four companies remained, and they were dispersed in heavily fortified bunkers along the Chiphwe road. We were to leave at 0830 hours the next day. Irregulars from villages near the enemy's bunkers would meet us in the forest, relieve the Lisu porters and guide us through their positions. Major Zau Chang had detailed two companies and a section to escort us, about 190 men in all, including our column, which, he stated, was more than a match for any resistance we were likely to encounter.

Seng Hpung instituted new arrangements attaching Mats and me to his mess, and that evening we went to his billet for a special dinner of bamboo shoots, turnip greens mixed with pork fat, chutney and rice. 'Tomorrow will be a little bit risky,' he warned. 'The path may be mined. Our boys are checking it now. You must walk behind me and Mats behind you – in my very footsteps. And we must keep always to the middle of the path.' The major, who dined with us, said nothing. He sat Buddha-like, his massive back against the wall, the light from the fire picking up his thick, placid features and playing over his oily, brown skin. It pleased me to fancy that he was contemplating the arrangements made for our security, but he was probably only weary from the social demands placed on him by the presence of a visiting colonel in his command area.

When we returned to our billet, three teachers came to us and told us about their school and their work. They were very proud of the little English that they spoke and of the KIO, for which they worked without remuneration. Their school took pupils up to the age of 13, and most of its pupils boarded in Jum Yang; it was the only school in the area, they said. That night insects crawled over us, and a baby cried relentlessly, despite his mother's embarrassed attempts at lulling him back to sleep. But, on the whole, it was a restful night.

* * *

A herd of cattle stampeding past our billet and the ping of a rifle shot awakened us next morning. We deduced that Seng Hpung had purchased a cow for us to eat in the jungle. I thought: 'This could be *my* last day too.' It was the Feast of St Valentine.

While we waited for the cow to be cut up, salted and packed, Awng Hkawng briefed us on the final plans for crossing the road. We would camp that night in the jungle and rendezvous the following day with KIA irregulars from Man Win, who would relieve our Lisu porters and take us through the Burma Army's lines. Some of our men would go forward to scout the enemy, while another unit made a diversionary strike at his positions west of the point of our crossing. After crossing the road, we would carry on for a few miles beyond it, establishing a rearguard to block pursuit.

By 1000 hours we were under way: a column of men, half from Third Battalion and half from the KIA's elite 253 Mobile Battalion, spread over the better part of a mile. As badges of their commando status, the 253rd's men wore red socks, red kerchiefs (captured from the Burma Army) and red patches on their uniforms, and some of them even attached red rags to their guns. To a man, they looked to be ferociously equal to any task assigned to them in any theatre of battle, and in particular, that in which they specialized, the jungle. Their weapons included 40 mm recoilless bazookas, two-inch grenade launchers that the men called M-79s, and Chinese machine guns.

Noon found us scattered around a leafy cluster of bamboo huts called Mung Hkum Yang, where the villagers were preoccupied with a rogue tiger that had killed one of their buffaloes. It had been cloudy all morning, but the sun now emerged from behind its cover and dried our shirts on our backs. There were many happy and unforeseen reunions as some of the men recognized friends with whom they had previously served.

Leaving Mung Hkum Yang, we tunnelled through dense jungle. Occasionally one of the lads would detect some edible plant growing in the verdant gloom, release a cry of jubilation, drop his load and sprint into the forest. We would hear a palm crashing through the foliage. Then the lad would reappear gleefully clutching his prize and race past us to resume his place in the column. In this way we supplemented our meagre rations with wild bananas, yams, clusters of small green pellets the men called curry, light brown mushrooms with a meat flavour, leaves that tasted like Dentine gum, and bamboo shoots. Seng Hpung greatly encouraged these predations, often carrying the men's packs while they foraged.

We reached the N'wan Hka and waded in and out of its cool water until the hollow, ringing sounds of *nhtu*s on bamboo announced that a campsite had been chosen and that we were about to harbour. Our men cut back the jungle on both banks of the river, and half a dozen fires were soon ablaze in the obscure light. They worked as a team. Some laid in stock for the fires. Some hacked *wara hpaw* into segments for use as *hka nhtung*s (bamboo hollows used for fetching water). Some crafted ground covers from another type of bamboo called *ura hpaw*, measuring it into six feet lengths, splitting it and shaving smooth the knotted joints. Some made spits for our pots and kettles or spoons for stirring the rice or bamboo cups. Others brought banana leaves and *lahpaw lap* and spread them for tablecloths, and others prepared the food. If sublimation to a Kachin was detonating a grenade in a pool full of fish, serenity, I now understood, was hacking at bamboo with his *nhtu*. All along the route by which we had come, and for several miles along that by which we would proceed, were the bivouacs of our enormous escort. If the Burma Army attacked, it would have to contend first with them before it reached the heart of the column, by which time we would have dispersed in the jungle. Philip stoked our *dap* and brought us coffee. Awng Hkawng presented me with a cinnamon leaf to chew. Alex and Paul, then San Awng and Seng Hpung's senior batman, Dau Gyung, joined us, and, as the forest's gloom deepened into dark night, we sat about settling the world's stupendous problems by dissolving them in our own private happiness. A full tummy and warm feet, a secure and comfortable

place to sleep, the gurgle o
reports of spirit-protected *nhtu*
of fire and bursts of laughter fr
much more of the same were
overcame for the moment all anxiet

A rumble of thunder. Everyone s
listened, intently. Another rumble of
menacing than the first, and, suddenly,
formed into a moving engine, noisily
everything in sight. Everyone knew exactly
in quest of *shataw hpaw* and *wa hpaw*, wh … into
our little perimeter, hacked into manageab … and split.
Some shaved *kawa hpaw* into two-millimetre s… to use as *pali*
(cord). Some measured strips of split *wa hpaw* and *shataw hpaw* and stood them at right angles to provide frames for shelters. Two-inch saplings were used as joists and purlins, and over these were spread the *plastiks*. The Lisu porters, who had no *plastiks*, roofed their shelters with leaves. No two shelters were alike. That night the rain bucketed down, but, in 20 minutes, we had constructed a village that kept us completely dry.

Dawn broke through dripping jungle over men still asleep in their *bashas* beside the sodden remains of their fires. I shaved from a trough of *kawa wara* that Philip brought me (embarrassed at being unable to supply a plastic basin), and, at 0700 hours, yesterday's rear escort marched past us in silence to take up their position as today's forward escort.

About an hour later we broke camp and continued in and out of the N'wan Hka, half the column barefoot or in flip-flops, the others in canvas boots.

We left the N'wan Hka and began to climb again, only stopping when we caught up with our forward escort resting in a clearing. They moved out at once. The lieutenant commanding them dropped back and took personal charge of guiding us through the next sector. If we were on a path, it was not discernible to me, but somehow our long column managed to keep together, as though linked by an invisible thread. We toiled steeply uphill. The thick bracken frequently obliged us to crouch or crawl, and *sumbwi* (thorns) seemed to cover every vine and creeper. Even leaves were wo miles or so of this ordeal brought us to a through a dark wood. The man in front of me wt!' (leeches). Later, on the Tawang Hka, after the first these little horrors would extend up to four inches in length d, after feeding, inflate to the thickness of slugs, but here, emerging from their cocoons in anticipation of the rains, they were tiny. Awng Hkawng predicted that we would cross the road today, ahead of expectations, but I knew that there might be a dozen revisions. Everything depended on the enemy.

At about 1330 hours we left the path and spread out in the forest. This was the site chosen for our rendezvous with the KIA irregulars who lived among the Burma Army bunkers. The place swarmed with mosquitoes and spiders; however, the worst part was that we had nothing to do but wait. I dubbed it Camp Hong Kong. We heard the drone of a distant aeroplane, and Seng Hpung observed indifferently, 'It is the enemy patrolling.' He told me that during the war Kachin mothers would cover their babies' mouths so the Japanese pilots could not hear their cries. Some of the villagers had maintained that the aeroplanes made so much noise that the pilots could not hear the babies anyway, while others argued that wireless sets could detect them, he said. I wondered if the aeroplane signified that the Burma Army knew about us. One of the men said that we were about three hours from the *mawdaw lam* and that, after crossing it, we would have a further march of two to three hours before we would be beyond danger. 'Enjoy your food,' said Seng Hpung. 'We won't eat again until we have crossed the road. This will be one of the longest days of your trip. Not *the* longest,' he added scrupulously, 'one of the longest.' The men distracted themselves as best they could. Mimo and Maran Naw climbed a banyan. Paul and Philip shadow-boxed. Mats found and examined lovingly a 2½-inch mortar among the men's weapons. I wrote up my diary.

Our irregulars arrived towards sundown. They were dressed in torn, dirty *longyi*s and flip-flops, but they were Jinghpaws, and their eyes shone with pride at having been selected to help what Seng Hpung told me they called 'their boys'. The irregulars' arrival was the cue for the Lisu to return to Zup Ra Yang, and they now came over to bid us farewell. Shyness had prevented them from approaching us before. San Awng doled out a canteen of rice to each of them, but they refused other compensation. Had we been Burmans, they said, we would have forced them to carry our loads and dismissed them without any rice for the return journey. Although night was fast approaching, they set out at once. Seng Hpung looked at me doubtfully and suggested, 'If you need help with your things, I can give them to one of the men.' My proud rejection of this sensible offer was to cause us several unnecessary and dangerous delays. Thus began another difficult but rather wonderful adventure. Except for rare and tensely brief moments, we would not break again until we reached what my diary calls 'Camp End-of-Toil' nearly 21 hours later, when it seemed scarcely possible that we had travelled no more than eight crow-flight miles.

We made good time while there was still some light and the ground was level, but darkness found us working cautiously around the side of a steep mountain. Unable to use our torches, we had to feel our way step by step, lifting each foot deliberately to avoid tripping on roots and vines and fixing it firmly before transferring our weight onto it. A slip could have been fatal. We proceeded in three main bodies, each accompanied by guides intimately familiar with the terrain. Most of the escort preceded the duty column, but we were in communication with them and with our rear guard by *matut mahkai jak*s (walkie-talkies). My orders were simply to follow Hkaw Ying, Seng Hpung's 15-year-old batman, and to keep as close to him as possible. Thus I spent much of the night staring fixedly at a pot hanging from his rucksack. Immediately in front of Hkaw Ying was Seng Hpung's other batman, Ma Htung, preceded by Seng Hpung and the escort's adjutant with our walkie-talkie. Behind me was Mats; behind him, Philip, trailed by San Awng and the others. The purpose of fixing our positions in the column was to enable us to account for each man at every stage of the march, what Americans call 'the buddy system'.

We were past the worst of the mountain now and descending towards another river. We were allowed the use of our torches here, as the mountain was between the Burma Army's positions and us. We reached the Lung Ga (Stony Field) Hka and, hopping from stone to stone, followed it for about three hours. The column halted. Everyone froze. A little moonlight filtered through a thin haze of mist. There was a crackle of talk over the *matut mahkai jak*, and I saw Seng Hpung's silhouette go forward to confer with the adjutant. He returned and explained that the guide was having 'some trouble finding the way'. More talk over the *matut mahkai jak*. Then we started to snake forward again, now onto the bank and into some bush, now back to the river, now up a steep bank and into wood, where fireflies floated reassuringly in the warm air and moonlight dappled the soft ground. Suddenly, a dog's barking heralded the approach of a village. Everyone extinguished torches and stopped talking.

To our left I could now see paddy and the contours of a house; to our right, a knoll. The forest had been cut back there. '*Enemy*!' whispered Philip. 'The enemy has a machine gun on that hill,' explained Seng Hpung.

We made a wide detour through tall grasses and, entering a sugarcane field, passed the house, which seemed deserted except for the dog. Still within range of the machine gun and tensely aware that the dog's ever more insistent barking might trigger its fire, we now crossed open paddy. Would they see us? If so, would they reckon their own chances of survival were best served by withholding fire? Through a clump of trees onto more open paddy, past somnolent cattle in a bamboo corral and over ground alternately stone hard and marshy.

The forward escort had reached a fence and was spread out along it for about 300 yards. We caught up with them. Then the rear escort arrived, and, suddenly, our entire column was together in one place, like a gathering of druids celebrating the new moon. I asked one of the soldiers who was half Gurkha and spoke Hindustani how much further it was to the road. He stared at me for a moment, wondering if I was taking the mickey; then, satisfied that I was in earnest, pointed at a hedgerow just beyond the fence and said calmly, '*Wuhan*' (Yonder).

Seng Hpung, Awng Hkawng and the adjutant had an urgent, whispered conference. They seemed to be debating the location of the Burma Army's guns and the best way forward; all were pointing simultaneously in different directions. Then they were pointing in the same direction. Some of the forward escort who had pushed ahead were recalled and sent off to protect our left flank, while we pushed through the fence and hedgerow to a ditch. Seng Hpung now turned to me and announced cheerfully: 'It's water-crossing time.' I removed my boots, sank into mud and buffalo dung and waded out and up the far bank of the ditch onto more open ground.

We were now moving at speed. Rather than delay the column, I trotted along in my bare feet. Tiny pricks of stubble jabbed at my soles. I ran forward to Seng Hpung and cried, 'I'm barefoot! I'm barefoot!' He looked at me, obviously completely baffled. What was the point of walking barefoot? Was I trying to *prove* something by walking barefoot? He looked at me again and carried on. On I raced over the stubble, expecting to be lamed at any moment. Again I overtook him and again proclaimed, 'I'm barefoot! I'm barefoot!' 'Well, put on your boots,' he said.

As the men behind us caught up they stopped to see what was happening. '*Jaldi, sahib, jaldi*,' said the Gurkha. 'Quickly,' echoed Seng Hpung, and, when, at last, I was ready to proceed, he added, 'Next time, walk through the water in your boots.' All around us were soldiers staring at me with disgust – *imagine putting their lives at risk because you did not want to get your boots wet*. It was a bad moment, and, compounding its awfulness, my foot slipped from a rock while I was crossing another ditch and plunged into the mud. 'All that lost face for one dry boot,' I reflected bitterly.

We crossed another two paddy fields, then took a sharp turn right, then a sharp left, over another fence, then diagonally left, then through another hedgerow – and, behold, the *mawdaw lam*. Men were trotting backwards across it to confound pursuit. A sergeant stood by directing them. I looked at my watch – 2315 hours – and remembered Seng Hpung saying, 'the later, the better'. Since that evening at Pajau Bum when N Chyaw Tang had first mentioned the *mawdaw lam* my imagination had steadily enlarged its size and importance; my map showed it as a major arterial route. I was therefore wholly unprepared for this narrow, dirt track with grass growing in the median, rutted from the wheels of bullock carts and little changed from the time when George Geis of the American Baptist Mission and Major Davies of the Burma Frontier Force tramped along it around the turn of the century. Pickets had taken up positions with heavy guns for about half a mile in both directions. Once we were across, they would fall in behind us.

There was more paddy on the other side. We turned right, negotiated another hedge, then left, past another paddy field, and onto a path and into a wood. Seng Hpung here whispered to me to be extra quiet and careful, as only yards separated us from the Burma Army. 'Tell Mats,' he said. Through a gap in the trees I could discern the timbered houses of a *nam kahtawng*.

We detoured into a copse and bludgeoned through it like rhinos, twisting through the dense, black undergrowth and fighting back the vines and thorns, blind to everything beyond reach. Without our guide's exact knowledge of the location of each tree, we would have been hopelessly lost. Then, suddenly, I panicked. Where was Hkaw Ying's pot? The tiny beacon of reflected moonlight had disappeared! I looked for evidence of his trail but found none and lunged forward but was met by an impenetrable wall of thorns. I lunged in another direction but was met by another wall of thorns. 'I'm lost!' I whispered. 'I can't see you! I can't see you!' I whispered more loudly, only to realize that the 15-year-old was staring at me – a hard, cold stare that proclaimed, 'Can't you keep up? We already know that you can't abide wet boots, but can't you use your eyes and ears? If you can't keep up, then don't take on a trip of this kind.' I followed him meekly, but more humiliation was still to come. A few yards on he turned to me and enquired if anyone was missing. '*Dep sai i?*' (Have you caught up?)

'*Dep sai i?*' I pronounced with deliberation, understanding not a word.

'*Dep sai i?*' he repeated with irritation. Not only was I an invalid inflicted on their otherwise healthy column, but, wonder of wonders, I could not even speak Jinghpaw. He scornfully hurled his query over my head, and someone behind Mats replied, '*N dep shi ai! N dep shi ai!*'

Hkaw Ying relayed the news to Seng Hpung, who passed it gravely to the adjutant. The exchange was then repeated back along the column – but only as far back as San Awng, when it struck me, finally, what had happened: we had lost our tail. The implications were very serious indeed. Tense, fear-laden minutes passed. Then someone behind us said, '*Dep sai!*' and '*Dep sai!*' (All present) ran joyously through the column in a diminishing whisper.

We went forward again in our lurching way, and then there was another awful wait for another tense tally. Finally, we regained the path and looked back wistfully at the spooky bunkers and houses of Man Win where Burma Army soldiers either slept unawares or watched in chilled silence our huge column defiling from the copse. I was too tired even to stoop down to do up a loose bootlace, and the men wanted to smoke, but we carried on regardless, climbing steadily until we felt safe enough to chance a respite. Hardly had we dropped to the ground, however, before we heard a fearsome sound, low, rhythmic and resonant, from some uncertain quarter. Everyone strained to listen. Was it the distant fire of our decoy's attack? Was it the Burma Army engaging our rearguard? The adjutant communicated fore and aft by walkie-talkie. Suddenly a grin broke over Du Kaba's face. It was Mats, snoring.

We climbed wearily on. I fell behind to glean from Awng Hkawng his version of our diverse fortunes but found him disinclined to postmortems, which, in any case, were premature. In addition to Man Win, he said, we had circumvented a Shan village called Malang, where the Burma Army was also dug in, and we were now probably beyond danger, climbing towards the Ka Le Pass between Seng Leng and Loingu (Jinghpaw and Shan for 'Jewel') Bum.[3] *Probably* beyond danger. The Man Win garrison might summon reinforcements and give chase.

We crossed a small ravine, summoned a little extra strength and scrambled up the inevitable far bank, and, suddenly, gloriously, all around us were wood fires and soldiers hacking away at the forest with *nhtu*s. For the moment at least our ordeal was over. The adjutant had called a *preekop*.

* * *

We ate some dried beef and chicken broth, grabbed some sleep and resumed the march at first light, dawn and the pellucid whistles of the birds reaffirming the beginning of better times. For about half a mile in the damp forest we passed the dying camp fires of our forward escort, some of them still rubbing their eyes, and were reminded yet again of the enormous effort made to

3. The almost identically shaped peaks are known as Brassière Mountain; the derivation is obvious.

ensure our safety. For the next two hours or so we climbed the steep slopes of Loingu Bum.

A picture snapped at Ka Le Pass hangs on the wall of my study. It is a solace to me when I am disappointed or downcast. I am standing in the centre of a crowd of men in KIA uniforms, holding aloft an M 16 (symbolizing victory) in my right hand. The men, in classic pose, stout and barrel-chested, are lying back on their packs, smoking. Moments before, when I had struggled into the clearing, they had roared with laughter, for nothing entertains a Kachin so much as the sight of a friend's discomfort, and in the moment captured by the photograph, we were all conscious of having just survived what my diary calls 'the Night of Horrors'. The picture has a general tint of green – green foliage, green uniforms, long, slender, dew-laden, green palm leaves – but my face and several others' are lit by shafts of gold and silver light. I can still hear the almost human voice of a monkey crying out at us from the forest. It is the Grecian urn of my collection of more than 250 photographs of life among the Kachins, celebrating a moment that lives on in my dreams. The danger, tension and uncertainty were behind us, and with a strong guard to protect our rear, everything from here on was downhill.

Seng Hpung now was relaxed and at peace. In addition to the physical strain, he had borne the worries and responsibility for the safety of the whole column. He strutted among the men telling stories and provoking laugh after laugh, everyone paying the keenest attention to everything that he said, none more so than our irregulars. They had never seen a KIA colonel before and felt that they were witnessing all the brilliance of the quasi-divine *duwa*s who had governed *Wunpawng Mungdan* when their grandfathers and great uncles were boys. It had been a tremendous privilege to serve under such a great man and to share in his triumph of demonstrating to the hated Burma Army that he could walk through their lines with impunity.

When we halted again it was for lunch beside the N'krawn (Unsmooth) Hka, and, while waiting for the food, one of the irregulars took my socks from me and washed them. Green leaves everywhere were shimmering in the vibrant light. Clean water was splashing over clean rocks. Then there was food, then sleep, and when we resumed the march for the last stage of the descent to

Camp End-of-Toil, I walked again in dry, clean socks and almost dry boots.

We slept for *eleven* hours at Camp End-of-Toil. Next morning, the soldiers who had camped ahead of us stood in their bivouacs and waved us on, prolonging and sweetening our sense of triumph. We were in low, sandy country now, the path wide and shaded by clumps of tall bamboo and wild coffee trees, the berries just starting to ripen. There were no hidden, trip-wire roots, no overhanging vines, and, most important of all, no *sumbwi.* My rucksack felt as light as air. Then, at about 1000 hours, Seng Hpung proclaimed: 'Shelby, I present to you the Nmai Hka.' We looked down over waving reeds and white sand upon a majestic, moving ribbon of granite-grey water, while the men rushed forward onto the strange and novel sand and gambolled in it like children. Major Zau Chang's escort was leaving us here. They fell out for a group photograph, and we thanked them for risking their lives for our safety. Awng Hkawng said that their return to base posed the greater risk, for once it was known that a large KIA unit was operating north of the Chiphwe road, the Burma Army would summon additional forces and try to intercept it. Nevertheless, he added cheerfully, there were many routes back.

A few miles downstream the Nmai (Bad) Hka joined the other senior stream of the Irrawaddy, the Mali Hka (Four Rivers). Even after five months of dry season, it was here about 70 yards wide and moving over rapids at about 15 knots. Four rafts constructed of tubes of *wara* lashed together with rattan and *pali* (Mats: 'the Kachin Navy') had been assembled to ferry us across it. We watched the first crossing with foreboding.[4] Sailors fore and aft pushed and steered with long poles, while a third amidships knelt and paddled. They worked the raft confidently upstream in the backwater close to the near shore for four minutes or so, then edged it out into the midstream current. The current locked onto it. It was now moving downstream at speed at a precarious angle to the current. Water sloshed over the gunwales. A tree, its leaves

4. The raft on which Arthur Thompson and his companions tried to cross the Nmai Hka in June 1942, not far from here, disintegrated, and they very nearly drowned (see Clifford, 1979: 131).

still clinging to its branches, and other driftwood floated past. The raft narrowly avoided some fearsome-looking rocks breaking the surface, the water foaming and bubbling angrily around them in vicious grey flurries. The raft started to spin, and for a moment success seemed to hang dangerously in the balance. But the sailors' skill was equal to the challenge, and it reached its destination. Its company of three soldiers waved at us triumphantly from the slither of sand and palm trees lining the far bank.

The next raft ferried San Awng across with Seng Hpung's baggage.

Now came our turn. Our sailors overcame manfully the same vicissitudes – but we spun completely round in the gurgling, raging rapids by the rocks, thrice. I distracted myself with concerns for my rucksack lashed to a platform amidships. The best thing about the crossing was its brevity. Each return trip absorbed perhaps twenty minutes, but, as none of the rafts carried more than six people, including the sailors, the entire exercise lasted about an hour. Then the sailors dismantled the rafts and hid their components in the forest to prevent the Burma Army from finding them.

Seng Hpung now sent for new porters and dispatched two men to contact the KIA's Fourth Battalion. While waiting for their report, he studied the hills on the south shore through his binoculars but detected only a band of small, stick-like people who, he said, seemed to be gold-panners. Reduced to our original strength and here lacking the cover of the forest, we felt very exposed. The Burma Army patrolled the Chiphwe road just beyond the hills.

We pressed on up the beach, labouring through soft sand and, towards sundown, reached Aura Yang, where we had intended to spend the night. However, the villagers feared Burma Army reprisal and asked us not to stop there. So we carried on for another 20 minutes and camped in the forest. Afterwards we learned that a Burma Army patrol had recently scouted Jubeli Yang (Jubilee Flat), site of the Kachin Baptist Church's fiftieth convention, which was half a day's march from where we camped. They had arrested three of the villagers and killed their livestock.

The next day we tramped through the valley of the Nmai Hka

over hard, sandy dirt and through high, undulating *kaing* grass, sugar cane and fields full of rosemary. I removed my boots to ford a stream and walked barefoot for about half a mile, which proved to be surprisingly agreeable. Eleven days of walking had toughened my feet. Our new porters were all women. They were barefoot and had firm, pronounced calf muscles and, unlike our previous porters, carried their baskets strapped over their foreheads. They said that we were the first Europeans they had seen, and I asked them if they thought us handsome. The younger ones timidly covered their faces with their hands and hid behind the shoulders of their more bosomy elders, who answered tactfully that they 'admired' the European look but would not want to marry a European. One of them eventually conceded that she could imagine such a thing if it came down to a choice between a European and no husband at all – provided, however, that the match comported with their rules of exogamy.[5]

We were met by a smartly turned-out KIA section whose orders were to escort us to Fourth Battalion's headquarters. While the sergeant major in charge briefed Seng Hpung, some of the men gathered small, reddish orange windfalls that John called 'Kachin plums' and shared them around.

We reached Gaw Nam Yang late that afternoon and camped on open ground next to a papaya grove. Philip had promised to mend a faulty strap on my rucksack, but I knew that he could not set up our *basha*, lay in wood, build our fire, make tea *and* deal with my rucksack before dark. There was a limit to what he could do, and, given my determination to conserve my own time for writing up my diary, I knew that the problem, which stemmed from Seng Hpung's order at Jum Yang detaching us from the students' mess, would recur. Therefore, when Seng Hpung came to me jauntily proclaiming that tonight was to be the first instalment in the promised curriculum of Indian history, I showed him the faulty strap and said, 'There are four lads over there looking after themselves but only one man looking after three of us, Du Kaba. Couldn't you give us one of them? It need not affect the existing messing arrangements.' I suggested Paul, and, more out of good

5. Our conversations with villagers were always conducted through an interpreter, usually, as in this instance, Philip (Hkyen Naw).

humour than conviction, he ordered Mimo to 'fetch the lad that the old man calls Paul.' This rather obvious measure solved the problem.

That evening the students sat with us around our *dap* drinking coffee. Coffee was a great luxury, and I asked Philip to invite Seng Hpung to join us, but Philip was reluctant to do this. John said, 'Mr Sheby, why you not go to Colonel Seng Hpung. If Colonel Seng Hpung come here, we all must leave. It is all right for you, but we are only soldiers.' 'Nonsense,' I countered and straightaway marched off to fetch our leader. The lads moved away from the fire and into the darkness as soon as he appeared. I laughed and said, 'They are afraid of you, Du Kaba!' As always, he was equal to the moment, accepting my offer of my rucksack to sit on and entertaining everyone with a succession of funny stories, only breaking off when Awng Hkawng came to report on intelligence gleaned from the villagers and on the arrangements that he had made for new porters.

I lay down in front of the fire while they spoke. Above me was a straight, ancient, naked tree rising about 70 yards into the sky and standing out spectrally in the moonlight, and above it was the moon and the firmament. Clouds floated in front of the moon and passed on; stars blinked at us through the drifts of silver mist; and frogs croaked down by the pebbly bend in the stream where I had bathed. The fire shed its warm glow and wood smell over us. I thought how happy I felt. The lads were now preoccupied with Mats. They seemed to like Mats, and their good opinion of him seemed to improve his spirits, which recently, I had noticed, tended to melancholy.

Seng Hpung and Awng Hkawng left. The lads were now talking between themselves in Jinghpaw, and I reflected that I preferred their banter when it was unintelligible. Then John asked me, a little hesitantly, if I wanted to go with them to drink beer in the village. I replied by asking him if he knew the story of Adam and Eve. All the lads laughed at first, politely, thinking that I was about to launch another joke, but I continued in dead earnest about how Adam and Eve had squandered their patrimony for inessentials like beer, and that was precisely what we had done in Europe and America. Their picture of the West was a glamorous delusion derived from cinema that concealed the loneliness, unhappiness and coldness among people and their distance from divine nature, I said. They listened respectfully and with understandable embarrassment. Then John said, 'Yes, Mr Sheby, but we are young. We can think about all these things when we are free. But, right now, we want our freedom.'

I thought of that dreary lot of dopeheads who followed Timothy Leary and Allen Ginsberg into oblivion in the 1960s and 1970s. They exalted Freedom. What would Freedom really mean for these lads? 'Even if you win your freedom from the Burmans, you might find yourselves saddled with other bad rulers, like Sama *Duwa* Sin Wa Nawng, who sold you out to Aung San,' I said.

'Mr Sheby, what would you advise us to do?' asked John.

The question implied a long discussion. I did not have any special answers, flattered though I was by their deference, and I replied that their leaders seemed to be handling things quite well enough. 'Even a year ago no one but a few specialists knew who the KIA were,' I said. 'And those few who did thought of you as bandits and narcotics traffickers trying to undermine a respectable government. Then came the riots in Rangoon and Mandalay, and the whole world changed its mind about Ne Win and his junta. The riots might not have happened but for the demonetization of the kyat, and the kyat would not have been demonetized except for the strain on the government's resources caused by the civil war. It seems to me that your leaders have led you well insofar as achieving freedom from Burman oppression is concerned. But you already have a freedom that is far more important than political liberties.'

There was a silence, then some nervous discussion between them in Jinghpaw. Everyone suddenly got up and called for Mats. The plan, apparently, was to take Mats into the village that evening without me. They were young; Mats was young. They wanted beer. That was the plan.

'Mr Sheby, we all thank you for your advice,' said John.

'Yes, Mr Sheby,' the others said, embarrassed. 'It is very good advice.'

Seng Hpung now came back for his 'lecture'. I had assumed that he had forgotten about it and was already half in my pyjamas. We roasted some rice cakes over the fire and ate them. Then I told him what little I knew about the Aryan invasion of the subcontinent, the fusion of their pastoralists' pantheon and the indigenous peoples' gods, and how a caste system arose from the Aryans' ambition to preserve their lightness of skin and martial power. He sat silent throughout this didactic torrent, and I was fast asleep when the lads returned from their pub-crawl.

* * *

We had time to idle next morning. San Awng shot a dove, and Ma Htung, Hkaw Ying and Philip picked green papayas and rosemary. We had the papaya as chutney for breakfast. It was not awfully successful. The slender pickings from the dove curried with the rosemary surfaced at lunch.

An old man from the village visited us. He looked poor, even by Kachin standards. His skin was scarred, as one who had suffered an attack of smallpox, and he was very thin. His *longyi* was in tatters and grey with age. He carried a flintlock muzzle-loading hunting rifle, which fired stones for bullets and which he had crafted himself out of some kind of metal tubing. He would have passed as a beggar anywhere else in the world, but here everyone greeted him enthusiastically. He was the local pastor.

We left Gaw Nam Yang at 0920 hours. While we had nothing so sophisticated as a compass, our route seemed generally northbound and rose steadily. After we had climbed for nearly an hour, we halted to dismiss a porter who had taken ill and was unable to carry on. Shortly before noon we entered an abandoned *yi* (dry rice or vegetable patch). Seng Hpung observed that two hours' march to the east was a Burma Army post and that the forest ahead afforded excellent cover for an ambush. We halted again, while he discussed our options with the sergeant major. They decided to scout the forest, and half a dozen men went ahead as a decoy to draw fire if the enemy was ensconced there. Awng Hkawng came forward to confer with Seng Hpung and the sergeant major. They debated between them with contradictory gesticulation, each man pointing excitedly in different directions; then our escort was recalled and sent to scout a path to the east. Turning to me, Seng Hpung said, 'We take rest here while the men gather information. There is a village ahead. We don't know if the Burma Army is there. We might be attacked at any moment. I put you on the alert.' I did not know quite what to make of this advice. Was he having me on?

'What do we do if attacked?' I asked.

'That depends on the situation. It will be better for you if you just follow me and keep very low and do not let the villagers see you.'

'Shall I tell Mats?' I asked.

'Yes. You should put him in the picture.'

I told Mats.

'I'm putting you in the picture. On no account must we be seen by any villagers, and, if attacked, we should keep close to Seng Hpung.'

We now came out of the forest into a clearing. All the trees before us had been felled, leaving chest-high stumps, and beyond the stumps was Jubeli Yang. Our escort had already surrounded the nearest house and were interrogating its occupants. Or perhaps the house was empty? At a distance of about 70 yards it was difficult to tell. The hills to the west, where the Burma Army might have had a lookout, seemed particularly sinister and menacing.

Seng Hpung went forward and entered the house. Mats and I detoured to the right, our hats pulled low over our faces, and hid behind the house. Then, suddenly, Seng Hpung came out of the house and strode brazenly into a *yi* below it, down to a clump of trees next to a brook. We followed at double march, sensing keenly our exposure. 'Here come some villagers!' Mats suddenly exclaimed in a tense whisper. Four women had appeared on the opposite bank of the brook and stopped to talk with some of our men. We turned away, hoping they had not seen us. Four more women appeared. 'They seem to move in units of four,' Mats observed.

We camped by the brook, and, when I went to Seng Hpung for another tutorial that evening, he put me in the picture again. 'The enemy is there,' he said with a vague sweep of his arm. 'I can't say exactly where or in what numbers, but we will avoid him, by another night march if necessary.' For nearly two hours we discussed the reign of Asoka (273–232 BC) and its special importance to the Hindu majority of the Congress Party, who imputed to it a utopia of 'self-rule'. 'Well, I suppose that's probably enough for one session,' I said eventually. 'No,' he replied crossly, 'you can continue for another quarter of an hour.' He was oddly sullen and taciturn, causing me to wonder if he was keeping troubling intelligence to himself.

We carried on next morning with new porters, leaving soon after dawn in a light rain. The path rose through mist-cloaked woods of uncommon beauty. We stopped someone encountered on the path and debriefed him. He was incongruously dressed in a khaki jacket and blue jeans and looked to be in his early fifties. I learned later that he was a KIA officer who had been demoted from major to second lieutenant for adultery. He had walked from First Brigade headquarters and was bound for Pajau Bum. Awng Hkawng had once served as his batman. He carried nothing himself and was accompanied by a young man with only a small pack and a hunting rifle.

We trekked on, stopping again for the porters' breakfast when we reached a stream. While they built a fire and roasted rice cakes over it, Mats discovered leeches feeding on one of his ankles and proposed a competition. We would keep tallies of the leeches that attacked us, and the victim with the lowest score would treat the other to dinner in India. 'That way,' he said, 'there will be something good about leeches!'

We pushed on, pausing for a sentimental glance back at the Nmai Hka and the twin, grey peaks of Seng Leng Bum and Loingu Bum of 'Night of Horrors' memory, and halted for the night at Gang Dau Yang (Gang Dau Family Flat). Its *yi* consisted of a few yams and pumpkins growing between charred stumps of recently felled trees. Its *dum*s (granaries) were empty, and its houses were tiny and in a state of precocious decay, their grey thatch full of vermin. No one was about except half a dozen barefoot old women minding filthy babies. They told us that the men and the younger women were away prospecting for gold, but I wondered if they had fled from us. In one of the empty houses was a pot of hog stew cooking over a fire. As we were well rested, I could not understand why we were stopping here. After conferring with the sergeant major, Seng Hpung explained, 'Better to stay in this village than in the jungle. We might be here for several days,' he added. 'We promised our Jubeli porters to relieve them here. We need to find replacements.' The 'less than four weeks' to reach

India forecast at Pajau Bum was becoming daily more of a mirage. As long as we reached India before the end of March I knew that Carole would be all right. But I knew also that any further delay would be very hard on her.

A Burma Army column had raided Gang Dau Yang recently and stolen their blankets and everything else they could find of use to them, so Seng Hpung called a meeting to elucidate the KIO's aims and report on the progress of the war. One of the women sought news of her grandson, as nothing had been heard of him since he had left the village to join the KIA. Seng Hpung informed her that he was safe at Pajau Bum.

Our tutorial that evening was about the dark centuries after Asoka, when India was ruled by petty rajahs who left no monuments or records of any significance, and how the arrival of Alexander the Great's army in the Punjab challenged local thought, as did also the evangelization begun with the Apostle Thomas's mission to Kerala. Seng Hpung seemed very pleased with my rolling generalities. 'It is just what I expected,' he said, 'Oxford in the jungle!' 'Do not worry,' he replied when I raised my concerns about Carole. 'The Chief of Staff has *ordered* us to arrive at the Indian border before the end of March.' After Hpaw Lam Hpya Bum (Mount Slaughtered Wild Ox), which would be one of the highest mountains in the whole trip, we would have the same porters for two stages. Thereafter, we would have no further porter problems, he said, consolingly.

I awoke next morning with a queasy tummy but found to my astonishment that seven sturdy-looking porters with empty *hting-gas* (baskets) had assembled. We moved off after breakfast and descended by an easy gradient through dense foliage to the Chyanya Hka. It was raining, but the forest cover kept us dry. We followed the Chyanya Hka's meandering route through a dark and stony canyon for the better part of an hour, then, climbing again, marched through the high grasses of abandoned *yis* and over ground recently cleared for cultivation and still deep in ashes. I asked Mats if he had elicited anything of interest from the men the previous evening. 'Specifically regarding what?' he demanded testily. 'Kachin ethnography,' I answered. He assured me that their discussions had encompassed only 'young men's talk'. We encountered some children returning to their homes on the lower Nmai Hka. They were fresh from taking examinations at a KIO school at a place called Bum San (Mount Clear), and their *nhpye*s (shoulder bags) were full of books. They had already walked for two days and still were three days from home. I used to hitchhike from school in Massachusetts for holidays in Mississippi and thought myself very superior to classmates who travelled home by train. But my father had always provided me with money for food and lodging. These children walked home and made their own shelters.

There now blew up one of those freak storms that can capsize the sturdiest vessel and easily might have wrecked my hopes of reaching India. We had been on the go for four hours and had anticipated *preekop*s both before and at the pass, but it was not until we reached the Nma (Wound) Hka in the valley below that Seng Hpung signalled the break. Then, suddenly, he rescinded the order. I had already taken off my boots and was removing the burrs from my socks. The column disappeared into the forest as I struggled to put my boots back on. Rage mounted within me as I thrashed about in the forest investigating different animal tracks, and when, eventually, I found the column, clearing a site, Seng Hpung resplendently at the centre of it dispensing instructions, I marched over to him and said: 'Now was that polite?' He looked at me, baffled.

'Walking off and leaving me like that,' I explained. 'I might have been lost.'

It was a moronic mistake. I had insulted him, and *in front of the men*. Very few of them heard it, but those who did were aghast, for they knew that the column's safety depended on Seng Hpung's authority and that he could not risk my undermining his authority in this way. They watched in silence, wondering how he would react. Mercifully, he withdrew from the confrontation, limiting himself to observing that he would not have abandoned even the least important soldier in the jungle and that his one difficulty with my accusations was understanding how it was possible to imagine such a thing.

A tender of apology was needed. Seng Hpung was now sitting alone under a tree nursing his rage. I went over to him and invited him to share our coffee. It was another mistake. He ignored me.

After a while he came over to me and said, 'This requires more discussion.' Courtesy to his foreign guest, he reminded me curtly, did not oblige him to share his decisions with me. We had shifted sites because there was not enough room to accommodate our numbers at the first site; but that was his decision to make and not mine. More important matters were at stake than the comfort of my feet. He would discharge his responsibilities as he saw fit with neither advice nor reproach from me. I urged him to sit down, but he refused. 'If I have something important to say, I stand!' he snapped. He concluded: 'Sometimes, Shelby, I get the impression that you believe that I have a *duty* to escort you to India. Let me explain to you something you do not know. You are here because, by chance, I had business in Second Brigade area and consented to let you travel with me.' It was all deeply depressing. Our friendship, so buoyant only a few hours before, had foundered on the shoals of petty vexation and silly remarks. The malevolent Nat of Wound River had holed it.

Awng Hkawng, who witnessed everything, was standing at the camp's exit, chuckling, when we resumed. 'Start climbing,' he said. Ahead of us was the notorious Slaughtered Wild Ox. A three-hour climb, said the porters.

We were soon counting each dreary step and estimating the fractions of ascent already accomplished and comparing them with that remaining. 'One-twelfth of the way! ... Two hours to go!' Arduous climbs like Hpaw Lam Hpya Bum have one commendation, I reflected: they deaden the senses to emotional pain.

On we trudged. After the first 40 minutes, we enjoyed a short respite of gentle gradient, raising the hope that the worst was over; that we had broken the Ox's back, so to speak. The lush, leafy vegetation and hot, humid air of the lower slopes were behind us.

Now we were among conifers. On we toiled into ever thinner air. Fallen trees and rotting and decomposing bamboo obstructed the path, which, in any case, was now scarcely wide enough for a foothold. At every bend we kept expecting deliverance, only to discern through the mists and gloom above our forward escort toiling stoically up another steep slope. Like toys with wound-up mechanical parts, we climbed on and on, our hearts thumping wildly, our damp, salty clothes clinging to our skins. The higher we climbed, the steeper the gradient became. Every few minutes I wiped the condensation off my brow and glasses.

Suddenly we were in cloud, and Awng Hkawng shouted exultantly: 'Half way!'

Another hour passed.

Night fell unnoticed in that unnatural light, and only my watch registered its approach. Finally, *nhtu*s hacking away at the forest announced that, although we had not reached the pass, we were stopping. Seng Hpung was pointing out various sites for locating our *basha*s. Everything had to be done quickly, as cutting wood at night risked offending the Spirit of the Forest. I took off my clothes, one dripping piece at a time, and hung them out to dry on the frame that Philip was constructing. Soon it was pitch black, and formless shadows were moving between the fires exchanging jokes about their trials. There were songs about Hpaw Lam Hpya Bum, which every Kachin knew. Now they had their own stories to tell, which, in turn, might beget more songs.

San Awng, who had also witnessed the scene at Wound River and shared my sorrow, brought me a potion concocted from some jungle plant that he called medicine. It was good for sleeping and potency, he said. Then he fetched *jumdwi* (sugar) from Seng Hpung's stock and made me a cup of tea. Maran Naw possessed himself of Philip's cassette player, and the dripping, brooding jungle soon throbbed with the pulsations of Big Beat. Slaughtered Wild Ox was another of those ridiculous ardours that the men would discuss and celebrate around their fires forever.

* * *

We made an early start next morning. When we reached the *hkyet* (pass), the mists were rising in thin white swirls from the pearled valley between us and the next range of hills. While we were drinking in the view, two beautiful Jinghpaw girls appeared. They were returning from visiting relations at Fourth Battalion headquarters and were bound for Wai Maw (Nearly Gone Village) near Myitkyina. They were about 25, well dressed and heavily made-up. They lowered their eyes discreetly and stared at the ground when speaking to us.

It was nearly noon before we reached the floor of the valley. We lunched and changed porters at Tsing Ja (Thick Grass) Yang and, now westbound, marched on to Hpung Gan Family Flat, where a bamboo rail fence had been erected to prevent livestock from straying, and harboured there overnight. The men fanned out into its *yi* and scavenged between the half-burnt logs and chest-high stumps for chillies, every man being entitled by their customs to take whatever he needed for his daily portion of food.

N'Lam Awng and Peter made the exciting discovery that the owner of the house in which they were billeted that evening, a man named Nlum Zau Awng, was their 'brother'. He was also, like them, a Hkahku or upriver Jinghpaw, who have a kind of Old Testament belief that they are superior to Kachins whose blood lines might have been debased through miscegenation with Shans and Burmans. During a punitive expedition against Hpung Gan Yang in 1987, Burma Army soldiers had seized Nlum Zau Awng and beaten him almost to death in front of his wife and three small children for refusing to identify the commander of their local guerrilla force. He was a fervent supporter of the KIA. His kinship to N'Lam Awng and Peter, their shared Hkahku pedigree and the general enthusiasm for the KIA called for a celebration demanding *tsa pi*, which is made by pressing a clump of fermented boiled rice repeatedly through a bamboo tube to extract the *tsa* (juice), which is then strained through a straw mesh to produce a sweetly acidic, intoxicating solution resembling dish water in appearance. Kachins are curiously proud of this revolting drink.

Next day we were slow in getting away, the main column following some distance behind the forward escort. This was prime ambush country, the next eight furlongs being the most dangerous. The path continued along the Darawng (Male God of Destruction) Hka. Occasionally, Seng Hpung would raise his hand, and the column would freeze; then he would pat his head as a sign to the rear escort to fan out around us, and we would wait for a communication from the sergeant major that the way ahead was clear.

We left the path, took cover in a tree-lined *hka hkawng* (ditch), followed it for about half a mile and emerged onto another path leading to a cane suspension bridge, where the sergeant major told us that a Burma Army column had successfully ambushed a KIA column. In a forlorn patch of high grass nearby had stood once prosperous Ntau (Gourd) Yang, now vanished without trace: the Burma Army had incinerated it.

We reached the majestic Jing Ma (Fulfilment) Hka sometime after noon and, while our escort reconnoitred the cliffs above it, halted for lunch. I have a photograph taken here of Seng Hpung proudly exhibiting a giant mahseer caught after being stunned by one of San Awng's bombs. Kachins rightly prize fresh fish above all other food.

Thereafter our route followed the winding course of the Jing Ma Hka through flat country abounding in primula, flowering clematis, convolvulus, honeysuckle and jasmine that scattered the sun's rays in a bauble of colour. But the men had eyes only for the sherry-dark pools and eddies where the fish lurked, and thoughts for missed detonation opportunities. We saw green pigeons, brown dippers, golden bee-eaters and peafowl and heard a bird whose song sounded curiously like a pinball machine.

The path broadened and was now pocked with the horny moulds of buffalo hoofs and pigs' feet. The bush was cut back from the path. A solid cane bridge with railings spanned a stream; there was even a notice at a junction manifesting directions and distances to different destinations. 'We are in a semi-liberated area,' explained Awng Hkawng. 'During the first decade after Panglong, when we Kachins still trusted the Burmans to fulfill the promises made to us, the government of Kachin State built a motor road over this sector.' We came to a guard post. Some of our escort exchanged greetings with friends there and, shortly before sundown, we marched into Jing Ma Yang.

Jing Ma Yang was the first village of any importance that we had seen since Jum Yang. A large herd of cattle grazed on an expanse of grass as smooth and green as an English lawn. There was an orchard of trees heavy with lemons and oranges and grapefruit; a papaya grove; a school; a shop; a chalk-lined football pitch and latrines discreetly concealed behind matted cane. Each house was bordered by flowers and fenced in its own compound. The women, fastidious about their appearance, wore burnished silver earrings and glossy red lipstick. Like the Shan women we had seen at Möng Ko, they piled up their hair to enhance their height. Their cheeks, foreheads and noses were covered with a luminous cream foundation paste made from ground wood of the *sanaphka* tree and streaked with white powder. Mats and I excited less curiosity than we had in other Kachin villages, although the ageing owner of the house where we were billeted pointed to a tiny grandchild and said, 'That's how old I was when the British were last here.' He told us that the Burma Army had raided Jing Ma Yang the previous year but had spared the villagers. 'They only killed our livestock,' he said.

Seng Hpung and I had not spoken since the insult at Wound River. Now Mimo came to me grinning, with the message that he was ready for another *lekcha*; and that evening, in the wan and uncertain light of his *dap*, we discussed the kind of life that had settled on India during the long centuries between Asoka and Genghis Khan, when the Ramayana emerged as the main source of popular folklore, and scientific investigation became the prisoner of Brahmanical texts. *Ahimsa*, caste strictures and the debilitating effects of climate had rendered India defenceless by the time the Mongols invaded, I said; and the Tartars, everywhere destructive, had left behind them a trail of mass murder, looting and arson. 'However,' I suggested, 'the Tartars had an unforeseen effect on India's future. They charted a route into India and took back to their bleak lands the pregnant message that rich and fertile country south of the mountains was ripe for plunder. The result was imperial conquest: Muslim rule lasting 500 years and British rule lasting for about a century and a half.' Seng Hpung was exhausted from instruction by the time I departed, but the insult at Wound River was forgotten. Ancient, neutral, eviscerated India dissolved our quarrel more effectively than any heart-to-heart.

When I returned to our billet, Mats and Philip had gone. They returned after midnight with John, Alex and Paul in tow, in boisterous spirits. 'Mr Sheby, he is sleeping!' cried John, aghast.

'I *was* – until the *Tsa Pi* Brigade arrived!' I retaliated, crossly gathering my things and moving outdoors.

Above me now floated the same glorious moon that those early Aryans had worshipped. Awng Hkawng found me thus the following morning, my sleeping bag soaked through with dew. 'Sleep well?' he asked politely, but on his face was a tight little smile that revealed what he was really thinking: 'This one's a raving loon.'

* * *

We halted at Mazup (Confluence) Yang, so named because the

Jing Ma Hka is joined there by one of its more important tributaries, the Htiyi Hka. It was the sergeant major's home village, which called for a celebration at his parents' house, both to mark his safe return and to welcome in the traditional way the VIPs that he had piloted from Jubilee Flat. *Tsa pi* was offered and I drank some, knowing that to refuse would be considered impolite — and at once regretted it. I remember N'Lam Awng explaining something important about our route and how the Burma Army managed secrecy and surprise by forcing local people to act as their guides; where it was more likely and where less likely to attack us, but, somehow, the specificities kept eluding me. I remember Awng Hkawng offering some seemingly interesting, seemingly astute observations about Kachin marriage customs, but what, exactly, were they? I believe that the sergeant major spoke about his village, but I do not remember anything he said. Mats broke off his conversation with our hosts to speak to me, but I remember nothing of what he said to me. The only thing that I really knew for certain is that I was *drunk*. Mercifully, in such a state benign nature protects you from more self-abuse. I suddenly keeled over and fell asleep. When I awoke, Philip was tugging gently on my sleeve, urging me to fetch my camera. 'Sheby, the ladies are ready.' *Ready for what?* Evidently, I had offered to photograph them. And there they were, gorgeous in their silver-studded velvet jackets and silver necklaces and high, embroidered *bawng bam*s, their lips painted bright red and their faces smeared with the yellow paste of *sanaphka* wood and streaked with white powder, ready and eager to pose.

Fourth Battalion headquarters was scarcely three hours' march now, but I could marshal no enthusiasm for this significant landmark in our trek north. We passed some females bathing naked above the waist in the Htiyi Hka. Their breasts were exquisitely turned and their wet hair tumbled down their jade-smooth backs, a Gauguinesque treat free for our inspection, but, still drugged, I was numb to enticement. They were one with the fantastical landscape; with Seng Hpung, Ma Htung and San Awng's groupie fantasizing about the fish lurking in the dark eddies; with the *laja* (chestnut) *hpun*, *maga latsen hpun* and coffin wood trees.

Protocol demanded that we afford Fourth Battalion headquarters opportunity to smarten itself up and prepare to welcome us properly, so we halted at Bum San (Mount Clear) Yang and waited for leave to proceed. I lay down in grass and, drowsily indifferent to the men scuttling about fraternizing with the villagers, fell asleep again. Two (?), three (?) hours later we marched into Fourth Battalion headquarters, a scattering of bamboo houses on a hill. Acting Commander Captain La Nan and his civilian counterpart, a *salang kaba* with hollow cadaverous cheeks and a bald head shaped like a bullet, were standing by to greet us in the middle of an entourage of smartly dressed junior officers and officials. Behind them, crowded onto the balcony of one of the houses, were some of our lads who had gone ahead of the column. As we were exchanging civilities with our hosts, a chorus of exultation arose from the lads at the renewed sight of their valiant drinking companion. 'Mats! Mats!' they screamed. 'Why were they calling for *Mats*?' asked Seng Hpung. 'Mats! Mats!' continued the unholy frenzy.

Mats, Philip and I were quartered in a house to ourselves. It had been an awful day, full of strange and confusing emotions. Mats and Philip had gone out, and I was looking forward to an evening alone with my diary and Jinghpaw wordlist, when Awng Hkawng appeared with La Nan and his colleagues and declared that there was to be yet another celebration. 'It is our custom to entertain visitors, and you are their special guests,' he explained in a way that barred all dissent. Tin mugs filled with neat spirit and tin plates heaped with a dark curry paste compounded of salted entrails that tasted like anchovies were soon circulating. Our hosts beamed with satisfaction. 'But where is Mats?' asked La Nan. 'I am sad your friend is not here to enjoy.'

'He will be heartbroken when he learns that he missed the fun,' I replied bitterly.

'Where is he?'

'He is with the students,' I said.

'We are only young once,' observed the bullet-headed *salang kaba*.

'Never again,' added La Nan. 'We can be happy knowing that they must be enjoying.'

They chatted for a while between themselves. The *salang kaba* scarcely spoke, but, when he did, I noted, his words commanded respect. He now turned to me and said that he had met another American, a technician installing communications apparatus. 'He was even uglier than you,' he said matter-of-factly. This strange experience, he said, had happened to him in China, where he had gone on a weapons procurements mission.

I enquired whether the route between Fourth Battalion headquarters and First Brigade headquarters was safe from ambush.

'The enemy is very quiet,' replied La Nan. Two years previously it had sent a large column against them, two entire companies, which they had prepared to ambush, but the column had gone by a different route, so there had been no engagement, no one had been hurt, and everyone's pride had been satisfied. 'It is the best kind of war,' he said.

'The Burma Army kills everyone suspected of helping the KIA,' observed the bullet-headed *salang kaba*, and, thus prompted, La Nan told the story of a woman from his village who had been obliged to precede a Burma Army column to detonate any mines that might be concealed along the path and who, after her ordeal, had been raped by every member of the column and then bludgeoned to death.

'What is vital to the KIA's chances of success, what is needed to bring the West on board,' I suggested, 'is a picture of an earless man. Random tales, like the story of this poor woman, sadly, make little impression, but one picture of an earless man would make a real difference.' A long, macabre discussion as to how to arrange such a picture ensued.

The conversation drifted to gentler topics. As the evening wore on I became conscious of an inclination to retire, yet no end was in sight. Then out of the dark and into our little circle of light Mats and John suddenly appeared, breathing new life into the party. 'Where have you *been*?' asked Awng Hkawng. 'We have been waiting for you *all evening*.' Mats sat down heavily on the floor next to me, folded his legs beneath him, lit a cheroot and said majestically that they had been to a neighbouring village to visit N'Lam Awng's 'brother'. John, however, seemed troubled and ill at ease. He laughed awkwardly, breathed heavily. Nor was he smoking in the smooth, urbane way that Mats smoked. After a while he said, 'Mr Sheby, I am very sorry for yesterday. Really, I am very sorry. All of us are very sad. Alex, Paul, N'Lam Awng, we are all very sad. We are very sorry, Mr Sheby, and very sad. Tonight we all say, Alex, Paul, that Mr Sheby is very angry with us.' He turned to Mats for confirmation, but Mats was unforthcoming. 'Alex, Paul, we all know you very angry with us for making noise when you are wanting to sleep.'

I assured him that I was not angry with him, but this did not content him. 'Mr Sheby, why you call me John?' he asked.

'Because you *introduced* yourself to me as John,' I answered. 'However, if you prefer, I will call you by your pagan name.'

'Last night we are drinking very much *tsa pi* and all the villagers give us presents. Philip invites us to make soup.'

I assured him that no further apology was needed and that the incident, although resented at the time, had left no lasting impression on me.

'Mr Sheby, I think you make it very important,' he persisted.

'Perhaps I did, Tu Lum, but it is now forgotten. I want you also to forget it.'

'I see you writing in your diary. You are writing about what happened at Jing Ma Yang, isn't it?'

'Yes, but only as a chronicle of the day's events. Don't let it trouble you. What *is* important are your beautiful mountains, your magnificent forests, swimming and bathing in your clean rivers, the many good moments that we have shared but will only share for a brief while longer. Believe me, I will cherish until the end of my days my time with the KIA.'

'Mr Sheby, why you now call me Tu Lum?'

'Tu Lum, John, which do you prefer?'

'Paul, Alex, everybody want to say they are sorry. But they do not know how. They say, 'Mr Sheby very, very angry with us.'

'Just tell them that Mr Sheby intends to carry on as before.'

It was past noon and blazing hot before we left Fourth Battalion headquarters and began climbing U Lup (Grave Bird) Bum, named after a type of fowl found there and at burial sites. From the summit we saw off to the east the great towers of the eponymous Shang Ngaw *shagawng* dominating a sweep of lesser but still imposing peaks bisected by the deep cleavage of the Tara Hka, and, far to the north, cloaked in mist, Lakawng Bum, on whose lower slopes was First Brigade headquarters. We would reach First

Brigade headquarters in two days, claimed Awng Hkawng none too confidently.

We harboured overnight in a village called Pang Sau Yang. Mats and I were billeted there with a young man who grew opium in a tiny patch adjacent to his house. He had been wounded in his hip and used it to alleviate his pain. Unlike heroin, raw opium can be no more than a mild sleep-inducing substance, a narcotic in the proper sense, and I felt confident that I could risk smoking it *once*. Although the KIA condoned drug use only for medical or veterinary purposes, Seng Hpung raised no objection. He even agreed to join me and, pointing out that we should not tax the wounded young man's store, ordered San Awng to supply some opium from the column's medical stores. So, it happened that, after discussing how Islam had opened a window and admitted the light of Greek and Persian science into the narrow closet of brahmanical dogma, we shared a pipe.

The conventions and rituals of opium use vary according to place and the type of opium available. Where, as at Pang Sau Yang, the resin hardens after harvesting, the user detaches a piece and immerses it in a tablespoon of water, boils off the water and mops up the residue with a ball of shredded, roasted banana leaf. He then inserts a piece of the saturated absorbent into the bowl of his pipe and, packing it with an ember from the fire, draws repeatedly. After three or four inhalations, he drinks a little tea, pinches off another piece of the absorbent, reloads the pipe and passes it on. Absolute silence is regarded as indispensable to a successful inhalation; indeed, speaking between pipes is deemed to be a gross impiety. I had smoked three pipes, experimenting with techniques mimicked from cigarette smokers, holding the smoke in my lungs before expelling it, chasing it down with tea, and was wondering why the only palpable sensation was a very slight dryness of the throat, when Mats swooped in upon us, boasting loudly that he had just enjoyed the most amazing chicken curry and all the *tsa pi* he could drink. At every house in the village the gentlefolk of Pang Sau Yang had regaled him with *tsa pi*. '*Tsa pi*?' I smirked. 'That's kids' stuff. How would you like to try a little *opium*?'

There were no rockets in the sky or hallucinatory dreams, nothing intense; simply the drowsiness that the drug slowly induces, the dulling comatosity of *papaver somniferum*. Still wondering, still expecting something more, I got into my sleeping bag and San Awng brought me some rice wrapped in *lahpaw lap*. The night was bitterly cold, the wind whistling through the porous *la mai tang* walls, and with my legs seeking the warmth of our *dap*, I very nearly ignited my sleeping bag. I awoke once or twice and was conscious only of a gentle but entirely spurious euphoria.

Pang Sau Yang is memorable for another reason: the oldest man in the world lived there: far and away the oldest – 160 years old! This claim might excite the reader's scepticism. The solid, plain, salt of the earth folk of Pang Sau Yang were not sceptical, however. Half of them were his progeny. If we suspend disbelief and work through the numbers, this enduring man was born soon after the First Anglo–Burmese War (1824–26), as Major Henry Burney, pursuant to the Treaty of Yandabo (1826), was about to take up his post as the first British Resident in Ava and abide the insolence, insults, treachery and intrigue of the Burman court. He was already 23 years old when the British conquered the chief towns of the Irrawaddy basin as far north as Toungoo and annexed Lower Burma (1852). He was 57 years old when they annexed Upper Burma (1886) and 110 years old when they completed the pacification of the Kachin Hills (1939). Such vital palaeontology clearly demanded a photograph, but the memory of the pacification gave difficulty here, for he remembered it all too well; he had just married for the third time. Photography had been the means by which the British had conquered them, and here I was up to the same old tricks. I assured him that the British had no further designs on Kachinland and that, in any case, the Kachins also had cameras now. The wife of one of his great, great grandsons (a mere child of 50) then coaxed him from the *dap*, where he spent the long sightless days alone with his memories, and gently assisted him onto the veranda, where, still suspicious, he allowed me to snap his picture holding the tiny hand of the youngest of his progeny in the male line, a great, great, great, great grandson. I hope that he hasn't fretted ever since about betraying the *Wunpawng* to the wizardly White Skins and their black arts.

Leaving Pang Sau Yang, the talk was all about opium: whether we considered it to be addictive; what sensation it produced; whether it weakened you in any way; would we continue using it?

From a position of near total ignorance of the subject we had catapulted overnight to the status of experts.

We halted to rest at a village that bore the odd name, U Kaw Yup (Where The Crow Sleeps). A huge white wooden cross marked the entrance. Other crosses crowned the roofs of many of the houses. On a hillock above the village stood a church. It was a Sunday morning. I climbed up to the church and peered inside. A young man was reading the Lesson — and, after a cursory glance at me, he carried on, as though the happenstance intrusion of an officious European was nothing unusual. Intergalactic emissaries were simply evidence, if further proof were needed, of the wonders of God's world. Half a century before no task would have been undertaken at Where the Crow Sleeps without first obtaining the *nat*s' consent by a complex divination procedure assisted by a *dumsa*. Had the villagers decided to erect a barn, for example, the *dumsa* would have taken a clod of dirt from the proposed building site, beaten it with bamboo and held the bamboo over fire until it burst. If it had exploded into the shape of a snake, the villagers would have understood that the *nat*s approved. Then the *dumsa* would have buried two eggs at the site. If the eggs did not decay, it was a further augury of the *nat*s' approval. Then the *dumsa* would have buried a clump of fermented rice on the site; if the rice did not turn sour, this was also auspicious. As a further test to determine whether the site was suitable, the *dumsa* would have buried an *ndum* of water there; if the water did not diminish, it meant that the *nat*s' had reaffirmed their approval. As a final test of suitability the *dumsa* would offer a root from the site to a baby to chew. If the baby cried, it meant that the *nat*s had changed their minds. Good harvests, safe and successful hunting and fishing, the choice of a wife or a husband, good health, life itself, all depended upon the will of these always capricious and often malevolent spirits as divined by the *dumsa*.[6] But there was no hint of their influence now.

We were following what might have been Arthur Thompson's route in his flight from the Japanese in 1942, for he states that, bound for the Columban Fathers' mission at Kajihtu, he crossed the Tara Hka where it was 'not more than 30 yards wide'.[7] We

6. See Fischer, 1980: 24 ff.
7. Clifford, 1979: 147.

crossed the Tara Hka at just such a place, by a bridge of matted *madang* cane suspended on cables of steel scavenged from the detritus of Commandos and Dakotas attempting 'the hump' during the Second World War. Seng Hpung said that his men could build such a bridge in two days.

We tracked the Tara Hka downstream to its confluence with the Pyang Hka, and the Pyang Hka as far as the *lam* (path) to Pum Pan, where the villagers beat a piece of hollow bamboo to summon volunteers, and we changed porters. The *agyi* invited us to pray with him. His petition, which was in Jinghpaw, was incomprehensible to me but, as Seng Hpung pointed out, not to the Deity.

Our Pum Pan porters took us on to Shau Kawng, which we reached late that afternoon, breathless, exhausted and miserable after zigzagging almost vertically down one side and up the other of a formidable canyon, and where we sheltered for the night. It was a delicately scented place of flower gardens, citrus and cherry orchards and concentric tiers of terraced *le-gwin*,[8] and its solid houses, each in its own compound demarcated by fences of prickly euphorbia, had an air of permanence. My *lekcha* that evening, which concerned the contribution of Persian craftsmen to Indian architecture, prompted Seng Hpung to observe that anyone trying to write a history of the Kachins would find only a wilderness, as they built everything with biodegradable materials that soon reverted to jungle. Later, sitting quietly with Philip, San Awng and Dau Gyung, we heard the beating of more hollow bamboo and the voices of the town criers shouting euphoniously, '*Zup hpawng*! *Zup hpawng*!' (hear ye, hear ye), summoning the villagers to discuss our need for new porters.

Next morning we fairly flew down to the Pyang Hka. Expansive *jahkya hpun* rained down on us sweet plums of tribute for much of the way. Our porters trussed their baskets from wooden yokes harnessed to their shoulders and necks and added a strap around their heads, a practice which would become more common further west and which, I believe, is unique to the Kachin Hills. Like the

---

8. A Burmese term for a type of cultivation revealing Burmese, Chinese or Shan influence. Kachins generally prefer slash-and-burn dry-rice *yis* to permanent wet-rice *le-gwin*.

Lisu of Zup Ra Yang, they seemed to regard us as softies. Without us, they said candidly, they could cover the distance in half the time.

We forded the Pyang Hka and climbed the hill beyond to Saboi Mare. This was Peter's home village, and we stopped there for a longish *preekop* to enable him to visit his family, their first reunion since he had joined the KIA. Although their tattered *longyis* contrasted sharply with his smartly tailored uniform, he beamed with pride as he introduced them to us. They served us grapefruit and cool water and warned us about the horseflies, which, they said, were daily more ferocious with the approach of the hot season. They advised me to change out of shorts into long trousers, and I am very glad that I heeded their advice. The brown Kachin horsefly common to this part of the Triangle looks innocuous, but it deals a mordant sting, and the bite of its fat, tiger-striped, green-eyed cousin, which we were to encounter west of the Mali Hka, would prove even more vicious.

We saw the modest cane and thatch buildings and flag square of First Brigade headquarters midway up the defoliated south slope of Lakawng Bum long before we reached it, nor could Xanadu have loomed grander in our imaginations. The final mile was done in complete silence, everyone savouring his own thoughts. Majors Kumhtat Gam and Latut Shawng, Captain N'Gawk Sinwa, *Salang Kaba* Gyung Zang and a host of other grandees were on hand to greet us; and we were reverently conscious that the whole of the Triangle answered to their command. Conscious, too, that we had just pulled off without loss or injury a march of nearly 300 miles through difficult and dangerous country, and this was our reward – lined volleyball courts, paths bordered with whitewashed stones, pressed uniforms symbolizing the hygiene and discipline that the KIA intended for all of Kachinland after it had cast off the Burmans. We felt ourselves to be part of a new, heroic order; and our hearts thumped wildly with pride at all that it promised. For a fleeting moment in our repetitive lives it was as though the admiring stares of everyone who cherished liberty, equality and fraternity were upon us alone. Moreover, for the few who had served in First Brigade, it was a homecoming; and, after they had traded news and renewed old ties, there would be feasting and drinking, even, if we were lucky, women and song and dancing.

5
Kumawng

Before leaving Pajau Bum, Mats and I had written, he to his mother, Berit, I to Carole, and given the letters to Zawng Hra to date and post when we reached successively First Brigade headquarters, Second Brigade headquarters and the Indian border. We hoped thereby to keep them informed of our progress. As soon as was decently possible, therefore, I asked Captain Kumhtat Gam to apprise Pajau Bum of our arrival at Lakawng Bum.

'That has already been done,' he replied, puzzled. Kachins were often away from home for months at a time, and their women did not worry about them; in any case, did our women not realize that we would be safe as long as we were with the KIA?

We were at Seng Hpung's quarters. As we were talking, N'Lam Awng appeared at the door and requested permission to speak. I knew that he had come to report that he was separating from the column and returning to his village. I was sorry to see him go, for I respected his independence of mind, and had already given San Awng money to arrange a farewell party for him. The son of a *dumsa* who had defied his father by converting to Christianity, he had then converted the rest of the village, beginning with his father. He had been the first of the students in Myitkyina to join the KIA, and this was his first leave after ten years in the KIA. He epitomized for me a kind of fierce integrity and fearless loyalty that I will always associate with the Kachins. As he was about to go, I said to Seng Hpung, 'Did you realize, Du Kaba, that this chap knows the names of 24 different kinds of bamboo?', which pleased him extremely.

Major Kumhtat Gam briefed us on the current state of hostilities in First Brigade area. Just before our arrival, they had received from a Burma Army warrant officer at Tara Yang such a large consignment of jerseys, cooking utensils, soap and .30-calibre carbine cartridges that he had been obliged to send the Brigade's elephants to fetch it. These arrangements, he said, suited everyone. The KIA got its supplies and, in return, drew a *cordon sanitaire* around the enemy depot. The new warrant officer at Tara Yang refused them ordnance other than bullets, but his predecessor and their counterpart in the Hpa Kan area, where Kumhtat Gam had served previously, had sold them carbines, G-3s, Browning pistols and 79-millimetre launcher shells. Rangoon's claim that it was fighting a war to defend the Union was just nonsense, he said. The senior officers knew what the junior officers were doing and demanded their share. He predicted, however, that the Burma Army would try to block us. 'They have brought up two columns, amounting to more than 160 men, and are clearing the bush on both sides of the *mawdaw lam*. I have sent a detachment to scout them and sent for the commander of Seventh Battalion, who will be able to advise you about conditions west of the Mali Hka.'

'We will rest here for a day, when a decision will be taken about our best route,' said Seng Hpung. 'But a day is all we can spare.'

Tuesday, 28 February, the last day of my fifty-third year, began with ceremonial gunfire signalling the slaughter of a buffalo for the 'special feast' that First Brigade were hosting for their 'special guests'. I had slept for over nine hours, and my first sight on waking was four elephants striding past our quarters, which were like the Pajau Bum guesthouse but smaller and lacking Zau Seng and Rocky. I now sat for a long time over morning tea, warming my feet before the fire and gazing through the open door at the sun rising over the hills beyond the valley where US Army Engineers had cleared a landing strip during the 'Japan War'. I wondered how Carole was. Kyi Myint had given me Bertil Lintner's telephone number, and I had included it in one of my letters written from Möng Ko, hoping that he would be able to allay her fears. I thought, 'If she could only see me now she would have no fears,' but, of course, she was frantic. Indeed, almost at that very moment she was inspecting the clothes in the window of a Bond Street shop, musing, 'If I'm a widow, I can buy everything in the shop.'

She wrote to me at a 'Hold until he arrives' address in Delhi about this time. The letter stated:

> My policy in times of trial is to worry as much as possible before the dreaded event in an effort to bargain with God that, now that I have already suffered, any additional catastrophe would be unfair. If you are reading this letter, then surely angels have watched over you. ... Nancy is soon off to Rwanda to see the gorillas. I thought [that] if you didn't come out of Burma I would join her. Michael Keane took me on a long walk over Otmoor on Saturday and to dinner. Peter Knapp-Fisher said that, if I became a widow, he would come up and relieve me of my estate and that I would not go about the world like *The Roman Spring of Mrs Stone*. But if something did happen to you, neither men, money nor gorillas could compensate for the pervasive sadness. It would hurt for the rest of my life. ... Feeling better today. Friends have been marvellous. I had lunch with Jo Farrell,[1] who loved your letters and also made me feel better about Burma.

Carole's 'bereavement' was the topic of jokey conversation at dinner parties that winter:

'Pal of mine disappeared in the Golden Triangle earlier this year.'

Second voice: 'Really?'

'Yup. Slipped across the Burmese border dressed as a Chinaman and made contact with the big chief of the drug business.'

'Goodness!'

'Sent a couple of postcards — in code, obviously — to his wife saying that he was going to crack the syndicate. That was the last she heard of him, until the box arrived.'

'What box?'

'They sent his big toe back in a box.'

'How awful!'

---

1. Mother of the late Irish novelist, J. G. Farrell. She was married in Burma.

'Both of them, actually. After that, boxes arrived at weekly intervals, each one a little bigger than the last. Until finally, the largest of all, a hatbox – though, obviously, it was far too heavy to contain only a hat.'

'How horrible!'

'Yes, he was daring, was old Shelby. Reckless, some would say.'

Third voice: 'Completely loony, if you ask me.'

'Thank you, Margaret. *I'm* telling this story if you do not mind.'

We had no duties except to ourselves, and once we had dealt with a few practical exigencies – Mats with an ulcerated leech bite on his right foot (a young medical officer at First Brigade headquarters had already cleaned the wound and treated it with tetracyclin powder), I with cleaning my sleeping bag by hanging it out in the sun – we were free to pursue our other interests. Not so Seng Hpung. Now, suddenly, we were startled to receive a summons from him. Come at once! Wondering darkly what this meant, we hurried to his quarters and found him surrounded by women and babies. I do not think that I have ever met a more tolerant man than Seng Hpung, who had none of those hazy preconceptions of how things *ought* to be, or known anyone more diplomatic. He was the master of the *mot juste* and had the right tools for coping with almost any awkwardness that might arise in the unpredictable arena of human concourse. But, by golly, the fellow was feeling the strain now.

The ladies moved aside politely to make way for us; then they presented us with a chicken bound miserably by its feet and half a dozen *ndum*s of *tsa pi.* Seng Hpung thanked them on our behalf and explained that it was the custom among Kachins, especially Hkahku Kachins, to bestow gifts on strangers. He asked us if we had anything to add. We expressed our confidence in whatever words he had chosen to convey our gratitude.

One of the ladies was the wife of Major Kumhtat Gam, who married her when she was 15. She must have noticed my surprise, for it seemed to throw her on the defensive. Kachin marriage customs allowed this where there was compatibility in blood lines and no feud between the parties' families, she explained. Women could marry as young as 12, but generally they waited until they were 20, and they always married above their age, men whom they could respect, she said. Marriages should be by parental arrangement, but in practice parents were often obliged to endorse a *fait accompli.* A groom who could not afford the price of his bride simply abducted her. Once married, he was in charge; nevertheless, Kachin wives only obeyed their husbands if they 'led well'. As it was an offence for either spouse to abandon the other, divorce was rare, although allowed when one of them committed adultery, or contracted leprosy, or, if after protracted efforts at composing their differences, they were unable to abide further cohabitation. A man could take a second wife only if he had his wife's permission, if she refused to follow him to the jungle, if she could not bear male children or if poor health prevented her from managing her responsibilities. 'A wife's health is the most important factor in the success of the marriage,' said Kumhtat Gam's wife. 'She has responsibility for building the house, sowing and harvesting the crops, winnowing the rice, spinning the cotton, making the clothes, mats and baskets, and conducting all the trading at the markets along the *mawdaw lam*, in addition to bearing and rearing children. A healthy wife can produce in a day, working without interruption, a mat that fetches 20 kyats [14 pence] at the *mawdaw lam*. She does everything that her husband cannot or will not do.'

'Aren't you frightened to travel without your husband?' I asked her. 'Who protects you when you go to the *mawdaw lam*?'

'What is there to fear?' she replied. 'Only the Burma Army, and when it is active, we do not go to the *mawdaw lam*.' Kachin custom allowed them to shelter in villages along the way.

'Kachins seem to enjoy excellent health and to be immune to sickness such as heart disease that afflicts Europeans,' I said.

'Our only illnesses afflict our stomachs, not our hearts,' she replied.

Mats asked if the differences in shapes and sizes of the baskets that he had seen and the different ways of carrying them had any tribal or clan significance.

'*Tribal significance?* Good heavens!' All the ladies roared with laughter. Seng Hpung asked Mats to repeat the question.

'In Europe, everyone is dead keen on cane baskets,' I explained. 'Ethnic artefacts are all the rage.'

Very well, said Kumhtat Gam's wife; she would try to help us, but, she warned, the subject was complex. First, there was the *shingnoi*, the standard, general-purpose basket. There were half a dozen of them in the room, and, as we could see, they were about two-and-a-half by one-and-a-half feet in size and closely woven. A *hting-ga* was about the same size as a *shingnoi* but loosely woven. Both these baskets were carried on the back, as was a *sawnghpai*, which had a curved top. A *mung* was much larger than a *shingnoi*, *hting-ga* or *sawnghpai* – about four by three feet. It could be woven closely or loosely and was slung on poles and used for transporting for short distances bulk produce like yams. A *mamka* was as large as a *mung*, closely woven and used for storing rice. A *ka tawng* was a loosely woven handbag with or without handles. A *pyem* was nothing but a pouch tied behind the waist like a *shingwai*, a child's basket. *Saw kup*s and *ka-pau*s were as tiny as grapefruits and were hung around the neck. A *jing pang* was the size of a man's foot and worn strapped to the waist and used for gathering the harvest. A *shingnoi garong*, though, was similar in size to a *mamka* and used for transporting the harvest. 'Do you want me to go on?' Kumhtat Gam's wife marvelled that ordinary everyday things were as much admired as the shiny plastic wonders that they saw at the *mawdaw lam*.

'Now you know about baskets,' said Seng Hpung, feeling that in some obscure way these genteel ladies had contributed to this new spirit of polyethnicity that was 'all the rage' in Europe.

The speeches made at the party laid on for us that afternoon were protracted, and, sensibly, hunger was sacrificed to comprehension, no food being served until everyone had his say. Seng Hpung came in for most of the praise – after one speech, we even stood stiffly to attention and saluted him – but we were not excluded. Mats was another Ola Hanson, another Bertil Lintner, and the happy comparisons drew loud applause. Lintner had crossed Kachinland from west to east. Now Mats was crossing it from east to west. It was hoped, therefore, that, like Lintner, Mats would enlighten their brothers in Sweden as to what was happening in Kachinland. I was a writer, and such an important profession charged me with special responsibility to tell the world that the Kachins burned with desire for harmony with their neighbours. Major Kumhtat

Gam concluded by deprecating the meagreness of their provision for us. 'We have only soup, rice, grilled buffalo, *tsa pi* and *lau hku* [a fiery red spirit distilled from *tsa pi*] to offer you,' he said. 'We have plenty of money but nothing to buy with it.' Then everything was dumped onto the table in one vast spread. We spooned down the contents of a soup tureen with a common spoon and competed with our fingers in the meat plate. The meat was greasy, and, on my right, Awng Hkawng smoked incessantly, while on my left, placed there because of a reputation for speaking fluent English, Major Latut Shawng kept repeating, 'I am join KIA in 1963. I am 52 years old.' The party lasted most of the afternoon.

Afterwards I sat on the veranda of our quarters in a folding canvas chair and watched the sun set. Mats was playing badminton with our hosts. As the shadows advanced through the valley where acrobatic American pilots had landed their DC-3s, L-4s and other light aircraft to supply OSS (Office of Strategic Services) Detachment 101, I could imagine them whispering their joyous encouragement. 'We were here also – in 1944. We had parties too. We, too, ate rice and buffalo meat and drank *tsa pi* and *lau hku*. It was one big party, man.' At 1810 hours, Seng Hpung came to me and said that he was still waiting for the commander of Seventh Battalion, who was expected any minute now, and, at 1945 hours, San Awng fetched a note from him advising that we were departing First Brigade headquarters in the morning. Two elephants had been laid on especially to transport Hoary-Headed Eldest Son and his companion, Clear Second Son, to the Mali Hka.

* * *

An unearthly rumble from somewhere quite near disturbed our breakfast next morning. I ran outside and beheld Sut Awng (Treasure of Success) ambling nonchalantly across our compound, a barefoot *oozy* (mahout) perched on her head and toe-tickling her behind her ears and an *enfant enchainé* named Lu Tawng (One Who Gets Solid) trailing at her hind legs. Lu Tawng's father, Awng Bu (Have Success), paused at the gate and fixed on us the two narrow slits of his piglet eyes. A soldier behind him barred retreat and to his left was a fence. For an anxious moment, Awng Bu considered. Should he risk the uncertain perils of these two white weirdos or breach the fence and incur inevitable punishment? He threw his head back to ponder the issue, and all at once everyone started shouting, '*Bri*! *Bri*!' (No, don't! No, don't!).

More elephants soon arrived, as our column was now assembling for departure. Their *hpa kawp* (saddlecloths) were made from burlap and rust-red bark. Their bamboo *waw* (panniers) were moulded to the shapes of their backs. *Le-bat* (yokes) secured the panniers in front, latticed cane *wum bat* girthed their bellies, and ovals of twisted cane (*hkam htawng*) looped their tails. '*Sambut*! *Bhutsam*!' commanded the *oozies*, and the elephants obediently couched, dropping onto their haunches and then onto their bellies with legs extended fore and aft. In a splendid book about these greatest of land mammals, Elephant Bill (James Howard Williams) tells how a calf is trained to accept human authority. After weaning, the elephant calf is lured, pulled, nudged or pushed into a wooden corral and placated with offerings of bananas, while his intended *oozy* waits suspended by a rope above him and his mother stands by for reassurance. The *oozy* is lowered onto his head. The calf struggles and is conciliated with more bribes, but as soon as he accepts that it is useless to resist the creature on his head, a heavy block of wood is lowered onto his back, which causes him to renew the struggle, bucking and rolling onto the ground, getting up and butting against the walls of the corral. Again and again the block is lowered onto his back until he sits down to puzzle out what is happening to him, whereupon the block is lifted, and the trainers shout in unison the first of their commands, '*Mai*! *Mai*!' (Get up! Get up!). The calf rises, and the trainers immediately lower the block again and shout the second of their commands, '*Sambut*! *Sambut*! (Sit down! Sit down!). The process is repeated until the *oozy* is able to remain on the calf's head and make him sit and stand without the aid of the block.[2]

---

2. 'Sometimes ... the game has to be kept up ... far into the night ... even till the morning. ... But however long it may take, the *oozies* never give in and never give the calf any rest until their object is achieved. The great lesson is that ... man will always get his own way, however long it takes him' (Williams, 1950: 78–9). Before an elephant is considered to be trained he must recognize at least 24 discrete verbal commands as well as commands imparted by gestures such as the *oozy* leaning forward or backward, stiffening his legs, hand-patting or knee-pressing against the elephant's neck, or toe tickling it behind his ears.

Above: Kyi Myint and Aung Gyi at CPB Northern Bureau HQ, Möng Ko.

Below: Sai Lek's wife, Kyaw Nyunt, Sai Lek and author at Möng Ko.

Ma Htung with boulder of raw jade worth $2 million at KIO HQ.

Zwang Hra, Kam Htoi, Tu Jai, author, Seng Hpung and Zau Mai at Pajau Brum.

Above: 'Castro', Chairman of the United Liberation Front of Ahom (ULFA) and his aides-de-camp.

Below: Poppy field at Shalawt Kawng.

Three soliders of KIA 253 Mobile Battalion on the south bank of the Nmai Hka.

Ata

We now had an opportunity to observe the *oozie*s' authority at close hand.

While they busied themselves loading their charges, Awng Hkawng put us in the picture. The Burma Army was moving a supply convoy of 78 vehicles and securing selected sites against possible ambush, which accounted for the unusual activity on the *madaw lam* previously feared to be aimed at blocking us. A platoon had been sent ahead to reconnoitre, but we should have no trouble crossing the road. We would ride the elephants as far as the Mali Hka, then send them back and continue by foot. The Putao road was less dangerous than the Chiphwe road, and we could risk crossing it with a smaller escort in daylight.

It was 1000 hours before the last loads were lashed to the panniers. The *oozy* commanding the largest of our elephants, a blue-black bull named Naw Tawng (Solid Second Son), ordered him to stand and proffer his trunk, and, as the trunk rose, skipped lightly up and onto his back. We mounted more prosaically by using the animals' extended front legs as steps, firming a knee against their withers, taking hold of the panniers and hoisting ourselves up onto them. Majors Kumhtat Gam and Latut Shawng were accompanying us part of the way. Captain N'Gawk Sinwa, *Salang Kaba* Gyung Zang and hundreds of others had gathered all over the hillside to see us off. Now swaying like maharajahs in our lofty perches, we bade them goodbye.

Naw Tawng led. Behind him rode Seng Hpung on La Mai, and behind her on Awng Shing, Mats, grateful for the opportunity to rest his ailing leg. My mount was a young bull named Tsan Yu after General San Yu of the Burma Army.[3] The *oozy* rode him straddling his massive neck, burying his legs beneath his floppy ears and using the hollows where his ears joined his neck for stirrups while holding on to a rope (*sai hkaw*) looped about his neck with one hand and sometimes brandishing an *nhtu* with the other. If the elephants manifested the least inclination to disobey

3. 'It is not uncommon to name pets and animals after top enemy leaders. It helps to put everything in perspective by showing contempt for the enemy leader/officer. The animals named thus always know their real masters!' (Stephen Morse, correspondence with author).

they received, instantly, a sharp, hard blow with the cutting sides of the *nhtu*s on the double crowns of their heads, a punishment repeated so often that the more truculent Tsan Yu's head was a mass of foaming blood. Regrettably, such cruelty was indispensable to maintaining the *oozy*'s authority. The 'great lesson is that ... man will always get his own way'. The animal must never be allowed to win even a temporary victory over his human master.

We were soon beyond headquarters camp and in the forest, moving in a majestic procession to the slow, shuffling tread of our mounts. It was 1 March – my fifty-fourth birthday – and here I was riding away from KIA First Brigade headquarters in a litter full of baggage, shotgun to a grinning *oozy* on an elephant. I thought: 'I might as well believe in the Tooth Fairy.' Ahead of me, Mats was experimenting with various postures to find one that suited him, alternately leaning forward, sitting erect and lying back in his pannier. Our mounts snacked continuously, working the sensitive feeler ends of their trunks around sprigs of green leaves, sheaves of *kaing* grass, branches of wild bananas and feathery tops of bamboos adjacent to the path and sweeping them voraciously into their mouths without once slowing their stride. All the while, they contentedly flapped their great ears and wagged their tiny tails. In the span of 24 hours each would consume up to 600 lbs of vegetables, most at night after the *oozie*s released them from their duties to graze unattended but hobbled in the jungle.

A mile or so from headquarters camp we stopped at Latut Shawng's house. His wife and Kumhtat Gam's sister were expecting us and served us delicious curried chicken, vegetables and cups of *tsa pi*, while their children competed in reciting the English alphabet and singing Jinghpaw songs for our entertainment. Kumhtat Gam's sister told us that while she was visiting relatives in Myitkyina the Burma Army had conscripted her and forced her to work in a road gang without wages. The Burma Army's euphemism for such slavery was 'contributed labour', she said.

We stopped again at N'rawng (Nothing in Sight) Kawng, a once proud village recently reduced to half a dozen houses by an incendiary visit from the Burma Army, and were greatly astonished to find N'Lam Awng there, visiting his great uncle, Sergeant Chyahkyi Hting Nan, who was living in honourable retirement with his son and daughter-in-law. Sergeant Chyahkyi Hting Nan had served under American officers in 103 Battalion the Kachin Rangers and under British officers in 2 Battalion the Kachin Rifles,[4] but after retiring from the army he had thought never to see another European and remembered little English or Hindustani. Then Bertil Lintner had visited him, and now we. We spoke about the Rangers and their role in the war, which, he said, had been the same as the Levies', to gather intelligence about the Japanese and interrupt their supply lines with hit-and-run tactics. He remembered the Americans and British with deep affection and respect as tough, brave and very disciplined soldiers. The Japanese were their equal as soldiers, he said, echoing what N Chyaw Tang had told us, but they had perpetrated atrocities on the Kachins in a foolish attempt to cow them. Consequently, when the British returned with the Americans, they found a flood of volunteers who were eager to serve under their colours. The Rangers had paid in rupees, not opium, although opium was distributed to the quartermasters and used for hiring coolies and financing intelligence gathering. Both the Rangers and Levies had participated in the siege of Myitkyina and, after Myitkyina fell, they were disbanded and re-formed as the Kachin Rifles.[5] 'After that,' said Sergeant Chyahkyi Hting Nan proudly, 'we were proper soldiers.' He showed us a mess kit, engraved with the words, 'MADE IN CINCINNATI, OHIO, 1943.' I have a picture of Sergeant Chyahkyi Hting Nan in a handsome black *taikpung palawng* (satin jacket) with a ceremonial silver *nhtu* strapped across his chest, holding up for us to admire his aluminium mess kit, proud souvenir of his wonderful bash-the-Japs days.

When we left N'rawng Kawng, dark clouds were banking up in the west. Seng Hpung, uncomfortable and disgruntled in his pannier, lost his cap to an overhanging branch, and I was fascinated

---

4. After returning to England I contacted the officer who had commanded Sergeant Chyahkyi Hting Nan's company in 2 Kachin Rifles, Captain (later Major) Robin Jellicoe, and relayed to him Chyahkyi Hting Nan's greetings. Jellicoe's family had lived in Burma for generations (see Fellowes-Gordon, 1957: 29). A schoolmaster in Rangoon when the war began, he joined Burma Regiment, a Gurkha battalion that fought alongside the Levies, and was later transferred to 2 Kachin Rifles. He now lives in Chelmsford.
5. See Note to the Author from Ronald Kaulback.

to see Tsan Yu ensnare the cap in his trunk without breaking his stride, march forward and obediently present it to La Mai's *oozy*, who returned it to Seng Hpung. Mats suddenly noticed the loss of his camera. Awng Shing went back and found it. Naw Tawng, leading the way, picked up and removed a log straddling the path as though it were a toothpick. We turned off the main path onto a *shat khat* over a mountain so steep and narrow that even mules would have experienced difficulties. But the elephants shuffled steadily up and over it undaunted, investigating the terrain before them with their trunks and dragging their massive hind legs down the descent. The *oozie*s made them trot the final stage, and, at about 1640 hours, to a crowd of children screaming their delight, we rode into N'Gum La.

N'Gum La, which according to Hanson means 'man flat on his face', was one of the grandest villages in KIA-liberated *Wunpawng Mungdan*, its 50 or so houses dispersed over a grassy plain about a mile long. News of our arrival spread quickly, and that evening there was a party for us at the house of the local headmaster, a bright, intelligent man who spoke excellent English and seemed to know a great deal about elephants. British merchants, he said, had imported Indian mahouts to work the teak plantations and, in consequence, most of the commands were now Tamil or Bengali words, but elephants had been used in Burma long before the British came. Indeed, a man's importance was judged by the size of his stable. Especially coveted were white elephants. Ambition to possess albinos had incited a war in the sixteenth century costing the lives of five kings. Albinos were even worshipped. There was a pavilion at the Burmese royal palace for the *Sinbyudaw* (Lord White Elephant), and if a white calf's mother died before it was weaned, human wet nurses sustained it.[6] 'The Burmese ladies competed for the privilege,' he told me.

Sitting beside me on the matted floor was an elder named Lahpai Zau Awng, who was much revered in the village and wore

6. This claim is well documented (see, for example, Williams, 1950: 69; and O'Brien, 1991: 24).

an honorific tiger's tooth in the strap of the scabbard sheathing his *nhtu*. He had represented N'Gum La at the Manhkring[7] Conference in November 1946, when the Kachins had resolved upon the policies fatefully pursued at Panglong. The delegates to the Conference, he told me, had been tricked by Sama *Duwa* Sin Wa Nawng into signing an agreement with Aung San and it emerged later that the two men had worked up a deal in private. In exchange for his support, Aung San promised to make the Sama *duwa* the first governor of Kachin State in an independent Burma. Commissioner Stevenson,[8] said Lahpai Zau Awng, had tried to warn them. He had advised them that the Kachins were not ready for independence and would be outwitted and exploited by the more politically adroit Burmans, and had offered them the option of a British protectorate, followed by independence after five or ten years. But the delegates to the Manhkring Conference, who numbered more than 1000 and represented every village tract in Kachinland and the Kachin Sub-State, had listened instead to Sama *Duwa* Sin Wa Nawng.

> He defined the issue in such a way that we thought that we were deciding between immediate independence or independence in five or ten years. We should have realized that he was sympathetic to the Burmans, because he was a Buddhist and the British had killed his father [during the 'pacification' of the Kachin Hills] and he hated them, but no one dared to oppose him. He was the greatest of our chiefs, and his father had led the resistance to the British. He later regretted what he did, but only after Ne Win refused him permission to go to London for treatment of his brain tumour.

---

7. Manhkring in 1946 was a village near Myitkyina and is now a part of Myitkyina. The name, which means 'the place where the Burmans were stopped', ironically recalls a Jinghpaw victory over numerically far superior Burman forces that left the Kachins the undisputed masters of the Kachin Hills (see Fellowes-Gordon, 1957: 112).
8. Burmans and British alike vilified Lieutenant-Colonel Henry Noel Cochrane Stevenson, OBE, Burma Frontier Force, then commander of the Burma Levies and the last Director of the Frontier Areas Administration, for predicting civil war – exactly what happened – if the British handed over their paramount responsibility for the Frontier Areas to the Burmans (see Smith, 1991: 75).

> His last words were: 'Ne Win is like a dog, not a human being.' The Sama *duwa* was foolish to trust the Burmans, and God has punished us severely for his foolishness. We should have listened to Commissioner Stevenson at Manhkring and not to him. We were very simple, just as Commissioner Stevenson said.

Talking with Lahpai Zau Awng was a joy. Here was someone who spoke not from some preconceived bias but from his own memories; he had personally witnessed the important events he described. But he told me this story with such deep sadness that I could not resist teasing him. 'Well, take heart, Lahpai Zau Awng,' I said. 'The British are resolved upon restoring their rule over Kachinland, and Mats and I are the advance party. We are determined upon reversing the mistakes of Manhkring and Panglong.'

'Oh, *Salang Kaba*, if only that were true!' he cried. 'The *Asoya* gave Kachinland good government. The *Asoya* was fair!'

Lahpai Zau Awng's ardent faith in the British caused me to feel a little uncomfortable. The British had jilted the Karens, the Indian princes and the Somalis, who, like the Kachins, had served them loyally. I had no doubt that they could have dissuaded the Chins, Kachins and Shans from going along with Aung San had they determined to do so, instead of trying to protect their commercial interests in Burma Proper. They had not been fair to the Boers, or the Arabs, or the Irish; and the Second World War arose from the unfair terms they and the French imposed on Germany at Versailles. To whom had they been fair? Yet they enjoyed this curious reputation for fairness. But I had no wish to disillusion Lahpai Zau Awng.

'Did they arrive by elephant?' I asked.

'No, by horse,' said Lahpai Zau Awng. 'And they all had golden hair.'

'Not white?'

'Some had white hair.'

Someone now intruded on our conversation. He had been waiting impatiently to tell me about an Englishman named Major Collins, in whose service he had once been employed, and could wait no longer. History has left no record of Major Collins, but the years that Brang Wa had spent in his service had made an enduring impression on him. Major Collins, after retiring from the army, had run the bank in Myitkyina, but the extraordinary thing about him, said Brang Wa, what marked him off as supernatural, was his teeth. They were not fixed permanently to the gums like ordinary teeth: he could remove and replace them at will.

By now many of the guests were fairly drunk. The headmaster rose, and the friendly buzz of conversation ceased. The *agyi* and several of the village elders got up and made speeches. They were well received. The headmaster made a speech. After a while I heard my name mentioned. The Teachers' Committee of N'Gum La had got up a gift to commemorate my birthday, which, said the headmaster prettily in English, he had the privilege of presenting to me. It consisted of two boxes of cubed sugar, a bag of ground coffee, a tin that was labelled 'milk' but in fact was a concoction of bananas and sugar, and a crate of biscuits.

More was still to come, for now it was the ladies' turn to honour my birthday. They advanced as one into the room, led by a strikingly beautiful young woman dressed in a *gumhpraw palawng*, and presented curried rice wrapped in banana leaves, boiled eggs, a caged chicken, *ndum*s of *tsa pi* and a silk Hkahku *bawng bam* (turban) to me and *bawng bam*s to Seng Hpung and Mats. I began a speech expressing my gratitude to which no one paid the slightest heed. But it hardly mattered, because Brang Wa was determined that nothing was going to detract from Major Collins's miraculous epiphany. It was as though history had moved to a *climatérique*. Major Collins's ghost had materialized in this very room: Brang Wa had merely to speak to commune with it, and, to mark the occasion, he had decided to show it how to put on its new *bawng bam*. When, at last, he stood back to admire the result, my head looking as though it had been bandaged, everyone applauded and cheered loudly. Major Collins's reincarnation was wearing his new turban! One of the ladies then did for Mats what Brang Wa had done for me, though more gracefully, and everyone pronounced this a success too. Mats said that he was very proud to wear a *bawng bam*, and that also went down well.

Throughout the evening I had sensed that John was eager to speak to me but could not find the words. Now he said, 'Mr Sheby, why you hate me so?'

'Tu Lum!' I cried, a little shocked. 'I thought that we settled this at Fourth Battalion headquarters, and here you are raising the same subject again. Why on earth do you continue to believe I hate you?'

'Because you say I commander of the *Tsa Pi* Brigade.'

I could not deny this, but it had not been said seriously. 'I was *teasing*, Tu Lum. However, you have to admit that you *are* our champion drinker. Such exceptional powers of consumption should be brought to Major General Zau Mai's attention.'

'Why you tell Major General Zau Mai?'

'Because I promised to report to him everything I observed on this trek that might assist the KIA in achieving its aim of total victory over the Burma Army. I am going to suggest that he raise a new Model Brigade – for drinking, not fighting – and appoint you as its commander.'

He groaned. 'Mr Sheby, I never drink before I come to First Brigade area, I swear to you. But here in Triangle, every person offer you *tsa pi*. They are very insulted if you are not drinking *tsa pi* with them. Mr Sheby, I stop tonight! I promise. From tonight, I drink no more *tsa pi*. I swear. You will see.'

'That is for you to decide, Tu Lum. But why are you telling me this? I will be with you only for a short time, and, after I leave you, no one will ever tease you again.'

Awng Hkawng, who had been listening, smiled weakly. He seemed to be sinking beneath the weight of so much revelry. He had been drinking and feasting and talking and smiling all evening. He had listened patiently to the conversation about elephants and translated for me when Brang Wa extolled Major Collins's dentures. He had endured the banalities of the birthday presentations and the speech that Seng Hpung made about the KIO's aims and its hopes for peace, which he had heard many, many times before, applauding dutifully throughout it. If the *agyi*, or Brang Wa, or the headmaster, or Mats proposed a toast, he had felt bound to join them, and now the headmaster's wife was pressing on him yet another *ndum* and more food wrapped in banana leaves. He did not have my choices. He could not escape. He was billeted at the headmaster's house, and his mattress lay unused and painfully inviting next to a *dap* encircled by revellers whose enthusiasm for partying on showed no sign of abating.

Brang Wa came over to shake again the hand of the shade of Major Collins. 'Good morning!' he said. He had not spoken English since the heady days of Major Collins's previous incarnation; he meant 'Good night'. This seemed an appropriate moment to end the purgation of the wounds between Tu Lum and me. Perhaps the Hkahku Kachins are more austere in their habits than appeared to me. That they should have marked our visits to their remote hamlets with special celebration is understandable. Nor was it odd that Tu Lum wanted to join in the revelry. There was little enough revelry in his hard life.

* * *

The platoon sent to scout the enemy reported that its convoy was stranded on the *mawdaw lam*, but the intelligence that they brought was insufficient, and Seng Hpung sent a section for further reconnaissance. While we awaited their report, he conferred with the commander of Seventh Battalion. Seventh Battalion had previously controlled the hills between the Mali Hka and the Kumawng. However, its strength had been depleted to reinforce Pajau Bum, and the Burma Army now patrolled there unchallenged. The battalion's headquarters was west of the Mali Hka and north of Sumprabum, about five marches from Lakawng Bum, but its commander had trekked the distance in less than three days. He had spent the previous night at N'rawng Kawng and risen before dawn to overtake us at N'Gum La.

The rest of us knew that our fate hung on this debriefing, and to divert us from our speculations one of the *oozie*s fetched La Mai and put her through her paces. He made her pick up a log and run with it and made her bow, present the log to Paul and salute; then he made her stoop for me to mount her. The extraordinary thing, again, was how placidly the beast took it all, ears flopping, tail wagging and closed eyelids shutting out not only the flies but our obnoxious presence as well. '*Za*! *Za*!' I commanded, simultaneously prodding her behind the ears with my feet and holding firmly to the *sai hkaw*, lest she should bolt suddenly. Her great bulk began to move. Children and soldiers swarmed under us wild with excitement, shouting and screaming as though a circus had come to their village. '*Za*! *Za*!' I repeated, prodding her with my right foot; and like a ship, she began to turn ponderously in a wide arch. '*Za*! *Za*!' I said, now prodding her with my other foot, and she turned in the other direction. It was almost *too* wonderful. Suddenly, however, her eyes opened. Was she about to do something *un*placid? '*Tut*!' I commanded, and she stopped. The *oozy* couched her and, to every child's disappointment and every adult's scorn and derision, I got down.

Later that morning, a gaunt old woman came to our billet and asked for me. Philip, who brought me the message, seemed embarrassed. She was waiting on the veranda, he said. 'Mr Sheby, better you not see this woman.'

'What is the matter with her?' I asked. 'Is she diseased?'

'Mr Sheby, this woman want to touch your hair. I tell her go away, but she not go away. This woman, Mr Sheby, may be she crazy.'

All was soon clear. In her adolescence the woman had fallen in love with an Englishman. The war had ended, Burma had got its independence, and the British had gone away – but in all those years, during which she had married, borne children, seen children born to her children, her young love had never died. Convinced that, some sunny day, she and her blond lover would be reunited, and hearing that a *shan hpraw* (white skin) was at N'Gum La, she had set out at once. She examined me thoughtfully, stroked my hair gently – it must have been blond once – smiled sweetly, and, having achieved her purpose, left to return to her village to await another sunny day.

A coded message was dispatched to Pajau Bum, and, while we continued to wait for orders, morning lengthened into afternoon. We skimmed the gossip brought by a succession of visitors. One of the elephants was lost, and his *oozy* had been searching for him since dawn. Mats was in a house at the other end of the village, ill. Awng Hkawng was asleep.

After Seng Hpung finished debriefing him, the commander of Seventh Battalion came over and introduced himself. He was tired from his forced march and had been drinking, and our conversation was bizarre and ended acrimoniously. He was compiling a history of the Kachins, he said, and he showed me a notebook that described nothing but victories that the Kachins had won against the British. 'Did you never *lose*?' I asked him. 'We always win,' he replied, but I knew that this could not be true. N Chyaw Tang had told me about the 'pacification' of the Kachin Hills after King Thibaw's surrender. And had the British not maintained garrisons at Bhamo, Mogaung and Myitkyina and established a chain of forts in the hills, Fort Harrison at Sadon, Fort Morton in the Sama hills and Fort Hertz in Hkamti Long? They presupposed some measure of victory. How could there have been British deputy commissioners at Myitkyina and Bhamo and assistant superintendents at Sinlumkaba, Sumprabum and Fort Hertz if the Kachins had never lost a battle? What about the engagement in which Sama *Duwa* Sin Wa Nawng's father died? The argument went back and forth, but we were never likely to agree. To a European, victory means forcing the enemy to retire from or prevent it capturing a strategic height, ammunition dump, bridge, airfield, railway, town, or the like. To a Kachin, it simply means suffering fewer losses than the enemy in a skirmish, raid or ambush.

Seng Hpung was in meetings all day and seemed a little troubled when I saw him at dinner. He said that he had been waiting for a reply to our message to GHQ. Normally, he said, he would not risk the column to the conditions now prevailing west of the Mali Hka, where the enemy's strength was superior to ours and its mobility allowed it to give chase at a moment's notice. However, further delay posed other risks. Therefore, he was seeking Pajau Bum's permission to proceed. He had already issued orders that no one was to be allowed to cross the Mali Hka for the next four days to reduce the chance of the villagers leaking intelligence to the enemy. And the boatmen who ferried us across would stand ready to ferry us back if we ran into an ambush. That evening I wrote in my diary: 'I think Du Kaba now regrets our presence in the column. We are too high profile. But, of course, he is too polite to say so.'

Pajau Bum authorized us to proceed, and we left next morning, almost everyone in the village assembling to bid us farewell. Lahpai Zau Awng wore his black satin jacket, an intricately woven and embroidered Hkahku shoulder bag called a *dawng hkun* and an *nhtu* made of tiger bone and silver. Some of the ladies wore *gumhpraw palawng*s. Brang Wa was sober and taciturn, almost diffident. It was, obviously, a moment of deep sadness for him – such a brief reunion! 'Good night!' he said, meaning goodbye.

A short walk along a ridge brought us onto a broad plateau where the path ran straight between multi-trunked banyans and kapok, a leafless tree with slender, blood-red flowers at the extremities of its naked branches. There were clusters of lilac-coloured flowers that might have been lacecap hydrangeas, wild cherry bright with pink blossom; and from a high ridge we saw for the first time the blue trace of the Mali Hka winding majestically between hills about three miles below us.

We rested at Hka Htu (Dig Water) for about half an hour. Peter pointed out a ball of wattled twigs in the high branches of a tree and predicted turbulent weather that spring. A type of black ant nested there. When the ants nested on the ground, there would be no storms, but when they nested in the trees, the storms always came, he said.

Tsan Yu's steady amble and the heat and lambent glare of the sun brought on a light fever, and I was glad when we reached Pan Lawng Yang Mare, where we were to swap our elephants for porters and spend the night. The lads retained energy enough to play *chinlon* with the locals, a curiously demanding game in which the participants face each other in a circle and endeavour to keep a cane ball in the air, using only their feet. After a few minutes they were all perspiring profusely, but they carried on until sunset.

Seng Hpung had promised to help me in my effort to understand Kachin tribe and clan classifications, but we had made many resolutions to each other on the trail never to be kept, and I entertained no hope that he had remembered this promise. However, he now summoned me and gave me a diagram he had prepared. Across the top of the diagram, in politically correct alphabetical order, were written the names of the Kachin tribes: Azi, Jinghpaw, Lashi, Lisu, Maru, Nung and Rawang. 'The Rawang used to be considered a branch of the Nung. Now the Nung are considered to be a branch of the Rawang. The other divisions are only linguistic,' he said. 'Mimo is a Maru, and I am a Jinghpaw. We speak different languages, but we are both Kachins. The Azi, Lashi and Maru can almost understand one another. The other languages are completely different.'

Below the tribes were the eponymous clans – Lahpai, Lahtaw, Maran, Marip and Nhkum – and, below them, 21 names of families. 'There are many more families,' he said. 'Not everyone knows what clan he belongs to, but everyone knows the relationship of his family to other families. The Hpauyu, Nangzing, Nlam and Tangbau families do not know whether they are Lahpai, Lahtaw, Maran, Marip or Nhkum, but they know that they are related. The Kumhtat, Lamung and Sabaw know that they are Lahtaw, and every Kumhtat knows that he may not marry a Lamung or a Sabaw, just as a Hpauyu knows that he may not marry a Nangzing, Nlam or Tangbau. Previously, a wife's brothers could not marry her husband's sisters, but the rules are not so strict now. Now, if they want to take a wife from her husband's family, they may do so, provided that a male buffalo is paid to the husband's family in addition to the normal bride price to compensate them for turning the tree upside down. If the wife's family aren't Christians, they must give two male buffaloes, a pig and some chickens in addition to the normal bride price. A tree grows from the roots up, Shelby. If a family that has taken a bride from another family is asked to change the natural direction of its tree's growth, so that it grows from the top down, by returning a bride to that family, then it must be compensated. For us it is very simple. It is systematic.'

Later, San Awng and Ma Htung came to my billet to assist me with my Jinghpaw. I was still struggling with sentences of the most rudimentary kind.

We departed from Pan Lawng Yang Mare late next morning in confident mood and descended the densely jungled wall of the escarpment. A man was sent ahead as a lookout. Seng Hpung said that our porters, all KIA irregulars, would be with us for several days, owing to the difficulties of obtaining porters west of the Mali Hka.

We reached the river. A section crossed by outriggered dugout to scout the opposite bank. The rest of the column hid in the forest. The scouts signalled that the way was clear. Then the boatman paddled us across in groups of three and four.

By 1140 hours we were all across, looking tensely about us. The hills here rose in a stepped sequence of knife-edged ranges running north and south. We advanced slowly up the first of them, cautiously stopping every 100 yards or so to wait in silence while the scouts reconnoitred the next sector. About two hours beyond the river, we reached Sharaw Kawng Nleng (Sharaw Clan Hill Hamlet), a sun-baked and somnolent place. Our new escort commander, Captain Sin Wa, who wore a stone charm in a cotton pouch hung from his neck, hid us behind a house, while Seng Hpung and Awng Hkawng questioned the villagers.

We walked on. Spring was everywhere apparent, with scarlet blossoms of the silk-cotton tree, fairy pinks and mauves of bohinia, delicate pinks and whites of wild cherry and pear and a riotous spread of purple and yellow convolvulus wherever the sunlight penetrated the jungle's canopy. From a ridge we looked back over cascades of some unknown mauve creeper. The Mali Hka was now a haze of heat rising from the valley beyond the range of hills behind us.

About an hour before sundown, we reached Shing Rai Ga, an abandoned village with an overgrown orchard of mango and fig trees. I climbed onto the porch of one of its houses and peered within. The furious, calcified eyes of a withered, smoke-blackened dead snake fixed to a *karap* (fireplace canopy) stared back at me. Flies with tiger-striped tails hovered menacingly an inch above my arm. Awng Hkawng, who had known Shing Rai Ga before, told me that it had once been a prosperous village; that the villagers used to cultivate orchids and collect honey, wild mushrooms and tigers' bones and trade them for salt and sugar at the *mawdaw lam*, but fear of the Burma Army had driven them off. Swallows and mynahs darted crazily between two giant banyans growing in a hollow beyond the orchard and their nests in the thatched roofs of the houses. 'We stop the night here, although it is a little risky,' decreed Seng Hpung. We were scarcely 12 miles from the road. We sheltered in a house that was all decaying bamboo infested with beetles, spiders and other insects. Dau Gyung boiled a local herb concoction for Seng Hpung, who complained of a pain in his shoulder that had troubled him since leaving Lakawng Bum, and, overlooked by a dozen pigs' skulls fixed to the roof joists, I had great difficulty getting to sleep. The lads told me later that the place where I slept was reserved for corpses.

We left Shing Rai Ga early next morning while the valleys were still choked with thick clouds. Concealed in the dense, liana-roped, mist-filled foliage, gibbons hooted mockingly and ghoulishly all around us. We were now moving due south at speed to evade the patrols associated with the enemy's stranded convoy. We passed two more abandoned villages before breaking for a lunch of palm hearts, rice and a stringy green vegetable resembling nothing I had ever seen, all scavenged from the jungle. Two propellor-driven aeroplanes flew over. Awng Hkawng said that one of them was the regular weekly flight from Myitkyina to Putao but that the other might be on a reconnaissance mission. We all stopped talking and listened thoughtfully; indeed, even the gibbons suspended their howling. The drone of the aeroplanes' motors, the first that we had heard since Camp N'wan Hka, sounded horribly near.

When we resumed, Seng Hpung sent scouts forward and issued orders for each man to march 50 yards behind the man preceding him, a command that Philip seemed incapable of obeying until it was pointed out to him that his neglect imperilled not just himself but everyone in the column. We were in a valley between rolling hills that were ideal cover for an ambush. More difficult still was the order to maintain silence. We whispered our few essential communications and avoided the pop and snap of stepping on fallen bamboo. Every ten minutes or so we stopped while Seng Hpung anxiously consulted Captain Sin Wa. Ma Htung pointed out a depression in mud and said to Mats, 'Bumma Ahmy soldier,' and Mats passed on the advice to me. The footprint was only that of a tennis shoe worn by one of our escort. About an hour before sundown, we left the path and hacked our way through thick undergrowth to a glade where our fires would be invisible to the enemy.

That evening we entertained ourselves nursing some orphaned chicks that one of our porters found. He gave one of the chicks to me and the other to Paul, but each blind, unhappy creature, hearing the chirping of its twin, kept struggling out of our hands and tumbling towards the fire. I tried feeding mine a baby frog, then wrapped it in a sock to keep it warm. But, sadly, with heart thundering forlornly in its tiny chest, it kept struggling free in its desperate yearning for its estranged twin, and, when I awoke and looked for it during the night, it was gone.

We resumed before dawn. 'We will cross the road about 1300 hours,' said Seng Hpung and added, ominously, 'If the Lord looks kindly on us.' 'Today, very dangerous,' added Philip. 'So, today, every time silence.' He had slept badly, owing to the dew that had dripped on him during the night. 'Too many snow,' he explained. So I christened the place 'Camp Too Many Snow'.

It was hard going that morning. We were in a scrub bush forest of the kind Burmans call *indaing*, all thorn, prickly bamboo and creeper. There were no paths, animal trails or features of any kind by which to orient ourselves. Nevertheless, our guides seemed to know where we were and where we were going. The ban on speech seemed otiose, as plainly not even the most determined enemy would ambush us here. Crossing a ditch, I tore the skin off my right wrist, narrowly avoiding more serious injury when my foot slipped on a mossy boulder, and a sharp wedge of bamboo thrust into my left eye socket, just missing the eye. I had a gruesome vision of myself returning to England as a cyclops. 'Pal of mine disappeared in the Golden Triangle earlier this year. His wife was frantic. He sent her a couple of postcards, in code obviously, saying that he was going to crack the syndicate. Then he came back with a pirate's patch over his eye.'

We halted at a stream and I bathed my wrist, daubed it with iodine and put a plaster on it. Mats detected a leech jack-knifing towards his foot and incinerated it in the ash of his cheroot. We carried on and crossed more open country, where there were haulms of fan-shaped, acid-green bamboo and clouds of tiny, bell-shaped white flowers and everything seemed a little drier. We came to another stream, waist-deep and about 12 feet wide, where Ma Htung, always the exhibitionist, cut a length of bamboo and vaulted over to the far bank, then challenged the rest of us to emulate him. The pole broke as San Awng tried, landing him backside down in the water, and everyone, including San Awng, roared with laughter.

We climbed onto a spur and halted again, while a section went forward with orders to scout the road and inspect it for footprints. Then we waited. The men smoked, and Mats practised making *pali* with his new *nhtu*; I wrote up my diary. An hour and a half went by. At 1215 hours the scouts returned. Captain Sin Wa reported that they had found footprints leading in both directions, but that the southbound depressions were more recent, and that there was no other sign of activity on the road. 'Maybe the enemy has come and gone,' concluded Seng Hpung. *Maybe*.

Seng Hpung extinguished his cigarette, and the men began putting on their packs. 'What's happening?' I asked. 'Motor road *very* near,' Philip whispered. We moved off, silently, through more thorn and lantana, and, suddenly, there it was: two parallel ribbons of yellow brown dirt and a median of pale green weeds, empty, silent and baking in the sun just as Fellowes-Gordon, Jellicoe and Fletcher and their Kachins and Ian Scott and his Gurkhas must have experienced it in 1944. It was almost *too* serene, as though a company of Japanese infantry might come tramping around the bend at any moment. The jungle had been cut back and the verges burned for about ten yards on both sides. We posted pickets north and south and hurried across. I tarried to take a photograph, waving forward those behind me to avoid delaying the column, and when I rejoined the column, Seng Hpung was furious. 'This is no time to take pictures!' he snapped. 'Security is more important than pictures!'

* * *

We regrouped in low scrub not 100 yards from the road, then marched west, then north. Then we descended into a dark, mosquito-infested gully and climbed a forested hill beyond, at speed. Suddenly, the column stopped, and the forward escort doubled back. Anxious looks all around. Seng Hpung and Sin Wa conferred with the guide, who was urging us vehemently to go back. We crept back to the gully and followed the meandering course of a tiny creek, leaving it after a quarter of a mile or so to climb another hill so steep that we had to hoist ourselves up it, clinging onto roots and vines while fighting through thorns, tangled bush and bamboo. Every step forced a decision – whether to lift that rotten lantana and walk under it, or waddle under it Cossack-style, or crawl; whether to hoist oneself up with the right hand, holding one's weapon in the left, or vice versa – and we were soon exhausted.

Again the column halted, and again the guide conferred with Seng Hpung and Sin Wa. 'What's happening?' I asked Philip. He shook his head, as though unwilling to answer. 'What's happening?' I persisted. 'We lose way!' he said scornfully, explaining that the guide could not find a certain tree that he had notched the last time he had taken a column through this thicket. 'Very bad,' he said. Steeply down again into another dark gully and into another meandering creek.

For two hours or so we marched and counter-marched, as though in a maze, wading through creeks and stumbling up and down hills through tangled forest. Down went a foot, and you began to transfer your weight onto it, but it slid back. You assessed the gain, which was never more than three inches, then tendered the other foot. Up another six inches and back three. Time and again I clung to scrub, head down and perspiring feverishly, raging at the heat, raging at the thorns, raging at the prickly bamboo, raging at the mosquitoes, raging at the guide's incompetence, raging at the truculent and intractable forest generally. Up another steep bank and, at last, there was a path! Or at least I imagined it was a path. Was I hallucinating again? But we soon lost the path and descended again to yet another creek. I turned to Philip and despairingly mapped our progress with a tour of my hand in the air. He sighed and, indicating the route we had just abandoned, said superfluously, 'That way no path.'

Even Seng Hpung seemed discouraged. There was another earnest consultation at which opinion was divided. The guide pointed repeatedly and ever more insistently in one direction, while several of the porters believed with equal conviction that our way lay further south.

Eventually the guide prevailed, and we turned downstream, having now come full circle. We reached a swamp (my diary generously calls it a 'marshy flat'). Seng Hpung, accepting an *ndum* of water from Ma Htung and suddenly remembering some rice cakes that the men had prepared for our lunch and recognizing that we had not eaten since breakfast, called a break. 'Here the danger is only 50 per cent,' he said. We ate. We rested. Then we resumed the trek, and an hour later I asked Philip to enquire of the porters whether they had the faintest idea where we were. He refused, so I asked them myself, managing with my limited Jinghpaw to communicate enough for San Awng to finish the task for me. To my astonishment, they calmly informed me that we were two miles from Hka Mai Yang and on a path. I had simply failed to notice the minute changes in the forest wrought by man that defined it as such.

Our phantom path soon joined a well-trodden *lam*. Philip's orders were to take us *around* Hka Mai Yang, but he led us *through* it instead. Some women saw us and abruptly broke off their conversation at the awesome spectacle of Mats's shadowy hugeness. 'Didn't I explain clearly that you *must not* be seen?' bristled Seng Hpung who was still cross with me for my unmilitary behaviour at the *mawdaw lam*. 'Do you not understand? The Burma Army has a post not four miles southeast of here, and an enemy column passed through here yesterday. It is obvious that you do not know the first thing about its tactics! The Burma Army tortures the villagers for information.'

That evening I learned that we had originally intended to cross the road near a lightly garrisoned enemy post but had abandoned this plan on the advice of one of the porters, who said that the enemy sometimes ambushed that route. It was also possible, said the porter, that the enemy was using that post to entice us into an ambush. Seng Hpung had therefore decided to cross further south, which was why we had spent the morning thrashing about in the jungle. Mats, Philip and I harboured in the forest, while the rest of the column put up in houses in the village. Seng Hpung came to us and asked if we were comfortable and told us to sleep lightly and to be ready to leave at a moment's notice.

Hkaw Ying brought us breakfast in the cold hour before dawn, and we left Hka Mai Yang as first light appeared over the hills behind us.

We reached the Daru (Crazy) Hka at about 0900 hours. We would meet it again as a narrow torrent near its source, but here it was about 40 feet wide, flowing sweetly over a pebble bottom between huge trees. We forded it, climbed its west bank and stopped to rest and congratulate ourselves on how well we were doing. We had now put more than eight miles between Hka Mai Yang and ourselves and were at least ten miles from the enemy's nearest post. To engage us now, the Burma Army would have to send a column up the Daru Hka.

A ridge took us most of the way to the next village, called Lahkra Kawng, where we halted long enough to change porters, which was accomplished very efficiently. Seng Hpung had sent men ahead to make the arrangements, our men secured the access paths, and Mats and I hid in the forest. I was sorry to see our Pan Lawng Yang Mare porters go without thanking them. They had knowingly risked their lives for us, like all the other porters who accompanied us.

We moved on quickly, soon reaching Hput Daw (Broken Knee) Mare. We lunched hurriedly in a wood beyond it. The heat was already intense, and every hour was hotter. My shirt was soaked through with perspiration, and its coarse, nylon-cotton fibres chafed against the skin. I blamed Seng Hpung's ill-starred concealment policy. It prevented us from bathing and washing our clothes, but had failed to conceal us. Those women had seen us at Hka Mai Yang. Some children saw us outside Hput Daw Mare. Now a stranger encountered on the path saw us. He discreetly lowered his eyes in a silent and pitiful plea not to eliminate him.

We passed through Tung Yang, a village abandoned by its inhabitants lest the Burma Army exact reprisals from them for aiding the KIA, and tracked a sinuous, undulating ridge for the better part of an hour under open sky; dreamily, as though we were afloat on an ocean swell, as though the earth were moving beneath us. The men said that the hazy peaks behind us were the ranges culminating in Shatnga (Sambur deer) Bum and that the pearled silhouettes off to the south were Bum Nen Bum and Bum Lang (Mount High) Bum. Ahead of us loomed the Daru (Crazy or Angry) Bum and cognate volcanoes of the Kumawng *shagawng*, with the sun still illuminating their near slopes. I knew that the Kachins had hymned each one of these great towers, and, later, Paul translated one of the songs for me with great feeling, though it sounded absurd to my ear. It was in the ingenuous style of *Winnie the Pooh*:

> 'We see so many mountains!' exclaimed Maran Naw (Pooh). 'They are Lakawng Bum and Ngaw Yi Bum, Ngaw La Bum, Kanau Kana Bum,' replied Kareng Gam (Christopher Robin). 'Every time we want to see the scenery!' cried Maran Naw (Pooh). 'All my home village, Mali-Hkrang Walawng, I so remember,' added N'Bawm La (Piglet). 'If you arrive at the Nbyen Tawng Sara you will never return to your homeland!' exclaimed Maran Naw (Pooh).

The sun was sinking below Kumawng as we tramped into Ga Pra (Clean Earth), set, as its name implied, in a high meadow grazed by goats. Philip chose a covered pigsty as a site for our bivouac, explaining his decision with these rudimentary words: 'This good place to hide. No one come here. No snow [dew]. No pigs. Mosquitoes not mind [were a tolerable nuisance].' He made a kind of mattress for us by fetching straw from the village and laying it over the dessicated manure. But the mosquitoes we very much did mind. Maddened by the salts in our dirty and glutinous clothes, they bit us mercilessly, until Paul built a fire, and we had a kind of bath from a shared cup of water. After the fire died, the mosquitoes returned. They carried the parasite of the most perniciously relapsing type of malaria in the world, 97 per cent malignant tertian reputedly, and we were defenceless against them. But we were now safely beyond range of the enemy's columns and were on target to reach Second Brigade headquarters five full days ahead of Kumhtat Gam's most optimistic prediction.

* * *

Next morning I counselled Philip about the dangers of malaria and tried to force antimalarials on him. 'After all the training that you have received from the KIA, it would be an awful waste were you to die of a mosquito bite,' I said, appealing to his finest sentiments, but he was contemptuous. 'We do not get malaria.'[9]

Since our exchanges at Fourth Battalion headquarters and N'Gum La, my relations with John had warmed, and he now brought the gleanings of overnight news. The village was deserted except for very old women and very small children; its other inhabitants were hiding from the Burma Army. Our porters had left us to return to Lahkra Kawng. Brang Shawng (our signaller) was having difficulties establishing contact with either First or

9. Malaria is less common at high altitudes than in the valleys, and above 5000 feet, theoretically, it does not exist. Many Kachins therefore believe that they are immune to it. When attacked by the parasite, however, they are prone both to catch and to die from it because of their limited prior exposure. The virulence of the plasmodium appears to strengthen as it passes through the bodies of the more resistant Shan and Chinese traders and Burma Army soldiers with whom the highland Kachins come into contact.

Second Brigade headquarters. Seng Hpung was pressing ahead. We were to follow as soon as new porters could be found.

Later, I noticed Philip counting and recounting the money I had given him to buy provisions for us. He seemed miserable, so I asked him what was troubling him, but he did not reply. 'There is a deficit for which he can't account, but he will resolve the problem and the cloud will lift,' I decided. However, the cloud persisted. Then he came to me and, solemnly tendering the balance of the money, asked to be relieved of these duties. He said that he would make up the deficit out of his own pocket. He was 25 kyats short, equivalent to about 17 pence in British currency. 'Philip, do not be tiresome,' I said. 'Mats and I can earn 40 times that amount in less than the time you have already wasted on these ridiculous calculations.' But our earning capacity was nothing to him. His honour was everything.

'It would be much more useful were you to do something about our laundry,' I said. I told him about the discomfort that my dirty shirt was causing me.

'Where it hurt?' he asked.

'Above the iliac crest.'

'How spell, iliac crest?'

'I-L-I-A-C. New word, C-R-E-S-T.'

'What mean, iliac crest?'

'It's a term used by doctors to confound their patients.'

'What mean, confound?'

As though on cue, half a dozen small children suddenly emerged from the forest less than ten yards from us and peered into our porcine sanctuary. Philip, now his old warrior self, bounded over to them and fiercely chased them away.

Seng Hpung and his party left, and, as we had nothing to do but wait, I talked on with Philip. He told me how the koel or Indian cuckoo (*Eudynamys scolopacea*), whose two short bell notes sounded at intervals we heard most nights, became estranged from the crow. The two birds were sitting side by side on a branch of a tree high on a mountain when they heard the beating of a *naw chying* (long drum) and a hundred gongs. 'What is going on down there?' queried the crow, to which the koel replied, 'They are dancing a *manau*,' a ritual dance. 'Let's go and join them.' So they made themselves up with the only make-up they could find, *latsut hku* (black ink). The crow painted the koel with exquisite care, but, when her turn came to paint her friend, his frisky impatience unsettled her and she spilled the ink all over him. Thus the koel is now very beautiful, while the crow, which is black all over, is very ugly. The koel escaped into a brace of thorns, and eventually her beauty transformed the crow's rage to love – which is why the koel sings at night. She is hiding from the crow.

At about 1130 hours Awng Hkawng came to us and plotted our itinerary on my map. The Indians would treat this 'sensitive map' (supplied by Blackwell's) as evidence of 'links with a global espionage network', but Awng Hkawng ridiculed its inaccuracies and its Burmese place names. Second Brigade headquarters, the map suggested, was about fifteen linear miles, or two stages from Ga Pra. Most villagers used the main *lam*, which traced the crest line two ranges north of us, said Awng Hkawng, but some had always travelled by the route that we had taken. The route had idyllic associations for him. He had travelled it five times, he said, but not for many years, and he was vague about distances. A few miles west of Ga Pra, we would cross the Daru Hka again and climb steeply to the Daru Pass. He remembered that the climb to the pass took about three hours and that, beyond Kumawng, the Supsa (Direct Flower) Hka would lead us to the Tanai Hka or Upper Chindwin. Second Brigade headquarters was on the Tanai Hka's west bank only a couple of hours south of the confluence.

The day wore idly on while the search for porters continued. Philip worked studiously on improving his English vocabulary, and Mats and I attacked our diaries. Maran Naw removed two small splinters from my hand, which, together with some scratches, scrapes and half a dozen sores from thorn wounds, comprised my few trophies of the road crossing. Awng Hkawng cleaned the carbine that he used for hunting. Lunch was cold, curried rice wrapped in *lahpaw lap*, and the flies were now as thick as the mosquitoes that had flailed us the previous night. We were at the point of resigning ourselves to another night in the pigsty, when our porter problem was abruptly solved by the appearance of a man in his sixties, two middle-aged ladies and two young boys.

We left Ga Pra at 1557 hours and spent the next half-hour

climbing, which, as we had just had lunch, was wheezy and purposeful. Then the path levelled, and our pace quickened.

An hour-and-a-half later found us beyond the first range and resting by the Bum Noi Hka. Trees 300 feet tall rose on all sides of us, and the water was clean and exhilarating. Awng Hkawng told me that he would like to spend more time here and recalled that, 13 years before, when the KIA transferred him from Second Brigade to Pajau Bum, he and his wife and their five-year-old son had stopped to spend the night at this very spot.

We sprinted up the next mountain and flew down to the Daru Hka in the valley beyond, where, shortly before dusk, we overtook Du Kaba's party camped along the river bank. The place was dark and damp and infested with leeches. Anticipating our arrival, they had already cut back the foliage and torched the ground to prepare a site for us that would prove an effective quarantine from the leeches. I greeted San Awng and Ma Htung and asked Seng Hpung if he required a *lekcha*, which he declined, and soon Awng Hkawng and I were comfortably installed beside a large fire. Mats and Philip left us to join the lads.

I had not asked Awng Hkawng about our confused meanderings after we crossed the Putao road. He now explained. We had chosen a point where the enemy would least expect us to cross, at about Mile 74, a mile and a half north of its post at Nam Hkam (Gold Water) and ten miles south of its post at Hkagaran (River Divide). But, after crossing the road, the guide and forward escort had reported that the enemy had laid an ambush for us, so we had turned back. While wading through the river at the bottom of the first gorge, he had heard footsteps and readied his gun to fire, but it was only the column's tail meeting its head. 'We were lost for only three furlongs,' he said. 'The guide found the path when we stopped for lunch.'

Alluding to the story that Philip had told me about the koel, I asked him if he knew this bird and, if so, what its name was. He replied, 'Every Kachin knows this bird. Some call it the *hkam hkam* bird, but others call it the *tat hkang*. It sings from sunset to dawn.' I pressed him: did he know why the *hkam hkam* lived at night and how the crow got its colours? I wanted to test his version of the story against Philip's. 'There are many versions of this story and many other such stories,' he replied. 'Some dishonest fellow in

Burma, a government clerk or a university professor, has published a collection of them and called them Burmese folktales, but they are not Burmese. They are our stories, handed down to us by the *myihtoi* [soothsayer].' Then he told me how the first *manau* (dance festival) came about and how the Kachins discovered that the leaf of the *mashaw* tree (*Clerodendrum nutans*) had medicinal properties.

Once upon a time, there lived an exceptionally handsome and intelligent boy called Ma Ding Yaw, who was disliked by the other boys because girls were so fond of him. They hung him upside down from a tree. The tree flowered and grew lots of fruit, attracting birds. The fruit that the birds did not eat fell to the ground, attracting butterflies. The butterflies appeared to be going about their ordinary business in the forest, but Ma Ding Yaw, because he was upside down, could perceive that they were really dancing. When his parents found him, he divulged to them the butterflies' secret. 'Our poor son has lost his mind,' they concluded and released him, but Ma Ding Yaw erected a pole and performed the dance himself. Other villagers lined up behind him and mimicked his jerky shuffle around the pole, believing they were mocking a madman – but they quickly realized that the pole dance imparted supernatural powers. The *agyi* and *bawmung* then implored him to teach the dance to other Kachins. Meanwhile, the birds flew off and danced this miraculous dance with the children of the sun, who had performed it long before Ma Ding Yaw taught it to the Sons of Wahkyet Wa. Then the birds danced the *manau* by themselves. The fan-tailed flycatcher, renowned for its excitability, superintended the preparations – exactly as the chief's wife always bosses her daughters about at the national festival. The quail, while pounding paddy, cried, '*Yik-yik*, *Yik-yik*', and the coppersmith, pounding meat, cried, '*Tok*, *tok*, *tok*' – just as the crowds attending the festival have voiced their excitement ever since. The white-crested laughing-thrush acquired its dusty appearance by poking about in the flour supplied to the dancers. The hornbill led the dancers, but the drongo soon replaced him, because he was a bad leader with an unmelodious cry inspiring little enthusiasm for dancing. Hence hornbills' feathers are worn and the drongo's whistle imitated whenever the *manau* is danced. It was first performed as a national rite at Hkrang Ku Majoi in about AD 1000. The Lisu at that time had not yet migrated from China and took no part; but they have participated ever since.

And this is how the Kachins came to learn that the leaf of the *mashaw* tree has medicinal properties.

God first provided for the Kachins a bleak and unpromising home. The Kachins migrated south, but their new home turned out to be another bleak place. Eventually they reached *Wunpawng Mungdan*, where one of their hunters, hearing strange music, found a pair of snakes fighting. The male snake killed the female and used her for his pleasure, but the pleasure that she gave him inspired love. He kissed her and declared his love, but, having died, she was unresponsive to his pleas for forgiveness. So he slithered sadly away, ate a leaf from a *mashaw* tree, and slithered back for a final kiss – whereupon she revived! The hunter deduced correctly that the *mashaw lap* in the serpent's saliva had revived her. He dug up the *mashaw hpun* and replanted it in Myitkyina, where, tended by the Mashaw family, it still produces the most potent *mashaw lap*.

We accord folklore status in the West. Ever since the publication of the Grimm brothers' *Kinder- und Haus-Mährchen* we have treated it as a branch of science. We examine collections of stories of the Graeco-Roman and Teutonic gods (mythology) and the origins of words (philology) to better understand our *past*. They recall a lost age, when our ancestors lived in great isolation surrounded by vast forests – not unlike the Kachins today.

Although half of Awng Hkawng's antecedents were Gurkhas, in outlook and sentiment he was fiercely Kachin and championed all their ways. When I asked him if he believed, as other Kachins, that otters were supernaturally priapic and that carrying around a dried otter's penis enhanced potency, he replied, 'My uncle has such a thing. He found it stuck in a piece of bamboo. The otter had tried to mate with the bamboo.' When I remarked that it struck me as odd that Kachin husbands slept separately from their wives, he answered, 'Wives are not birds. They do not have to share their husbands' beds.' If some Kachins in Myitkyina were dishonest, he said, it was because contact with Burmans had corrupted them; indeed, his motive in joining the KIA was to preserve a way of life threatened by Burmanization. As we talked on in the wan light of our *dap*, a feeling of profound well-being crept through me. I was where I wanted to be, with men I respected deeply. Whatever they said concerning the minutest detail of their language, beliefs, values, traditions or customs interested me more than anything anyone had ever said to me before. That evening spent in Awng Hkawng's company by the Daru Hka was one of the most agreeable of the trip. We shared a packet of biscuits that were infested with weevils. The two middle-aged ladies bivouacked next to us. Although it was very cold, they simply stoked a fire, lay on the ground and went to sleep with no cover save their clothes – alone, as they slept every night. Life among the Kachins was hard indeed.

* * *

We moved on early next morning, tunnelling through a green world to a chorus of jeering gibbons. Our porters, whose number had increased during the night, now included a mother and her pubescent daughter, half a dozen boys aged between eight and ten, and a tough, stag-like 60-year-old with a stubble of grey whiskers named Gam Seng. They wore dirty, tattered *longyis* and cotton shirts and walked barefoot. Their ankles and calves were covered in sores from the bites of blood blister flies, which they treated with a white powder derived from a jungle plant called *mawau*. For the first two hours we looked vertiginously up at Daru Bum through gaps in the dense roof of the forest; first from the east, then from the south, then from the west. We crossed a saddle and, after a further climb, reached the aptly named Bum Noi Hka (Hanging Mountain Stream), the hill beyond presenting us with another almost vertical climb. I hoisted my rucksack onto my shoulders to spare my chafed back, but the unfastened waist strap had an irritating habit of slapping against a leech wound on the ham of my right leg.

About noon we reached a flat watered by a small brook and dappled with clusters of tiny purple and white flowers called *lahkrang pu* (*Smilax aspera*?). Our escort had already stopped for lunch on Sin Wa's orders, but Seng Hpung overruled him and ordered us onward, and when, after another long climb, we did break for lunch, it was at a waterless place where we were obliged to picnic on rice cakes and weevil-riven biscuits. Mats recalled a time when, after leaving school and before he joined the Swedish

Army, he worked as a baker's delivery boy and was allowed all the hot buns, cakes and pies he could eat. '*That* was paradise!' he proclaimed with great feeling, and we all laughed at the idea that Nature's provision for us was so capricious. One of the escorts had wounded a gibbon and hobbled its feet. Men and beast stared at each other, the gibbon not in fear so much as fascination. It would continue with us in harness, grabbing at passing branches in bids to free itself, until its final moment, when it would be pinned squealing to the ground, decapitated, skinned, gutted and cooked.

We had hoped to reach the Supsa Hka before sundown. However, two of the boy porters began showing signs of exhaustion, so we camped instead at a place called Nhku (Knife Handle). Gam Seng said that there was a spring there, but it tested dry, sparking a bitter row when I went to Seng Hpung's site and asked Mimo for the tea I had come to expect at the end of each stage. He grinned and pointed at Philip, who in turn grinned and pointed back at him.

Mats was lying on the ground beside Philip with his head against his rucksack, smoking a cheroot. There was a smug and, I thought, incriminating look on his face. Next to him were both our mugs – empty. And in the bottom of *my* mug were some soggy tea leaves.

'Mimo!' I flared, but again he pointed at Philip.

Ma Htung, who witnessed this exchange and understood its darker implications, gestured in the direction of the spring, and Mats, who also grasped the implications but resented my confronting them in this way, held up a thumb and forefinger a centimetre apart to indicate how little water they had been able to sluice from the spring. By now, however, I had already drawn my conclusion. The four of them – Mats, Philip, Mimo and Ma Htung – had obviously colluded in stealing *my* tea.

I seized an empty canteen and marched off in quest of corroboration, only to find that the spring was dry, exactly as they had suggested. This still did not explain, however, why there were *two* empty mugs. I hurried back to confront them again.

'You not believe me!' cried Philip, pained by my distrust.

Dinner intervened. Philip's pain was eloquently evident to everyone – and it wasn't fair. He had laboured ceaselessly to keep us dry, warm and safe. He had bought biscuits for us (albeit infested) out of his meagre salary. He had slept rough every night, while we lay warm and snug in our sleeping bags. Seng Hpung broke the tense silence once, speaking softly to his boys, and, once, Ma Htung glanced at me, surreptitiously. I smiled to show willingness, but he immediately turned away, embarrassed. A vague suspicion that I might have erred began to trouble me, and after dinner, when Dau Gyung and Mimo were cleaning up, scraping the pans with stones, and after everyone else had dispersed, I went to Seng Hpung, who was in his *basha*, smoking. 'Du Kaba, something rather nasty has arisen,' I began. He smoked and stared up at the sky through half-closed eyes as I spoke, and, when I had finished, he said nothing. Then he laughed. 'All this over a small cup of tea, Shelby?'

I should have left it there. By now, I might have deduced what had happened. The spring had yielded only enough water for two thimblefuls of tea. Mimo had divided the tea between our mugs. Mats had requested more. Philip had given him the tea in my mug, and Mats had allowed it because he had not realized that no more water was available. But I was still reluctant to let go.

Seng Hpung continued. 'My boys came to me and said, "Du Kaba, the old man seems to be very angry." "Why is he angry?" I asked, and my boys said, "It is because of tea." A storm in a teacup!' he added, delighted with his donnish joke. He then said that he had offered to sacrifice his own tea to resolve the difficulty but that his boys had opposed this solution as contrary to their custom, which forbade serving me from a cup from which he had already drunk. '"Du Kaba," my boys asked me, "have you already drunk from the tea?"'

I stammered feebly, 'Du Kaba, it is not *just* about tea. I have some difficulty in *believing* Philip.'

'Why should you think that Hkyen Naw would lie to you over such a small thing?' he replied, as though in his long experience of harmonizing discord he had never heard anything so preposterous.

'Because all three of them laughed when I asked Mimo what had happened, and Mimo *pointed* at Philip. There were dregs of tea leaves in *both* mugs. This isn't the first time that tension has arisen between us.'

'How do you know that Mimo was pointing at Hkyen Naw?'

We went around in circles, Seng Hpung ridiculing me for raging against the spring's niggardliness and I maintaining that the issues were more complex. Eventually, I allowed that at least an apology was owed to Philip. 'Leave it to me,' said Seng Hpung. 'It will only make a small thing big if you speak to him. Moreover, it might be helpful if, in future, you and Mats composed your problems between yourselves without involving the men. You upset them with your quarrels.' I rose to leave. 'One more thing,' he said. 'Don't be so serious!'

I found Philip and Mats at our site staring at our fire in silence. Philip had spread my sleeping bag for me. Having witnessed such scenes from me before, they had evidently decided to allow time to do its healing work, but the issue was still very much alive with me. I looked at Mats and said that I wished to speak to him 'in private.' He shrugged his shoulders wearily and got up, and we walked a short distance together in silence, until we were out of Philip's hearing. Then I said, 'Seng Hpung wants no repetition of what happened this afternoon. His boys reported that you drank my tea.' Mats replied that he had not intended to drink my tea.

'That's all very well,' I snapped. 'The fact remains, Mats, that you drank the tea in *both* mugs and said exactly nothing when I accused Philip of lying.' He tried to answer, but I intruded: 'Keep your voice down! Someone might hear us quarrelling. I've already told you that Seng Hpung wants no tension in the group over this. This is between you and me!'

'Shelby, we have an expression in Swedish, "Don't make a chicken farm out of a feather." '

It was very dark now, and, through the leafy night, we could hear the lads' musical laughter. Seng Hpung had summoned them for a briefing. Later, after Mats abandoned me to my rage, I joined them at their *dap* and explained to them what I felt required elucidation. That, contrary to what they might have been told, I did not despise them. That I did not eat with chopsticks to manifest my superiority: I simply disliked eating with my hands. That during meals I sat on a log or on my rucksack instead of squatting on the ground as they did because I was unused to squatting and for me it was uncomfortable. That I gave my laundry to them rather than wash it myself because I wanted to conserve the time for my diaries. That I refused their offers of *tsa pi* because I did not enjoy drinking alcohol and because the missionaries' example of abstention seemed to me important and worth emulating. That my tutorial sessions with Seng Hpung were spent discussing Indian history and not disparaging them. Finally, that I wanted with all my heart for them to remember me fondly, as I would remember them. They heard me with respect, and, when I had finished, Tu Lum said simply, 'Mr Sheby, Mats is your friend.'

Philip was still awake when I returned to our *dap*. I went over to him and apologized unreservedly for having accused him of lying. 'It was an appalling accusation, and I have no excuse,' I said. 'I can only ask you to forgive me.' I ate the biscuits he had put out for me, took two sleeping pills and managed to go to sleep.

We left Knife Handle on empty stomachs in the cool dawn air and did not rest until we reached the Supsa Hka, a shallow river flowing through wide beds of polished, white rocks. Elephants had been there to water that morning and commemorated their visit with monstrous, lumpy piles of green dung. Awng Hkawng loaded his carbine and went off to hunt them (prompting me to wonder how one 'bagged' an elephant). We heard the harsh, rutting ngawk-ngawk-ngawk-nu-waw of an *u tawng* (peacock); *u hkung-rang* (hornbills) squawked at us, and fantailed warblers and fat, little green *u ra* (pigeons) patrolled the pink sky. I shaved and washed my shirt, and, as I sat there on a stone by the river, cooling my feet in the water and pounding the soap from my shirt, Ma Htung plucked some fungi bedded in the sand beneath me, which surfaced later in our breakfast. The great Kumawng *shagawng* was now behind us, and everyone seemed rested and cheerful.

After breakfast we followed the Supsa Hka as it trickled west through a hot and muggy forest of soaring trees, and, not for the first time, I regretted that I had wasted my early life studying law instead of botany. My *Salang Kaba* (Revered Elder) status seemed a cruel hoax: fortunes had been spent on teaching me what I did not need and could not use. The lads were able to identify everything, but only by its Jinghpaw name, and, as the names varied in different parts of Kachinland, as often as not they disagreed. Not even our university-trained botanist, Philip, knew the English or Latin names. 'My ignorance oppresses me,' I complained to my diary. 'I only see and can describe what a child would notice: *kadung hpun* (red flowers); *hpungi hpun* (small leaves, smooth white bark);

labyi hpun (yellow fruit, long, slender leaves — excellent for making posts, says San Awng).' In front of me in the column, strapped to the back of one of the escort, the wounded ape on its terminal journey struggled desperately against its hateful bondage. Occasionally, for a hopeful moment, it would succeed in retaining a hold on a passing branch, only to be yanked brutally back by its collar.

Shortly after noon we stopped again. San Awng detonated a grenade, and the fishing brigade charged into the Supsa Hka, our child porters at the head of the stampede and Gam Seng directing the attack from the branch of a tree overhanging the river. Philip stayed back and boiled up some tea for us. Mats and I had not spoken since our quarrel, and I had been anxious to avoid him. I now heard him behind me, slurping his tea and thought, 'Good Lord, he's *trying* to provoke me!' But, again, I was mistaken. He had come to venture reconciliation. 'Shelby,' he said softly, 'I suppose that you now know what happened yesterday. San Awng told Philip to give me your tea, but, of course, I did not know that it could not be replaced. Had I known, I would not have drunk it.' He was completely sincere. 'Of course not,' I said and proffered my hand. 'How stupid of me.' A few minutes later, I heard him chatting cheerfully with the lads. What role Philip, Tu Lum or Seng Hpung might have played in mediating this reconciliation, I would never know.

A little further downstream the Supsa Hka debouched into the Tanai Hka, and, on flat, hard clay near the confluence, lay Sut Awng (Treasure of Success) Yang: half a dozen modest houses on poles scattered amongst palms and *kaing* grass and clumps of bamboo. The village was deserted save for a few goats and chickens wandering about among the sandflies and a woman weaving at a loom contrived from bamboo slithers stuck upright in the ground. A baby was asleep in an *nbat* on the ground beside her. A few feet away a child of eight or nine operated a primitive cotton gin, feeding the bolls through wooden rollers that separated the fibre from the seeds. The heat was overpowering, though merely a foretaste of worse to come, for this was the Hukawng Valley, where temperatures in April and May exceeded 100°. Although Second Brigade headquarters was less than eight miles from us, Seng Hpung ordered a halt. Our porters were committed to come only so far, he said.

On a wobbly altar in the empty house where we were billeted were a Bible and a coloured photograph of Pope John Paul. Our female porters visited us there, placidly squatting on the floor and, out of habit, facing the rough palms of their hands towards the *dap*, though it had nothing in it but cold cinders. They said with offhand affability that they thought we were very peculiar and that our strangeness reminded them of a party of Nagas who had passed this way bound for China. These marvellous Nagas, evidently, had known even less Jinghpaw than we and could only manage to say, '*Kaja i?*' (how are you?) When I remarked on a revolting smell emanating from a pile of yams, the little girl got up and serenely disinterred a dead rat. Conversation faltered, and I soon left them to seek Awng Hkawng. I wanted his help in understanding the Kachin clan system, with which I had been grappling without much success since First Brigade headquarters, when Philip confessed to me his ignorance of his 'sister's' name.

Next morning I rose before the others and saw Awng Hkawng leaving the village with his carbine. His cavalier attitude towards killing wild game ('If I see an elephant, I shoot it. If I see a bird, I shoot it') puzzled and disheartened me, and when he returned I asked him, 'Exactly what do you do with a dead elephant, Du Jum?' 'I eat it,' he replied sharply.

We were waiting for orders from Second Brigade headquarters. About noon a pair of magnificent bull elephants sent from Second Brigade headquarters arrived. We loaded our baggage onto their panniers and resumed the march. Our route was now along the Tanai Hka, here, at the southern end of the Hukawng Valley, flowing peacefully northwest through gorges in the Kumawng and navigable only by shallow-draft vessels. Later, joined by the watershed torrents of the Patkai divide (including the Tawang Hka and Tarung Hka), it would bend around to the south, spurning the Naga Hills, and leave the Hukawng. From then on as it continued south – past most of the 'Japan War' graveyard routes into India; past Homalin, Taungdut, Mawlaik and Kalewa; through bottomless valleys riddled with fevers; past the unbroken forests of the Chin Hills – it would be known as the Chindwin, after Chinthe, the lion-headed dragon of Burmese mythology. It flowed for 550 miles, finally merging with the Irrawaddy about 50 miles west of Mandalay, near the ruins of Pagan.

We tramped through a forest of low, fat-leaved trees, out-pacing the elephants, and behind me John (he was not Tu Lum today) and Alex joined me in singing a song about the Seine they had asked me to teach them. '*Elle coule, coule, coule de Montmartre jusqu'à Poissy*,' I sang, and they repeated the words after me. We crossed to the west bank of the Tanai Hka. '*Elle roule, roule, roule, en passant le Pont Poissy*' – ignored by a pair of wild elephants cavorting in the river downstream. Loudly and more loudly we sang. '*Elle chante, chante, chante, tout le jour et la nuit*.' The sun sparkled on the water, which was a rich bronze colour veined with streaks of pale blue. Behind us, our elephants began to ford; behind them were Kumawng's blue peaks. '*Car la Seine est une amante, et Paris dort dans son lit*' and, not for the first time since leaving Pajau Bum, it occurred to me that here was paradise. It was even more beautiful than the Seine from the Quai des Grands Augustins on a foggy, wintry morning. Every step now measurably reduced the distance to our fairy-tale goal, and at every bend in the path we felt a little stab of anticipation.

On we went through tall *kaing* grass and banana palms. Women were now bathing in the river, combing their straight, long, black hair, the sun gilding their wet bodies.

We emerged from high grass onto hard ground. Confronting us were a pair of houses in a poppy field. Half a dozen people inside were sitting on their haunches staring dreamily at the ground. Seng Hpung coyly called them 'gardeners', but in fact they were opium farmers. Their opium is less valuable than that grown further east, is slow to solidify and has to be mopped up with cloths, which are hung out to dry. The user tears off a piece from the impregnated cloth and immerses it in a spoonful of water, then boils off the water to obtain the sticky distillate he wants for smoking or eating; hence, it is known as 'cloth opium'. Here, as elsewhere, the KIO licenses its use only as medicine and to certified addicts, most of whom are already old.

We stopped at a village called Gaw Nan, where a very old man renowned for his piety invited Seng Hpung to pray with him. While they prayed for the success of our mission and the final triumph of the Gospel in Kachinland, Mats and I swam in the Tanai Hka. On the far shore KIA *oozies* were training a baby elephant, marching it up and down the beach alongside a *koonki* (or 'schoolmaster', an already domesticated older elephant used to allay the baby elephant's fears and lead him through the *oozy*'s commands) and singing lullabies to it. John opined that they were singing in 'elephant language', but Awng Hkawng said that it was a mixture of elephant language and Shan. Some Burmans on a raft, sheltering under a flimsy canopy with their livestock and household goods, saw us and waved as they glided past on the swift current. A couple of almost naked Europeans bathing in the Chindwin's Ultima Thule must have struck them as *very* odd, and afterwards we wondered if they would report us to the Burma Army.

Nearing sundown we heard bells tinkling in the forest and sighted other elephants hobbled by their front legs with leather *htungs*. The path widened, and the thatched roof of a building appeared. Then there were more buildings and a football ground.

6
The Rivers

We were under orders to reach Pinawng Zup (Binuzu), a Lisu settlement near the Indian border, before the end of the month, but as no one had ever ventured anywhere near there save a few Lisu who traded between Hkamti Long and the Hukawng and we could not measure our likely progess by them, no two views agreed as to how long this last sector would take. Opinions varied between eight and fourteen days. The 'mini-rains' would start soon, but no one knew exactly *how* soon. The rivers were already rising from the melting snow, and the rains would slow our progress still further, might even stop us altogether. The time we spent at Second Brigade headquarters was therefore critical. Moreover, I had my own reasons for wanting to press on. First, Carole was expecting to hear from me by the end of March 'at the latest', and hearing from me meant ringing her from India. Second, I wanted to reach India within the ambit of my visa. It had expired on 9 March, but I had extended it by 20 days by inserting a '2' in front of the '9'. It was already 12 March.

We expected no delay, but we depended on La Roi, Second Brigade's *svelt*, track-suited civilian administrator, for intelligence and procurements. However, for security reasons, he had been left in the dark about our intentions and had made no preparations. There were two routes to Pinawng Zup. The easier route led through the Hukawng Valley and up the Tarung Hka, but strong Burma Army garrisons blocked it at Tarung and Namyung. The other route was top secret and, as the column would have to return by it, had to remain so, but it was known to be extremely difficult, and no column as large as ours could prudently attempt it without elephants. So elephants had to be organized. But elephants would exacerbate the security risk, and greater risk meant a larger escort. So that too had to be organized, including supplies for feeding everyone, because much of the route was uninhabited. There was also the important matter of a guide. A teacher named Hpauwung Tanggun reputedly knew an *oozy* who had taken an elephant through this *terra incognita* and was thought to possess a map charting a vital and sensitive part of the way. But he lived in a village called Awng Lawt, which was 25 miles from Second Brigade headquarters. So we had to send and wait for him.

Hpauwung Tanggun arrived in camp during the afternoon of 14 March. His younger brother, Lieutenant Hpauwung Yaw Htung, had died defending the Nationalist Socialist Council of Nagaland's GHQ when it was harbouring Bertil Lintner and his wife, and, after Seng Hpung and Awng Hkawng debriefed him, he came to our quarters 'to meet Bertil Lintner's compatriot'. He was a young man of grave demeanour wearing thick bone spectacles who had learned English by reading aloud with the aid of phonetic symbols from books supplied to him by Jehovah's Witnesses. His father had been the headmaster of a mission school in Sumprabum, and he and all his brothers had been educated there, but, he said, in those parts of Kachinland now controlled by the Burma Army, Buddhists had replaced Christian teachers and Scripture lessons were prohibited. It was Ne Win's expulsion of the missionaries and the BSPP's nationalization of their schools and hospitals and other attacks on their religion that had driven them to revolt. It had come as a great shock to him to learn from Bertil Lintner, whom he had met at Second Brigade headquarters, that not all Europeans were Christians. 'If Europeans do not believe in Christ, what do they believe?' he asked me. 'Do they worship idols?' He said that he had joined 'the revolution' in 1964 and that three of his five brothers had sacrificed their lives for it. 'To this day we not tell our mother that Yaw Htung die. She has weak heart. She might die if she learn that Yaw Htung die,' he said. He predicted that it would take us 12 to 14 days to reach the border. The path was difficult even for elephants. 'Never mind,' he said. 'God will take care of you, and I will find you an *oozy* who knows the way very well.' My photograph of him, snapped in front of the fur-textured, rusty red hibiscus marking the borders of our compound at Second Brigade headquarters, shows him in a *taikpung palawng* of black silk appropriate to a senior schoolmaster standing at the centre of a group of soldiers. I called him *Sara Kaba* (Great Teacher).[1]

We spent five days at Second Brigade headquarters. Five days of sweets and sumptuous meals and flirting with Maji, a Lahpai from Kutkai, and Hkawn Shawng, a Maran from Bhamo, two pretty corporals with long, black hair flowing from their khaki caps and down the backs of their khaki shirts assigned to look after us. Inevitably, they were Philip's 'sisters-in-law'. They washed and ironed our clothes and served us plates of early potatoes and curried fried chicken, *tsa pi*, cheroots and Chinese cigarettes. Five days of proper tables, proper chairs, proper beds, proper blankets, vacuum flasks of hot water, bags of chicory sweets, bowls of biscuits and rice doughnuts fried in brown syrup. Five days of botanical (*myng pan*, name flower) and ornithological (*myng u*, name bird) expeditions into the forest with Philip and San Awng. Five days, too, of anxiously searching the skies for black omens of rain. It was hot during the day and muggy at night, for we were in a hollow between two fingers of the Kumawng, dominated on the east by Janbai (Sun Returns) Bum. In the morning a multiplicity of Chinese lantern colours played across its cosmic shoulders. Cirrus cloud alternated with bright blue skies.

'Next month flowers everywhere, but today not so many,' observed Philip on one of our botanical strolls. We collected specimens (which I later abandoned) of *aya pan* (like a large dandelion or small marigold); *shaba pu* or brinjal, a five-petal purple flower with a yellow centre; *u jaw ban* (rooster's crown) *pan*, a yellow, orange or crimson flower shaped and textured like sea coral; *nwa pan*, tiny, three-petalled and crimson; and the bird-pollinated *su hkrang pu*, a five-petal white hibiscus with a yellow tongue. Through Seng Hpung's binoculars we fancied that we saw the plain-backed sparrow, black-throated and yellow bellied; the tiny, black and white *pasi tum u*, whose song is a long, melodious whistle; the brown, crown-headed, tailless *u kataw* or bulbul, with

1. Bertil Lintner's book about his trek across the Kachin Hills, *Land of Jade*, presents a fuller account of Hpauwung Tanggun's family (1990b: 121–3) and of the circumstances of Yaw Htung's death (1990b: 1–5, 96–102).

a red spot at its rear, whose signature tune is a persistent series of hiccups; the sultan tit, with its distinctive yellow crown, black back, bright yellow breast and white-tipped tail feathers; the tiny, green *u tu* that sounds like a croaking insect; eagles whose call was three whistles, two long notes and one dipping melisma (a chorus of sounds that Philip dubbed 'natural music'). And throughout the long nights we heard the constant 'tu tu' of the *hkam hkam*.

Mats and I had been with the KIA now for more than six weeks and paid for nothing except a few sweets. There was a shop at Second Brigade headquarters. I wanted to exchange some dollars for kyats and buy some biscuits for the men. I also coveted a certain *nhtu* that I had seen at the shop. However, La Roi refused to change my money; and, one afternoon, when I returned to our quarters from one of my *myng pan-myng u* rambles with Philip, the shop's entire stock of biscuits was waiting for me there. 'Present from KIA,' announced Philip proudly. Thus began the Battle of the Biscuits, which raged for the better part of two days before I was allowed to pay for them.

A parallel engagement over the *nhtu*, however, ended in my rout. Seng Hpung bought it and presented it to me as a gift.

'San Awng will fit the strap and show you how to wear it,' he said. 'When a Kachin gives you an *nhtu*, which he uses both as a tool and a weapon, he becomes like a father to you. He assumes responsibility for your safety. It is like adopting a son. That is our custom.'

The *nhtu* was a proud specimen of Kachin swordcraft, nearly two feet long, engraved with the design of a tiny pistol representing the *si nat* or death demon and riveted with copper to repel the other *nat*s. Accompanying it was a bright red *nhpye* (shoulder bag), trailing black tassels and embroidered with sequins. As Kachins keep their money in their *nhpye*s, this further gift signified that Seng Hpung also assumed responsibility for my prosperity. In effect, he explained, he had adopted me into his clan, and, as he was a Dauje, henceforth, the incongruity of my name notwithstanding, I would also be treated as a Dauje.

Proudly wearing my *nhtu* and *nhpye* over a shirt neatly pressed by Maji and Hkawn Shawng, I went to Seng Hpung early on our last evening at Second Brigade headquarters, and we galloped over the remaining syllabus of my *lekchas* on Indian history: the means by which Britain had conquered and ruled India; the causes of the Mutiny; the final expansions east and west; the princely states and the principle of 'paramountcy'; the foundation of the Congress Party; Gandhi and the peaceful resistance path to *swaraj*; Nehru, Jinnah and the Muslim League; the role of the Second World War and the postwar Labour government in precipitating independence; Mountbatten's partisan interference in the work of the Boundary Commission; the Partition massacres and the ensuing wars between Pakistan and India. Throughout my long discourse Seng Hpung nodded and frowned and smiled. Contemporary Burma was never far from his thoughts, and, when I had finished, he asked me, 'Shelby, what is meant by "psychology of domination"?' I knew what he was after because, among his few possessions, in a cellophane sack, was a Mentor paperback edition of *The Prince*, so worn from use that the pages had come unstuck. Its mixture of cunning and pragmatism might have served as a set text for my *lekcha*. He wanted to know whether the statecraft the Muslim dynasties and British Raj used to govern India was the same formula that Ne Win and his junta were using to rule Burma? 'The artifices and stratagems that Machiavelli describes might have worked in sixteenth century Florence, but I very much doubt that they would work today,' I said. He asked me to make a reading list for him and was particularly keen to know if there was a modern equivalent of *The Prince*. I replied that I knew of none, except possibly works of Bolshevik tacticians that I had not read, and that modern politicians were no more honest than his illustrious mentor, only too pious to confess their dishonesty. He seemed to understand this.

Almost ten years have passed since then. The nights are black now. Frost lies hard on the ground. Cats prowl the spines of cold brick walls and raid plastic rubbish bins. I wake and remember the moonlight on the *u jaw ban pan*, the long silence broken only by the owl and the *hkam hkam,* and wonder how many of my favourite titles Du Kaba has read on his jungle paths. I wonder to what possible use he has put the potted Indian history of those extraordinary *lekcha*s. Should he ever read this, I want him to know that I will always cherish my *nhtu* and *nhpye* as tributes to his friendship and always remain a Dauje.

* * *

A large crowd assembled for our departure. We were two companies and eight elephants. The morning was overcast, and we could hear distant thunder reverberating in the mountains to the north. Had the mini-rains started? We thanked La Roi and his staff for their many kindnesses and, on 16 March, left Second Brigade headquarters happily ignorant of pending danger.

We stopped briefly at Gaw Nan for a final blessing from the saintly elder there. He promised to pray for us. At Sut Awng Yang a man staring dumbly and blankly at the cinders of a cold *dap* was exactly as we had left him five days before, as though frozen. He might have been suffering from acute depression; alternatively, in some drug-induced state, a legacy of the time when the banks of the rivers of the Hukawng were extensive poppy fields. According to Geoffrey Rowland, who was a missionary in the Hukawng for almost 16 years, the opium harvest was a great celebratory event and was often the occasion for initiating children in the use of the drug. So many families deserted their houses for their opium garden huts that in their villages 'not even a chicken clucked'.

North of Sut Awng Yang a soldier plucked a capsule from some poppy and ate it. Breaking open a capsule, Philip explained that the soldier was only eating the seeds. '*Very* delicious,' he said. Philip also pointed out a five-petal bright red flower called *bum panlawng* in Jinghpaw and *khaung yan* in Burmese; the *hkunmau pu*, whose petals half resemble and smell like honeysuckle; the *chying hkrang pu* or mustard flower; the *nam lachyut pu*, a tiny double-petalled, purple flower; and the large yellow dicotyledon known as *woi shamyen pu* that grows on a creeper fond of open, sunny places. If a plant was edible, he explained, it was called a *pu*; if not, it was merely a *pan* even though it might be ravishingly beautiful. We had picked *nam lashawt pu* by the Jing Ma Hka and *chying hkrang pu* the day that we crossed the *mawdaw lam*, he said. 'You not remember, uncle? You not *remember?*' But the main topic of conversation that day was my *nhtu* and *nhpye*. It was along the lines of 'Don't laugh, but the old man now thinks he's a Kachin!' The forest thickened, and, occasionally, through the dark foliage, we would catch glimpses of the Tanai Hka, silver at noon and a tawny copper in the late afternoon.

We stopped the night at Tanai Len Mare. A woman there presented me with two white eggs. Philip claimed that they had a very deep meaning, but he did not explain what the meaning was. The woman had wrapped the eggs in a leaf. This, too, apparently, had mysterious implications.

Spring was already well advanced in the Hukawng, and next morning we saw the trunk and branches of a *hpun lahken* covered in bright orange fungus. We also saw the *lagat hpun,* with its large, dark red flowers resembling poinsettia, and the glorious bloom of the *langu hpun* (wild banana), fleshy and white, the texture of a Mississippi magnolia. After crossing the Hkamaw Hka, we saw starlings and rollers, ducks and herons, and a bird with brilliant green feathers about the size of a dove that flew in long dipping patterns. Two *langda* (vultures), huge and black with snake-like necks and long beaks and yellow markings near the tail, made a sinister whirring sound when on the wing that prompted Ma Htung to call them 'little aeroplanes'. Awng Hkawng identified for me the *kadawn pu*, a thin, white sliver of tree blossom, and the *shalap pu*, a round, white bush flower with a yellow centre whose name means 'sour-tasting leaf flower'.

We rested briefly at Sara Kahtawng (Teacher's Settlement), a village that enjoyed a reputation for antiquity because it had retained the same name for more than three generations, but, I learned afterwards, it was about ten linear miles east of the village of that name on the 1942 reprint of the 1926 *Survey of India*. Fixing the location of Kachin villages according to their places on maps is all but impossible, as John Masters, who led a Chindit column into these hills in 1944, discovered. 'When the soil round a village becomes exhausted', he wrote, 'the villagers move to another site, one or fifteen miles away, burn twenty acres of jungle, plant their crops, build a new village, and call it by the same name as the one they have just left. Ten years later, the soil again exhausted, they move again.'[2]

We reached Awng Lawt just before 1300 hours. As we entered the village we saw mausolea carved with large crosses and the letters 'RIP'. Hpauwung Tanggun accompanied us, but not even he knew what 'RIP' signified. It was enough that all missionaries'

2. Masters, 1961: 227.

tombstones bore the same inscription, he explained. One of the mausolea evidently harboured the remains of a man of mixed beliefs, for a genealogy engraved on it traced his descent from a sky *nat*. The temperature was now close on 100°.

By Jinghpaw standards, Awng Lawt (Victorious Freedom) was a metropolis, spreading for about half a mile over a meadow grazed by the only goats we saw in Kachinland and dotted with lemon, pomelo and grapefruit trees. The brother-in-law of the KIO Foreign Secretary lived there, and it was at his house that the *agyi* and *bawmung* assembled to greet us. We dispersed around his *dap* as protocol decreed: the owner of the house next to the shorter wall, Seng Hpung next to the longer wall, and the rest of us in descending order of rank with our backs to the women. Had a man of the cloth been present, he would have displaced Seng Hpung. No one would have dared disturb these arrangements. The terrible squealing, the desperate gasping for air of a fatted hog tugged by its ears and stabbed through the jugular portended another special lunch.

After the special lunch, Hpauwung Tanggun took me to his house and showed me proudly the 'largest library in the Hukawng', which he kept in a tin trunk. The library proper comprised almost exclusively books published by the Jehova's Witnesses' Watchtower Press with titles such as *Did Man Get Here by Evolution or by Creation?* and *Your Youth: Getting the Best Out of It*. But here, also, was the map thought to be vital to our success, a quadrant of *Survey of India* quarter-inch that stated ominously, 'Path *appears* to follow the bed of the river'. And here, too, were Hpauwung Tanggun's family photographs, including pictures of Yaw Htung and his other dead brothers, all handsome men. There was a letter from Bertil Lintner written at Pajau condoling Yaw Htung's death, and a bloodstained shirt and green sash taken from Yaw Htung's corpse. 'A Naga soldier bring me these things,' said Hpauwung Tanggun. 'I have to take out and dry during rainy season, but they are safe here from ants and my children.'

We spent more than 24 hours at Awng Lawt, throughout which time our orders were to stand to for immediate departure. However, Hpauwung Tanggun's *oozy*, our indispensable guide, was two days' march from us: two days to find him and two days to fetch him; and, further complicating matters, one of our elephants went missing. Extreme care had been taken to conceal our destination. Now everyone down to the smallest child knew that we were bound for Pinawng Zup. We could only hope — and pray — that this intelligence did not reach the Burma Army. Seng Hpung was the moody, solemn stuff of indecision: should we push on and hope that our errant elephant would be found and that the guide would catch up with us? Or should we wait here? He suddenly resolved his indecision. The escort snapped on their cartridge belts and grabbed their guns. We were on the move again.

We harboured that night at a bend in a river, which Awng Hkawng represented to me as the 'Gap Dup' Hka. We would follow it to its source, there pick up the 'Tongli' Hka and follow it to its confluence with the 'Bi' Hka[3] and follow it to the Tawang Hka, which would take us to within a day of Pinawng Zup. I bivouacked alone, disdaining the stony ground that San Awng had selected for us. A clump of trees obstructed the view above the bend. Downstream, patches of a succulent ground creeper that the Jinghpaws call *hka kinji* grew in the white sand.

About sundown, Seng Hpung came over to warn me to take care that one of our elephants did not tread on me during its nocturnal grazing. He enquired if I was comfortable, then asked me if anything was wrong.

'As you know, Du Kaba, there have been unforeseen delays, and I am concerned about my Indian visa,' I said. 'If I cross the border without a valid visa and the wrong Indian authorities catch me, they might hand me over to the Burmans. I don't know if you have ever had dealings with Indian bureaucracy, but it is in a class of its own. Those *babus* concern me at least as much as the

---

3. Many in the KIA, including Major N Chyaw Tang, linked the attack on NSCN headquarters at Longva resulting in Hpauwung Tanggun's brother's death with intelligence that the Indians gave the Burma Army, and Seng Hpung had to allow for the possibility that the Indians would capture us after we left the column. As the column had to return to Awng Lawt by this route, therefore, he may have ordered the men to falsify the names of the rivers. Alternatively, the men might simply have differed in their opinions of the rivers' names. In any case, none of the names given here in inverted commas are in the existing cartography for the area, such as it is.

Burma Army. Would you have any objection to my pressing ahead on my own?' I had raised this idea with him at Tanai Len Mare, and he hadn't rejected it out of hand.

But he was in no mood for this discussion now and had already got up to leave. 'All right! All right,' he said peremptorily, 'I am concerned too. But we have no guides.' And suddenly he was gone.

All at once, as though they had been waiting for my visitor to leave me alone with them, frogs started croaking all around me. The sky was clear and full of stars, and a nearly full moon sailed serenely over the grey, jagged line of mountains to our east. Occasionally, one of the escort, Hkaw Ying or Ma Htung would go to the river to fetch water, and I could see moving about some of our escort who were camped downstream. I compared my position with that of my friends at home, all of whom were queuing up to be grandfathers, and none of them, I concluded, knew the freedom I knew. Hang the Indians, I decided. What was there to worry about? The Good Lord would take care of *everything*, and never again would I be as happy as I was now. Then I descried the shadowy outline of an intruder.

It was Awng Hkawng. '*Kaja i?*' he said, and after I returned the greeting he sat down beside me. We sat in silence for a while listening to the frogs. Then he explained that, knowing my intense interest in Kachin genealogy, he had worked up this analysis tracking the Jinghpaws back to the first man on earth, and here it was. I perused it by the light of his torch. It began, '*THE EXISTANCE OF HUMAN According to oral history of Kachin, every Dumsa recited as follows the existance of Human*' and told how First Human's male progeny through 14 generations had all married the daughters of demigods, spirits and monsters. It spoke of how a fifteenth generation descendant, Sumpawng Yaw, had married the hearth god's daughter; how from this union had sprung the progenitors of the Chin, Rawang, Nung, Lamun-Lisu, Tang Bau Tang, Wan-Maru and Lashi; and how Sumpawng Yaw's youngest son was Tingli Yaw, the first Jinghpaw. It was, plainly, something to which he had given most thoughtful and serious care, to which he attached the gravest importance, and which deserved the most careful and earnest study – which was more than I was able to manage there on the beach beside the 'Gap Dup' Hka.

By the time Awng Hkawng left me, it was quite cold. The moon was directly overhead and the frogs were in full throat. There would be dew tonight, I decided, and carefully folded part of my ground sheet over my sleeping bag. The sand was soft but firm beneath me. Then came the first buzzing in my ear – mosquitoes!

* * *

The frogs continued all night. I would wake, hear them, and fall asleep again, reassured. They stopped at first light as abruptly as they had begun. The *oozie*s were up before anyone else, rounding up their mounts[4] and fetching them to the river to scrub down their backs with *dohnwe* creeper and bark. The sight of these huge grey beasts emerging from the water, the *oozie*s standing on their dripping gleaming backs, balancing themselves like acrobats, is a wonderful thing never to be forgotten.

We got off to an early start and soon found ourselves wading up the 'Gap Dup' Hka – a painful ordeal, because my flip-flops kept snagging rocks and floating free, obliging me to about-turn on the ball of one foot in strong current to snag them before they floated off. They were too thin to cushion my soles properly and too short to protect my toes. The rocky bottom seemed brutally intent upon punishing the same toe, the big toe of my right foot. The more care I took to protect it, the more it was hammered. I began to limp, which seemed ridiculous and provoked Philip to disgust. 'Please hurry,' he said, screwing up his nose. 'You always last.'

We encountered some Lisu who had come down the Tawang Hka from Putao to pan gold. They excited little curiosity at the time, but, later, our Indian gaolers would impute to them a sinister significance. ('Putao is long way from where to travel to pan gold, Mr Tucker. I am thinking they are not gold-panners.') They seemed almost wild, inhabiting huts of sticks and leaves, but they were the last people we saw for several days. We stopped at one of their camps. Hpauwung Tanggun was waiting for us there, having

4. Although trained elephants often meet and consort with wild elephants during their nocturnal foraging, they appear to exhibit little disposition to return to their former freedom (see, for example, Peacock, 1958: 47).

found not only his *oozy* but another man as well, a Lisu named Adi, to act as our guides. He had made a copy of his map and highlighted our route with red crayon. We parted without bidding him farewell, for we did not realize that we would not see him again. I have often thought of Hpauwung Tanggun and his much bereaved family since then. I wonder if we would have succeeded in reaching Pinawng Zup without his help.

The elephants, which had fallen behind, caught up with us and halted head-to-tail, ears flapping. Their arrival was the signal to push on. The 'Gap Dup' Hka narrowed as we continued upstream, low hills rising all around us, for we now appeared to be leaving the Hukawng. Gibbons played with languid athleticism in the overhanging foliage; monkeys and peafowls screamed abusively at us, and the pain in my big toe was excruciating.

We left the river, climbed a hill, and then descended to what I expected to be the 'Tongli' Hka. However, the direction of its current asserted that we were still on the 'Gap Dup' Hka. Then, suddenly, the lads began hacking out a clearing in the forest. '*Ndai kaw yup na i?*' (We sleep here?) I asked Dau Gyung incredulously, as a good three hours remained in the day. '*Ndai yup kaw na, re*,' he affirmed. I turned to Philip for an explanation. 'Elephants too slow,' he explained. Night had begun to fall before the elephants caught up with us again. Dinner included the roasted offal of a hog deer hind that one of the men had shot.

Seng Hpung visited our bivouac that evening, which he did rarely. I was alone with Philip when he appeared. He had been moiling over the subject that I had tried to discuss with him the previous evening and said, 'I don't know what to think. Zau Mai told me to allow eight days from Second Brigade headquarters. However, the guides now advise that it will take us at least another ten days – from here. I have therefore decided to send you ahead, so that you can reach the border before your visa expires. But are you sure you *want* to take this risk? You won't have any porters. You won't be able to buy rice along the way. It will be very difficult for you, and a little dangerous.'

'More difficult than what we've already experienced?' I asked.

'Much more so.'

'Dangerous because of the enemy?'

'No, because of the terrain and the wild animals. If you are determined to go ahead, you must travel as lightly as possible, taking nothing that you do not strictly need. The rest can follow with the elephants. You don't need to decide now. You will have until tomorrow night. Think it over carefully, Shelby — and also,' he paused and scrutinized me intently, '*pray* about it.'

'Can Mats come with me?' I asked. 'He doesn't have an Indian visa and it occurs to me that it might help both of us were he to accompany me as my servant. That would seem plausible to the Indians. Have you spoken to Mats?'

'Is it not enough that you speak to him?'

'We haven't discussed it until now because our plans were uncertain. I'll ask him what he wants to do.'

Mats was with the students. I had not visited their *dap* since Knife Handle and they were surprised to see me, moving aside almost nervously to provide a log for me to sit on. Paul, who had never found me very intimidating, tried on a joke about finding a wife for him in England, and I replied in kind. Everyone laughed. They seemed to enjoy this kind of banter. I offered them some of my biscuits, but they refused them, pretending that they never ate while smoking to spare me the embarrassment of being told that they could not accept what they believed had been a present to me from La Roi. Then I repeated my conversation with Seng Hpung, to which they listened transfixed. They were extremely fond of Mats, and what they had long feared was now about to happen. 'Mats, the choice is yours,' I concluded. 'You can come along with me, or you can stay with the column and take your chances with the Indians later on your own. Seng Hpung thinks that you will incur less risk by staying with the column, but he may not appreciate just how tricky the Indians can be. You have tonight and tomorrow to decide what you want to do.'

I was in my sleeping bag when Mats returned to our *dap*. Philip had waited up for him. There was a brief, whispered conversation between them. Then I heard Philip laugh, joyously, and knew that Mats had decided not to accompany me.

I was awake a full hour before dawn contemplating my Big Decision. It was the last day of winter in Europe and, assuming that Seng Hpung did not change his mind, would be my last with the column. All the dramas of choosing a route, of selecting a campsite, of eluding mines and ambushes, were about to end. I would return to Europe, and there would be no one with whom I could share the experience. *Walked across northern Burma with a bunch of insurgents, eh?* At about 0530 hours the *oozie*s dispersed into the forest to retrieve their charges. Hkaw Ying and Dau Gyung got up and started preparing breakfast. Ma Htung stirred. I knew that I would miss them hugely. They were immediate and real to me now, but, all too soon, they would be one with so many fantastical memories of mists and gibbons.

Mats got up. 'If you have any further questions, now might be the time to raise them,' I suggested. He confirmed that he had decided to stay with the column.

I reported to Seng Hpung at breakfast. 'Mats is taking his chances with the column.'

'I know,' said Seng Hpung.

'I expect he will be all right on his own,' I said. 'I wonder if you could help me with a few provisions? I will need a torch, a needle and some soap. I will need to change some money. And will it be all right if I walk with Awng Hkawng this morning? I want to question him about the route.'

'If I send you ahead,' he replied, 'I will send some of the men and a guide to accompany you.'

This was excellent news, for I had somehow assumed that I would be on my own. But the *if* alarmed me. Perhaps he had already changed his mind?

We broke camp at 0810 hours and delicately picked our way up the last of the 'Gap Dup' Hka through a damp, gloomy tunnel of foliage full of leeches. Pointing at the spongy ground at the pass, Seng Hpung said, 'Here is the beginning of one river. It goes that way – back to Awng Lawt. And here is the beginning of another river. It goes that way – towards India.' I took our new river to be Awng Hkawng's 'Tongli' Hka. We followed it down, watching it grow steadily from a barely discernible trickle into another raging torrent bounding over grey boulders. Now, for the first time, I waded in my boots and it was my turn to mock the others as they stumbled on the tricky surfaces, banging their toes and chasing after fugitive flip-flops. Mats was in excellent spirits, rejoicing in his rising leech count.

'Are you counting the ones you see in the forest?' I asked him.

'Only those I pick off me,' he replied.

'Obviously, they prefer Swedish blood!'

'Because it is so sweet!'

When we stopped for a *preekop*, I found half a dozen of them under my socks, already bloated with my blood, two more on my wrist, two others at my navel and another buried in my groin. Everyone's clothes were bloody.

We broke again at noon. The route led down amphibiously, onto land and back into the river again. At the foot of the mountain the 'Tongli' Hka disappeared into the broad, shallow, southbound 'Hka Taw' or Tabyi Hka,[5] which we followed upstream past wide, sandy beaches and *theke* grass until 1400 hours, when we halted for lunch. The elephants caught up with us, and the *oozie*s unloaded them and let them out to forage. One of the bulls, disconcerted by ticks, repeatedly scooped up sand with his trunk and sprayed it over his back and had to be restrained from tramping on our bags. I sat on a rock, nursing my stomach cramps and a mild fever. Seng Hpung now came over and, with a troubled expression on his face, asked me if I remained intent upon going ahead. 'I must repeat what I have already told you,' he said. 'It will be very difficult and very dangerous.' Was he about to renege on his promise, or was he merely making sure that I fully understood the dangers? Nothing was certain with this enigmatic and complex man. Events would prove how right he was to caution me.

The Tabyi Hka now led us west, past sun-bleached boulders and silver sand and tall, grey reeds rippling in the wind. It had been cloudy and cool all day. Now delicate pinks of late afternoon sun emerged from behind the clouds. There were clumps of trees to our south, open *kaing* country to the north and, upstream, low hills shrouded in mist. It was a pleasant change from the raw, wild mountains of the Kumawng and the Triangle.

We camped under some trees on hard sand. At about 1900

---

5. The distinguished Scottish cartographer, John Bartholomew, having compared the topographical, chronological and directional detail in my diaries with existing cartography, has concluded that the 'Hka Taw' was the Tabyi Hka. My diary records four different names for it: 'Hka Taw Hka', 'Hkamaw Hka', 'Hpunging Hka' and 'Timying Hka'.

hours I went to Seng Hpung to ascertain whether he was still willing to send me ahead. I said that I wanted to brief the men who were to escort me while there was still someone available to act as a translator. 'No, no,' he protested. 'You will only confuse them. If it is possible, I arrange everything.'

If again!

'Very well, Du Kaba. Then please tell them that I want breakfast in time to start hiking about an hour before dawn, so that we can do eight to ten miles before the heat sets in.'

'You must not think of yourself!' he retorted.

Seng Hpung's order reached me by the gossip relay I called our Nine O'Clock News. There was no if now: Awng Hkawng, his two batmen, Tu Lum and Maran Naw, four soldiers from our escort and our Lisu guide, Adi, were taking me to India, and we were leaving early next morning. Mats's feet were in worse condition than mine, so I gave him most of my remaining plasters as well as half my remaining Maloprim tablets in return for some chloroquine, keeping for myself the iodine, which, anyway, he had always disdained. I knew he was keen to see the last of me, and my feelings towards him were none too generous. But believing it to be our last moment together, we made a special effort to be nice to each other, and I now experienced the charm he had conferred on everyone except me since Camp Four Papayas. We both reckoned that we had more to lose than gain by another open rupture and, as things turned out, that proved to be very sensible.

* * *

'Ready?' said Awng Hkawng, slinging his rifle over his shoulder. We were off. Men with whom I had travelled for nearly two months, now preoccupied with their breakfast, scarcely looked up. Were they, too, glad to see the back of me? It was the first day of spring, and, back in England, the crocuses and daffodils would be drinking up the dew. Our apple tree, framed by the kitchen window, would be in blossom again. The days would be getting longer, and Carole would be planning her garden. In a week or so it would all be over. The telephone would ring; she would answer and know I was safe.

I was more heavily laden than the others in our little column, carrying a stocking of rice looped about my neck in addition to my usual load. Things began to go wrong almost at once. The strap of one of my bags broke loose from its brass eye. The blue nail of my battered toe, now clinging like a dead leaf in a cold wind, fell off. (I found it later in my sock.) It started raining.

For exactly an hour and forty minutes we waded in and out of the Tabyi Hka, fording it at pebbly shallows above the bends whenever the going on the opposite bank seemed easier. Then we rested for exactly 20 minutes on some rocks under a wall of trees draped with pink myrtle blossom. We waded on and, after another hour and forty minutes, climbed onto a sandy bank, where a peacock called out to us. Some Lisu who had camped there had cut back the bark of a tree and inscribed the directions and distances to various destinations in charcoal, but they were no help to us, as our only Lisu, Adi, was illiterate. Then we turned away from the Tabyi Hka into scrub forest and tracked a tributary of the Tabyi Hka, whose bottom was all soft sand and mud and full of hornet leeches. Here and there we scrambled on to the bank to follow an animal track or a gold-panners' path, pausing only to scrape off the leeches. We reached a pass, picked up the dark trickle of another incipient stream and carried on until it was deep enough to allow a drink. Thereafter, we were harassed mercilessly by leeches, which marched up our trousers and dropped on us from the overhanging foliage.

Wading waist-deep in a strong current, I suddenly had the unsettling sensation of being alone, a feeling reinforced by tiny birds chattering thinly in the treetops. Adi had gone to the *nam dum,* relying on me to maintain our link with the column. The others had taken a *shat khat*, and I had distinguished myself by losing them. Adi was now wading towards me with a look of disgust on his face. After much thrashing about blindly in thorns, we found the others, who had realized what had happened and were waiting for us. The experience brought home to me how utterly dependent I was on the Kachins and how silly it had been to consider attempting this sector on my own. When, eventually, we made camp, I moaned whingingly to my diary:

> Awng Hkawng says that 'tomorrow will be difficult', as though today has been easy. He has taken himself off with

> his carbine to shoot an animal. Adi, who is addicted to opium, has prepared a pipe. I suppose this will be our pattern from now on. We walk from early morning to dusk. Adi and the lads establish camp. Awng Hkawng goes shooting. Adi has a pipe. I bathe my sores. Eat. Then sleep and resume after breakfast. One of the men has used a kettle instead of a *hka nhtung* to fetch water, thereby offending the river *nat* Bareng. Bareng has retaliated by visiting us with a cold wind.

Tu Lum and Maran Naw were up most of the night keeping the fire blazing.

Next morning, we came upon a landscape unlike any we had seen before – vast stretches of white sand and pebbles and tall grasses with feathery tops waving in a light wind. It seemed odd to look up at so much open sky after so much dense jungle. Awng Hkawng called it a 'different world', and we sat down to ponder it. As we sat there under this tremendous sky, a pair of heron, half-concealed in reeds, took flight and a flock of northbound geese flew over. We had reached the Tawang (Undercutting) Hka, here pouring out of the hills to the north in a wide bend. When we resumed, we encountered the tracks of elephants, bison, rhino, bear, sambur, barking deer, wild pig and what might have been that strange cross between a goat, a donkey and an antelope, the serow (known here in its black subspecies) or the even rarer Feae's Mountjac. We were in a kind of animal paradise, an Okavango or Ngorongoro, where food and water and visibility abounded. Awng Hkawng, whose fanatical kills so far had counted only a few miserable pigeons, was inconsolable. 'Those [depressions] were made by a stag! They were made by a doe and her fawn! They were made yesterday! They were made today!'

We emerged from grass and saw three grey hulks about half a mile distant advancing on us. We waited, our eyes straining in the bright light. They were moving in procession. We thought they were sambur or hog deer. Slowly they came, upwind from us, apparently ignorant of our presence; but we knew that, at any moment, they might stop, sniff the air, pick up our alien scent and bound off. Awng Hkawng caressed his carbine in anticipation of a kill, and on they came through the ethereal void. Then, quite suddenly, we realized that these grey creatures moving soundlessly through the empty wind were other humans, a man and two women, and that the man, in addition to his *shingnoi*, carried a long pole. Awng Hkawng surmised that they were villagers bound for Tarung, but they turned out to be Lisu from Pinawng Zup who had been commissioned to deliver a letter to the KIA. Awng Hkawng took delivery of the letter and persuaded them to join us.

The man's name was Ati. He was tall and thin, about 30 years old, with a faintly discernible wisp of moustache, and, in addition to his pole, which was a plastic fishing rod, he carried a camera. Even more incongruously, he wore plastic shoes, meagre signs of affluence by most standards but conveying to us an impression of effeteness that proved to be entirely misleading. The women, whose names were Ata and Anna,[6] were a good ten years younger than he, and they deferred unreservedly to his leadership, which he exercised with considerable delicacy, carrying the heaviest load and making all the decisions affecting their safety: where to camp, what kind of shelter to build, where to ford the rivers, and so on. Fording the rivers, he would assume the upriver position, Ata clutching his hand and Anna hers, his long fishing rod bobbing in the air as a mace of his protective authority. When a *shat khat* was attempted, he would pioneer a route over it and come back and fetch them.

Ata was both innocent and mature, her best feature being her mouth, which she sometimes painted crimson. She had wide, almond-shaped eyes and long, black hair, which she sometimes wore in a French roll. Made up or unadorned, she seemed to me to be almost intolerably beautiful and had a kind of grace that transcended her wild surroundings, through which she strode in a leisurely, sinuous lapse from pose to pose, laughing and singing from morning to night. Once I saw her remove her shoes and scamper up a rock face to pluck an edible plant growing in a cleft there. Once a chute of stones, every one of which was lethal, whizzed past our ears, but, seeing my dismay, she roared with laughter. Anna had buck teeth and was cross-eyed, and her timidity was in complete contrast to Ata, who led her around like a

6. Lisu appear to have a predilection for names beginning with *A*.

child, chatting with her when every one else ignored her, encouraging her when her confidence failed, and chiding her when, as often happened, she was frightened. Ati, Ata and Anna were cousins and, at night, slept together under a *plastik* and a blanket. They were devout Christians. This was my first encounter with Lisu of Hidden Valley and they made an enduring impression on me.

They immediately disabused us of the notion that our white world augured an easier route, pointing out that it had taken them six days to walk from Pinawng Zup. It was true that sickness had delayed them; but, they said, sickness was inevitable on the Tawang Hka. The Tawang Hka would become a raging torrent, overpowering us if we weren't careful. Worse than the river, they warned, would be the *shat khat*s.

We rounded the bend, forded our new challenge for the first time, and were soon fording it every few minutes. Two of the men slipped and went under. Then I nearly went under – with appalling implications for my diaries and film. The diminutive Maran Naw had to be towed across with a length of rattan. Every quarter of a mile or so we stopped to empty the sand from our boots. Some of us tied our laces loosely, which was more comfortable but allowed in more sand. Others tied them tightly, in a kind of tourniquet, which admitted less sand but choked the feet. Late that afternoon, tempted by a patch of flat land abounding in wild flowers and butterflies, we tried to camp but were driven off by ferocious ants and finally harboured at the site that our new companions had first suggested. Adi and I now learned that we both spoke Hindustani. This transformed my relations with Tu Lum and Maran Naw. Previously, they had evinced a certain unfriendliness, as though they resented waiting on someone with whom they could not speak. Now, able to communicate with me through Adi, they eagerly made tea for me and, after I braved the chilling river for my bath and shave, brought me more tea. They fetched me a candle, and, sitting up with my legs in my sleeping bag, I wrote in my diary: 'God willing, only five more days to India.' Then I heard a noise like thunder rumbling slowly down the river towards us. I called over to Awng Hkawng to ask him what it was. It was the echo of the Lisu singing hymns.

* * *

Next day Ata put on lipstick, a minute attention to appearance that disturbed our orderly, if unromantic, regime. A great ball of cloud rolled through the steep gorges. Then it started to rain, delaying our departure. By early afternoon, the rain was belting down. Adi and Ati were magnificent, time and again returning to help the others with their baskets after ferrying their own across the foaming river. Many days would pass before we would ford the river again.

We came to the first of a succession of perpendicular rock faces, seemingly impassable. Ati and Adi treated it with contempt. Fingers splayed against the stone like lizards, they soon disappeared, chatting, into the cloud above. The rest of us started up, warily. Nearing the top, a cleft in the rock face allowed a considered assessment, but this was more disconcerting than helpful. I could see Ata and Anna waiting patiently 100 feet below. Adi peered over the ledge above me to offer encouragement. 'Do not be afraid, Master. There's nothing to fear,' he coaxed ungently in Hindustani. 'Come along now.' He extended his hand and pulled me up to him. 'See how easy it is?'

Now I was on a narrow rock ledge, and Adi was behind me. The ledge ended at a fault line, confronting us with a gap of about four feet. Adi said, 'Jump, Master!' Resignedly, I jumped and landed on a patch of moss that mercifully offered some traction but might just as easily have not.

The next sector was a traverse along steep hillside, consolingly simple after the rock face and the fault line, nevertheless difficult. For support, we clung to saplings, vines, roots, rocks, always testing their strength before proceeding. We were shrouded in *plastik*s as cover from the rain, and my rucksack, packed to ensure that camera and lenses remained dry during the river crossings, was dangerously top-heavy; adjusting it, however, seemed too much trouble at the time. All of a sudden, I sensed a sharp, hard blow to my head. The mountain had collapsed beneath me.

Recurrent nightmares keep this memory fresh in my mind. I was hanging by my left arm from a sapling over a cliff face. First thought: would the sapling hold its ground? Fifty pounds of pack with most of the weight concentrated at the top and 150 pounds of me about three feet up the trunk of the sapling translated into perhaps 800 pounds of force at its roots. Adi was leaning over the abyss between us, offering me his hand. With my free hand I reached down and secured my staff, which had slipped from my grasp and caught in some bushes, and passed it back to him. He groaned. He wanted my hand, not this worthless piece of bamboo! My next thoughts were for my hat, knocked askew by the blow to my head, and my spectacles, clinging by one arm to my right ear. Adi impatiently took them from me and renewed the offer of his hand. The tail of the column had linked itself to him in a human chain ready to pull me back to safety.

I considered my position. It seemed to me that three options were on offer: two aft and one forward. I might twist round counter-clockwise, facing the mountain, or swing round clockwise with my back to the mountain and try thereby to reach Adi's hand. The latter manoeuvre would entail releasing my grip on the sapling – and, if I reached Adi, would the human chain hold? Or would someone panic and let go? Committing strength aft, moreover, might leave me with insufficient strength to attempt the remaining option, which was to try to span the gap of some five feet to the next possible foothold. A thin sliver of lantana dangled enticingly in front of me. Could it support my weight? Was it taut? Or would I find myself swinging free 30 feet down the cliff face? Gut feeling told me to go for it. Adi again renewed his plea for my hand. '*Apka hath, sahib*! *Dediye*!' I reached for the vine and sprang to safety.

A few hundred yards on, we made camp on a beach. I then noticed the loss of my Oyster Perpetual. This was no ordinary timepiece and I remembered only too vividly how it had come into my life: a *cantina* in a village in South America; an invitation from a stranger accepted all too naively; a black alley from which there was no retreat; the dwarf with a big *sombrero* pulled low over his ears brandishing a machete who relieved me of its predecessor; the kind but unhelpful policeman to whom I reported the crime (*Son sin verguenzas, señor. No tienen ningun respeto por los estranjeros*);[7] the sensible shopkeeper in Panama City who suggested a replacement that could be concealed in laundry soaking in the sink of my hotel room as proof against other

7. 'They are shameless ones, sir. They have no respect for foreigners.'

bandidos. I had worn my cherished Oyster Perpetual for 18 years, and, like the rucksack that had accompanied me around the world (now, by provision of my will, waiting to be buried with me), it spoke of all the sunny places where we had travelled together. It symbolized for me what could *not* be replaced, the adventures of a once young traveller. (Should Rolex feel disposed to replace it, I hereby declare that it gave me 18 years of untroubled, unremitting and nearly perfect accuracy.)

My first inclination was to impute the loss to my misadventure. Further reflection convinced me otherwise. Having worn the watch on the wrist of the hand gripping the tree I could not imagine how it might detach itself. Moreover, Adi advised me that he had *seen* it on my wrist. Therefore, I deduced, it must be somewhere between the cliff face and our campsite, difficult to find perhaps, but the men would help me. I would offer a reward and with a little patience and luck... I was hallucinating again. The men were indifferent. What did they want with either my money or my watch? Awng Hkawng ordered Maran Naw to help me, and Adi joined us because he felt sorry for Maran Naw. We retraced our steps and thrashed about without much conviction in the wet, leech-infested bush, making ourselves thoroughly miserable, until, eventually, I called off the search. 'Revered Elder, it is in the Tawang Hka!' the men cried with delight. They saw the Tawang Hka as a fitting bier for something that proclaimed its own perpetuality. The only thing perpetual about it, they said jubilantly, was that it would tumble on and on in the current, rewinding its waterproof innards for the benefit of dumb fish until some delighted gold-panner found it and traded it for a packet of sugar. Many years later, after the war ended, they said, I might see my Oyster Perpetual in a shop in Myitkyina, Mandalay or even Rangoon. 'Who knows, Revered Elder, maybe it is part of God's plan that you meet again!'[8]

It was raining hard now. I sat under our *plastik* watching the

---

8. After returning to England, I claimed compensation under our home insurance policy, designating 'Kachinland, Northern Burma' as the 'Place of Loss' on the form sent to me and alluding to 'the attached copies of relevant pages from the claimant's diary' to explain the 'Circumstances of Loss'. In due course an adjustor called on me. She was, she said, 'sceptical but nevertheless open-minded'. The claim was allowed.

men soggily discharging their tasks, envying their cheerful fatalism. More firewood appeared. I changed into dry clothes, put out my wet clothes to dry and wrote up my diary.

> We *could* reach the border by midnight the 27th, but I am not optimistic. The Lisu insist that the worst crossings are ahead of us. The more it rains, the higher the river rises, the more 'shortcuts' we'll have to take, and the slower our progress. We are already into the fourth hour of this downpour, and every hill on both sides for fifty miles is draining into the Tawang Hka. However, there is food enough for the moment, and I have somewhere dry to sleep.

That evening after dinner I asked Awng Hkawng his opinion of our prospects. He was pondering a desperate alternative to future *shat khat*s that envisaged one of the men swimming the Tawang Hka with a length of rattan in his mouth and anchoring it to a tree. I visited the Lisu's *dap* and discussed our prospects with them. Ati was tucked up in blankets like King Farouk. The Farouka was flirting with one of the men, who had faked a chest pain, and was rubbing his chest with some kind of oil. Cross-eyed Anna behind her was experiencing it all vicariously. Clearly, *they* weren't bothered. I returned to Awng Hkawng and said, 'I'm not worried.'

This interested him. 'Why not?' he asked.

'Because the Lisu aren't worried.'

'Nothing ever worries them,' he replied wearily.

'At least one good thing has happened,' I said.

'What?'

'I found them.'

A packet of sweets that I had bought for us at Second Brigade headquarters had gone missing.

'Where?'

'Maran Naw had them. I saw the blue bag.'

'The blue bag contains *toffees*. Why didn't you say toffees? You said *sweets*.'

'Never mind. Let's celebrate.'

'You'd better have them.'

We decided that it might be too early to celebrate, and I bade him goodnight. When I returned to our *basha*, Adi was smoking his pipe. This was, after all, the moment that *he* lived for. That night the storm broke. The whole sky was rent by the violence of its fury, black one moment and lit up with forked lightning the next, the mountains quaking with thunder as rain and hail in half-inch pellets pounded down upon us. A corner of our *plastik* tore loose and flapped in the wind. But I was snug and secure in my sleeping bag, and Adi, beside me, was already asleep, dreaming whatever thoughts the bubbly brown opium inspired. Our fate was in God's hands, as evidenced so plainly on the cliff.

* * *

I did not remain snug in my sleeping bag for very long. I woke with a start, aware that Adi was sitting up. A look of consternation was on his face, and his keen eyes were fixed with animal intensity on something behind me. As the rain was slanting down, it was difficult to see what he was staring at. I crawled to the edge of the *basha* and peered out into the storm. He muttered something about the river. We had camped well above it. It was now about 20 feet from us.

In typical Kachin fashion he saw no reason to leave our dry, cozy *basha*, but I had spent my childhood by the sea and remembered only too vividly the snakes twisting frantically in the flood waters of Hurricanes Betsy and Camille; the uprooted water oaks; the sections of railway trestle swept miles inland; the steel drums left stranded in gardens and streets. Camille had picked up the ferroconcrete bulwark (purpose-built to protect our yacht club from wind-driven water) and smashed the club to bits with it. Camille had so thoroughly devastated our village that, after the floods receded, I had difficulty locating our house. All that survived of it were five brick steps. My Hindustani was not up to explaining to Adi the force of these 'cataclysms', so I tore some paper from my diary and wrote a message to Awng Hkawng suggesting we evacuate to higher ground at once and tried to induce Maran Naw to take it to him. Maran Naw looked at me mutinously; then at Adi for support. Wasn't *Salang Kaba* off again on another of his looney-tune hallucinations? Adi heaped scorn on my alarm and went back to sleep.

Reckoning that we had a quarter of an hour's grace, at most, I got up, changed into my bathing costume and went myself to Awng Hkawng. He had heard my shouts of frustration and listened calmly. 'Cataclysm' was an exciting new idea for him but one that was altogether too fanciful insofar as *our* safety was concerned. Evacuation would oblige us to rebuild our *basha*s, he said. That would involve dragging wood at night, which would antagonize the *nat*s.

The river was now perhaps three yards from us. He could do as he liked, I said. I was shifting to higher ground.

'Then you had better go *there*,' he conceded, indicating a shelter built over some rocks at the edge of the forest whither the Lisu had shifted. I repeated my warnings about 'cataclysms' and urged him to *order* the others to move.

'It is all right. It is all right,' he said. 'You stay there with the Lisu. I will oversee everything.'

I went to the Lisu. Tu Lum had preceded me there and was stretched out in a channel in the rocks. I wedged myself in alongside him. He was shivering and, desperate for warmth, wrapped his legs and arms around me. Then, suddenly, he jerked violently and cried, '*Wawt*!' He jerked again. Now it was my turn. I plucked a leech from my forehead, then another. One crossed my face in what felt like a march of slime, then another. One stung me in the centre of my chin. It was to be a night unlike any I had ever experienced. Out of the forest they came with appetites sharpened by a lifetime of privation and maddened by the promise of our blood. I now realized why we had not camped higher up the beach in the first place.

I summoned my courage and resolved to get through it. *You will go to sleep, Shelby, and tomorrow you will carry on*! But phantoms rose up on all sides of me, gaining in reality and awfulness as the night wore on. The river was now too high to be forded, and the only exit was more *shat khat*s. Sooner or later, there would be another landslide, the next one fatal. Even were I to survive the *shat khat*s, we would exhaust our supplies of rice. We had provisions left for five or six days, at most. Seng Hpung would assume that we had outpaced the storm and already reached our destination; and, in any case, he would reason, he could do nothing for us. No one could blame him for abandoning us. He had the rest of the column to consider. He had advised me not to leave the elephants. What man in his right mind would walk across Burma? It was no achievement to cross this unforgiving, leech-bound land at the cost of a comfortable home and a beautiful wife who loved me. I remembered the 'darling' sequence of my many broken promises to Carole. 'If there's any *real* danger, *darling*, I'll turn back. No avoidable risk is acceptable, *darling*. ... Don't worry *darling*. ... There is really *nothing* to worry about, *darling*.' My modest, unpretentious house in Oxford, uncluttered, with rooms knocked into one and light pouring in through the Victorian windows onto sanded and polished timber floors and plastered walls lined with bookcases. Our yellow kitchen with fermenting, homemade wine emitting comforting blips, opening onto a flagstone patio and high walls clad in wisteria, grapevine, clematis, climbing roses and passion flower. Our back garden shaded by an old bramley. Our little community of Jen Teales, Roger Cashes and Gideon Upwards, a few Stowcrats among the Definitely-Disgustings, and my allotment across the street. Cosy, cloying, ridiculous domesticity suddenly assumed an astonishing importance to me – and pervading everything was my precious Carole. Carole in her apron. Carole on our aluminium stepladder in her size three wellies pruning the roses. Carole in the living room with no one to cook for, watching the Nine O'Clock News, *alone*! Carole who had trusted me unreservedly and invested everything in me – I would never see my dark-haired, brown-eyed Carole again. She would never know what had happened to me. I could never explain ... while, jack-knifing through their blind, slimy paces, the leeches swarmed all over us. '*To the thresholds of our dread ... In the nights when you must lie ... Heartsick for the Jungle's sake*.'

The pink light of dawn. The sound of Ata singing a familiar hymn. It had stopped raining. The leeches were gone. '*Awake! For Morning in the Bowl of Night, Has flung the Stone that puts the Stars to Flight*.' I wondered for a dizzying moment if I had already crossed over and was grateful (and a little surprised) that I had reached the right side. Ata was singing *What a Friend We Have in Jesus*, celebrating another day among these majestic mountains, and everywhere shadows were receding. What were a few leeches in the night to her? Leeches were part of Divine Creation too. She sang in Lisu, of course. I sang the first line of another hymn and looked at her as though to say, 'I'll bet you don't know *that* one.' She sang the rest of the hymn. I sang the first line of *Rock of Ages*, which, recalling my moment of peril on the cliff face, seemed entirely apt. She smiled condescendingly and sang it through too, and so on until I had exhausted my limited repertory. At no point did she hesitate or stumble over the words. She knew the text of every verse of every hymn.

Awng Hkawng told me later that, before the missionaries brought the Gospel to Kachinland, the Lisu used to be the most savage of all the Kachins. Ne Win's expulsion of the Morses, he said, took from them their shepherd.

Who were the Morses?

7
Hidden Valley

The text of Russell Morse's sermon on the Sunday morning in December 1965 when he announced to the congregation in their church in Muladi, a village about seven miles south of Putao, that the Rangoon junta had ordered him, his wife Gertrude and their family to leave Burma, was Matthew 10:23. 'When they persecute you in one town, flee to the next; for truly, I say to you, you will not have gone through all the towns of Israel, before the Son of Man comes.' The 500 Lisu in the congregation responded by singing in four-part harmony, 'He leadeth me, He leadeth me; by His own hand He leadeth me,' for they shared their elderly mentor's certainty that whatever happened to them was the will of God.

Sometimes God's will was obscure. Then Russell and Gertrude would consult Scripture for precepts and examples apposite to the decision confronting them. If a text did not comport with 'common sense' or prevailing orthodoxy, they deferred to it nevertheless, relying on the Lord to reveal its hidden truth to them in His own time. The mere fact that the expulsion order had issued from a hateful regime was not in itself sufficient reason to ignore it. Paul had faced this issue when the world was governed by pagans and answered it with Romans 13:1–3. 'Let every person be subject to the governing authorities', whom God had appointed as His 'servants' for 'our good'. Jesus had answered it with 'Render unto Caesar what is Caesar's.' But 'the governing authorities' had forbidden their adopted Tibetan daughter, Drema Esther, who was eight months pregnant, to accompany them on the aeroplane. Did the Lord really intend them to abandon her? It seemed strange, moreover, that God should want them to leave Burma.

They had served in the mission field for 45 years: first in Tibet (to assist the work of Dr Albert Shelton, who was murdered six weeks after they joined him); then among Tibetans and Lisu living on the Upper Mekong; then on the Upper Salween; eventually in Hkamti Long. Their children, Eugene (born 1921), Robert (born 1923) and LaVerne (born 1929), were as fluent in Tibetan, Yunnanese and various dialects of Rawang and Lisu as in English; and their grandchildren David, Joni, Tom, Stephen, Ron, Sam, Bobby, Deedee, Margaret, Marilyn, Jeannette, Camille, Genevieve and Lucy were already learning Rawang, Lisu, Jinghpaw and Burmese.

The only alternative to abandoning Drema Esther, within the ambit of the expulsion order, was to make for the Indian border and try to persuade the Indians to grant them entry. Russell and Gertrude were nearly 70 years old, and it was 70 miles to the border, over some of the most challenging mountains in Kachinland. But the Lord had seen them safely through other vicissitudes. In 1949 Russell had been seized and held for three years by the communists. All contact with him had been lost. Then, following a week of continuous prayer held for him in California, he had reappeared. Gertrude and LaVerne were in Hong Kong investigating his disappearance and had postponed their departure to explore a belated lead, when the missionary friend with whom they were staying received a local telephone call. 'This is J. Russell Morse,' said the caller. 'I have just arrived from China and wonder if you have any news of my family.' Now, as then, it was only a matter of consulting God's wishes and reposing their confidence in Him.

On a moonless night just before Christmas, they left Muladi, assisted by more than 100 Lisu porters. Half a mile away was a military police post; Burman officials had visited their compound a few hours before. They stole down the steep embankment behind their house to the Namlang River and picked their way delicately over the rocks along its bank to a place appointed for ferrying them across. Their porters were already crossing on the bamboo rafts assembled for that purpose, while the rare silence of the dogs on the west bank confirmed God's blessing on the enterprise. Their next task was a 4000-foot almost vertical climb. A few days later, at a junction of elephant trails and assisted by Eugene's wife, Helen, who was a trained nurse, Drema Esther was delivered of her baby.

Their next stop was a flood plain at the foot of the Chaukan Pass, where Robert was already negotiating with the Indians. The Indians procrastinated and, while they waited for a decision, other Lisu joined them – 5000 Lisu, a quarter of the population of Hkamti Long. As in the original Exodus story, some of the people began to grumble. All this talk about deliverance from Ne Win and his *Burmese Way to Socialism* – where was the milk and honey? Weren't they better off back in Hkamti Long? Beyond the next range of mountains was the Tawang Hka, but its flood plain, though rich in salt and game, was capable of supporting no more than 50 families. Forty miles to the west of the Tawang Hka was Hidden Valley, the domain of head-hunters and cannibals. Only two of a party of 50 Lisu who had gone hunting there some years before had survived. Again, they sought God's guidance. Then someone delivered them a message sent by Lisu they had taught in China offering them a home in Binuzu, alias Pinawng Zup.

Approaching Hidden Valley, with all its dark associations, the Morses experienced a momentary exhilaration.

> [We] sensed that we were free at last. We seemed to be at the top of creation, with open land spreading in every direction as far as the eye could see. How could anyone but God keep us from taming this land to our needs? It is difficult now, back in civilization, to evoke the sense of freedom that comes upon a man when he stands on a mountaintop and looks out over tens of thouands of acres of fertile and unexplored land in the valleys below. It is only then that a man knows that, given the wit and will to survive, he need not bow his head to any government, to any ideology, to any small-minded men who feel that they control the essentials of his existence.[1]

The Morses spent six years in Hidden Valley, but the most testing was the first. They had scarcely arrived when they heard elephants in the jungle near them trumpeting wildly. They turned up their radio, and the crackly sound of Alistair Cooke reading his 'Letter from America' drove away the danger. They lived on nuts,

1. Morse, 1975: 64–5.

birds' eggs, berry jam, wild fruit, honey, fish, sago and the detoxified pith of a tree fern called *ahteu*, a sodden, rotting and fermenting mess that tasted 'rather like some form of garden compost'. A few worms and bugs 'added protein', they would inform the congregations supporting them in America. The combs that the wild bees concealed in the high cliff faces supplied them with honey and wax. Once, as they hid in the forest to elude the Burma Army, lightning began to strike the trees around them, but to Robert and Betty's eldest son, Joni, the explanation was obvious:

> 'Satan is testing us. I wish Gabriel would knock his teeth in.' Just then ... lightning ... struck a tree [next to them], stripping it naked of bark clear to the ground [and t]hunder, erupting almost simultaneously, shook the ground. When the reverberations from the thunder died away, Joni's voice broke the tension. 'Thank you, Gabriel,' he said.[2]

In this wild setting the third-generation Morses grew up learning to distinguish edible and inedible leaves; to make gunpowder from charcoal, saltpetre and sulphur, and arrows tipped with aconite; how to entice deer within range of their crossbows by imitating their calls; and when a tiger was friendly or angry. They stalked gibbons, monkeys (which they called 'tree pork'), rats, deer and other antelope. Life in the jungle, nevertheless, remained tedious and claustrophobic, and, after the long monsoon, many of the Lisu left and returned to Hkamti Long.

> [S]urvival ... was as much a matter of mental attitude as of experience. ... [Y]ou needed a kind of pride, a feeling that nothing could defeat you. In many people, this pride was often coupled with a dream, a goal, a drive or a new life free of the fears and repressions they had suffered in Putao. But even this sense of pride and motivation was not enough without still something more: an openness to new

---

2. Morse, 1975: 79.

> experience, a willingness to improvise, [and] a capacity to trust in Providence.[3]

Eugene and Robert shifted their families from Binuzu to new clearings in the jungle further west: Eugene, to a place they named Ziyudi (Zion Plain), and Robert, to Chinquapin Hill, where his youngest daughter, Genevieve, was born. The Lord then tried their faith again, visiting on their crops a caterpillar pestilence. They tried to contain it with measures of their own devising, such as releasing their chickens into the fields.

> The chickens ate the caterpillars, but ... hardly a dent was noticeable in the caterpillar population. They just marched forward in a mad frenzy to eat all they could. ... [O]ne family ... went with baskets ... from early dawn till late at night, picking up the caterpillars. ... When one basket ... was full, they dug a hole and buried them. In just one day one family gathered three bushelfuls [*sic*], from only one field.[4]

It was not until they confessed their abject dependence on God's sustaining and preserving power and toured every field imploring Him to save them that the caterpillars departed, marching off as though under orders.

Russell was an accomplished horticulturist, and stocks from his nurseries already supplied citrus growers all over northern Burma. His skills were now put to use in Hidden Valley. The Lisu fetched cuttings from Hkamti Long, and he grafted them onto a local species of wild lemon. Grandson David made a generator out of a pair of magnets scavenged from the wreck of a Dakota by rigging them to a geared system of wheels driven by water sluiced through an aqueduct.

The Morses had other practical skills to contribute to the community. About 80 pupils attended schools that they opened in Ziyudi and Strawberry Hill, some commuting great distances through the jungle. There were three forms: kindergarten, middle

3. Morse, 1975: 93–4.
4. Morse, 1975: 121.

school and seniors, grouped according to prior education. Kindergarten included 16-year-olds and the senior school 10-year-olds. Drema Esther taught Bible, her husband, Jesse, English, and David, who at 18 was younger than some of the pupils, mathematics. David was reluctant at first to take on this responsibility, but Ziyudi's headman overcame his scruples: 'Most of the pupils in our school don't know their ABCs in Lisu, let alone in English. Instead of knowing arithmetic, they can't even count "one, two, three, four". If you know arithmetic and ... your ABCs, you already know plenty to be a teacher in our school!'[5] The school steadily expanded to six rooms and an office, accommodating a staff of six offering up to fifth standard (eighth grade) Bible, arithmetic, science, anatomy, history, geography, music, Burmese, Jinghpaw and English[6] to nearly 80 pupils. The pupils sat three together on wooden benches and wrote on banana leaves with pieces of slate. Their blackboards were slabs of chinquapin wood painted with a compound of egg whites and carbon from exhausted batteries. For chalk they used clay, refined, rolled into round strips and baked in the sun. Helen and a Lisu teacher worked up a series of English and Jinghpaw readers printed on paper with stencils and a Gestetner duplicator brought from Muladi. For the children's recreation, they made badminton rackets strung with fishing line, shuttlecocks of a wood resembling balsa and chicken feathers, and volleyballs of tanned deer hides and thread spun from hemp.

Meanwhile, the industrious brethren stripped the aluminium from the wrecks of Commandos and Dakotas that lay scattered about the forest, melted the aluminium into portable ingots, remelted it and poured it into moulds of sand and clay to produce bowls, kettles, pots, pans and spoons. Relatives and others visiting from Putao recognized the superiority of their kitchenware to the mass-produced products sold in their shops, and traders soon followed with cloth, tea, salt, canned foods, seasonings and

5. Morse, 1975: 160.
6. One of the most extraordinary experiences that Mats and I had crossing Kachinland was being addressed in clear, fluent English by a Lisu of Hidden Valley who had learned his English at the Morses' school in Ziyudi.

medicines to barter for it. God's presence was something that they sensed constantly.

> The moon was our natural calendar, just as the sun was our clock. Planting, hunting trips, journeys and assemblies were all governed by the phases of the moon. These natural measures of time seemed to us much more in accord with His plan for man than the mechanical devices by which man drives himself in most of the modern world.[7]

By the end of the harvest of the winter of 1968/9 their granaries were well stocked with rice, maize and yams. They had chickens and eggs, pork and wild game, *tsumu* (mushrooms), *peimu* (Latin *fritillaria*, a medicinal bulb prized by the Chinese), a medicinal root called *si chyee* and musk; and they exchanged their surpluses with an ever-increasing number of traders from Putao and Namyung. Christmas that year, which they called 'The 1968 Birthday Convention for Jesus' and celebrated in a harvested rice field at the base of Chinquapin Hill, was a festival of thanksgiving attended by Lisu from all parts of Hidden Valley, every village producing its own choir.

However, the Morses always knew that their days there were numbered. Too soon, they knew, they would have to submit again to 'the ideologies of small-minded men' who presumed 'to control the essentials of existence'. In 1969 Robert and Betty's house caught fire and burned down. The children's teeth required dentistry unavailable in Hidden Valley, and Betty was now suffering from acute arthritis and beriberi. She, Joni and her four younger children were the first to go. Joni took them over the border, where they were arrested and, after six weeks of more fruitless haggling with Indian officials, deported. Then the Yangmis left. Jesse had already begun his translation of the Scriptures into Lisu. He now enrolled in a Bible college in the United States, the better to equip himself for further work among the Rawang and Lisu. Meanwhile, the Burma Army, which was fighting the Nagas, came ever nearer. Other strangers appeared, Burmans and Indians sur-

7. Morse, 1975: 186.

veying the border; and some of the traders began to evince ambivalent loyalties.

Robert's other son, Stephen, left in 1971 by the same route as his mother, brother and sisters, and finally, not long afterwards, the remaining Morses left – after being arrested by a Burma Army column sent from Namyung.

A helicopter that landed on the volleyball court next to the school flew out Russell and Gertrude, Helen, her two youngest daughters, and Robert. Hundreds of Lisu assembled to wish them farewell with their characteristic double hand clasp, the equivalent of an embrace. 'Once more my father [Russell] chose the hymn traditional for such occasions: *He Leadeth Me*. ... [W]e then sang *God Be With You Till We Meet Again*. ... The wild freedom my children had learned to take for granted in Hidden Valley had suddenly been curbed by the gun of authority.'[8]

Eugene and his three sons and eldest daughter were marched out on foot down the Tarung Hka, which had already claimed the lives of three of their escorts, and, after some months in various prisons, they were finally deported from Burma. But that did not conclude their mission to the hill peoples. Robert completed a Rawang translation of the New Testament begun in Hkamti Long, then translated the Old. Jesse finished his Bible college course and completed a new Lisu translation of the Scriptures. Eugene and Helen, Robert, Jesse and Drema Esther went to Chiang Mai and established the North Thailand Christian Mission, which today includes a tribal children's hostel accommodating more than 300 children drawn from the Lahu, Akha, Lisu and other hill communities nearby. After adjusting to a world in all ways stranger than the wild jungles and 'monkey people'[9] of their upbringing (devices like doorknobs baffled them at first), most of the third-generation Morses joined their parents in their new work. The Yangmis' eldest son married a Christian Lahu, David a nurse who worked with them as a volunteer, Joni a Rawang Christian whom he had known since childhood, and Eugene and Helen's second daughter, Marilyn, a Lisu evangelist. Robert and Betty's youngest

8. Morse, 1975: 211, 217.
9. Term of opprobrium sometimes used of Lisu by Burmans.

son, Bobby, married a Chinese Christian and now runs the children's hostel.

Although Russell and Gertrude were 77 and 76 when deported from Burma, they continued in their vocation to the end, spending their sunset years raising funds to enable their progeny to carry on the work they had begun. She died in 1977, and he in 1991.

For six years, then, this unassuming but exceptionally brave and devout family ministered to the Lisu of Hidden Valley, and their work there continues through those to whom they have handed on.[10] 'Perhaps the most tangible evidence of our contribution', suggests Eugene ingenuously, 'was that fruit trees were now blooming in Hidden Valley'.[11] And what effect had Hidden Valley on them?

> After gazing out across the snow-capped top of the world, we find the concrete horizons of even the greatest of cities limited. After living in houses open to wind and weather, we feel stifled in the airtight boxes that are the wonder of modern architecture. After sharing a simple Christian fellowship with our Lisu friends, we are put off by the complexities of religion in the Western world. But, wherever God leads us in the future, we feel grateful to Him that He gave us these years of hard but rewarding service in one of the most spectacular regions of all His creation.[12]

* * *

We broke camp and plunged at once into another Gehenna of leeches. 'Better move fast,' counselled Awng Hkawng, briskly plucking them from his trousers. 'They even drop on you from above!' I would detach 87 of them from me before the day ended. We made only half a mile that day.

The river receded during the night, and the following morning,

10. Compare 2 Timothy 2:2. 'What you have heard from me ... entrust to faithful men who will be able to teach others also' (Revised Standard Version).
11. Morse, 1975: 208.
12. Morse, 1975: 223–4.

the wonderfully mind-concentrating war with the leeches resumed. We were a little more hopeful.

We climbed an escarpment where the footholds were loose shingle or crumbly earth, only to find a rock face on reaching the top. A jump of some five feet onto a knife-edged shaft of mossy stone offered a way around it. One of the men, while declining to attempt the jump himself, urged me to try, but I prudently held back. Ati found another way. However, it led to another rock face. Adi, sedated by opium, bounded up it obliviously and beckoned the rest of us to follow, but Awng Hkawng, agreeing with me for once, judged it to be too dangerous and told the men to fell a tree and fit a monkey ladder. Once this was in place, Adi dropped a vine to us.

At the next cliff, I gave my pack to Adi, backsided down a chute, swam across a narrow backwater and lay down on the beach beyond to dry myself in the sun. It was a moment to take stock while the others made their way slowly over the cliff. The sand below me was firm and warm. The sky above me was clear as glass. There were no leeches. I closed my eyes – and opened them to a kind of heavenly choir. John, Alex, Paul, Philip and Mats, all dressed in shorts and carrying only shoulder bags, like a party of day trippers on a weekender, were shouting at me from the edge of the escarpment above the backwater. The main column had caught up with us.

That evening Awng Hkawng brooded. He had failed to fetch me to India before my visa expired. Nevertheless, he conceded, we had shared a 'big adventure', however pointless.

'Weren't you worried that we might have died?' I asked.

'Not worry,' he said.

'In any other army you would have been court-martialled for constantly buzzing off and leaving the rest of us to follow, willy-nilly.'

'Willy-nilly?'

I explained.

'My main concern is *you*!' he retorted, pointing out what was undeniable: that at all critical junctures I had been the problem. 'I ask myself, if the rotten bush is strong enough for my weight, is it also strong enough for you?'

Next day, a Sunday, the beaches were longer and the *shat khat*s less awesome, although once, in over-confident mood, my foot slipped on a glassy wall of rock and only the traction of my weight prevented me from slipping over the edge.

The elephants revived the option of avoiding such risks by fording the river, and, watching them now, it seemed to me extraordinary that we had been so rash as to attempt the Tawang Hka without them. They plunged majestically into the river at the *oozie*s' bidding, carrying men on their heads and rumps and towing still others clinging to their *waw*s and *wum bat*s, never once evincing the least displeasure at all these parasites. What was a feat of extreme daring for us, was to them a casual stroll in their ponderous trek through life. Their superior height, strength and weight and their four legs enabled them to ford at much greater depths and against much stronger currents than we could manage. With their trunks they explored the always-tricky bottom before committing themselves, and, whenever need arose, they were superb swimmers. After each crossing, the *oozie*s would about-turn them to fetch stragglers. However, we had already advanced so far up the Tawang Hka that we soon found that we were able to ford the river again unaided.

By early afternoon we were tramping over a broad flood plain bounded by low, round hills through a forest of poplars. We halted for lunch on a sandy beach, where a small but robust tributary joined the Tawang Hka from the east. We had entered the southern end of Empty Valley and were nearing Yangmi Junction, where the Morses had camped and received the message inviting them to Binuzu. Awng Hkawng said that a village had stood here once, but recurrent avalanches had eliminated all trace of it. A party of Lisu overtook us. They told us that they had been looking for a place to resettle where the Burma Army would not trouble them.

A crowd of young admirers gathered around Ata that evening. They were like young people anywhere, but far from wine bars and discos their bright young faces shone with a freshness and innocence all their own. Ata presided over them like royalty, the Queen of Young Hearts, her shapely body straining the buttons of a jungle green shirt patched with the insignia of the KIA that one of her subjects had bestowed on her. I told her that in Europe and America she would be celebrated as the girl who skipped fearlessly up rock faces with a pack lashed to her head and a sword slung over her back, singing hymns.

Adi prepared an excellent site for us on soft sand, and I stayed awake a long time wondering if I should write a book about our adventure and what I would call it. *Baw Hpraw Gam in Wunpawng Mungdan*? More simply, *Among the Wunpawng*? The Tawang Hka, I decided, would require a special chapter. *With the Queen of Young Hearts on the Tawang Hka*? Even Awng Hkawng admitted that the Tawang Hka was 'special'.

We rose before dawn and dressed in darkness. A party of scouts moved out of camp before the rest of us. We were a march away from the Putao–Namyung *lam*, and, if we were to be ambushed, this was the most likely sector.

The sun rose, the sky was clear, and all went smoothly until we reached a gorge where the river was too deep and the current too swift for the elephants to ford. The elephants left us to find a way through the forest. Later, we halted to wait for them. The volcanic cones of Bumpa (Barrel-shaped) Bum and Matsihku (Tabletop) Bum emerged from a nimbus of cloud to exhibit momentarily their wild, inaccessible beauty.

There was a long delay. Two men were sent back to investigate. They returned and reported that there was no trace of the elephants. Seng Hpung consulted Adi, who had lain down on the sun-bleached beach with a mug of tea beside him, his head thrown back against some stones and partially concealed by exhalations of opium smoke. In his euphoria, Adi had only the most optimistic advice to impart: the elephants would arrive 'soon'; they were very resourceful and many alternative routes were open to them.

Another worrying hour and a half passed. Then the elephants filed into camp, wet up to their panniers but trumpeting their own triumphant welcome. Having failed to find a *shat khat* on the east bank, they had swum the river below the gorge and found a route up the west bank. We resumed the march, harbouring that evening among some poplars near the ruins of a Lisu village.

The *oozie*s awakened us next morning before dawn with their shouts of 'Shoo! Shoo!' and 'Tut! Tut!' and we carried on, now walking barefoot, while the elephants proceeded in the river, so that anyone who found our depressions would think that we were nothing more sinister or complex than an exceptionally large band of Lisu on the move. Puffs of white cloud floated in a pale blue sky, and monkeys frolicked in the bush.

We halted for breakfast at a *zup* – probably the very spot where the Yangmis had established a depot to assist the exodus from Muladi. Nothing grew there save some struggling strands of *theke* grass, while huge, ugly landslides scarred all the hills about.

At about 1100 hours, now westbound on the Putao–Namyung *lam*, we crossed a bridge, not the usual withy of driftwood but two massive trees that had been cleaned and fitted with a rail to provide a crossing above the flood line (the Lisu's version of an all-weather bridge). Then, leaving the elephants to continue by the river, we began the long ascent over Shiransam Bum.

Five hours later, we were again among rhododendrons, and tiny, blue, bell-shaped flowers (Campanulas?) carpeting islands of sunlight, and could hear again the clear, clean, crisp noises of birdsong and wood snapping beneath our feet. The lads broke ranks and began eagerly pulling up plants, stripping them of the stalks and eating them voraciously. '*Salang Kaba*! *Salang Kaba*!' they shouted in their frisky, proud impatience to show me another esoteric delicacy. It tasted like celery blended with rhubarb.

We harboured that night in cloud, in a clearing in a forest of dwarf trees strewn with the charred wood of dead campfires, and here, for the first time, filled our *hka nhtung*s in the Tarung Hka (River of Death). Seng Hpung, in better spirits now that the Tawang Hka was behind us, said that he had been thinking about what Mats and I should do after we crossed the border.

'It seems to me we have three choices,' I said. 'The first is to present ourselves to the authorities in Vijayanagar and ask them for permission to proceed to Delhi. The second is to make for the airport and try to board a flight out, hoping that no one will challenge us. The third is to by-pass Vijayanagar altogether and make directly for Miau.'

'Where's Miau?' he asked.

'Twelve miles from the Assam line. Once in Assam, we can board a train for Delhi. Assam is a restricted area, but so many European technicians work there that we would probably go unremarked. Ati says that a Lisu can walk from Pinawng Zup to Miau in five days but that it would take us nine and that the path passes a police post at a place called Sherdi, where everyone's papers are checked. There is no way of evading this post, he says. However, he also discourages the airport idea. He says that there is only one aeroplane a week and that no one can board it without a permit. He thinks that our best hope is to give ourselves up and appeal to the *bara sahib* for clemency.'

'Who is the *bara sahib*?' asked Seng Hpung.

'He's head of the Special Branch of Arunachal Pradesh Police. Ati says that he comes to Vijayanagar in a helicopter, not like the other policemen.'

'How does he know?'

'He says that he works for Special Branch.'

If Ati worked for the Indian police, what was he doing with our column?

* * *

We marched all next day and camped on damp ground on the north bank of the Tarung Hka, now a boiling torrent. The site, which even the stoical Awng Hkawng (who chose it) disavowed, was full of mosquitoes. 'Where are Adi and the Lisu?' I asked him.

'They have gone ahead. They told me we would spend tonight in Pinawng Zup. They have no idea of time or distance.'

'Where are the elephants?' I asked.

'They will arrive.'

They will arrive. But what if they *did not*? What *was* the point of outpacing them? I felt the chill of a fever coming on, and my pullover, anorak, sleeping bag and even our *plastik*s were with the elephants. They would never find their way at night. The air was heavy with precipitation. Our fires gave off more smoke than heat and had to be fanned continuously to keep them alight at all, and everything that we touched smelled of mildew. I tried to help Tu Lum and Maran Naw collect more firewood, but the few pieces I contributed were so rotten they crumbled with handling. My left ankle was inflamed from leech bites, and a cane-gored gash in the calf of my right leg was septic. There was swelling, too, around a scar on my right leg, and for several weeks I had been suffering from dysentery and praying that I would be spared the dreaded scrub typhus. Now this.

A dinner of rice and soup improved matters somewhat, but afterwards the shivers resumed. *KIA take care of everything*. Yes, I thought, but what could they do about my coming down with a fever? It would start raining soon, and we had not even put up *basha*s. The rain would put out the fire, and without a fire? We sullenly swatted mosquitoes and waited. Then we saw them, a wall of massive shadows moving through the black foliage and into our circle of light, eyes half-closed, ears flapping unconcernedly, now ringed by men noisily retrieving packs, and, almost at once, the skies broke. It rained most of the night, but I was warm in my sleeping bag and protected by the *plastik*, confident that I would live on for another day. We were too high here for leeches.

It was still raining next morning when we broke camp. Everyone protected himself as best he could. Seng Hpung was resplendent in hat and American field jacket under an umbrella. Once, slanting down a disingenuous rock face, I slipped and tore the palm of my left hand and received a blow to my head. Once, rocks whizzed past my head. Awng Hkawng shouted to keep my head down, and Ata, predictably, roared with laughter, as though to say, 'Revered Elder, it is only a landslide.'

We left the Tarung Hka, tramped over soggy ground through more leech-infested forests, and, shortly before sundown, reached a mud flat a little to the west of where the Pinawng Hka spilled into the Tarung Hka. This was our destination – Pinawng Zup, Binuzu, the Eldorado of all our labours since leaving Second Brigade headquarters, eerily silent and unimposing after our many anticipations. Awng Hkawng commandeered a barn as shelter from the rain, and John and Alex joined us there. I was glad of their roistering company.

* * *

Dawn brought another grey, drizzly day and the melancholy news that the elephants had not arrived. Dense, black cloud filled Hidden Valley. Five tiger leeches attached themselves to me *en route* to the *nam dum*. It was now the last day of March, the limit of the time advised to Carole for reaching India.

As noted in my diary, a delegation of Lisu elders visited our camp that morning.

> They are solid, respectable men, with open faces and forthright manners, most of them Church of Christ pastors. They have come from Adehdi, a village on the escarpment above Pinawng Zup, and other parts of [Hidden Valley] to confer with our leaders. Our visit poses awkward problems for them. Pinawng Zup lies midway between Putao and Namyung, and both of those places are garrisoned by the Burma Army, which, if it learns of our presence, might send a punitive expedition. Even showing ourselves to their own people entails a risk, for some of the traders who come here are spies. Therefore, they want us to leave and, pending departure, to hide. Their lack of enthusiasm for the KIA contrasts sharply with the keen support that we have found everywhere else. They even refuse to help us to find a guide. Money is not the issue. 'We value our freedom more than money,' they told me. There is a spring about an hour this side of the pass, they said. I will have to travel by day to avoid the tigers that hunt by night. The Assam Rifles patrol the path, and if they catch me they will lock me up and *whip* me, which seems preposterous. ... Mats and I have decided that I will proceed to Vijayanagar without him and that, failing to hear from me within three days, he will avoid Vijayanagar and make directly for Miau.

The elephants arrived that afternoon, having swum the river half a dozen times. One of them had capsized, and his *oozy* had nearly drowned. Next morning, April Fool's Day, we left for the border.

We passed through Adehdi, where Russell and Gertrude Morse had lived for their first two years in Hidden Valley. As we tramped past its houses, which were grander and more sophisticated than any we had seen since leaving China (one of them even had a glazed window), a gap in the cloud cover indulged us a view of Lohpa Bum, far to the south but looking so near that it might topple over on us. Wisps of cloud caressed its icy rocks and seams of eternal snow. The Kachins call it 'Master Lohpa Bum'.

> Another muddy, slippery path obstructed by fallen trees and tangled, dead bamboo. More rocks shifting as you step on them; more roots and vines ensnaring your feet. And always

> leeches — hair-fine when they squeeze through your button–holes, and bloated and squashy when you remove them. The hollow of my navel has a special attraction for them. All the enthusiasm felt during those first weeks after leaving Pajau Bum seems to have deserted me. The jungle, once so rich with wonder, is now full of dread. Then it was always luminous, pierced by limpid shafts of tawny light slanting through its cindery foliage. Now it is perpetually dark: dripping, mouldy, leech-infested; the caterwauling of black gibbons, the hoarse cry of a peacock, the crash of an elephant plunging through bamboo or tearing up a banana palm, all smothered by a dripping, gloomy forest. A tree soaring a hundred yards into the sky still excites interest, but not the intense, romantic fascination that I felt during those first weeks. I remind myself with every painful step that it *is* the *very last* mountain! I have to remind myself, too, that the ten soldiers in tattered T-shirts and Chinese plimsolls worn through and exposing the toes, rolling strips of newspaper into slug-shaped cigarettes, are *not* savages.

We were climbing Monkey Tree Hill, where the Robert Morses and Yangmis lived before they moved to Chinquapin Hill.

We stopped for a *preekop*, but, as I was pondering whether to take off my boots and remove the ganglion of leeches feeding at my ankles, the soldiers suddenly began shouting, 'Yup! Yup!' up, up, greatly amused by the idea that they were speaking English. *Magwi*, they explained, laughing uproariously. The elephants had been unable to negotiate the ravine above Adehdi and we were going back there — April Fool!

We went back. Twice I slipped and fell on my bottom in the mud. *The old man has slipped and fallen on his arse again. Have you ever seen anything so funny*?

The rest of the column was dispersed along the bottom of the ravine, all ready to take up the joke. Carole was now scarcely more than a telephone call away. Muddied and irascible, I went over to Ati and asked him to take me over the pass. Seng Hpung winced — and I suddenly remembered the Nat of Wound River. Seng Hpung had his own reasons for sending me on as soon as possible. He had already made the arrangements, and, a few

Our column's second-in-command, Captain Awng Hkawng.

Elephants fording the Tawang Hka.

Farewell to Seng Hpung at Camp Mound of Blessings.

The Four Adeus in jungle near the Vijayanagar Track.

Pradip, Mats, Sanjay, guard, author, HP sauce, Mej and Prem Bahadur at Changlang Rest House.

KNU and DAB Chairman, Bo Mya, 1990.

Above: ABSDR recruits undergoing training by KNLA, Manerplaw.

Below: Carole and author on their wedding day, Zanzibar, 1976.

minutes later, I left for the pass with Awng Hkawng, Ati, Adi, Paul, Tu Lum and Maran Naw.

That night we harboured by the spring that the Lisu elders had told us about, which must have been very near to the site where the Robert Morses and Yangmis had built their houses. Tu Lum and Maran Naw set up a separate *dap* for me. Paul joined me, eschewing the excitement around Awng Hkawng's *dap*. 'Where is your raincoat?' he asked. I used my poncho as a groundsheet. 'I gave it to Seng Hpung,' I replied. He found some leaves, toasted them over the fire, fetched his plastic raincoat, his proudest possession, and spread it over the leaves. I offered the Lisu the remains of the noodles and raisins I had bought in Dali, but they would not eat food that was unfamiliar to them. Paul sat with me for a long time, talking of his ambitions to learn Chinese, Japanese, French and German after perfecting his English. 'Then I can go everywhere,' he said sweetly.

Next morning it was still raining. Maran Naw, his shirt drenched from sorties to the spring, was preparing our breakfast, as usual. I returned his torch, a ritual, re-enacted now for the last time that we had played out each morning since my torch had packed up at Camp Tawang Hka 3 and Awng Hkawng had ordered him to supply his. Tu Lum was in the forest scavenging wood to stoke the fires. Adi was deep in his addict's heaven under his *plastik*. Awng Hkawng was reading the Scriptures, beside him a cup of tea prepared by Maran Naw – all reassuringly familiar. My unonerous chores this morning, as every morning with the KIA, were to dress, roll up my sleeping bag and repack my rucksack. Then Awng Hkawng said: 'The border is about an hour from here. What do you want to do? Ati and Ata are going to Vijayanagar, and you can go with them. But I warn you again, if the Indians catch you, they will beat you and they will put you in prison, the Lisu say for two years, maybe longer. Maybe they will never release you.' Notwithstanding N Chyaw Tang's advice that the Indians had kept him for two years, I had a naïve confidence that they would treat me differently (like those waiting rooms in Indian railway stations reserved 'for Europeans only'). In any case, I believed that torture was not in my stars. I repeated what Mats and I had decided.

Thus just over an hour later, at precisely 1020 hours Burma time, by Awng Hkawng's watch, on 2 April 1989, I reached the cresting, jutting peaks of the Patkai divide and so achieved my dream of 27 years. Whatever now lay in store for me, *I had walked across Burma*.

'Here, we say God bless you,' said Awng Hkawng. I presented to him my Lonely Planet *China: A Travel Survival Kit*, a gift I had planned at Second Brigade headquarters when he borrowed it from me, and inscribed it: TO CAPTAIN AUNG HKAWNG, VALIANT WARRIOR, DISTINGUISHED GENEALOGIST AND THEOLOGIAN, AND COMPANION OF THE ORDER OF THE TAWANG HKA. FROM SLG. KABA BAW HPRAW GAM. 'I want you to remember me for something other than all the grief that I caused you,' I said. Ati snapped a picture of us straddling the ridgeline and, as though to mark the moment, the sun broke through the clouds.

We were now just Adi, Ata and myself. We did not halt again until we reached the far side of a small river at the base of the mountain, which might have been the Noa Dihing, when, suddenly, Ati whispered, 'Wait here.' He climbed the bank and cautiously peered beyond it; then he turned and beckoned Ata and me to follow. We silently followed him onto a road marked with tyre treads and with stacks of sawn timber piled on its verges; then, after sighting the goal posts of a football pitch, to an unused barn standing alone in what had been cultivated land but was now forest. He and Ata left me there. I did not know that I would not see her again.

Ati returned a few hours later with a Lisu whom he introduced pseudonymously as Noah. Noah, who made a meal for us, looked to be in his fifties but might have been older and, though he had come to Vijayanagar through the Chaukan Pass in the first wave of Lisu to flee Hkamti Long, he spoke no more than a rudimentary Hindustani. He seemed to fear and despise the Indians and, once he established that I understood what he was saying, repeated over and again, 'They are very, very bad men.' I never succeeded in learning *how* the Indians were very bad men, but to Noah the *cause* of their evil ways admitted of no doubt: they were pagans.

The following morning passed in great anguish, for I was now three days beyond the time Carole expected to hear from me.

Ati visited us again that afternoon and now brought with him two other Lisu, one of whom had also worked for 'Special'. He advised me to return to Hidden Valley. The Indians would not understand about my wife's fears, he said. They would not accept that I had demonstrated good faith by obtaining a visa. None of it would make any sense to them. The Indians were pagans, repeated Noah. On no account must I go into Vijayanagar.

It was the same the next day, with the added complication that I now had a boil on the heel of my right foot. Boil or no, my companions were united in their conviction that I must go back to Burma. I quarrelled with them. It would only be 'for a season', they said, pronouncing these words in English. 'But you haven't explained *why* I should go back, or *how* the Indians are bad men, or *why* they would imprison me and beat me,' I objected.

They spoke between themselves to make sure they had understood me correctly. Then Noah said, 'The Lord will give us an answer.' He referred me to the Epistle of James, chapter 1, verses 5–8,[13] and suggested that we leave off talking about what I should do and pray for guidance.

'What if I can't walk?' I asked.

'The Lord will provide a means to transport you,' replied Noah.

As we were arguing back and forth in this manner, a small party of Lisu arrived and delivered a chitty from Seng Hpung. It said simply, 'I suggest that you return to Burma,' and was signed with his Christian name, 'James'.

'You see?' said Noah. 'God gives us an answer.'

* * *

Next morning before dawn, uncomprehending and dejected, I left with Ati and two other Lisu to return to Burma. I was now five days beyond the 'expect to hear from me by' date advised to Carole and knew that this detour would prolong her fears for another ten days at least. I wrote to her again ('Have met with

---

13. 'If any of you lacks wisdom, let him ask God, who gives to all men generously and without reproach, and it will be given him. But let him ask in faith, with no doubting, for he who doubts is like a wave of the sea that is driven and tossed by the wind ... unstable in all his ways.'

temporary obstacle. Can't explain, but don't worry. Just know that I am safe and in good hands') and gave the letter to Noah to post for me. Would he understand its urgency and know how to get it past the Indians?

We crossed the playing fields. Smoke rising from some houses caused me a moment's hesitation. Wasn't I merely deferring a problem that would resurface as soon as I reached the *mawdaw lam*? Awng Hkawng had said that if I ran into 'obstacles' the KIA would send me by 'another way'. What was this mysterious 'other way'? Why not break ranks and go for it?

Dawn came slowly through cloud as we crossed the river and started to climb, but the leeches were curiously inactive, and the boil wasn't all that painful. I reproached myself for resigning my rucksack to a porter. It somehow seemed wrong, effete and self-indulgent. Noah had persuaded me to accept the porter's help, presenting him to me as the Lord's provision for my lameness. My thoughts kept reverting to my options. The man who had worked for 'Special' had confirmed that a unit of Assam Rifles garrisoned Sherdi. He had also said, however, that there were other routes over the Patkai that joined the road to Miau west of Sherdi: routes from Adehdi via a place called Geu Sadi that could be done in 11 stages, and down the Tarung Hka via Midi (Mile Long Plain), Sadodi (Three Stream Plain), Geudi and Ngalung Ga that entered India somewhere east of the Ledo road.

We reached the pass early that afternoon and soon found the column. It had shifted to the site near the spring and transformed it into a small village that Seng Hpung later christened Wun Gaw Kawng (Mound of Blessings) complete with latrines; the lads were putting the finishing touches to a capacious house for him. No one paid any special attention to me, merely reciprocating my greetings, as though I had never been away. Seng Hpung, who was with a delegation of Lisu elders, looked up and said, 'I'm glad you decided to come back. It was in your best interest. We will find a way for you that is not so dangerous. You will leave tomorrow, but I want first to be sure you will be safe.' He informed me that Mats would be going with me. I was pleased. I had missed Mats's counsel and valued his support in moments of danger. Our bickering had nothing to do with my respect for him.

'The Lisu say that there is a route that joins the *mawdaw lam* five days east of Miau and avoids the military post at Sherdi,' I said.

'We are discussing these matters just now,' replied Seng Hpung. 'I will let you know what I think is best for you.'

That evening paranoia romped triumphant. I accepted that Seng Hpung *wanted* to send us on. However, I knew also that he had the safety of the column to consider. If the Indians caught us and thought we were narcotics traffickers, gem smugglers or gun-runners supplying one of their insurgent groups, like the Nagas or ULFA, or suspected we were linked in some way to the Chinese, they might alert the Burma Army, putting the column in jeopardy. I confided my fears to Mats. 'In persuading me to come back,' I said, 'the Lisu used an odd expression, which they must have got from Ati, who must have reported back to Seng Hpung after leaving me with Noah. My returning to Burma would only be "for a season", they said. What did they mean? Did they mean until the column leaves to go back to Second Brigade headquarters? Maybe Seng Hpung intends to return us to Second Brigade headquarters?' 'Du Kaba has kept all his other promises to us,' Mats reminded me, sensibly.

Seng Hpung summoned us shortly before noon next day, having spent the morning discussing our options with some Lisu elders. Nevertheless, I remained convinced he intended to keep us in Burma. 'It occurs to me that we do not need to burden the KIA further with our problems,' I said. 'The river at the foot of the mountain leads straight to Sherdi. If we leave now, we could reach it before sundown, then continue along it in the dark, reaching Sherdi by noon tomorrow. I can't imagine the river route taking us much more than a night. Sherdi is only nine miles from Vijaya-nagar by road, and I'm confident we'll be able to sneak past the Assam Rifles posted there. We haven't learned anything from the KIA if we haven't learned how to avoid detection!'

'I would prefer you not do this,' he replied gently, and presented a plan that he had worked up with the Lisu elders. We would leave after lunch, harbour until sundown in a house above Adehdi, and pass Adehdi, Hkalue and Hkasher after dark. It was, he stressed, of paramount importance for both the column's security and to avert reprisals against the Lisu that no one should see us. San Awng, Philip, Paul and one of the elders would accompany us as far as Hkasher and hand us over to some Lisu there, who would take us on to the *mawdaw lam*. The Lisu would carry my rucksack and some of Mats's things as well. They would set up camp each night, supply all food, do all the cooking and cleaning up, lay in wood and stoke the fire at night. The all-in cost, including rice sufficient for our onward trek to Miau, would be Rs 800/–, payable to the elders now for handing over to our guides upon presentation of our written release.[14] 'They wanted to charge you nothing, but I have insisted on paying them,' said Seng Hpung. 'And we won't release you unless you agree to let us pay them. As long as you are in the KIA's protection, the KIA will take care of you. We have discussed all possibilities, and I believe that this is the best plan for you and Mats. I hope you agree.'

'Please ask them to pray for our safety,' I said. The elders seemed pleased with this reply.

We had shared with Seng Hpung something few men would ever know, and parting with him was not easy. His last words to us, characteristic of his warm but practical concern for us throughout, were to counsel us never again to couch our concerns in terms of a woman's fears for our safety. 'This kind of talk makes a man look ridiculous,' he said. He would stay at Camp Mound of Blessings until the rains ended in September.

Everything now went as planned. We were taken to a house that was like all the others in which we had sheltered (chickens strutting the ground beneath the floor; a hog fattening in a pen; a *yi* guarded by some very odd-looking scarecrows but sprouting the first green shoots of the new season), while our companions went ahead to make the onward arrangements. They returned to fetch us as night fell, bearing the butchered remains of a pig they were taking back to the column. It was a moonless night, with an overhang of low cloud, and our silent, torchless procession through Adehdi (*adeh*, type of bamboo, and *di*, flat place) seemed a little spooky. We could hear voices in all the houses. Later,

14. As the journey would take at least eight days (allowing for our guides' return trip), this amounted to Rs 25/– or about £1 per guide, per day, including their food.

passing through Hkalue (Old Village), some people talking on a veranda sensed our shadowy presence and fell silent. Then we heard someone hailing us from an unlit house, saw his shadowy silhouette and stopped. As he drew closer, I recognized him as one of the elders from Camp Mound of Blessings. He was called John and, strangely, spoke English.

Outside Hkasher (New Village) we stopped again, and another, younger man joined us. His name was Adeu, and he spoke Hindustani. San Awng, Philip and Paul now handed us over to John and Adeu and left to return to the Mound of Blessings. I gave Philip my Swiss Army knife, which he had often admired. It was a trifling recompense for his many kindnesses, but he would have been insulted by the offer of money, and I had nothing else to give him. We would not see them again, at least as KIA soldiers in uniform. We spent the night luxuriously in a *dum* about 20 minutes beyond Hkasher. Adeu found two large mats and, clearing some straw from a platform, spread one of them for us and the other on the ground for John and himself. It was already 2300 hours, and everyone went rather suddenly to sleep.

* * *

When we woke next morning, Adeu (hereafter 'Adeu Hkasher') had already built a fire and prepared some diluted cane syrup for us. While we were drinking this *chai* (his Hindustani derived from a childhood spent in Vijayanagar), another Lisu appeared. He was also called Adeu and thereby became 'Adeu Hunter', to distinguish him from Adeu Hkasher. He was a lean, powerfully built man of 39 with a wisp of mandarin moustache and beard and was armed with a crossbow and a quiver of poison-tipped arrows. His straight, sharp nose and alert, almond-shaped eyes gave an immediate impression of intelligence and self-assurance. He wore a shabby, old KIA cap, which, I learned later, was a legacy of conscripted service with the KIA. Another Lisu, Afoi, now arrived. His responsibility was to fetch two men from Midi who knew the way to the *mawdaw lam* and bring them to Geu Sadi (Winter Green Tree Field). He and John would leave us at Geu Sadi and return to the Mound of Blessings to report to the other elders.

We broke camp as soon as Afoi joined us and laboured uphill

for the better part of two hours, not stopping until we reached a brook, where we made another fire and ate roasted rice cakes and rice flavoured with strips of dried beef and drank more diluted cane syrup. Mats's ankles were already swelling badly, but he was too proud to let the Lisu carry his rucksack. 'I don't feel the pain as much after walking,' he said. Adeu Hunter found a cinnamon tree and extracted some of its root for us to eat, pointing out that the root was the most succulent part. Unlike the Jinghpaws, I noticed, none of these men smoked.

After this pleasant breakfast, we carried on warily, as we had now rejoined the main Namyung *lam*. Once, John went forward to confound a party of traders bound for Putao, while the rest of us took cover. Luckily, they did not see us. Afoi left us, and, shortly afterwards, we abandoned our path and cut a way through prickly bamboo down a steep hill to Sadi (Old Field), a substantial village in the Morses' day but now overwhelmed by jungle and wasps, its orchard grown rank in tall grasses and its church a heap of timbers eaten through with termites.

We reached Geu Sadi late that afternoon. It was a smelly, black, marshy flat full of tiger leeches, tucked into a bend of the Kindrin Hka. The village that once stood there had become uninhabitable and three youths, John's nephews, were clearing the site for a new village. Some of the tree stumps were still smouldering. The first paddy would not be planted before the onset of the rains and the first house not built until after the rains. Meanwhile, they had sunk *wara hpaw* into the soft ground, tied a bamboo platform to them and roofed it with thatch. We spread our things on the floor of the platform, and that night I slept untroubled for the first time in a week.

Next morning began idly in the quietly gaining and reassuring realization that we were now irrevocably India-bound. Afoi was to fetch the guides to us here, and, while we waited for them, we passed the time talking with John about the Morses, to whose school at Ziyudi he owed his English. He told us that Ziyudi was on our route, but all that remained of it were some lemon trees whose fruit was bitter. He said that all of the Morses spoke Lisu fluently and brought many Lisu to Christ and that Robert's sons, Joni and Stephen, used to hunt tiger and elephant, once going as far as Namyung. 'They shot elephants for their tusks and traded the ivory in India for salt and soap,' he said. 'Robert continued working as a missionary after he left us, but he is now a professor of English in Kunming, and Russell is still living, although he has lost the use of his legs.'[15]

Afoi, who had pledged to rejoin us ere we finished breakfast, was as good as his word, but he brought disappointing news. He had found only one of the two men who knew the way over Patkai; the other man was somewhere in the forest. I perceived a difficulty. If we were to be a man short, I would have to carry my rucksack, which, considering my lameness, seemed unwise. John proposed that we take his nephews with us, stating that he would make up the deficiency himself were he not already committed to report to the elders at the Mound of Blessings. The two younger nephews would accompany us only for a day, he said, but the older one (Adeu Nephew) would continue with us to the *mawdaw lam*. They were superb fishermen and would supply our meal that evening, he said. Knowing that it would take us at least four days to reach the *mawdaw lam*, another five days to reach Miau, and at least three more days for our escort to return to Geu Sadi, I perceived a further difficulty. Did we have enough rice? Adeu Hkasher replied sternly that, if need be, Lisu could do without rice.

The anticipated guide now arrived and was greeted with a fanfare of cheers. His name too, astoundingly, was Adeu, and we would call him Adeu Guide.[16] He was old and frail, with a sallow face and a loose, protruberant tooth, which he tested continuously by prodding with his tongue. We had expected a younger man. Our misgivings, however, were soon dispelled. Adeu Guide had hunted in these forests all his life and was utterly fearless.

Our route from Geu Sadi followed the Kindrin to its confluence with the Kanmachyi (Belly Ache) Hka[17] and continued north to the Kindrin's headwaters along what the Lisu call the Muhpa Lo (Big Valley River).

---

15. Russell died three years before this conversation. Robert died in March 1993.
16. The Lisu number their sons chronologically and often use the number as a name. Adeu means second son.
17. The name of this river derives from the fact that it is so silted with chalk in late spring that drinking from it causes stomach pains (Stephen Morse, correspondence with author).

We alternated between river and bank. Adeu Guide, bearing a full load, struck a brisk pace, hopping lightly from stone to stone, while I, now carrying only my two small shoulder bags, struggled to keep pace. Even Adeu Hkasher found the pace difficult. It was a cloudless day, and the sun-bleached stones and clean, white sand of the Kindrin's banks were a little hard on the eyes. Blue and grey and black and white kingfishers and small round humming birds with rust-coloured short tails hovered above schools of tiny, scintillating fish. From time to time, at a sign from John's nephews, we would stop and wait, while they patrolled an especially promising part of the river in goggles and rubber fins. Once, eerily, we detected fresh depressions of human feet.

We reached the confluence and waded on up the Muhpa Lo, a charming little river cutting through serene jungle full of birdsong, until we found firm, flat land on the bank and made camp. The chat round the *dap* that evening was about the poison for Adeu Hunter's arrows, which he procured from Meugahpi (Snow Mountain), a conical peak east of Sherdi. Going into India was always risky, but this special poison repaid the risk, he said and he proudly showed us his arrows, expertly crafted from two-foot lengths of bamboo and fitted with steel heads and feather fins. He hunted all year, he said, including the rainy season, and had even killed a tiger with this poison. John's nephews lay on the ground behind us, sharing a sheet for warmth and taking no part in the conversation. Then they began singing a hymn in three-part harmony and the rest of us fell silent and listened.

Next day, 9 April, was the Sabbath. Adeu Hkasher asked me if we should proceed, and I replied that we could delay departure for an hour to hold a service. He consulted the others and they decided to scrap the service, so we bade goodbye to John's two younger nephews and continued upriver.

About 1000 hours we came upon two magnificent silver-grey sambur, a stag and his hind, drinking in the river. They eyed us disdainfully with enormous, liquid eyes, then retreated with dignity up the hill and into the forest. We halted to ponder the moment and to excise the leeches from our ankles; then we climbed up a steep escarpment.

At the top of the escarpment was Ziyudi. As John had warned, nothing survived of the timber buildings that had once stood there:

the houses, the church, the school, the volleyball court next to the school where the Burma Army helicopter had landed and their Lisu brethren had bid Russell, Gertrude, Helen, Marilyn and Jeannette farewell with *God Be With You Till We Meet Again*. It was another orchard returning to jungle and a meadow whose tall grass had been stamped down in places by elephants and was strewn with their droppings. We picked some wild lemons and ate them, tempering the bitterness with raw sugar Afoi had brought us from Midi.

Adeu Guide had travelled this particular route only twice before and not for a decade and knew only its general direction, but it never occurred to any of us that he might lose his bearings. Whenever we would ask impatiently how much further it was to the border, he would point northwards at an almost indiscernible and perhaps entirely imaginary dent in a faint line of distant ridge. We cut through thorns; found an animal path and tracked it; and hacked through more thorns. Once or twice the mouldy stump of a tree hinted at a human antecedent. Once I suggested gloomily that there would be rain. Adeu Hkasher looked thoughtfully up at the sky and agreed, '*Ji, sahib*.' The rain would excite the leeches, I said, and he roared with laughter. We camped that night on ground spongy with decomposing vegetation at the head of Muhpa Lo. It started to rain. We dined under *plastik*s on curried potatoes and *tsumu*, which tasted like beef.

It was still raining next morning, and when we resumed our trek our thoughts were preoccupied with the enhanced difficulties of hacking through wet cane.

What happened now was surreal. I am the last in the column, the others suddenly start shouting, and I crane my neck to see what is happening. '*Meugeu*! *Meugeu*!' they are shouting. *Meugeu* is a Lisu word. I have heard it before, but I can't remember what it means. '*Meugeu*! *Meugeu*!'

Adeu Nephew trots back, calmly drops his load and slithers up a palm tree. Adeu Hkasher follows him up the same tree; then, looking down at me still on the ground, sweetly explains, '*Magwi, sahib*.' *Magwi* is a Jinghpaw word, more familiar than *megeu*, but neither can I remember what it means. Adeu Hunter, with Mats following close behind, races past me, clambers up a boulder and implores me to join them, and now Adeu Hkasher is waving at me and saying, a little more energetically, '*Magwi*! *Magwi*!' Then, sensing my incomprehension, he shouts yet more emphatically,

'*HATHI, sahib*! *HATHI*!'

Hathi I can recall, or rather unearth, for it lies buried beneath the sands of time. It is an Urdu word. My thoughts fly back nearly a quarter of a century (but it might have been a century) to a summer in the green hills above Mussoorie and the Landour Mission Language School, where Shri Das Guptaji, forlorn child of the Raj, was my *munshi* (teacher). He took such pains over my clumsy attempts to master his beautiful language, patiently cutting and sharpening quills for our pens and dipping them in the black ink with which his thin fingers were permanently stained. Only quill pens were acceptable, and every stroke had to be done just so, 'like so, *sahib*'. I hear a flapping sound, the flapping of a large ear, and a few feet from me, half concealed in foliage... Bloody hell! *Hathi* means *elephant*.

The beast emerges and glares at me, breathing heavily. I can climb neither the palm nor the boulder, for the criss-crossed straps of my two bags have locked me into a kind of harness. Mats reaches down and hoists me onto the boulder. From this still precarious position I turn and stare directly into the beast's tiny blood-red eyes, thinking: How much further are you going to take this? We can hear the rest of the herd crashing through the jungle distancing itself from us. The bull had stayed back to ward off any attempt at pursuit. Finally, convinced that his family is beyond danger, he turns and disappears.

We resumed our trek – chastened, however, and now carefully assessing the jungle at every turn for possible refuges should there be a recurrence. The animal track that we were following circled back on itself, then plunged into a stony nullah. Adeu Hunter and Adeu Nephew dropped behind and, after a while, I began to wonder if we had lost them. 'Shouldn't we go back for the others?' I suggested to Adeu Hkasher, to which he retorted with gentle dignity, 'A Lisu *never* goes back.'

Eventually, the others caught up with us. Adeu Nephew was grinning and Adeu Hunter had a gibbon slung over his shoulder, which was dripping blood down his back. We made a fire and, while we scorched off the gibbon's hair, laughed at our narrow escape and melodramatic alarms; after which Adeu Hunter led the column, the spreadeagled, roasted, hairless and now bloodless ape strapped to his *shingnoi*.

We climbed through dense cane the steep north bank of the Muhpa Lo, an exhausting climb, which, however, rewarded us at the end of our labours with the kind of forest that Kachins love felling and burning for their *yis*: trees 200 feet tall, the boles sweeping up straight and clear to the first branches, then spreading out into giant canopies topped by red and white creeper. That evening we camped beside the Geucherdi (Sand Flat) Lo and, after an omelette of gibbon brain, our companions sang hymn after hymn in perfect four-part harmony of the most compelling beauty. When it started to rain they got up and hastily erected the *plastik*. Later, when troubled by nocturia, I found that, despite all the hasty rearrangements, Adeu Hkasher had remembered to place his torch beside my head. Thunder roared through the nullahs and the hills shook violently. I was back in India.

* * *

Five inches of rain fell during the night, filling Mats's bamboo cup, which was empty when he went to sleep.

Next morning it was still raining. The men lay in, singing beneath their blankets, then got up and, somehow achieving a fire with damp wood, heated the remains of the gibbon. We ate it under the *plastik*, while mist floated thickly through the dripping forest and thunder rumbled in the distance. Then we waited for the weather to clear, for, it hardly needed to be said, Lisu travelled to no one's agenda but their own. They chatted and sang hymns, and, contrasting their serene patience with our frenetic eagerness to get on, we were once more enviously aware of the price we had paid for our complex lives. How would it be when we were among our own again?

It was past noon when, at last, the sun peeked bravely through a hole in the clouds and we broke camp. Our way now led straight down the Geucherdi Lo. Mats's legs, infected by leech toxin, were so swollen that he was obliged to go barefoot. We had not gone far, however, before Adeu Hkasher suddenly dropped his basket and announced that we were stopping. Why stop now, I asked, amazed? Why not carry on? A good two hours of daylight remained! It was a clumsy, insensitive blunder, and it had a galvanizing effect on Adeu Nephew. He immediately picked up my pack, which he had only just put down, and made off down the mountain like a hare, thereby proclaiming all too clearly: 'You wish to substitute your judgement for ours. All right. Then, let's carry on, and this is how it's done, Revered Elder – this is how a *Lisu* would do it. However, the time to stop is *now*. This is tiger country. They begin prowling as soon as it is dark and fear nothing except fire. We have to collect our firewood and water *now*.' I chased after him, desperately imploring him to turn back and eventually, still smarting from my crude impertinence, he stopped. Then we climbed back to where the others were already making camp. Adeu Guide reported consolingly that the road was 'near'. The Lisu were reluctant to rig up the *plastik* that evening, for they did not expect rain, but I insisted on shelter, and, for once, I was right. By midnight it was raining again.

Next morning, while Mats soothed his inflamed legs in the cold river, the Lisu made breakfast. Adeu Guide said grace; then we crouched in a circle, as we always did, and ate rice curried with smoked fish, *tsumu* and other gleanings from the forest. It was our last meal together. However, my thoughts were entirely taken up with the proximity of the road. While the Lisu tidied up, cleaning their few utensils and packing them neatly into their baskets, I composed the release for them to present to their elders and a letter to accompany it.

We now resumed our descent of the Geucherdi Lo, hopping from boulder to boulder through a pergola of trees and vines until, suddenly, we found ourselves on gently sloping dry ground. Adeu Hkasher and I went forward and, through a hole in the foliage, looked down with surging emotions upon what in that tense moment almost seemed like an optical illusion: a double-rutted, dirt track with the bush cut back on both sides. '*Ji, sahib*,' Adeu Hkasher affirmed gently, '*rasta hai*'. We were at about Mile 71 and not, as anticipated, 20 miles further west – but never mind; what were another 20 miles to two such jungle-tested swells? In any event, Adeu Hkasher assured me, we would have no trouble catching a lift. A sound of voices on the *rasta* muted our jubilation. After sharing the jungle with no one, this intimation of another world seemed intrusive.

Mats and the others caught up with us. I now insisted on

reading the release and letter, taking pains to ensure that Adeu Hkasher translated my words faithfully. The letter restated the arrangements made at the Mound of Blessings and lavishly praised our companions' skills and the cheerful spirit in which they had honoured these arrangements. They listened dutifully, and, when I had finished, Adeu Hkasher, amused that our customs should require such grave formalities, said simply, '*Ji, sahib*'. They knew their worth; why this silly encomium? And as to keeping the terms of their bargain, their word would suffice. They posed for the final snap with mixed expressions on their sweet, strong, clear faces, and, quite suddenly, for the first time since those miniature soldiers of the People's Army intercepted us near Hkai-lekko, we were on our own.

Scarcely had we emerged from the forest and shed our KIA uniforms, however, before more Lisu appeared. Their western clothes, contrasting so sharply with the Adeus' torn and tattered *longyi*s, seemed absurd, almost like fancy dress. I *namastay*ed and greeted them in Hindustani as casually as I could, but I do not think they were deceived. They returned the gesture and informed us that they were bound for Gandhigram, using the Indian name for the village that the Lisu call Sherdi,[18] and announced that it would take us four days to reach the *rasta*. 'Aren't we already on the *rasta*?' I asked. 'You are four days from the *rasta*,' they repeated, and we marched on, puzzled.

We would soon be taking for granted the ugly detritus littering the path (a discarded match box, a Cadbury's Milk Bar wrapping, a milk bottle, a burlap bag, a scrap of egg carton), but now we stared at these empty horrors with fascination. We encountered other people, carrying shiny, tin suitcases and wearing shiny, chrome watches and plastic shoes. The great ramparts of the Patkai *shagawng* towered above us, and the Noa Dihing, already swollen with water and mud from numerous tributaries, roared and smoked in the valley below us, but what claimed our respect were these sad products of our 'civilized' world. We marched in 30-minute phases – 20 minutes walking and 10 minutes extracting the leeches. We had believed, somehow, that leeches were

18. Sherdi means 'grass flat'. A Mishmi village called Mi-Lo-Xi-De once stood on the same site. Mi-Lo-Xi-De also means grass flat.

peculiar to Burma, but, at our first *preekop*, I discovered that my feet were black with them. I would pick 241 of them off me before the day ended. Mats found one in his nostril. With his legs and ankles now a hideous mass of boils, Mats had expected to be able to wear his flip-flops, but the road was too muddy and glutinous for flip-flops.

We trudged on through mud four to six inches deep and laced with tiny, razor-sharp rocks. After the second stage, however, Mats looked at me grimly and said, 'I can't go on. I'm turning back.'

I did not answer at once, as to have done so would have seemed dismissive, but turning back had to be avoided if at all possible. In all likelihood the Indians already knew of my aborted attempt on Vijayanagar, and we would be walking into a bonfire of suspicion. They would want to know why I had hid from them if I had nothing to conceal. Moreover, we would be dealing with junior officers too concerned with their careers to risk them on a wrong decision, who would refer the decision to their superiors. It would take months, if not years to sort out. I turned over in my mind how to explain it all to Mats. Then I had a go. He was unimpressed.

'Maybe. Maybe not,' he said. 'This is speculative.'

Pointing to a narrows ahead where the Noa Dihing appeared to have forced a route between the Patkai and the ramparts to the north, I suggested that we would find the start of the jeepable sector of the road there, a notion supported by nothing more substantial than the fact that the two ranges converged there. 'How do you know this?' asked Mats. 'How do you know *where* the road is? Those Lisu said that we are four days from the road. I can't manage another four days, Shelby.'

'To be precise, they said that we were four days from the *rasta*, which does not necessarily mean "road". I suspect that they were referring to the beginning of the asphalt.'

'You don't know this for a fact,' he persisted stubbornly.

'No, of course I don't know it for a *fact*. But you don't *know* how far back it is to Sherdi, either. All that either of us knows is what Adeu Hkasher told us, and he said that we would find inspection bungalows and PWD camps, which suggests to me that maintenance work is being carried out on this track. They wouldn't need to maintain it if jeeps didn't use it, would they?'

'*I* didn't hear Adeu say anything about inspection bungalows and PWD camps.'

'Of course you didn't. Because you don't speak Hindustani. My views might be speculative, Mats, but please don't complicate the issue by distrusting me.'

We decided that if we hadn't reached the jeepable sector of the track by sunset, or learned before then that we wouldn't reach it by sunset, I would go back to Sherdi for help.

I often saw Mats under stress during my six months spent in his company, but he was never more manly than now. My advice reflected the bias of one whose legs were in a fitter condition than his. Nevertheless, once we concluded our discussion about what we should do, he raised no further objection. Instead of converging on the path at the narrows, the Noa Dihing slipped away to the north. We now fortified ourselves with the delusion that we would reach the road at the 'line of those hills'. But the 'line of those hills' came and went.

A tubby, round-shouldered Bengali accompanied by a broad-backed Lisu toting his suitcase informed us that we were at approximately Mile 65 and that the jeepable sector of the 'road' was another two hours away. Moreover, he said, at Mile 49 we would find a PWD camp with proper buildings and permanent staff. We felt ashamed of ourselves for befriending him while ignoring his servant and wanted to tell him that he was too fat; that, in a world that apportioned privilege according to manliness and purity of heart, he should be carrying the Lisu's suitcase; but we held our tongues. We heard later that he alerted the authorities to our presence. A rumour that he started would overtake us in Miau: Arunachal Pradesh had been infiltrated by an elderly American and a giant Negro employed by the Chinese!

We marched grimly on, every step now an act of steely resolve. Above and behind us, etched melodramatically against a Prussian blue sky, was the white cone of Meugahpi, where Adeu Hunter scavenged for the poison for his arrows. The Bengali's 'two hours to the road' lengthened into three, and we could conjure up no other mirage to sustain our hopes. Shadows were now gathering in the valley where the Noa Dihing clawed interminably at its ragged banks. We knew that we would have to stop soon to prepare our shelter and food.

We passed several plausible sites for bivouacking, some showing the charred wood and tinfoil leavings of erstwhile campsites, and were about to quit when our determination was at last rewarded. A bend. Beyond it, another nullah. Beside it, a well-constructed bamboo shelter with firewood already in place. The tracks of a bulldozer. A metal sign proclaiming, 'Chief Engineer, Jaraimpur'. A log bridge with a balustrade nailed to it, and, beyond the bridge, a graded road — the jeepable *rasta*.

* * *

Camp Mile 61 was the first place since Wanding where we were responsible for our own shelter, and it was waiting for us. We dined on noodles purchased centuries ago in Dali, flavouring them with rock salt supplied by the Adeus, and resumed walking next morning feeling rested and optimistic. Patches of vibrant blue sky windowed through the tangled tree cover augured a fine day.

We met an Indian (not so fat and oily as the first but still overweight) who imparted the astonishingly erroneous advice that we would suffer no further attacks from leeches and tried to cadge a cigarette from us. Then we encountered a man and woman with two children — tribal people who, however, wore shoes and carried tin suitcases strapped to their backs. The woman spoke Hindustani and said that they were bound for Gandhigram, calling it (I noted again) by its Indian name. She carried a lighter load than her husband and had to be coaxed by him across a log spanning a nullah. She also smoked. She might have been from a lowland tribe who had married into the Lisu. She told us that we would find the IB (inspection bungalow) at Mile 39 — not, as previously advised, at Mile 49 — and confirmed that Miau was two to three days' walk beyond it. One of the children was pushing a bicycle procured in Miau. We would follow the tread of its tyres for the rest of the day.

We carried on, our regime unchanged — walk for 20 minutes; stop for 10 to pick off leeches. By noon, our high expectations had degenerated into a dull, myopic trance. We limped past a jumble of huts standing empty in high grass. Was this the ghost of one of Adeu Hkasher's PWD camps? A black snake about a yard long, with a tiny narrow head and darting probing tongue, slithered across the path in front of us. It seemed a bad omen. Another slithered ominously across the track. We then noticed depressions of boots and a jeep's tyres! The depressions were *fresh* and faced east and west, as though someone had walked thus far and turned back. We rounded another bend and suddenly confronted a pair of inert bulldozers and, beside them, a bright orange canvas tent. In the tent were the startled faces of half a dozen incredulous men staring out at us. Mats whispered to me, 'Soldiers.'

As luck would have it, we had stumbled not upon soldiers but upon PWD workers awaiting a part needed to repair one of their bulldozers. A Nepali named Som Bahadur seemed to be in charge. He was about my age and his English was fluent; however, his manner was reticent and unfriendly. He confirmed what the Adeus had told us, that Vijayanagar was at Mile 96 and Gandhigram at Mile 87. He said that we were now at Mile 51½, from which we deduced that our Sisyphean ordeal, although it had seemed much longer, had lasted only about 20 miles and that, when debating whether to turn back, Sherdi and the bulldozers must have been almost exactly equidistant. Whatever the fate of Mats's feet, therefore, at least we had made the right decision in carrying on. Then he asked us suspiciously, 'Where from you are coming?'

We could not risk the truth, but we had been with the Kachins for so long that I had almost forgotten how to lie. 'Vijayanagar,' I replied awkwardly.

'What are you doing here?'

'We are tourists,' I said absurdly.

'How did you get here?'

'We flew to Vijayanagar and decided to walk back. But we had not reckoned on the leeches.'

He pondered my answer for a very long time. Then he asked, 'You have passports?'

'Of course we have passports,' I replied. 'Would you like to see them?' How effortlessly I had slipped back into form.

'You have Inner Line pass?'

'Obviously,' I countered, bluffing wildly. It was the first time that I heard the term. '*No one* comes here without an Inner Line pass!'

While we were talking, a party of Lisu passed. They were

dressed in dirty, tattered *longyis* and were barefoot. Their *shingnois* were full, their foreheads gleaming with beads of sweat, but their silence and averted eyes showed that they wanted nothing to do with us, as though our trinkets and love of ease would contaminate them. I knew then that we had already crossed the divide separating our lives from theirs and had already exchanged the freedom and integrity that we had known with them for trivia and mendacity. Careless of their contempt, Som Bahadur asked them if they had seen a jeep. They replied that a landslide had blocked a jeep at Mile 34. 'These Lisu are dirty people,' said Som Bahadur when they were gone. 'They do not seem to want what we want, but they are highly principled and fear no one. You must never insult them. My advice is to leave them alone. That is best. Leave them alone. Come, take your rest,' he said, now a little more welcoming and inviting us into the tent.

A handsome young Bihari named Chaunday Saur and a barrel-chested Zo named Zaua Mizo now sprang forward to help us remove our packs. The Zos or Mizos live on both sides of the border and in Burma are known as Chins. I knew that their *bawis* (chiefs) had participated at Panglong and, like the Shans and Kachins, had gambled on Aung San's promise that the hill peoples would not be discriminated against in his Utopian vision of a Burma free from foreign rule.[19] Yet they had not been accorded even the theory of their own state. I knew also that there had been cross-border cooperation between the Mizo National Front and the Chin insurgency groups, of which one, the Chin National Front, was a member of the NDF. I longed to question Zaua Mizo about these matters and to ask him about joint operations between the Indian Army and the Burma Army, but I had first to contend with Som Bahadur, who was still suspicious. 'What are your plans?' he asked.

'If you do not mind, we would like to wait here for the jeep that you are expecting and catch a lift with it to Miau. We have our own rice, and we won't be a burden on you,' I said.

'Better you go,' he answered simply. 'You go *aste*, *aste*' – by gentle and easy stages – and he painted an attractive picture of

19. 'If Burma receives one kyat, you will also get one kyat' (quoted by Smith, 1991: 78).

what we might expect: after another five miles, an improvement in the condition of the road; beyond Mile 47, no more mud; shelter in PWD camps at Miles 47 and 43; and at Mile 39 an inspection bungalow. 'Proper IB, and, after Mile 39, road is metalled!' The camps were not staffed, but they were in sound condition, he said.

'You don't seem to understand, Som Bahadur. My friend can hardly walk. It is a miracle that he has got this far. I can't ask him to carry on.' However, he was coldly unsympathetic. 'We are sorry that fitness is not there, but that is misfortune, isn't it?'

'All right, then,' I persisted, 'how about hiring us two of your men? With their help we might be able to make it as far as the IB. Then I could go on to the jeep alone and tell them about my friend's condition. Money is not a problem. We will pay whatever is reasonable.'

'These men are assigned to these bulldozers,' he replied. 'You arrive here telling that you are coming from Vijayanagar, isn't it? But we do not know where from you are coming. I am working in Arunachal Pradesh since twenty years, and this is first time I am seeing foreigners here. It is area forbidden to foreigners.'

'*Sahib*, Zaua Mizo and I will take you to Mile 39!' suddenly cried Chaunday Saur. 'We will leave tomorrow! Road is easy. You will see! We carry all!'

Chaunday Saur and Zaua Mizo prepared dinner over a Bunsen burner. We offered to contribute what remained of our *tsumu*, but Som Bahadur refused it, calling it 'jungle food'. Instead, we ate onions and potatoes supplied from burlap bags, mixed with ghee from a tin. Chaunday Saur poured diesel over a heap of damp logs and torched it, but the fire provided more smoke than heat and little light. And that night we heard the deep wanton growl of a tiger. It had come to water at the spring where we washed ourselves before retiring.

* * *

A burning wick of cloth floating in a ghee tin of diesel kept the tiger at a distance, and, as so often before during these past two months, I lay awake thinking about what the future portended. Whatever danger lay in store for us, and however cringing our response to it, I thought, we would eventually boast to anyone willing to listen to us about our Big Adventure and how brave we had been.

The jeep arrived next morning as we were about to leave. It had taken more than two days to travel 16 miles. Its driver and four passengers had been obliged to get down and unload it and extricate it from mud every few hundred yards. An equal number of Jinghpaws or Lisu could have carried the same tools and spare parts the same distance with less discomfort in less than half the time.

The jeep fetched a young engineer named Devi Singh, who was now in charge. 'These bulldozers cost crores of rupees, and they are standing idle here now four days,' he said. 'I am taking them to Dewan with me.' Dewan was at Mile 17. 'They will clear the way if we get stuck.' Devi Singh was jolly and modest when he was not vaunting his Rajput ancestry or his native Benares ('where every Hindu wants to die'), but what lifted him above ordinary mankind was his gullibility. Cynicism was a stranger to him. He *believed* our story of simple-minded tourists who had strayed into difficulties. It was from this excellent young man that we first heard that splendid term of art, 'sortie from Dibrugarh'. Henceforth, when asked how we happened to reach Vijayanagar, we would be able to reply, 'by sortie from Dibrugarh'.

The men soon succeeded in starting the bulldozers, and after lunch we left for Miau in convoy, Som Bahadur, Mats and I travelling in relative comfort in the jeep, Devi Singh more nobly with the others and the baggage on the bulldozers. Every half mile or so we would stop and wait for the bulldozers. The sun made a feeble stab at penetrating the cloud cover but gave up, and it started to rain. We passed the deserted PWD camp at Mile 47 and looked with wonder upon its prefabricated window frames, its doors of planed wood hung on steel butt hinges and its corrugated tin. Night fell, confining visibility to the sleet slanting through the beams of our headlights. Once we came upon a boulder straddling the road. A bulldozer roared forward, raised its blade and nudged the intruder over the side of the mountain, reminding us in a curious way of the ease with which our elephants had managed the Tawang Hka.

Then a force six gale blew up, as though we had motored into a wind tunnel. Devi Singh got down and hailed us out into the stinging weather to enjoy the view. 'This place is called Burma Nullah, and this is wind from Burma!' he shouted as we clung to each other for anchor. 'Here we are only 12 miles from Burma! May I be knowing what places you may have visited in India?' He was wet and cold and, clearly, starved for want of conversation.

'You'd better ask Mr Tucker!' shouted Mats. 'He understands India!'

'I am thinking India must be very different from Sweden!' shouted Devi Singh. 'Is Sweden kingdom or republic?'

'The hill people probably track this nullah as a route into India!' I interjected.

'*No one* crosses border!' countered Devi Singh indignantly. 'Indian Army is *patrolling*!'

I demurred. 'Perhaps not!'

We braved the gale a while longer. Then Devi Singh shouted resignedly, 'We must leave bulldozers! Bridge is not strong enough! Bulldozers will cross down there!'

'Where?' I asked, and he indicated the black chasm below us.

In five or ten years an all-purpose bridge would span this nullah, and other Europeans would come here to admire the wild people previously known to them as costumed figures in ethnographic museums who had once used the nullah as a route through the forest. For the moment, though, standing out against the icy blast from Burma, I found it impossible to summon any great enthusiasm for it.

We crossed the nullah and drove on without the bulldozers and, a few minutes later, motored past a Shiva *mandir* and up a winding gravel drive. The IB stood on the summit of a small hill, its moonlit gables like a gothic palace in a fairy-tale. The *chowkidar* heard our approach and was waiting for us on the veranda. Soap and towels, and a bath from galvanized buckets of warm water by the light of a storm lantern in a room with a trowel-smoothed cement floor; a hot meal brought to us on trays; mirrors, curtains, carpets, tables, chairs and wardrobes; window reveals and doors painted in prime, undercoat and gloss; beds canopied with mosquito nets, pillows and blankets: we had motored back into 'civilization', and it was all a little confusing.

Mats's legs continued swelling during the night, and, when I looked in on him next morning, his feet were standing in a bucket of salted tea heated to scalding to allay the pain. 'I don't want to be cripple,' he said despairingly. 'I don't want the doctor to say, "If you came to me last week, I could help you, but now it is too late. I will have to amputate your legs".'

'Why don't you sit out on the veranda?' I suggested. 'The sun has come out, and the *chowkidar* has set up a table on which you can write up your diaries.'

But he preferred to nurse his wounds alone. I gave him some streptomycin sulphate powder that Seng Hpung had supplied to me; the faded letters on the bottle stated: 'Made by Burma Chemical Industries'. 'Mats, do you remember where we were this time last week?' I asked.

'Wading up the Kindrin Hka with the four Adeus,' he replied.

About noon the jeep returned with Devi Singh and Chaunday Saur. They had been at the nullah all morning and were wet and muddy. The bulldozers were still on the east bank and the water in the nullah was chest high, but they were confident of success.

Nevertheless, next morning, we abandoned the bulldozers and drove on.

At Dewan, Devi Singh gave us tea at the galvanized steel and concrete bungalow where he lodged when not with the bulldozers and exploited the moment to expound his Hindu chauvinist's admiration for 'Mahatmaji'. My thoughts reverted to Seng Hpung. Was he still at the Mound of Blessings, or had he already started back to Second Brigade headquarters? We had discussed Gandhi in our 'briefing' at Second Brigade headquarters and he would enjoy Devi Singh's panegyric, I thought. But he would not fancy my condoning the notion that 'Revered Great Soul' was a saint. I knew that in this part of India Subhas Chandra Bose, who had rejected *ahimsa* and fought with the Japanese against the British, had as many admirers as Gandhi. Subhas Chandra Bose had remained loyal to the Japanese even when they were in full retreat, after Aung San and his Burma National Army deserted them. It seemed to me that the Kachins were more like Subhas Chandra Bose than they were like Mohandas Karamchand Gandhi.

We left Devi Singh at Dewan. Later, Mats and I wrote to him and apologized for having deceived him. He did not reply.

After Dewan the road was paved and, as we sped over its

smooth asphalt, my mind turned over the options now open to us. Our party now comprised Som Bahadur, Chaunday Saur, two mechanics, the driver, Mats and me. Only one of them was stopping at Miau. The others were continuing on to PWD headquarters at Jaraimpur by a road that traversed a corner of Assam. If we did not stop at Miau after advising them that we were bound for Miau, would they report us at the Inner Line checkpoint? The police there might inspect the jeep anyway. If we got down at Miau and proceeded on our own, we would reach the Inner Line about midnight; but was it fair to impose this extra effort on Mats? What if his feet really *were* at risk of amputation? The thick cloud that had enveloped us all morning lifted, revealing lush green forest sloping down to the now Amazonian Noa Dihing and carpeting the greenish blue hills beyond. One of the men said that we were in a bird sanctuary. We came to a checkpoint, but the guard, cold and mute at his post, only raised the barrier and waved us on. We reached another checkpoint and stopped for some formal clearance involving registration of the vehicle. One of the mechanics went into the guards' quarters with the documents, while we waited in the jeep, apprehensive that someone would come out and inspect – Baoshan all over again! There was a hospital at Miau.

It clouded over again and started raining. We drove past an Indian Army lorry parked beside the road. A section of soldiers looking bored and miserable in thick, woollen, army-issue trench coats and hats preoccupied themselves with keeping dry while they fatalistically went through the motions of carrying out their orders. We learned later that their orders were to intercept us.

We passed two more checkpoints undetected and, just after 1600 hours, drove into Miau and, on Som Bahadur's officious instruction to the driver, drove straight to the house of the local medical officer, a Dr Mukerji. Half an hour later we were at the hospital, and Dr Mukerji, freshly bathed and scented and wearing a smart white coat, was dressing Mats's feet. 'Actually, I was asleep when you arrived,' he said. 'Sunday is my rest day.' The lights failed. 'In no time flat, as soon as penicillin takes effect, your feet will be back to normal,' he said reassuringly, fetching a lantern. 'Amputation is not there,' he predicted confidently.

The first uniformed, armed men now appeared. We saw them

assembling in the shadows outside the door, fixing us with unfriendly looks. Then someone burst into the room and demanded, 'Where have you come from? How did you get here?' His abundant, wavy hair was brushed into a duck's tail, and he wore a neat, tailored, cutaway jacket and a silk cravat.

I had already lied to Som Bahadur, to Devi Singh and to Dr Mukerji. I now lied to him. 'We have come by sortie from Dibrugarh.'

'Then you must be having Inner Line PASS!' he screamed. 'I want to know *who you are* and *who these men are*!'

'We met them at Mile 51½ on the Vijayanagar–Miau track, camped next to two broken-down bulldozers. We know very little about them, only that they were a gift from heaven.'

Then we were escorted to Circuit House and locked in a room named Dawn Calm. Our imprisonment had begun.

8
Arrest House

It is now time to return to Carole as she was after we parted in Canton. For her, 1989 began as a frosty day walking over the Great Wall of China and through fir-clad woods. There was a light fall of snow. Thick clouds concealed the sun. She had missed her return flight to England.

Several anxious days followed. She wanted to beg me again not to go to Burma but deferred ringing Canton until Aeroflot had clarified that she would not be charged a penalty and, when she did ring, Mats and I had already left for Dali.

I had sprung my 'Burma idea' on her at a christening party the previous year, and fear had marred her happiness ever since. That outrageous announcement had triggered a campaign of attrition that extracted from me pledges to seek a companion and incur no unacceptable risk, but its main achievement, she believed, was my admission of the difficulties. Such were the difficulties, she had reasoned, that, once confronted by them, I would change my mind. Her spirits thus plunged even further when she now discovered that we had already departed for Dali.

Her great bear of fear sat beside her on the long flight back to England and was with her when she resumed work. Someone said, 'Carole, is it communist over there?' 'Yes, Marion, since 1949,' she replied. That was the world to which she had returned.

My mother suffered a heart attack. This was a melancholy development and horrid news to pass on to me, but at least, Carole thought, it would trump my Burma plans, if only she could reach me in time. She sent a telegram to me at a contingency address in Hong Kong, but it never reached me.

She was used to my going off to wild places, but this was over the top. Our friends' well-intentioned efforts at consoling her ('Shelby can look after himself') carried no conviction. What did *they* know about Burma? One of them confused it with Borneo. The newspapers had spoken of demonstrations in the streets of Rangoon and Mandalay. Someone said: 'Burma's the largest concentration camp in the world.' Everyone said: 'Isn't Burma embroiled in some kind of civil war?' A general breakdown in public order meant that anyone might kill me for my possessions. And what would happen if I fell ill in the jungle? There would be no doctors, no medicines, and no one to look after me.

As January, then February passed, the fear persisted, her diary reflecting her efforts to come to terms with something that she could not understand.

> I am tied to a person walking into a minefield. ... It has occurred to me that I could divorce him, but that is really no answer. He's too bound up in my life. And suppose he gets through? Then I would have made a fuss about nothing and a great mess of things. It will be very hard on both of us if he is taken prisoner.

She received the letters I sent from Dali and Möng Ko, but they only exacerbated her fears.

> Letters continue to come in, while Shelby is going into the eye of the cyclone. There is no way of responding to them. My last cry of 'Do not go' lies suffocated in some unregarded heap in Hong Kong. But he has provided me with the telephone number of Mats's mother, who is also tied to someone who has done this foolish thing. Berit will be a great consolation during the months ahead.

The first letter of significance, posted from China on 15 January but written at 'CPB Northern Bureau headquarters', reached her during the first week in February. It began, 'Incredible as it may seem, I am writing to you from Burma', and described our hike from Wanding to Möng Ko. She and Berit were horrified to read of climbs over 'sheer drops', conversations with peasants who 'chewed heroin' and many changes of 'armed escort'.

> More important than what the letter says is what it conceals. There are coded references to 'ranking brass' and 'exiting via Thailand'. The letters are tender and touching, but tenderness counts for very little at this stage. All our friends agree: it's madness.

She clung to the words 'nicest people I've met anywhere' and prayed intensely.

But the chat was unrelenting. One of her advisers was friendly with the wife of the brother of the British ambassador to Burma, who told her: 'Opinion in Rangoon is strongly opposed to his going. The roads have not been repaired for 50 years.' Peter Carey, an Oxford don with obscure Burma credentials, put her in contact with Michael Aris, who asked her, 'Don't you know who I am?' and, 'Why did your husband go to Burma, Mrs Tucker?'

'He thought it might be fun,' replied Carole, trying to sound cheerful.

'Burma is not about fun,' said Dr Aris.[1]

The next letter Carole received, also written at 'CPB Northern Bureau HQ', announced our intention to proceed northwest to India rather than southeast to Thailand. 'This is slightly more consoling. Shelby promised me that, under no circumstances, would they go through the Golden Triangle.' The next letter, sent from Pajau Bum, stressed the importance of completing the trek 'before the end of March, when the rivers of the west of Burma swell with the spring rains'. It tried to console Carole with numbers, comparing the KIA's strength with that of the other insurgent groups in Burma, and suggested she contact Bertil Lintner for 'independent assurance about our safety'. However, Mats wrote to Berit from Pajau Bum that we had been 'smuggled' through China. 'Are they mice caught in a hole? They both have perfectly good Chinese visas and could return by the way they came. Why are they going all the way to India? Berit says that Mats's biggest worry is that he doesn't have a visa for India!' Channel 4's *Dispatches* showed students vomiting from

---

1. Dr Aris, who died in 1999, was married to Daw Aung San Suu Kyi, who, a few months after this conversation, was placed under house arrest in Rangoon and not released until nearly six years later.

> a form of malaria peculiar to Burma that responds to no treatment. ... I caught a glimpse of Aris's wife and surmised that I had made a *faux pas*. ... My social life is enforced bravery. It is no consolation that I now have something to talk about. Last weekend at the Wadsworths I walked across fields and marvelled at the sight of snowdrops peeping through the snow, and an hour later I was standing in a crowd with my back to the fire in the inglenook fireplace thinking that Shelby would still be walking in the cold. A late night film of prison torture in South America kept me awake all night.

The next letter to reach Carole was that posted by Zawng Hra from Xima when we reached '1 Bde HQ' announcing that we had arrived there on 27 February and that, 'to guarantee our safety 100%', we were taking the longer of two routes to the Indian border and proceeding part of the way by elephant. 'This is the only aspect of the trip that I envy,' noted Carole.

Towards the end of March the second letter Zawng Hra posted reached her. It confirmed our departure from Second Brigade headquarters on 16 March, which encouraged her somewhat, as I had previously estimated that it would take us only seven days to reach India from '2 Bde HQ'. However, when, on 10 April, she received Zawng Hra's letter confirming arrival at the Indian border, she and Berit knew that something had gone wrong. They could understand our silence as long as we were in Burma, but India had telephones and telegraphic and postal services.

She now rang Bertil Lintner. His efforts at consoling her only deepened her despair. He surmised that we were probably 'stuck in Nagaland', having been stuck there himself for three months 'hiding in a room the size of a lavatory'. 'Frankly,' he said, 'I don't see how they can get out through India. The Indians share intelligence with the Burmese government and are sure to catch them.' Carole's diary here alludes to us as 'exiles among leeches, marooned by rivers swollen by the spring rains'; our 'only hope' was to wait out the rains, return to KIA GHQ and exit through China. 'But the Chinese will arrest and keep them for a long time and confiscate their diaries and film,' warned Lintner. Carole asked him why the Chinese had released him. Because, he explained, he was a journalist and the Chinese did not want adverse publicity; also because the Chinese 'have a high regard for family', and he had been accompanied by his wife and infant daughter. After this dismal conversation, Carole wrote: 'It has been the worst day of the whole ordeal.'

It was now the end of April and nothing further had been heard of us. In desperation, she turned to an elderly lady who had spent the early years of her marriage in Burma.[2]

> Jo said a very Irish thing: 'People who plan seem to have all sorts of disasters, while those who embark on scatter-brained adventures always succeed. Look at my friend Dervla Murphy. I have a feeling that Shelby will succeed.' In a funny way this brought me a little comfort. It just shows, I suppose, that I am willing to grasp at any straw of hope, however irrational.

She rang Bertil Lintner once more and learned that, since their previous conversation, he had conferred with the Kachins. 'I'm afraid that nothing has been heard of them for a month now,' he said. 'But', he added, 'not hearing anything is not quite as ominous as you might think. It's not unusual for the Kachins to go to ground. This would happen if the Burma Army were in the vicinity. A Japanese [Yoshida Toshihiro] spent *three* years getting out of Kachinland. Don't worry about your husband, Mrs Tucker. He will be safe as long as he is with the Kachins.'

She began mentally to prepare for a summer of uncertainty.

* * *

Our *svelte* hospital inquisitor, Assistant Deputy Commissioner Bhattacharjee, came along purely for the fun, for he had already decided what to do about us. He would pass us on to the Deputy Commissioner in Changlang, and now that decision was off his chest we were simply an evening's entertainment. The others who followed us into Dawn Calm were answerable to other masters, and some of them were already in trouble. The officer com-

---

2. Jo Farrell.

manding the unit whose men we had passed west of Dewan was a solemn Punjabi named Lieutenant Sharma. He attended the interrogation in Dawn Calm to glean what he could about how we had escaped detection. Inspector Mamio's simple task was to inventory our possessions. He was a jolly, uncomplicated Mishmi from the Tibetan borderlands. The villains of the piece were Inspector Ravi of the Arunachal Pradesh Police, two junior detectives who wagged their heads in assent to everything that he said, and their squad of constables – underemployed, undervalued career thugs trained to beat up anyone so unlucky as to wander into their custody, who felt wasted on the crimeless hill people inhabiting Miau. Their frustration was evident throughout.

Inspector Ravi began the investigation with flattery and jocular banter as soon as we had finished bathing; he then disputed everything we said, however irrelevant or unimportant. It was the technique of attrition through repetition, the tacit assumption being that whatever we said in reply to his questions was dishonest.

To Mats: 'Where are you meeting Mr Tucker?'

'On the train from Moscow.'

To me: 'Where are you meeting Mr Larsson?'

'We first met on the Trans-Siberian Express.'

Ah, a discrepancy! One of the prisoners says, 'train from Moscow', and the other says, 'the Trans-Siberian Express'.

'You must be knowing Mr Larsson before?'

'We met on the Trans-Siberian Express.'

To Mats: 'I am thinking you are knowing Mr Tucker before?'

Silence.

Another discrepancy!

To me: 'How is it you are not knowing him before?'

To Mats: 'Were you in China?'

'Yes.'

'Did you meet Mr Tucker in China?'

'Yes.'

'You are saying that you are meeting on train from Moscow, and now you are saying that you are meeting in China?'

'I first met Mr Tucker in China on the train from Moscow, and I met him again later, in China.'

The two detectives smile. Their boss made it all seem so very easy. He was *such* an astute interrogator.

To me: 'I am thinking you were in China? You must be meeting Chinese?'

I made a sudden, unpardonable descent into sarcasm. 'We met *millions* of Chinese, Inspector Ravi. It was a job not to trip over them when we left our hotel.'

'Mr Larsson, are you meeting Chinese?'

Silence.

To me: 'Why is your friend not admitting that you are meeting Chinese?'

'Perhaps he doesn't understand the point of the question. You can't travel in China without meeting Chinese, Inspector Ravi.'

'I am thinking you are working for Chinese.'

'We weren't working for anyone.'

'I am believing you, but it is *just not convincing*!'

Then, 'Why did you not go back to China, where you are having valid visa, Mr Tucker? Visa is there.'

'Why should we return to China if our objective was to walk across Burma, Inspector Ravi?'

'Are you having Burmese visa?'

'No.'

'Then why must you be wanting to walk across Burma? You must be knowing that, without Burmese visa, you cannot walk across Burma?'

'We've just walked across Burma without Burmese visas.'

'Why are you not obtaining?'

'If our objective was to walk across Burma, and the Burmese authorities would not allow us to walk across Burma, then what was the point of obtaining Burmese visas?'

'I am believing you, but it is *just not convincing*!'

'Inspector Ravi, must you ask the same questions over and over again?'

'I am just asking, why is it you must be coming to India without visa when you are having visa for China, isn't it?' The junior detectives wagged their heads. Their boss was such a *shrewd* judge of character.

Lieutenant Sharma eventually placed a restraining hand on Ravi's shoulder. Never mind, nodded the inspector to his disappointed subordinates. He would have another go at us later.

Inspector Mamio and his men then proceeded with their inventory. They removed all our possessions from our packs, spread them on our beds and examined them with meticulous care, while Inspector Ravi looked on, hopeful that somewhere in all these calling cards, credit cards, credit card vouchers, ballpoint pen refills and bamboo souvenirs of our time among the Kachins he would spot something incriminating. Two policemen grabbed at the same piece of paper simultaneously and tore it in two. Then a fight broke out between them.

'Please, gentlemen, *please*!' I protested. 'There's plenty of time for each of you to examine each and every item.'

After the inventory was completed, Inspector Ravi said, 'I am thinking there is something else.'

'Well, you sleep on it,' said Mats.

Bhattacharjee now invited us to dine with him, and, over a table laid with linen, silver, crystal, curried chicken and *chapattis*, the first wheat on offer since China, Lieutenant Sharma whispered, 'If anyone should ask you, will you say that I intercepted you? I am hoping for promotion to captain. Actually, we have been following your movements since 4th April. We received a report of an American-looking man and a black man.'

'My mother is going to be very surprised when she hears that I've been mistaken for a Negro,' interjected Mats.

'Did you not see our truck on the road?'

'There was a lorry parked beside the road a few miles west of Devan,' I said.

'That was mine. How did you get past it?'

'It was raining hard, we were in a jeep, and your men, who were trying to keep out of the rain, simply didn't see us. Can you tell us why you are making all this fuss over us?'

'It is restricted area.'

'There's nothing here but leeches. Surely you don't apprehend a threat from Burma?'

After dinner, now locked in Dawn Calm, armed soldiers standing vigil outside the door, a tall, elegant, Kashmiri pandit whose skin was the colour of Nehru's appeared. It was Lieutenant Sharma's commanding officer, Colonel Sapru. 'I did not catch your name,' I said. 'Never mind *my* name,' he replied sharply; 'it's *you* we want to know about.' I mentioned that I had once taught at the Tyndale-Biscoe Mission School in Srinagar. He had once been a pupil at the Tyndale-Biscoe school, and that eased matters, but only for the moment.

Next day we were transferred to Changlang. A convoy of jeeps assembled for that purpose. We rode in the forward jeep with Sharma, Mamio and two armed policemen. Behind us was a jeep full of more armed policemen and soldiers; behind it, another jeep with Bhattacharjee and an entourage of local grandees. Bhattacharjee was even more resplendently turned out than on the previous day – straw hat, Kashmir wool sweater, silk kerchief – and carried a silver-tipped staff of lacquered bamboo. It was raining hard. I rode between the driver and Sharma. The rain slanted through the jeep's open side on to him. I offered him my poncho for protection. 'This is a little awkward,' he said. 'Strictly speaking, you are my prisoner.'

Miau's tin-roofed buildings, the logging operations beyond, the flat country after the cramped weeks in the hills: everything was strange and new. There was plenty of cover on both sides of the road and, when we reached the 'Inner Line', I noted that the checkpoint was manned by no more than half a dozen guards. They would be asleep soon after the traffic ceased that evening, and eluding them would have been a piece of cake had we carried on instead of stopping for Mats's legs. Their little building backed on to more forest.

After the checkpoint, the road passed through several more villages. Film music blaring from loudhailers; emaciated rickshaw wallahs pedalling their passengers through dung-littered streets; obese *dukandar*s presiding over their merchandise. We roared past them.

At Ledo there was a level crossing and hoppers full of coal reminiscent of Danang. This was the railway that, had we evaded capture, would have taken us to Gauhati and on to Delhi. We passed through Margherita, the entrepôt for the Second World War concentration that had preceded the retaking of Burma, and signs everywhere brandished the colours of different units and the locations of their officers' messes. Uniformed Sikhs without turbans in a jeep at a petrol station and roadsigns indicating Likhapani and Dibrugarh and other towns that had figured in our aborted plans.

After we recrossed the Inner Line the road began to bend and twist as it rose towards the crest of the Patkai *shagawng*, which here ran south into Naga country. I felt quite sick.

* * *

We expected some perfunctory formalities before being sent on to Delhi, three or four days convalescing at Circuit House in the company of interesting men like A. K. Bhattacharjee. Instead, we were taken to a gaol on the outskirts of Changlang and there frisked, handcuffed and paraded before the Superintendent of Police, C. P. Mansai. Nearly two centuries of British rule had wrought little change for those who knew how to work the system, and it just wasn't on that these two Europeans – two pampered, privileged and *rich* Europeans – should get off scot-free. No, it just wasn't on. On the wall behind the SP's desk was a catalogue of his normal fare: homicide, involuntary homicide, arson, rape, dacoity and burglary. We appealed to Bhattacharjee, but this exquisitely dressed, exquisitely groomed, exquisitely mannered man now disowned us without even a sigh of regret. We were no longer his responsibility; the investigation must pursue its course. Through barred windows, we watched them leave the police station together – arm in arm, as it were. I bitterly noted my diary: 'SP: *bête noire*. ADC: traitor!'

That night we slept in a room full of dusty papers. 'I am too much embarrassed, *sahib*, but what to do?' lamented Sub-Inspector Deori. '*Kia karega?*' Better this, however, than the *en suite* concrete cube cum tap and hole in floor, with its leaking roof and damp and filthy walls and the mildewed blanket for a bed that Mansai had intended for us. Next morning at dawn our fellow prisoners in striped, grey pyjamas swarmed out of their cells for their daily exercise in their common room corridor. We gave them a tiny glimpse of hope, and they clustered at the bars at the end of the corridor giving access to their cells and glared at us with wide-awake eyes. Deori had granted favours to us. Why not them? Perhaps we could help? One of them, quite plainly deranged, shouted over to us that he had been in detention for two years awaiting charges.

Breakfast was cold lentils. Then Deori and a colleague, Sub-

Inspector Sikiani, took our statements. 'Where do you want me to begin?' I asked.

'You may begin when you are departing your native land.'

'I left England on the 24th of November and flew to Berlin.'

'That is 24 November 1988?'

'Correct.'

'When did you arrive Berlin?'

'That same day.'

'That must be 24 November, isn't it?' ...

Then we were escorted to a large, modern building in the middle of the town and there handed over to a man named Bora. Bora presided over a multitude of secretaries, sub-clerks and *chaprassis* shuttling files. He was, proudly, the chief clerk. He served on us a warrant of arrest.

'Arrested for what?' I asked him.

'That is up to Magistrate,' he replied.

'A warrant of arrest should state the grounds for arrest,' I said.

'Maybe for violation of Bengal Eastern Frontier Regulation of 1873? Maybe for entering restricted area without Inner Line pass? Maybe for violation of Foreigners Act, entering India without valid visa? I am only Clerk of Court.'

'What is the maximum punishment?'

'That is up to Magistrate.'

'May I see the statutes?'

'I am having it,' he said proudly and produced a fat, yellow paperbound volume. The powers of a magistrate, I read, depended upon whether he was a Magistrate First Class or a Magistrate Second Class. Our magistrate, Mr Bora informed us, was a Magistrate First Class. He could imprison us with hard labour for up to five years. I asked Mr Bora what he *thought* would happen. 'That is up to Magistrate,' he replied.

'Yes, but drawing on your experience as the Clerk of Court, Mr Bora, what do you think will happen?'

'Rupees 200/–, *bas*!'

'Who is the magistrate?' I asked.

'Madam Deputy Commissioner.'

'And who presents the state's case?'

'Madam Deputy Commissioner.'

We asked to see her.

The work of the DC of Changlang District, whose office was a few doors from Mr Bora's, falls mainly on the ADC. In the spring of 1989 this was one Narayan S. Meyan, who, when we intruded on his busy regime, was in conference with his transport officer, a Mr Gogoi.

'Mr Meyan, we accept that it is your responsibility to punish us for any offence that we may have committed in Changlang District,' I began pompously. 'We understand this. But this matter bears on the tender feelings of other people, who are guilty of nothing but worrying about their loved ones. I am referring to Mats's parents and my wife. We have not been able to contact them since January, and they were expecting to hear from us by the 1st of April. Three months is a long time to live in uncertainty, especially considering that, from their point of view, we were venturing into a civil war. Have you a wife and children, Mr Meyan? If so, as a family man you can appreciate just how worried *your* wife would be had you not contacted her under similar circumstances, just how worried you would be had *your* son not contacted *you*. Is it too much to ask, therefore, that we be allowed to contact our loved ones and tell them that we are alive and safe?'

'Mr Tucker, you are prisoner for only few days. I am smoker. I am prisoner for *life*,' he replied.

Even now, at our very first meeting, I felt that Meyan was going to be our friend.

'We are also puzzled as to why we are being detained,' I continued. 'We understand we may have committed two quite minor offences under Indian law. Entering a restricted area without an Inner Line pass, which carries a maximum penalty of a fine of Rs 200/– and two months' imprisonment. And entering India without valid visas. The first offence is your responsibility, and the second is Delhi's responsibility. Can't you just accept our plea of guilty on the first count and, on payment of the fine, hand us over to Delhi?'

'Better you speak with Madam Deputy Commissioner,' he answered.

'Think about it, Mr Meyan,' I persisted. 'What are the other incriminating possibilities? We might have been engaged in subversive activities. But that's absurd. Have you seen the jungle through which we've passed? What or who is there for us to subvert? What information might it yield up that is not already common knowledge? Second and third possibilities: we were arms suppliers or narcotics traffickers. But did you find weapons or drugs on us? Or a stash of money received in exchange for weapons or drugs? Fourth possibility: we were saboteurs sent here to blow up bridges and railways. But there are no railways, and, had we blown up any bridges, you would have known about it. Did you find on us explosives or the means of making explosives, saltpetre and detonators? No! Fifth and final possibility: we were couriers. Now I ask you, Mr Meyan, had someone in China or Burma wished to communicate with someone in India, would he have chosen for that purpose two highly visible Europeans when any Lisu, Naga, Mishmi, Singhpo or Hkamti able to travel unnoticed along that same route would have done just as well? Of course not. There is one more thing that you ought to take into account. Had we been engaged in a criminal enterprise, would we have *volunteered* ourselves for arrest? Of course not. Seriously, we believe that we are entitled to a better reception than we've got. Think about it, Mr Meyan.'

By a sequence of nods, grunts and *accha*s, the ADC indicated his understanding and sympathy. In the twilight of a long career in government service, he knew the Kafkaesque implications of our predicament. He had seen many times that octopus of administrative and juridical processes that swallowed its victims whole, that mindless hydra of procedural punishment of the innocent — and, when I had finished my presentation, he repeated, 'Better you speak with Madam Deputy Commissioner,' and personally escorted us into her office.

Kum Archana Arora, like Meyan, was a seasoned bureaucrat. But she was more suspicious and, unlike him, not approaching the end of her career. She had more to lose by a wrong decision. I should have come straight to the point. Instead, I began by unctuously contrasting our detention with that of Pandit Jawaharlal Nehru, who, while detained by the British, had been accommodated in such an unobtrusive manner that he was able to write *Discovery of India*. 'Don't tell me about the British,' she retorted. 'My mother was *gaoled* by the British.'

If my opening tactic caused offence, what followed was even worse. 'Suppose, Madam, that, upon reaching the summit of

Everest, Sherpa Tensing and Sir Edmund Hilary had been met by a babel of *babus* demanding to see their Inner Line passes.' An expression of unutterable pain came into her soft, grey eyes.

I then told her about our adventure. Told in the round without interruptions it seemed almost plausible, and here I seemed about to win her sympathy. 'Madam, whatever crime you accuse us of,' I added, unnecessarily, 'there remains this mountain of a fact. We *walked across Burma.*' Her response afforded us our first glimpse of the wall of indifference that would greet us at home. She decided on the spot and against Meyan's advice to refer our case to her superiors. If we were not subversives, spies, arms traders, drug traffickers, saboteurs or couriers for a foreign power, then let *them* release us. Meanwhile, as concessions in deference to her ADC's advice, our clothes and toiletries were to be restored to us and we were to be detained under guard at the inspection bungalow.

That night at the IB two policemen shared our room, and two others slept outside. Whenever the guards outside needed to use the *nam dum*, they unbolted the door and came through the room, exchanging banter with their colleagues. They were urologically or otherwise infirm, and there was loud coming and going throughout the night. Thus ended our third day of captivity.

* * *

We were allowed to wander next morning as far as the dining room for toast and butter and tea. Then Deori and Sikiani took us to the hospital, though not for any medical purpose. To complete their reports they needed my employment history, and the hospital offered a venue safe from competing investigators. Until weariness defeated them, they noted the particulars of the snowball business I ran from a stand in front of my house when I was 12, the soft-drinks concession I ran at the ferry landing when I was 13, the paper route I had had when I was 14...

When we returned to the IB, a round faced man professing to represent the *Immi*gration Department of the Ministry of Home Affairs' and operating under the pseudonym 'Lama' was waiting for us, furious that we had gone off with Deori and Sikiani. He had the Nelles map of Burma that I had entrusted to Gogoi. He and two assistants examined me in the dining room, while two other assistants, jolly tribals from Assam, took Mats off to the bedroom to examine him. Sensing from Lama's oily manner that the SP had already convinced him of our inherent criminality, I said rude things like, 'Don't you feel a little demeaned, Mr Lama?' and, 'Aren't you just abetting a process that encourages the national paranoia?' and, 'Who on earth is ever going to read your report? What will you call it, the Tucker/Larsson Report?' Meanwhile, will you kindly tell me *what you are doing with my map*?' They seemed chiefly concerned to establish when Mats and I had left Europe and how we had met.

All of a sudden a convoy of jeeps roared into the compound and out of it sprang two army majors, a Sikh captain and half a dozen other ranks: Colonel Sapru's men. A sharp mêlée arose over who was supposed to have the 'first crack at us'. Lama allowed that he had 'jumped the queue' but maintained pragmatically that he was 'nearly finished. ... Just a few more questions, please,' he said wagging his head piteously. 'How *many* more questions?' 'Half hour, *bas*!' Majors Banhot and Sinha watched contemptuously from the veranda while their Sikh subordinate handled the haggling. Service life had taught them the important virtue of patience, but deferring to a nerd like Lama must have vexed them sorely. Nevertheless, they decided to let him continue.

His inquisition lasted until well into the afternoon, by which time the valiant majors were nearly comatose with boredom. They opened their interrogation by presenting to us bags of sweets and disclaiming malevolent intent. 'Please understand, Mr Tucker, we are not here to punish you,' they said. 'The Indian Army would never resort to torture to get at truth. We want only information.' They asked us if we had seen Nagas in Kachinland.

'No,' I answered. 'The Naga Hills are west of the Hukawng Valley, but, on reaching the Tanai Hka, we turned north and skirted the eastern side of the Hukawng.'

Mats and I had known that, if captured, we would be questioned about our route, especially about the sector from Second Brigade headquarters to the border, and, to protect the column and any other KIA force using that route in future, we had decided to conceal it. We had also decided to suppress Mats's military background and my venture into Vijayanagar but to tell the truth about all else, loading it with as much detail as possible, partly to enhance an appearance of veracity and partly to reduce the time available for unearthing inconsistencies. We had rehearsed our stories carefully and were fairly confident that we would not be caught out. But it was true that we had seen no Nagas. 'Then why have you marked the location of the headquarters of the National Socialist Council of Nagaland [NSCN] on your map?' asked Major Banhot.

'That was done by someone else, a sergeant at KIA GHQ [Awng Seng La] before we knew our exact route. He thought that the KIA would take us through the Hukawng and hand us over to the Nagas, but they didn't. I have no idea how he knew where Naga headquarters is or if the site he has marked is accurate.'

'Why did you avoid the Nagas?'

'We were not consulted about the route. If there were any intention to avoid Nagaland, it would have been because of the unsettled conditions there. Apparently, a schism has erupted between their two main groups, and they have turned their guns on each other.'[3]

'You must have heard of Phizo?'

'I believe that he was the leader of one of the Naga groups, that he lived for many years in London, and that he is now dead. I know nothing else about him.'[4]

'You did not meet Phizo when you were in London?'

'No.'

'Your trip had nothing to do with contacting the Nagas?'

'The sole purpose of our trip was to walk across Burma.'

'Did you see any Nagas when you were at KIA GHQ, Mr Tucker?'

'No; and it would surprise me to learn that there were Nagas there.'

'Are the Kachins supplying the Nagas with arms?'

'I have no idea, Major Banhot, but I shouldn't think so. The KIA

3. At various times and in varying degrees the CPB succeeded with its policy of 'minority fronts' in dividing the Karen, Karenni, Kachin, Rakhine, Shan, Chin, Naga, Pao and Wa insurgencies (see, generally, Smith, 1991).
4. Angami Zapu Phizo founded the National Naga Council (NNC) in 1946 and led it for many years. In 1979 Thuingaleng Muivah challenged his leadership and formed the NSCN, which is now the main Naga insurgent group.

needs all the arms it gets. Its Chief of Staff told me that the only limit to the number of soldiers that they can put in the field is their ability to provide them with arms.'

'Who is the KIA's Chief of Staff, Mr Tucker?'

'Major General Malizup Zau Mai.'

'Did you notice a KIA presence when you were in Pinawng Zup?'

'It was my impression, Major, that the Lisu living in that area do not particularly like the KIA or the Burma Army. My impression was that the Pinawng Zup Lisu want only to be left alone.'

'Did you see any Nagas at Pinawng Zup?'

'No. And, again, I don't think there were any. There might have been the odd trader, but if so we did not see any. ... Can I ask *you* something?' I said, shifting the onus. 'Why is this border so sensitive? No one who has interrogated us has been able to explain this to us. The Lisu of Pinawng Zup threaten no one. Their only weapons are crossbows and cap guns, which they use for hunting. The KIA hardly ever visits there, and then only on public relations exercises. And no other insurgent group operates there. As I've said, our impression is that they want only to be left alone.'

He suggested that the Nagas might use the Vijayanagar corridor as a route into India. Then he said, 'Mr Tucker, you must have formed some idea about what will happen in Burma?'

'We weren't in Burma Proper, Major Banhot, and in our trek across the Kachin Hills we met very few Burmans. But I can tell you how the Kachins see the future. They believe that Burma's prospects of lasting stability hang on the elections. If the elections promised by the junta bring only cosmetic change, then the violence and chaos will continue. But if they lead to real change, there can be stability. Sooner or later, the Kachins believe, a government in Rangoon will have to meet the hill tribes' demands for some measure of control over their own affairs. Perhaps the Burman students we met at Möng Ko and Pajau Bum and the ABSDF student-soldiers along the Thai border will serve as a conduit of understanding between Burmans and the hill tribes, and this generation won't repeat the mistakes of the past.'

'You seem to sympathize with the insurgents, Mr Tucker?'

'My sympathies are with everyone caught up in this brutal war, Major Banhot: both Burmans and insurgents.'

'Am I right in thinking that you would like to go back? That you would like to visit those groups that you have not already visited?'

'Right now I never want to see the jungle again.'

'But in a few months you might feel different, isn't it?'

'What are you suggesting?'

'Let us suppose that you had the opportunity to visit the Nagas. If you had such an opportunity, would that interest you? I am thinking that there might be possibility that you might be wanting to go back to Burma and there might be possibility that we might help you. Would that interest you?'

'Are you suggesting that I spy on the Nagas, Major Banhot?'

'The Indian Army does not employ spies. It's just an idea, Mr Tucker.'

'The Indian Army and the KIA should be talking with one another. There are areas of common concern to be pursued here, and I would be glad to use any influence I might have with the KIA to arrange for you to meet them. But I could not spy on the Nagas or on any of the other hill tribes of Burma.'

'What might be these areas of common concern, Mr Tucker?'

'A power vacuum is developing in Burma. A stable Burma is in India's interest. ...'

* * *

The Army finished with us late the following afternoon. Now a tall, stout Pathan appeared. He professed to represent, symmetrically, the *Emi*gration Department of the Ministry of Home Affairs and identified himself as 'just a human being', but his whole manner proclaimed him to be much more important than any of our other interrogators. His voice was like one of those machines that addresses you dolefully from the wall of a lift ('fifth floor; sixth floor'), and his fierce stare and monotone style of examination had a curiously corrosive effect on your nerves. He was chiefly interested in learning what we had told the others of what we knew about the border and what leverage a rival investigator could exert to extract this information from us. We learned later that he came from the Indian Prime Minister's office. His pseudonym was Khan.

'Mr Shelby, you are telling me that the Chief of Staff of the People's Army ...'

'*Not* the Chief of Staff. General Kyi Myint was the Northern Bureau's *Vice*-Chief of Staff, Mr Khan. Let's get this correct.'

'You are telling me, Mr Shelby, that the Vice-Chief of Staff sent you to India?'

'No, I did not say that he sent us to India, Mr Khan. He contacted CPB GHQ, and they indicated that they were sympathetic to our idea of travelling to the Thai border through areas the CPB controlled.'

'Did you have a visa for Thailand, Mr Shelby?'

'Yes.'

'May I see this visa?'

'It is with the SP. He has seized our passports and all our other documents.'

'If I obtain your passport, will you let me see this visa?'

'Of course.'

'Mr Shelby, I believe that you are having a camera?'

'We both have cameras.'

'May I know what kind of camera?'

'A Minolta SR.'

'You must be having fillum?'

'Indeed, seven rolls of exposed film.'

'Where is this fillum, Mr Shelby?'

'The SP has them.'

'If we develop this fillum, would you let us see the pictures, Mr Shelby?'

'You are very welcome to see them, but I can tell you now, they contain nothing that implicates us in any crime. My one difficulty is how would you develop them? They are critically important to my work and I cannot risk losing or spoiling them. At the very least, I would insist on their being developed by Kodak in my presence.'

'What *is* your work, Mr Shelby?'

'I write novels and travel books.'

'May I know who may be publishing your books, Mr Shelby?'

'No one.'

'*Why* are they not publishing your books, Mr Shelby?'

'Because I haven't offered them for publication.'

'Why haven't you offered your books for publication, Mr Shelby?

'I'm too proud to offer them for publication.'

'If you had a visa for Thailand, Mr Shelby, why are you not going to Thailand?'

'The CPB advised us that hostilities at the Thai border meant that they could not guarantee our security.'

'Who told you that you could not go to Thailand, Mr Shelby?'

'No one told us that we could not go to Thailand. CPB GHQ said that it could not guarantee our security over that route.'

'How long were you at CPB GHQ?'

'We were not at CPB GHQ. We were at CPB Northern Bureau headquarters from 14 January to 28 January.'

'Did you meet any other generals at Communist Party headquarters?'

'We met the titular Chief of Staff of the CPB's Northern Bureau armies in Möng Ko.'

'May I know his name?'

'General Aung Gyi.'

'Ongee?'

'*Aung*, A-U-N-G and *Gyi*. It is pronounced "Gee" but it is spelled G-Y-I.'

'How old a man was General Ongee?'

'Fifty-eight.'

'You are having Indian visa and your friend is not having, Mr Shelby. Why is it?'

'We first planned to enter Burma from Thailand and to get Mr Larsson's Indian visa in Bangkok before crossing into Burma. But after travelling in China we decided, rather on the spur of the moment, to try to reach the Burma border through China. As the area through which we had to pass was restricted, we rated our chances of reaching Burma by that route as too remote to justify delaying our departure to obtain an Indian visa for Mr Larsson. I already had an Indian visa, and, we reasoned, if we happened to reach the border, we would carry on to Rangoon and obtain the visa there. This was hopelessly naïve, of course. There was not the slightest chance of eluding the checkposts and patrols on the Kutkai road, but we did not know this at the time. After the CPB discouraged us from proceeding south, the only option remaining to us was the one we took. By then, however, it was too late to obtain an Indian visa for Mr Larsson.'

'Have you written anything about your trip through Burma, Mr Shelby?'

'While we were waiting in Möng Ko for a decision from CPB GHQ about our onward journey I started writing an article.'

'Where is this article, Mr Shelby?'

'With my other documents.'

'May I see this article, Mr Shelby?'

We were about to retire for the night when Lama reappeared, pretending that he had been sent to fetch us to the police station for the purpose of handing over our dirty clothes for passing on to the *dhobi*. 'You and Mr Khan want to see my article,' I said. Lama smiled in his oily way.

Meyan, Khan, Mansai, Bora, two clerical assistants and half a dozen armed constables crouching in the perimeters were waiting for us at the police station. The generator was down and a hurricane lamp provided the only light. Meyan requested the keys to my rucksack, then peremptorily threw them back at me and ordered me to open my rucksack and exhibit the contents. His anger alarmed me. I deduced that he had turned against us, but, unbeknownst to us, he was only annoyed with the DC for having ignored his advice to ship us on to Itanagar. '*It is because Madam herself is being transferred. She will leave Changlang, and I will inherit this mess. One wrong decision and I am ruined*,' he was thinking.

Bora made another inventory, carefully noting and correlating everything with Mamio's inventory. I caught Khan purloining a page from the notes that I had made of my interview with Sai Lek and protested to Meyan.

'Mr Tucker, why are you not bringing everything with you when my orders were to bring everything with you?' said Meyan. I had left my sleeping bag at the IB.

'Mr Lama didn't say to bring anything with us,' I replied. Meyan scowled.

'*There* they are! *There* they are!' cried Mansai suddenly.

The films had surfaced. Khan raised again the question of developing them. 'We will give you negatives, Mr Shelby. We will not keep negatives, that is promise. We only want copies,' and, before I could respond, he added, 'Mr Shelby, why are you not wanting us to develop this fillum?' Meyan scowled again. We were guilty!

'Mr Khan,' I said, 'you are making a great fuss about nothing. As I have already told you, these films are snaps of mountains, rivers, jungle, villagers, Mats on an elephant, me on an elephant — the kind of pictures one takes on holiday. There is nothing in them that will interest you or anyone else in the Indian government. My one concern is that they are developed by Kodak in my presence.' Meyan's expression softened. Mansai was wrong. We were innocent!

'They must be having laboratory in Calcutta,' said Khan.

'Kodak's laboratory is in Bombay, Mr Khan — not Calcutta. You must know that.'

'Bombay, Calcutta, Delhi, they must all be having laboratories, Mr Shelby.'

'I think not, Mr Khan, but, wherever the laboratory is, only Kodak has the proper equipment for developing this film.'

'Kodak will develop it. That is promise, Mr Shelby. You have nothing to worry. It will be done in two days, maybe four. That is promise. I will send special courier — four days.'

Meyan's expression hardened again. He had been deceived! If it took only four days, why *shouldn't* Khan see the film? 'I will *make an order*!' he shouted.[5]

After completing the inventories we went with Khan and Lama to Circuit House to 'finish it off', and everything was suddenly jolly again. Khan dispatched a car to Margherita for chicken and whisky, the staff of Circuit House prepared an almost sumptuous meal for us, and I was invited to speak on the topics dearest to me. The KIA's history and aims. The universal support that the KIA enjoyed among Kachin villagers and its invincibility in the theatre of war where it operates. *Wunpawng Mungdan*'s intractable forests. Past hostilities between various hill tribes and the ever mutating pattern of their various alliances. When religion was and was not a factor in the war. The Chinese factor. The narcotics factor. Relations between the ethnic insurgencies and the CPB, and between the CPB and the CPC (Communist Party of China). Prospects of peace. And the implications of the Burmese Civil War

5. Meyan did not carry out this threat. Further reflection must have reinstated his first opinion that we were innocent, and Khan, having vindicated his power, did not allude to the matter again.

for India. I was in full flood when Meyan, exhausted and dispirited by the intrigues of colleagues, his own vacillating suspicions and inventories, appeared, only to disappear without a word to any of us. And after dinner, when we resumed the interrogation, even Khan's big, brown-sugar eyes began to glaze over. His questions betrayed signs of drift. His deep, monotonous voice grew fainter ('sixth floor; fifth floor; going downnnn'). He stopped listening. We would not, after all, continue through the night to 'finish it off'.

* * *

'Mr Shelby,' Khan asked me on resuming the interrogation next morning, 'can you explain this letter?' He had seen a draft of the letter to Carole that I had entrusted to Noah. It bore the heading, 'Vijayanagar, 4 April 1989'.

'This is a draft of a letter I wrote in Pinawng Zup. I wrote it thinking that I would be able to post it from Vijayanagar. In the event, I gave it to some Lisu to post for me. As you can see, Mr Khan, it reflects my concerns for my wife's fears for me.'

'*Accha*,' he said, relieved. I learned later that he already knew of my venture over the border and was testing whether my alibi would withstand the scrutiny of rival interrogators. 'Mr Shelby,' he continued, 'can you prove to me that you are not working for China?'

'I can't prove such a thing, Mr Khan, because I can't prove a negative. I can only *assert* that we were not working for anyone.'

'Mr Shelby, I have stayed over especially to finish my report. You must be knowing that I was supposed to be in Khonsa today.'

'We are grateful, Mr Khan.'

'I have set aside my other duties to finish my report. The ADC wants me to finish my report. I have promised him that I will finish my report. But, Mr Shelby, you make complications.'

'What complications, Mr Khan?'

'Why is it that you are not able to prove to me that you are not working for China, Mr Shelby?'

'Can you prove that *you* are not working for China, Mr Khan?'

He asked me no further questions.

Now it was my turn. 'Mr Khan,' I said, 'I am an old man, and it would be a matter of very deep sorrow for me were I not allowed to return to India. India was where I became a Christian. I have taught in a mission school here. India is an important theme in three of the books I have written. I therefore have a favour to ask of you. If you believe that we have done anything sinister, please confront us with your suspicions now. Otherwise, please don't allege anything against us in your report that might prejudice our chances of returning to India.'

'You are not an old man, Mr Shelby.'

'We have just spent two days with you, Mr Khan. We are real to you. But, to your superiors in Delhi, we will only be two disembodied names in a pile of documents that will drift from one office to another for months, maybe even years. No one will want to assume responsibility for taking a decision. Everyone will initial the Larsson–Tucker file and pass it on – unless and until someone takes an active interest in pressing for a decision. Will you do that for us? Will you take an active interest in pressing for a decision?'

'Once I have filed my report, Mr Shelby, it is out of my hands.'

'Is there nothing you can do to push this matter along, Mr Khan?'

'I have done what I can, Mr Shelby.'

'How long are we likely to remain in Changlang?'

'That is entirely up to the state authorities.'

'It is my understanding that Changlang wants to transfer us but can't do so without first obtaining your clearance. Can you give us this clearance, Mr Khan?'

'You will have to ask the DC.'

'I understand that she is leaving Changlang within the next few days.'

'Then you will have to ask the ADC.'

'I fear that he has turned against us. How long will it take you to make your report?'

'I will dictate the report tomorrow. It will be typed. I will read it and make corrections. Then it will be retyped. The answer to your question is, maybe two days.'

'After you have posted the report, how long will it take to reach Delhi?'

'Only one day.'

'And after that, how much longer are we likely to be in Changlang?' ...

With Khan's departure went our best hope of escaping the yawning shadow of *babu*dom.

That evening we were in our room dolorously pondering our predicament when Lama appeared. This was purely a personal visit, he announced, dispelling the impression that he had come to take us off to the police station again. No, he said pleasantly, our adventure had awakened in him thoughts of his lost youth.

His thoughts, he went on, had reverted to the time when he was a schoolboy at a mission school in Kalimpong, then a centre for the Tibetan wool trade. The traders with their apple-red faces, conical, scallop-brimmed hats and felt boots with pointed toes had inspired him with a determination to see their country, so he had borrowed money from a family servant to finance an expedition and persuaded a school chum to accompany him. They had crossed the border into Sikkim and spent a month there wasting a great deal of their money. Then four days' climb had brought them to the pass, beyond which they had found the first Tibetan village surrounded by tattered prayer pennants and elaborately wrought brass prayer wheels fluttering and revolving in the strong wind. Thereafter, every day vouchsafed something new: silken-haired yaks grazing in tall grass; processions of monks swathed in padded gowns; pink-walled monasteries endlessly circled by pilgrims mumbling muted incantations; columns of shaggy ponies collared in bells and scarlet yaks' tails defiling across wind-blasted immensities and threading precariously through deep gorges. On reaching Lhasa, however, they had received their outraged fathers' peremptory summonses to return to school.

A year later they repeated the trip by Land Rover, dismantled and carried over the pass by porters and then reassembled. Now they learned that war was about to break out between China and India. There was a run on petrol, so they entrusted the Land Rover to a local Bengali merchant and walked back to Kalimpong. The merchant reported later that he had also been obliged to flee and had abandoned the Land Rover with his own possessions.

The route to Lhasa was now closed. There were no more long columns of mules bringing their wool to exchange for Indian wares in the market at Kalimpong. But, if Lama had done it, we mused after he left us, why couldn't we? Mats was keen, and I was *only* 54. Lama's uncovenanted visit was a very special treat. It restored our confidence. It renewed our hopes. It was as though we were back tramping over hills and through forests. But it was only an hallucinatory interlude.

The interrogations resumed next day with the return of Majors Banhot and Sinha and their teams, predictably and typically while we were at breakfast. 'Good morning, gentlemen,' I said, cheerfully. 'Why do you have such long, disapproving faces this morning? I thought that we parted on friendly terms.'

'You are interviewing the Chairman of ULFA, isn't it?' screamed Major Banhot. 'I am asking if you had seen any Nagas, Mizos or Assamese, and you are saying you are not seeing any Nagas, Mizos or Assamese! I am remembering it specifically. Why are you not telling us that you are interviewing the Chairman of ULFA?'

'You asked us if we had seen any *Nagas*. You didn't say anything about Assamese. At any rate, your questions triggered no connections with Castro.'

'I am talking about ULFA! *Why* are you calling the Chairman of ULFA Castro?'

'Because he resembled Castro. We told Mr Khan about him. If you also want to hear about him, very well, we will tell you too – but *after* we have finished our breakfast.'

'Where were you on 4th April? Where were you on 4th April?' They had learned of the letter that I had entrusted to Noah.

'Dear me, Major Sinha. Whatever has wrought such a transformation? We were under the impression that you entertained kindly feelings towards us. Now you are consumed with horrible suspicions. Please sit down. As you would say, take your rest.'

We told them all about our meetings with Castro, and I repeated my story about the letter.

After the majors left, two men, a Mr Nath and a Mr Gupta, came to the IB and quietly emphasized that we would be taken to Delhi and handed over to our embassies. When, we asked? Soon, they replied. They had no questions for us except to ask how well we were being looked after.

After that, there was silence – the silence of hope. Each day we woke wondering if this would be the day of the silver chopper descending from beyond the rim of hills to the north to collect and fly us to Dibrugarh for a connecting flight to Delhi. But nothing came of Nath and Gupta's prediction. Then we learned, a little disconcertingly, that they had no authority from Meyan to visit us. Then there was the kind of silence that prisoners know – the silence of fear.

Our room opened at one end on to the IB's main corridor, living room and dining room, and, at the other, on to a veranda. Gradually, as our gaolers became more accustomed to our presence and less paranoid about our chances of escape, we were allowed to sit out on that veranda. Goats and pigs strolled about the grounds scavenging for food, and birds cavorted in and out of the frangipanis. Several hundred yards below us was the Tirap or Changlang River, from which the district had taken its name. Beyond it were the green and blue foothills of Patkai *shagawng*, invitingly near, and, beyond them, Burma, the cause of our present distress.

Most mornings, the hills were wrapped in clouds – huge black and purple, rain-filled clouds. Late in the afternoon and into the early evening we could hear cymbals and chanting from a temple in the valley. Most nights it rained, sometimes all night, the heavy, pounding rain of the advancing monsoon, thunder shaking the sodden earth and lightning illuminating the murky heavens.

About this time I wrote a letter to the DC predicated on the already overworked assumption that the two heroes in her custody were biding the moment when their achievement would be recognized. It concluded with a number of requests: to be allowed to speak with our loved ones; to be allowed to speak with our embassies; for certain medicines obtainable in Margherita but not in Changlang; for English-language newspapers; for the use of a table and some scrap paper 'so that I can get on with my writing pending completion of your procedures'; and for verification that 'all of the documents and other materials lent to the various people who have examined us have been returned'.

Meyan visited us at the IB soon afterwards and informed us that moves were afoot to transfer us, not to Itanagar, where we would be subject to further indignities, but to Delhi, where everything was more efficient. He gave us some biscuits and took us to the Changlang public library and urged us to borrow books on his ticket. A large, gift-wrapped box of *barfi* arrived from none other than Mansai. Then we began receiving obsolete copies of *Indian Express* and *The Statesman*, and the local people began calling on us to solicit our autographs. Mats's ankles returned to normal; the purple scars of half a dozen jungle sores were all that remained of my wounds; and, with the unremitting succession of meals (*puris*, curried vegetables and onions), we were almost content.

But nothing happened. Then Meyan gave orders disallowing further visits and disappeared to Tinsukia (where, we learned, he was building a house), and we were alone again with our guards. Then someone sympathetic to us discreetly informed us that we were to be taken to Dibrugarh and from there flown directly to Delhi.

'Why that's *wonderful* news!' we cried jubilantly. '*When?*'

'In two or three days,' he said.

But the DC was at that very moment preparing to hand over to a young man who proved to be even more pusillanimous and indecisive than she was.

* * *

Another week passed and another, and soon we were in the middle of May, still staring dumbly at the fungus on our plaster walls and the verdigris on the iron bars over our windows. Why were we still in Changlang? Did anyone *know* where we were? Why hadn't our gaolers let us contact our loved ones?

Because I had tampered with my Indian visa, its ostensible expiry date was 27 March, implying that the date of issue was 28 December. If Delhi contacted their Peking consulate and learned thereby that no visa had been issued to me on 28 December, they might deduce that my visa was forged. By whom, they would ask, and wonder if my passport was also false. This fantasy gave us recurrent nightmares.

To hide Mats's military past, we had stated that he had worked in Sweden as a bakery delivery boy, as he had for a brief time. But my diaries alluded to him as 'Lt. Larsson' and 'Capt. Larsson'. Sooner or later, we feared, our gaolers would discover the truth. Our diaries also revealed that we had come up the Tawang Hka (and not the Tarung Hka as we had told them) and that the KIA had accompanied us as far as Pinawng Zup (and not only as far as Second Brigade headquarters). Once these discrepancies were exposed, our gaolers would wonder what else we were lying about – and, specifically, why a professional soldier was accompanying me.

Most worrying of all was whether someone would deduce from the date on the draft of the Noah letter and the corresponding bare pages in my diary that I had crossed into India on 2 April. In whispered, coded conversation after the guards retired (lest the room was bugged; 'V' was Vijayanagar), we concerted an alibi to account for my diary's silence. The memory of that venture haunted me. Why were those Lisu suddenly so insistent that I turn back, and why their odd, frightened looks when I hesitated? Why their nervous refusal to explain the necessity for turning back, and why the audible exhalation of relief that greeted my eventual acquiescence? We could not avoid the thought that something was happening along that border – something we knew nothing about but from which innocence alone would not protect us. In our isolation we looked inward, and our troubled imaginations were quick to supply an answer – *drugs*. We were clear, at least, that neither the KIA nor the Hidden Valley Lisu had any such involvement, but we knew that Khamti Long Shans also traded across that border, and there might be others. If *they* trafficked in drugs, their contacts on the Indian side would have unmonitored resort to the sortie from Dibrugarh, in which event there would be accomplices within government. What chance would we have against such powerful adversaries? It was not *what* we knew but what they might *think* we knew.

Our fears now took on a chillingly new dimension. The mysterious Nath and Gupta suddenly reappeared with a rather sinister man who was obviously their superior. He refused to disclose his name, so we called him simply the Capo. 'Mr Tucker,' he said menacingly, 'you were in Vijayanagar.'

Had he deduced this fact from the Noah letter? What did he really know? I fought to conceal my panic.

'You were seen there on the 2nd of April with three other men.'

There *had* been three men, and I *was* there on 2 April. 'I intended to go to Vijayanagar but went only as far as the border, where some Lisu warned me to turn back,' I said.

He smirked. 'How did you know where the border was?'

'We reached a ridge that one of the Lisu said was the border.'

'Who were these Lisu?'

'Just Lisu. I didn't enquire into their particulars.'

'Where did you meet them?'

'In the forest.'

'How convenient. You just met them in the forest? You went for a stroll and there they were. What were they doing in the forest?'

'I don't know. I suppose they were merchants.'

'Did you meet them before or after the river?'

'Which river are you referring to, the creek about half a mile above Adehdi?'

'The Noa Dihing.'

'The Noa Dihing is in the valley. I didn't get that far.'

'Why did you proceed as far as the ridge if you made the decision to turn back before reaching it?'

'So that I could say that I had walked from China to India.'

'You are not telling the truth, Mr Tucker, and I demand that you tell me the truth. You went to Vijayanagar. Why did you go to Vijayanagar? And *why* are you not telling me the truth?'

'I haven't the faintest idea what you are driving at, sir. But if you wish to believe that I went to Vijayanagar, so be it.'

'You were seen in Vijayanagar with three men on the 2nd of April. I have received a report that you were in Vijayanagar.'

'Then you were misinformed.'

'Stop pretending, Mr Tucker. Stop pretending.'

While the Capo was occupied with me, Gupta and Nath were interrogating Mats. They told him that they were trying to catch a ring of smugglers, and even knew who the smugglers were, but needed our evidence to prosecute them. 'Did they tell you what the smugglers were smuggling?' I asked him later.

'Drugs.'

Mats and I had often talked about our 'luck'. We needed a great deal of it now. In this hothouse of germinating speculations we discussed the implications, fusing reality and fantasy. Details like the confidence that these men exuded and the expensive watches they wore stoked our paranoia. Either they were bona fide investigators – in which case, why did they interview us secretly and without Meyan's permission? Or they were testing us to see how much we knew about their activities and whether we had the wit to sustain our alibi? If they were gangsters, as we suspected, they would have to decide whether the risk of exterminating us outweighed the risk of our disclosing what we might know. To put us away forever, they needed only the perjured testimony of two or three hired witnesses that we had, for example, collaborated in smuggling heroin, impossible to controvert, because no one would believe that we had walked across Burma purely from motives of adventure. And once formally tried and convicted, nothing would induce our governments to intervene.

I would be the first to wake each morning, usually at 0330 hours, and lie for an hour or so haunted by fear. After revisiting the implications of the Capo, Gupta and Nath, my thoughts would turn to our gaolers and investigators. What would they do if they could not find my visa? What would they think when they found no evidence of my writings? Would they send more investigators, to breed more reports? We had given the cook, Mej, some letters to post for us. Would Meyan discover this and conclude that we were using these 'other channels' to communicate with our 'principals'? I knew that this tendency to wake up early and fret was symptomatic of depression; that, if not checked, it would become self-perpetuating; and I would try to distract myself by listening to a radio borrowed from Prem Bahadur, the cook's assistant. But this merely aggravated my sadness by its dreary repetition of political rectitudes. Once, lying there with the rain pounding on the tin roof, I even wondered if I *wanted* to be released. Then reason would reassert itself, and I would recognize such reflections for what they were.

At about 0500 hours I would rise, driven by the knowledge that if I imposed no discipline over myself, indiscipline would assert its own agenda. I would then focus on tasks, hoping, like the narrator in *The First Circle*, that they would get me through the day.

My first task was to bath. If I bathed before 0500 hours I bathed in darkness, but after 0500 hours the generator functioned and I could switch on the amber glow of a 20-watt bulb. No one competed for the hot water at this early hour, and it was so hot that it had to be mixed with cold water in a plastic bucket. The sill of the barred window on the wall above our shower was littered with scraps of desiccated soap and a broken toothbrush. The glass there and on the other window was opaque with dirt. The walls were painted dull blue.

After bathing, I shaved, dressed and made up my bed. I was now ready to wake H. P. (Harinder Prasad) Singh, the police sergeant known to us as 'HP Sauce' who, with the other guards, slept dispersed on the sofas in the living room next to our door. I would tap on the door, lightly to avoid disturbing Mats but loudly enough to rouse HP Sauce and, moments later, would hear the bolt slide in its casing. HP Sauce would then go outside and unlock the veranda door – and, while he was thus engaged, I would sneak into the living room and nick an article of his clothing. It was a little game by which we paid tribute to our common predicament.

The use of the veranda was our most cherished privilege; and the most agreeable part of my day was the half hour or so after dawn spent sitting on a wicker sofa there watching the dark clouds tumbling through the valley below us with the night's unspent rain. Tucked into a bend in the road winding up to the IB from Circuit House lay Meyan's baleful little bungalow, and further down the road was the State Bank of India, perpetually guarded by the Central Reserve Police in their woollen hats. Beyond the bank was the bus stand with its agenda of two departures a day for Margherita – always, I would reflect, without us. I would hear the motors revving, then hear the buses roar through the town's narrow streets, stopping briefly at the post office to take on more passengers, the trail of sound ever more faint until it ceased altogether at the gap in the hills by the police station.

About 0600 hours Pradip, who lodged permanently at the IB, emerged to float about the grounds in his *dhoti* and flip-flops smoking. He was always extremely cautious about speaking and sometimes stood quite still and erect, like a Magritte casket. Then Prem Bahadur would bring me a thermos of tea, walking around the house to avoid waking Mats. In the first days of our detention, before Mej took over as cook, our tea was boiled together with milk and sugar and tasted like syrup, an economy achieved at our expense to pay for the former cook's drink. Now it came *ulug ulug*, each of the constituents in a separate container so that we could sweeten or dilute it according to taste. Mansai's nephew lodged in the neighboring room. About 0700 hours he would come out onto his veranda to resume his surveillance, and, soon afterwards, HP Sauce would make his first proper appearance.

HP Sauce's smoker's recce around the grounds was the signal for the IB's remaining inhabitants to rise. They were overnight guests who were not sufficiently important to stay at Circuit House. Those with early business at Government House had priority claim on the other bathing facility, an outside tap. (Ours was a dedicated bathroom.) Mats would rise about 0745 hours. Then Mej and Prem Bahadur would serve us breakfast – dates, *anda* (egg) boiled, *anda* scrambled, toast and more tea – which we took on the veranda. They were heroic in their eagerness to please, but the eggs were always rubbery and the table inevitably deficient in forks or salt. After breakfast, Mats had his bath and made his bed, then settled down to read the latest newspapers received from our gaolers, while I beguiled the long, hot hours composing the first drafts of what was then called *In the Land of the KIA*.

In our after-lights-out, coded conversations, Mats and I often discussed 'E' (escape) as an option open to us if all else failed. Then one evening, during our right-to-enjoy-guests dispensation, two diminutive, but solidly built men came to our veranda. They hung about waiting for an opportunity to speak to us discreetly and, when we were alone, they announced, 'We are Nagas,' as though further explanation was otiose. Our first thought was that the KIA had sent them. They told us that they would help us to escape. The report of our trek across Kachinland had touched their own desire for freedom, they said.

We did not pursue the proposition further that evening, but they returned next evening with a square-shaped pugnacious man who asserted fiercely that overpowering our guards would not be difficult for them, that Indian policemen were no match for Nagas. Once free of our gaolers, they said, a party of trustworthy men would escort us past the Inner Line, and a car would drive us to a place where we could hide until the search for us was abandoned, then drive us on to Bengal. Mats assured them that resort to force would not be necessary. He had already examined the screws fixing the bars to our windows and was confident that he could remove them. Having raised these tantalizing possibilities, the Nagas went off to make the arrangements, and we heard nothing more from them.

We also canvassed a plan of escape with a Bengali contractor who befriended us. He would visit us in our room, hoping for salacious conversation before going on to a Tongsa woman with whom he was prosecuting an affair in a shed behind the IB.[6] It was obvious even to us that his mistress was fonder of the drink and money he gave her than she was of him, but that did not seem to discourage him. Indeed, nothing ever seemed to discourage him. He was one of those fortunates who perceive their *raison d'être* purely in terms of arranging things. The guards got used to him and, after a show of monitoring our conversation, left us alone. On the mornings following these visits we would watch him from our veranda leave the IB for Government House, sober, though a little wan, shoulders thrown back and with briefcase in hand for another exciting day at brokering deals. He was exactly the sort of jolly company that in our dolours we relished most, and in one of his more ebullient moments he too proposed that we escape. 'If I were you, I would just up and off,' he said.

His plan, if anything so rash deserves to be called that, was to make a dash for Nepal. Such flights were common, he told us reassuringly. He himself had a cousin–brother who had escaped from fiscal difficulties by decamping to Nepal. There were no road checks and no border guards, he said. All we needed was someone willing to drive us to the border – and who better able to render this small service than himself? He would charge us only $10,000 – *cash*.

Kum Archana Arora departed for her new post. Then, in the last week of May something unexpected happened: we received a visit from an American diplomat named Haynes who was the vice-consul in Calcutta. Meyan and the new DC, Arun Goyal, escorted him to the IB after entertaining him to lunch at Circuit House. He brought gifts (a tube of Colgate toothpaste, two dozen plastic razors, a book on Chinese art) and news (Carole's job in Witney was 'going well'). However, when I asked him, 'Precisely what is the State Department

6. The Tongsas inhabit the hills around Changlang. They resemble those pictures of Nagas in the library of the Pitt Rivers Museum: heads shaved at the sides and hair swept back and rolled into buns; togas worn over their chests, cotton bandaging their crotches; all the men armed with bows and arrows. Very few of them have converted to Christianity.

doing to secure our release?' he spoke worryingly about respecting 'the paramountcy of Indian law'. 'I will try to visit you again within the next three to four months,' he said, but, turning the warm beam of his personality on our gaolers, added, 'If you are still here.' He grinned. They chuckled. It was better than anything that they could have hoped for.

Haynes went to some trouble to visit us. He meant well. And his visit established that Berit and Carole knew that we were alive. But our spirits sank to a new low after his departure.

Matters stood thus at the end of May. A month and a half had elapsed since our arrest. Although some of the restrictions on us were relaxed (now we were allowed biscuits with our tea and police-escorted walks beyond our compound), all else was immobility and stagnation. We were not charged. We were not tried. But neither were we released. And in our moments of bleakest pessimism we imagined that Meyan was taking his orders from the mysterious Capo. My thoughts vacillated between memories of Carole and the mounting dread of not seeing her again save in the visitors' room of an Indian prison. At this juncture we were presented with another mirage.

'Operation Bust Out' was Sanjay's idea. From almost the beginning of our detention, Pradip's roommate had taken an unusually sympathetic interest in us. Whenever we were in a mood for venting our grievances he always seemed to be present. His was the kind of handsome, open face that one trusted intuitively, and he was as cheerful and garrulous as Pradip was surly and taciturn. Moreover, he provided us with curious titbits of almost plausible counter-intelligence. It was from him that we learned that our 'neighbour with the telescopic eyes' was Mansai's nephew. Slowly he gained our confidence, and, when the moment was right, he unveiled his plan: we should make for the Burmese border. It was, he said, a march of only two days. He would supply us with a map and instruct us how to get there. He would also supply a plastic sheet, a *dah*, matches, rice, dates, bags to replace the equipment the SP had impounded and, all importantly, puttees. ('You *must* protect yourselves from the leeches.') He would buy all these things in the market for us. If we procured them ourselves, people would talk. He would even hide them for us, handing them over a few hours before departure – which was to be midnight the following Saturday, when Meyan would be in Tinsukia and HP Sauce and his men would be asleep. We would slip down the embankment at the back of the IB, circumvent the bank guards, hike as far as possible before dawn and harbour in the forest until it was safe to carry on. His map would indicate where we might encounter soldiers or police and where we could hide if pursued, and he would obtain for us a week's supply of rice 'just in case. But you won't have any trouble at all,' he said.

Such was our desperation that we did not dismiss Sanjay's plan out of hand. Mats was never very keen on it though. If we eluded our pursuers and succeeded in reaching the border, he pointed out, we would still have the problem of reaching the Kachins. We would have to rely on the Tongsas to lead us to the Nagas; on the Nagas to apprise the KIA; and on the KIA to escort us to Second Brigade headquarters, as they had done for Bertil Lintner. We had also to consider the rains. And, if we failed to reach the border, there would, of course, be no more IB (dismal as we thought it to be); no more Mej and Prem Bahadur; no more books from the public library; no more biscuits with tea and dates and *barfi*. It would be straight into Mansai's *en suite* cell and then on to prison.

Meyan put off his trip to Tinsukia, delaying implementation. That delay proved critical. We gave Pradip some letters to post for us, but when we asked him about the letters, he confessed that he had diverted them to Meyan. 'You gave them to me in Sanjay's presence,' he said. 'Sanjay is spying for Meyan.'

On Mats's face was the satisfaction of one who had known all along.

'Trust no one,' counselled Pradip. 'It is motto of modern India.'

* * *

Mats was not a turn-the-other-cheeker, while I must confess I have always found greater solace, if not doctrinal consistency, in the un-biblical 'The Lord helps those who help themselves' than in the Sermon on the Mount's exhortation to forgive your enemy. At any rate, the attempt at enticing us to escape seemed to both of us a declaration of war. 'We can't let them just walk over us.'

A school head staying overnight at the IB provided us with our first chance to strike back. I met him in the dining room and enquired if he happened to know the SP.

'Mansai?'

'Curious fellow, isn't he? I understand that he's up to his neck in it,' I said.

'Up to his neck in what?' he answered, puzzled.

'Do I have to spell it out for you? Wasn't he the SP at Vijayanagar before they transferred him to Changlang?'

I briefed him on how we had come to be at the IB. He listened politely but uncomprehendingly, then said, 'But what does that have to do with Mansai?'

'Let us understand each other, sir. You know that *I* know, and I know that *you* know, so we don't have to pretend. Our instructions at KIA Second Brigade headquarters were to contact Mansai as soon as we reached Vijayanagar. We were told that he would get round whatever problems arose, only we must contact him before any other Indian official got to us. Mansai is the Nagas' contact man. *Everyone* knows that.' We relied on Changlang's bush telegraph to complete the business. Thereafter, *Bête Noire* gave no further trouble.

Meyan was always going to be the more difficult target. Even the Bengali contractor, an extortion and peculation expert, conceded that he was incorruptible. 'Dishonesty is not there. He is dolphin among eels,' he told us metaphorically one evening *en route* to his assignation in the shed. The ADC had to be got at in other ways. Thenceforth none of our 'clandestine' letters was without reference to an ambassador, a senator or an MP. I even alluded to the President as 'George'. We reckoned that Meyan and, more importantly, his wife would deduce that our friends included some of the world's most powerful people. '*My love, why are you letting that bitch* [Kum Archana Arora] *do this to you? She has buzzed off to Itanagar, leaving you holding bag. You do not need this in your condition and at your age, my precious Narayan. Listen to me, my love. In another 18 months,* bas, *you will retire. Give this case to someone else. You have suffered enough. Now let somebody else suffer. Sooner or later, Mrs Tucker will inform the American ambassador, and he will inform President Bush, and he will inform the Prime Minister, and scandal will break over this whole nasty business. Then everyone will say that you didn't even let Mr Tucker write to Mrs Tucker. Why should you take the rap for what these buggers are doing, my precious?*' Meyan, hypertensive, operating on one kidney and far too busy with the many complex demands of his job for reflective detachment of the kind demanded by the Larsson/Tucker file, wanted rid of us. Hence the crude ploy to entice us into a trap. We were not indifferent to the pain that we were inflicting on him, but neither were we prepared to resign ourselves to indefinite wretchedness.

We further exploited his loathing of the Larsson/Tucker file by harassing him with legal processes, which was not difficult, for his three-hatted role of judge, prosecutor and gaoler was legally untenable. In detaining us, he was abdicating his duty to prosecute us. If he prosecuted us, he would have to recuse himself from his role of judging us. First, we applied to 'the Court' (Meyan) for an order directing 'the custodian of Defendants' personal property [Meyan] to spread out and expose same to sunlight and take all feasible measures necessary to ensure that no damage is caused to same through the corrosive effects of mildew or humidity'. We then moved for an order directing 'the State [Meyan] to produce for Defendants' examination and, if need be, copying, any and all police reports or other documents pertaining to Defendants' guilt or innocence in any proceedings that may be brought against them'. Next we sought an order directing our 'gaolers' (Meyan) to release us from detention; alternatively, directing 'the State' (Meyan) to define the charges against us; then, warming to the task, an order setting our case for trial, an order appointing counsel to represent us and an order granting us 'access to whatever law reports, legal textbooks and other legal publications Defendants need to prepare their case properly'. We filed a motion to dismiss 'any charge made against [us] under Section 14 of the Foreigners Act, 1946' (we had as yet not been charged with any offence under any statute), contending that the Act was 'on its face and as applied, impermissible, null and void, and violative of [our] fundamental civil rights and [our] rights of due process and procedural due process, as guaranteed by the Constitution and laws of the Republic of India and the State of Arunachal Pradesh'. We then filed a motion to remove our case to the High Court of Assam, arguing in a 'supporting memorandum' that 'the gravity of the alleged offence and the interests of the administration of justice require that this matter be heard by a tenured Judge rather than by an untenured Magistrate who, however impartial in fact, is nevertheless perceived in his administrative capacity to be responsible to the Government of the State of Arunachal Pradesh'. The consummation of our campaign of interlocutory harassment was a Petition for a Writ of Habeas Corpus and a claim for damages for false imprisonment addressed to the High Court of Assam.

And still we were not finished with this decent, honest man. We now set about preparing and dispatching letters addressed to *India Today*, *The Statesman*, the *Hindustan Times*, *The Telegraph*, *Indian Express*, *The Sentinel* (Gauhati), the *Times of India* and, for good measure, the Indian Prime Minister.

> The Miau authorities might have allowed us to proceed to Delhi and there seek Home Office permission to exit the country, the usual procedure in cases involving visa deficiencies. Instead, they floated the fantastical notion that we had 'links with a global espionage network' and were 'part of the CIA's network'. Miau passed us on to Changlang. But 'global espionage' was too much for the Deputy Commissioner here [Kum Archana Arora but, effectively, Meyan] and her even more irresolute young successor serving in his first IAS post [Arun Goyal but, effectively, Meyan]. They should have examined the evidence and released or charged and tried us accordingly; instead of which they sought instructions from Itanagar, thereby discharging *administratively* judicial powers vested in them as *magistrates*. So much for our right to an independent and impartial judge and to confront our accusers. Itanagar sought instruction from Delhi, and thus was born a Frankenstein of bureaucracy. Twenty-nine people representing ten different agencies of State and Central government and the military have investigated and rendered reports already. It scarcely seems to matter that *all* of them have pronounced themselves satisfied that we are not spies. The decision must rest with their superiors, and the magistrate won't release us until they have decided. A passes the matter to B who passes it to C who passes it to D, as report

breeds report and one person's endorsement demands another's. In reality, no one wants to take responsibility for clearing two people who *might* have 'links with a global espionage network'.

Whatever else our disinformation and scheming may have achieved, they gave us the illusion that we were engaged in useful activity. Three of our dispatches reached the newspapers to which they were addressed and were published almost verbatim under the headlines, 'Why are foreigners suspect?' (*The Statesman*, Calcutta, 19 June 1989); 'Victims of red-tapism' (*The Statesman*, Delhi, 20 June 1989) and 'In Kafka country' (*Indian Express*, 28 June 1989). By then, however, our circumstances had changed.

* * *

Meyan's superiors had ordered him to hang on to us, and hang on he did, despite our frightening his dear wife half out of her wits. But he reckoned without that engine of radical change – the female infrastructure.

Sometime before Haynes's visit a party of schoolgirls called at the IB to check out the many exotic rumours then circulating in Changlang. They were allowed to visit us because their fathers had important posts in the local administration. 'Your wife must be very worried about you,' one of them exclaimed.

'Indeed. She must be *very* worried,' I replied. 'She does not know whether I am dead or alive.'

'You are not writing to her?' asked the schoolgirl indignantly.

'I write to her every day. But your fathers intercept our letters.'

'Why?' asked the schoolgirl, horrified.

'Why are they intercepting our letters? We've asked ourselves that question. It is absurd, but they seem to believe that we pose some kind of threat to India's security.'

She furiously tore a page from a school exercise book, handed it to me and whispered: 'Please, sir, what is your wife's name and address?'

Meanwhile, Carole had been busy. Learning that her former history teacher, John Hubbard, was now the US Ambassador to India, she rang his office and, to her surprise, was put through to him – and within the hour someone at the London embassy with a New Jersey Italian accent rang her. 'Mrs Tucker, what's your husband's passport number? ... I'm afraid we can't do anything until we know that he's an American citizen.'

The New Jersey Italian rang her again some days later. 'We've got something to tell you, but we don't know exactly what to make of it. Maybe you can tell us something. We've had a report from Calcutta about a Swede and his English girlfriend who were arrested after crossing into India from Burma.'

'Shelby wasn't going to Calcutta.'

'I didn't say that they are in Calcutta, Mrs Tucker. I said that we received a report from Calcutta. We have a consulate in Calcutta.'

'Where are they now?'

'At a rest house.'

'In Calcutta?'

'We don't know that, Mrs Tucker. We only know what's in the report.'

'What is a rest house?'

'We cannot say that, Mrs Tucker. All we can tell you is what's in the report.'

'Well, my guess is that the Swede is Shelby's companion and that the "English girlfriend" is Shelby. Shelby is ambivalent.'

'What do you mean by that, Mrs Tucker?'

'Shelby is neither male nor female.'

'We're not interested in your husband's orientation, Mrs Tucker.'

'I'm talking about his name, not his orientation! The name Shelby can refer to either a male or a female. And "rest house" must mean "house arrest".' She noted in her diary: 'I will always remember today as Hallelujah Friday! He's in India and will not go to prison in Burma or be killed or perish or remain land-locked. I called Berit and Shelby's mother and bought a dress at Liberty's. Ranjit and Sara [Banerji] have invited me to dinner to celebrate.'

Then she received an anonymous letter from Assam. Notwithstanding the delicacy of their fathers' positions and at great personal risk to themselves, the schoolgirls had managed to elude the censor. Whether they posted the letter themselves or gave it to a courier to post for them, we shall never know. In any event, Carole now knew exactly where we were. After months of uncertainty and apprehension suddenly everything seemed to be falling into place.

The celebratory dinner at the Banerjis, however, took an unexpected turn. 'I hate to tell you, Carole, but you should know the facts,' said Ranjit after one of his pensive silences. Ranjit's advice was to be respected. He had grown up and worked in India, including Assam. 'Their problems have only just begun,' he said. 'They are in an extremely sensitive area. Don't ask me why it's such a sensitive area. I can only tell you that I was allowed there only because a friend with a house in Nagaland invited me to visit, and no one else was given this permission. Mats's youth will protect him, but they won't assume that Shelby is innocent. Somehow you'll have to convince them that he is exactly what he is, and that won't be easy. They won't believe that he's a lawyer, because he doesn't work in a law office. They won't believe that he is a writer, because his books aren't published. Call your ambassador again, and contact anyone else you know who may be able to help. You will need all the help you can get.'

The first offer of help came from Bob Pelletreau, who had been my classmate at Andover and my roommate at Yale and was then the US Ambassador to Tunisia and the Arab League. Carole rang him and told him what had happened. He promised to contact Haynes's boss, with whom he had once shared a posting. 'I will vouch for Soph,' he said, referring to me by my Andover nickname (derived from the jazz singer, Sophie Tucker). 'That will at least resolve the credibility problem. He'll know that Soph's not some petty smuggler. But involving the State Department too closely at this stage might be counterproductive. It might be best to leave most of the running to the Senate.' Pelletreau also promised to consult the Indian Ambassador to Tunisia. 'Perhaps he'll put in a good word for Soph.'

Carole's next offer of help came from another of my Andoverian Yale roommates, Ray Lamontagne. 'Senators? Sure. No problem,' said Ray. 'But you need influential Indians. I've never needed them, thank goodness. It is one of the very few problems in life that I have been spared. However, I am bound to know someone who can help. I will get back to you.'

Carole then rang my cousin, Nancy Gentry, who was friendly

with Senator Wilson. ('Nancy, I need your help. Get out of bed.' 'I've already tried four times.' 'You must try again. Shelby is under house arrest in India.')

She then contacted a local friend whose father, Prem Bhatia, had been a distinguished newspaper editor in India and who was able to arrange a meeting with the Indian High Commissioner. Carole's diary describes her sensations and apprehensions on entering India House with its vivid frescos, arched balconies, potted palms and pierced screens: 'How odd everything suddenly is. This time last year I was simply a wife and a lawyer. Now I have to convince this man that my husband is not a spy or a drug baron.'

She found the Indian High Commissioner at lunch, eating out of a paper bag. He had snow-white hair and great, round, dark eyes and was seated beneath an enormous picture of Indira Gandhi. She placed what she called a credibility bundle (my letters to her from China and Burma, our Christmas round robin projecting my walk across Burma, my curriculum vitae and the manuscript of *The Last Banana*) on his desk. This he perused thoughtfully over the long, bony incline of his nose while tea was served to her in a delicate, porcelain cup. Then, smarting suddenly, he summoned an assistant on his intercom. 'No, I do not want Bhutta. It is Darawalla I want. Send me Darawalla as soon as possible.'

A small, dark man now entered the room. Carole was introduced to him as 'a friend of Prem's daughter'. 'Tell him', the High Commissioner said, 'what you have just told me.' What interested Darawalla were not my credentials as a traveller. It was her description of me as a writer. 'I believe I have heard his name, Mrs Tucker, but, please remind me, what has he written?' Carole referred him to the manuscript of *The Last Banana*.

The High Commissioner listened with a kind of avuncular sympathy. He was himself something of a novelist *manqué* and, when Carole had finished explaining why literary recognition had eluded me, he directed Darawalla to cable Delhi. 'If necessary, Mr Darawalla, the highest powers.' Darawalla was to state that the High Commissioner had inspected my work and was convinced that I was a genuine writer who writes 'regardless of discouragements'. Moreover, he added, there was every reason to believe that I would not repeat the offence of entering a restricted area of India without permission. 'You put it in your own words, Mr Darawalla. You will know how to phrase it. It should be polite but firm.' Two hours later she was back in a courtroom behind a barrister cross-examining a witness, still musing on the strangeness of life.

She always stayed in a friend's flat in Elgin Crescent when in London on a case. There was a flutter of messages for her on his answerphone that evening. 'Please call Senator Wilson'; 'please call Senator Lott'; 'please call Senator Dole'; 'please call Senator Moynihan'; 'please call Rennie Smith at the US Embassy in Delhi'; 'this is the US Embassy in London. Would you please tell us exactly where Mr Tucker's passport was issued'; 'this is the US Embassy in Delhi again. Would you please call Rennie Smith.'

* * *

When Consul Haynes rang Carole to tell her about his visit to us, he seemed to her to be

> full of bounce and vigour, with newsy things to report – but *without* Shelby and Mats.
>
> Were they in good health, I asked? Excellent health, he replied encouragingly. Mats's infections had cleared, and he was just about to ring Berit to tell her so. Were they being held in cramped conditions? 'Mrs Tucker, don't worry about that at all. You could say that they are in an ideal place for taking a retreat.' There is even a library at the 'retreat'!
>
> I offered to reimburse him for the gifts that Berit and I had requested, but he replied that the State Department 'maintains an emergency fund for incidentals relating to US persons in custody'. I pressed him as to why he was not planning on returning to Changlang before October. 'It's getting wetter by the minute,' he replied. He stressed that the Embassy had already 'done a lot', which I don't dispute. He also said that he [Haynes] was the first American to go to Arunachal Pradesh. 'No, not the first,' I said. Shelby gave him a power of attorney to pass on to me, which he is stamping with his official seal and sending to me.

Carole now wrote to me every day, and her letters, intercepted and read by Meyan and vaunting the names of the VIPs who had espoused our cause, must have caused him further annoyance. She also decided to enhance my credibility bundle, sifting through her address book and ringing everyone who might be supportive. It was the shotgun approach to testimonials.

People whom she contacted in this way rang others, and, before long, they too were professing their concern. Some seemed genuine enough but said depressing things like, 'I've known Shelby since we were at Camp Leconte together in 1946. He always had a *real* gift for getting in trouble. I am *so* sorry to hear that he's in prison. But you know *Shelby*.' Most were simply curious to know what had happened. She varied her approach according to each person's particular personality. For example, to the mellow-voiced aide to Senator Lott, she said, 'My name is Carole Tucker. My husband and I live in England, but we come from Mississippi originally. I was born in Cleveland, and my husband and I have a farm in Shelby. I used to work for Senator Eastland on the Senate Judiciary Committee' – alluding to a minor clerical job lasting part of a summer during her youth. Long absence from the South had not dimmed her memory. People who went directly to the point were pushy.

'You don't say, mam. That's *real* interesting!'

'I'm sure you know Ann Bode. She worked on Senator Lott's campaign in Pascagoula and Gulfport. She was Ann Morrison before she became Ann Coopwood. They divorced, and she married Paul Bode. Ann used to live in Shelby, but now she lives in Pass Christian. I've known Ann all my life.'

'That name sure rings a bell, mam. What can I do for you?'

'Last year my husband decided to walk across Burma.'

'Did you say Burma, mam?' ...

Meanwhile, on Ambassador Hubbard's instructions, Rennie Smith was bombarding the Indian Ministry of Foreign Affairs, the Indian Ministry of Home Affairs, the Indian PM's office and the Governor of Arunachal Pradesh. 'What news have you on the Tucker/Larsson case? When are they going to be released?'

Meyan must have felt the vibrations, for his behaviour vaccillated wildly. One moment he was conciliatory, all sweetness. He even consulted me about what he should do. ('If you really want my opinion, Mr Meyan, I would send us to Delhi without delay. You don't need to wait for Delhi's approval. You have that power under section 11 of the Foreigners Act.') The next moment he was fiery and threatening.

One evening, after we had been in detention for almost two months, a little man wearing the loose-fitting khaki cottons of a government *chaprassi* appeared at the IB and presented some documents to us. Mej and Prem Bahadur were in the kitchen preparing our dinner, and Mats and I were alone on the veranda sitting in darkness. There was a light on the veranda, but we preferred darkness to the swarms of moths, flying beetles and other insects it attracted. I signed a receipt for the documents, and the *chaprassi* departed. I went inside, read the documents and returned to the veranda.

'Good or bad?' asked Mats.

'I suppose it's good. A date has been set for our trial.'

'When?'

'Tomorrow morning.'

'What are we being tried for?'

'They don't say, but never mind. We've been offered the right to retain local counsel.'

'When do we find local counsel? *Tonight*?'

'Meyan seems to be concerned about tidying up the record. Ordinarily, we would have nothing to fear. The untimeliness of the notice of trial would appear in the docket sheet and furnish summary grounds for reversing any conviction. But who knows *what* may happen here?'

We decided to plead guilty whatever the charges and I worked late into the night on a plea in mitigation. Either the system worked properly, in which case we could plead guilty with impunity. Or the system did not work properly, in which case it mattered not a tittle what we pleaded.

* * *

For our trial Meyan wore a new shirt (not one that was frayed about the sleeves and collar) and a clean necktie (not one stained with spittle). And his neatly parted, slicked down and darkened with brilliantine grey hair looked wonderful. 'All stand!' proclaimed Mr Bora as the ADC strode chest-proud into the courtroom.

It had been six months since Mats and I first set foot in Burma. Neither of us would have predicted that our adventure would end in this larder-sized Indian courtroom. We stood, our backs to the wall, beneath a picture of a pink and blue, loin-clothed, hunchbacked, bespectacled Mahatmaji. Meyan sat on a bench behind a lectern above us. Bora was at right angles to him, less elevated.

'The Court of the Judicial Magistrate, First Class, Changlang, is now in session, the Honourable Narayan S. Meyan presiding!' Bora proclaimed, and Meyan rapped the lectern with a wooden mallet. Twice! Hard! Exactly as judges do in Hollywood films. 'Now,' he began, looking benevolently down at us as though we were his oldest and very dearest friends, but, suddenly, he stopped. 'No, Mr Bora, do not write this in your book. I want to tell our foreign friends what I think they should do. You want to know my opinion, Mr Tucker? And Mr Larsson ... let us *not forget Mr Larsson*. Frankly I will tell you what my opinion is!'

His opinion was that we should plead guilty; his reasons complex and protracted. The crux was that, by so pleading, we would spare everyone, including ourselves, further delay. After he had spoken for some minutes, I interrupted. 'May it please the Court!' There was a breathless pause. Meyan had worked hard at preparing this speech and had not anticipated an interruption. Were we about to torpedo his masterplan ere it was launched? He stared hard at me. 'The Court ought to know,' I said, 'that the defendants have decided to plead guilty.'

'You are pleading guilty?' asked Meyan.

'Yes, Your Honour.'

'You are pleading guilty?' he repeated, incredulously.

'Your Honour, we are pleading guilty.'

His whole frame stiffened with instinctive suspicion. Then, as realization settled upon him, he broke into a weird kind of joy. 'I am so glad, Mr Tucker. Really, I am *so* glad. So very, very glad — because I have already decided what my sentence will be!' He turned to Bora. 'I am sentencing the prisoners to three months. Sentence *suspended*! My judgment will be ready in two days! Thank you, Mr Tucker.'

We felt a little ridiculous, and more than a little contrite, for by now we knew that we had demonized this rather simple, decent, hard-working and sadly neurotic man. For weeks, he had been sending daily cables to Delhi and Itanagar pleading with his superiors for directions.

'Mr Bora,' he continued as one blowing away the last lingering puffs of Doubt, 'you will please note that the defendants have pleaded guilty. *Guilty*!' He banged the lectern again with his mallet. 'Finished!'

'I will bet you ten Swedish *krone* that he changes his mind,' whispered Mats.

'Not this time,' I said.

As we went to trial that morning a young man named Chris Cohen, who happened to be staying at Ray Lamontagne's house, spoke over the telephone to his father, Senator Bill Cohen.[7] Chris had overheard Ray lobbying senators about our difficulties and wanted to enlist his father's help. Senator Cohen spoke to Ray. 'What's this I hear about your friend, Sophie?'

'The Indians suspect Soph of CIA connections,' said Ray solemnly. 'Bill, aren't you the senior Republican on the committee that monitors the CIA? ... So what? So it seemed to me that a contribution from you might be counterproductive.'

But Cohen knew something unknown to his son's host. P. K. Kaul, the Indian Ambassador to Washington, had recently contacted him regarding a $29 million grant to the Indian military that was contingent on the approval of another committee on which Cohen sat. 'Ray, you leave this one to me,' he said.

About an hour after our trial ended, I was summoned to Meyan's bungalow. He was waiting for me at the back door. All the curtains were drawn, as though there had been a bereavement in his family. 'Come in,' he whispered, his face twitching. 'Quickly! No one must see you here. Do you know what they will think if they see you here, Mr Tucker? They will think that I have taken a bribe from you! *Jaldi*!'

'Why do you care what they think?'

---

7. Who is now (1999) the US Secretary of Defense.

'I care,' he replied.

'It would never *occur* to us to offer you a bribe.' This was untrue. Mats and I had considered but rejected the idea as too fraught with risk. 'You would never accept a bribe, Mr Meyan.'

'You do not know these people, Mr Tucker. You do not know how they are thinking!'

We went to a small room at the far end of the house beyond the hearing of his wife and servant, where he offered me a bowl of nuts. 'Does Mr Larsson know you are here?' he asked.

'Yes.'

'What did you say to Mr Larsson?'

'That I was going to your house. He was present when your servant handed me the *chitthi*.'

'Did you tell him the purpose?'

'What *is* the purpose, Mr Meyan?'

'If I reveal purpose, will you not tell Mr Larsson?'

'If that is your wish.'

'Promise that you will not tell anyone purpose.'

'I promise that I will not tell anyone. But what do you want from me, Mr Meyan?'

'Mr Tucker, you write very nice memorandums. I have read your memorandums. You know something about the law. Because you are having legal background and training, isn't it? I want you to help me to prepare my judgment? I must show reasons for imposing light sentence, or they will think that I have taken bribe.'

'There are sound, legal reasons for imposing a light sentence on us, Mr Meyan. No one who studies the case will think that you have taken a bribe.'

'Do your best, Mr Tucker! Write it very nicely! But you promise that you will not tell anyone?'

'I will do my best. And please be assured, I will not tell anyone.'

'Do not come to my house again, Mr Tucker. I will send servant to IB at seven o'clock with envelope. Seal judgment in envelope and give it to servant to bring to me. And, please, Mr Tucker,' he smiled imploringly, 'do not say anything about this to Mr Larsson.'

'What did he want?' Mats asked when I returned to the IB.

'He has asked me to write the judgment. But you are not to let on that I've told you. He's worried that someone will suspect him of having taken a bribe.'[8]

Following his conversation with Ray, Cohen sent a telex to Kaul. 'Reference your request for a meeting, the $29 million grant in aid to the Indian Defence Forces, agreed in principle by the Congress, will not be paid until US citizen James Shelby Tucker, Jr, under detention in Changlang, Arunachal Pradesh, is released. There will be no further discussion regarding this grant until our citizen is released.'

A week after our trial (not two days later, as announced in his first flush of euphoria) Meyan radiantly presented to us certified true copies of his judgment, having revised the wording so skilfully that no one but a clairvoyant could have divined my authorship. As anticipated, we were charged with contraventions of the Foreigners Act (maximum punishment, five years with hard labour), Passport Act (three months' imprisonment) and Bengal Eastern Frontier Regulation of 1873 (two months plus fine). After reciting the charges, the judgment continued:

> Both the defendants entered India, somewhere in the vicinity of mile 68 point on Gandhigram–Miau track in Vijayanagar administrative Circle of Changlang district of Arunachal Pradesh on 10th April, 1989 and proceeded to mile point 51, where persons employed by Public Works Department took them by jeep to Miau, a Sub-Divisional headquarters of Changlang district on 16th April, 1989. The defendants presented themselves to civil authorities and requested the local Administrative Officer, Shri A. K Bhattacharjee, Extra Asst. Commissioner to allow them to proceed to Delhi and make application to Home Secretary, Government of India for permission to leave India. ...

8. Meyan's request was not unusual. American counsel routinely proffer orders for judges to sign, and the judges routinely sign them and, moreover, rely on counsel's written submissions in crafting their opinions, often adopting the language of these submissions verbatim.

Investigation and Proceedings

Investigation were carried out by Arunachal Pradesh Police subsequently experts, specialised in the art of interrogation conducted interrogation. Expertise of Subsidiary Intelligence Bureau/Special Bureau/SSB/Department of Central Excise and Customs/Military Intelligence/APP(SB)/Assam Police had also put their brains but no evidence had emerged from any of the above agencies that could prosecute the defendants with gravity except those charges with which they have faced the trial.

The *Times of India* on 17th May, 1989 in its issue(Ex-1) gave some grounds of suspicions that they have links with the 'Global Espionage' and are part of the 'CIAs' network' nothing of the kind revealed in the investigation report which this court has studied carefully, and it appears inherently improbable that persons engaged in Espionage would present themselves voluntarily to the authorities of the country in which they were spying or that the trans-border groups would engage for that purpose two conspicuous foreigners and bring them all the way from China. The *Times of India* further published news item that 'some sensitive maps' were found in their possession. Court has examined the maps in their possession and none of them were related to India. Person in this country are not prosecuted on suspicion only, the court must proceed on evidence that is legally admissible and consistent with law. Ample powers are vested with the Central Government to continue these defendants in custody under secton 3 of the Foreigners Act 1946, the Foreigners (Inernment) Order 1962 and other connected laws, if grounds unknown to this court, exist. But it would be improper and this court shall not detain them further on the pretext of punishing them against the contingency that they might be guilty of other offences except for three offences with which these proceedings are concerned.

Findings

The defendants had walked from China through Burma to India, in itself, that is not a crime within the purview of law of India. In the absence any evidence to the contrary, the court has no reason to disbelieve that they undertook this journey for purpose of adventure. Such a purpose is consonant with J. S Tucker's career as a writer of the travel books.

Before entering Burma one of the defendants J. S Tucker had obtained from the Embassy of India at Beijing, a visa for entering India. ... Had Tucker arrived India before expiration, this Visa would have permitted him to remain in India for three months. But by no fault of his own and circumstances beyond his control, he was unable to reach India before its expiry date. ... Mats Larsson was prevented from obtaining a Indian Visa by 'Force Majeure'. The defendants were *en route* to Rangoon to decide upon which route to come out from Burma and apply at the appropriate Embassy for a Visa, when they were taken into custody by armed soldiers belonging to People's Army (The military wing of the Communist Party of Burma) diverted the defendants against their will from their destination. All these facts are substantiated with the Diaries carefully examined by the court which were in their possession.

... [D]eficiency of this kind and magnitude of the offence, normally would be regarded as an offence of insufficient gravity to warrant more than the administrative rectification by the Central Government ...

No reason exists for imputing the defendants about the knowledge of any sensitivity attaching to the route by which they came to Miau. Those groups hostile to India, with bases perhaps in Burma – the underground Nagas, Mizos etc operate several hundred miles South of this route, while the areas bordering China are well North of it.

The defendants did not sneak surreptitiously into India, on the contrary proceeded openly along a public way and offered [themselves] voluntarily to the civil administration. The facts have been substantiated from various sources and may weigh exceedingly in the evaluation of the court about the defendants intention. Further, they had succeeded to cross northern Burma undetected by Burmese authorities, who they intended to evade, there is no reason for supposing that they could not have evaded detection over a short distance of 33 kilometers to reach Assam and proceed to Delhi by commercial transport, had they felt so. But they had behaved as one would expect of a bonafide travellers with Visa deficiency. The court, therefore, has all inclinations to believe that's what they are.

The facts also weigh heavily for the court to evaluate of the allegations of sensitive maps and other incriminating documents found in their possession. Had they entered India with some sinister motives or purpose, they would have destroyed any evidence likely to incriminate them, before surrendering to the civil authorities at Miau.

Appreciation of Law

... Such being the story of the instant case and the evidences adduced before the court R. B Sethi's *Law of Foreigners and Citizenship*, 3rd edition at page 217–219 makes it abundantly clear that the punishment for these offences should be light. 'It is essential that the punishment must fit the crime' states Sethi. 'The principal object of punishment is the prevention of crime ... punishment should be made as moderate as is consistent with that purpose aimed at ... to shut a man up, in the prison longer than is really necessary is not only bad for the man himself, but also it is useless piece of cruelty economically wasteful and source of loss to the community'. Therefore, the court should take into consideration the circumstances under which the offence was committed and whether the criminals are first offenders or habitual offenders or professional offenders. Here, in the instant case, the defendents have not deliberately violated the Foreigners Act or Bengal Eastern Frontier Regulation and their offence against the Passport (Entry into India) Rules seems unavoidable. 'A day's imprisonment to an honourable man' says Sethi 'will have more deterrent effect than a life spent in durance-vile by a hardened criminal'.

The defendants have already suffered more than the sufficient punishment for their unintentional, unavoidable and obviously, the chance of recurrence of offence appears remote, under three charges.

Judgement

... The evidence adduced before the court, in the instant case do not warrant a severe punishment for the crimes which the above named defendants have committed. Moreso and beside all, the defendents have prayed court's mercy for a lenience and this court is inclined to adopt a lenient view.

Having read the charges to the defendants and considering that they have pleaded guilty at their own volition the court hereby find them guilty and order that they be fined Rp. 50/– each and confined to prison for 90 days in respect of charges under Passport (Entry into India) Act and 60 days for other two charges and sentences to run concurrently with credit that the period of pre-conviction detention i.e. of 66 days from 17th April to 21st June 1989 may be set-off against the sentence now awarded.

It is further ordered that the remainder period of their sentences be suspended for the conditions listed below in the larger interest:-

(i) The defendants are to be escorted to Itanagar and handed over into the custody of the Inspector General of Police, Arunachal Pradesh within the purview of section 11 of the Foreigners Act 1946.

(ii) The Inspector General of Police, Arunachal Pradesh shall make immediate arrangement for transferring the defendants to the Commissioner of Police, New Delhi under Police escort.

(iii) The defendants shall be detained in Police custody at New Delhi for the remainder period of sentences unless the Home Secretary or his delegated officer, Ministry of Home Affairs, Government of India, New Delhi orders otherwise for their longer detention as the competency of the Central Government is clearly final and is unchallenged and such binding nature of the order cannot be questioned. Therefore, the Home Secretary may take such suitable action against the defendants under Foreigners Act or under any other provisions of the law which may be applicable to them for the purpose of either deporting them or otherwise dealing them as is thought fit.

Meyan's judgment removed the awesome danger that one or the other of the powerful agencies investigating us would use the Foreigners Act as a pretext for sending us away for five years while they elaborated their more exotic theories of our guilt. Our possessions (including a roll of film that the die-hard Mansai tried to keep back) were returned to us, and we spent our last day in Changlang entertaining scores of people who had supplied us with bits of information useful to our case or simply encouraged us to hope.[9] Most touching of all, H. P. Sauce and every one of our guards called to bid us farewell. Mej and Prem Bahadur confected a special dinner for us, and, on our final night at the IB, we slept behind unlocked doors for the first time since Mile 39. We were free men once more — for a short while.

In ordering the Arunachal Pradesh Inspector General of Police to 'make immediate arrangement for transferring [us] to the Commissioner of Police, New Delhi', Meyan acted with almost reckless bravery and pre-empted a repetition of the paralysis of indecision that had prolonged our stay in Changlang. He also neatly finessed the technicality of who was to pay for our transport. We were driven to Itanagar at Changlang's expense, driven on to Gauhati at Itanagar's expense, and put on a train for Delhi at our expense.

Three policemen escorted us. At Dibrugarh, we exploited our mini-freedom to post a letter about the Capo to the Swedish Ambassador. We still felt too insecure to leave anything to chance. It explained in melodramatic detail our wildest fears for our safety.

The risk of ULFA ambush or mined roads obliged us to abandon the shorter route from Itanagar to Gauhati in favour of a safer route south of the Brahmaputra.

At Gauhati we tried ringing Berit and Carole but found the lines cut. 'Never mind, we'll send a cable,' we said and laughed. We laughed because the dispatch clerk had no idea that we had met at Pajau Bum the leader of the 'terrorists' who had cut his lines. We laughed all the time now, for, in our euphoria, everything seemed

9. For obvious reasons, they must remain anonymous.

risible. We laughed about everything and nothing at all. It was exhilarating to buy our own food and to pay for our lodging again, even though we shared the rooms with our custodians and the beds were often infested with fleas.

We boarded the Assam Mail, the other passengers tensely suspicious of us and irrepressibly curious – why the armed escort?

We rode into the night, battling for a refuge of sleep in the crowded carriage. The clank of steel on steel, and dawn streaking pink and blue over green rice paddies; tea in expendable clay goblets and *samosas* sold through the barred windows. Oddest of all was the Frenchman outside our window at Siliguri. He was a pale, goateed man with a rucksack experiencing India: something that might have happened to us on another planet where even the air was different.

Already running late, we reached Katihar at 1455 hours; Barauni at 2150 hours; and, some hours later, after crossing a steel suspension bridge over the purifying Mother of Rivers, Patna. Porters gleaming with sweat with mountains of luggage piled on their heads streamed through the bodies crowding the platform. Then dawn again, the light spreading over a land more desolate than any we had seen since Mongolia. Kanpur at noon – old and decaying like so many Indian towns, the heat crisp and dry.

Our three policemen smartened themselves up as we rode into New Delhi. There was a battle to leave the train with our luggage and dignity intact; another battle for a taxi to Arunachal Pradesh Bhavan, where we were installed in great comfort and style in an apartment normally awarded to VIPs. It was air-conditioned and equipped with a telephone, bathroom and kitchen. The sofas and armchairs were upholstered in silk. The refrigerator was full of Coca-Colas. But there was a hitch. It also came with a dozen investigators dressed in dark suits and neckties whose leader was a moon-faced, betel-chewing man who introduced himself as Chandra. 'Never mind what the others have asked you,' said Chandra. 'You are not out of the wood yet.' They were, according to the Indian High Commissioner in London, the 'big fry'. He clarified the position for Carole. 'The small fry have questioned them. Now the big fry must have their turn.'

Our detention at Arunachal Pradesh Bhavan throbbed with contradictions. We were free to move about, provided we did not stray from our rooms. We were free to use the telephone, but only to communicate with the dining room. We could order food and drink from the dining room, but were forbidden to take our meals there. Our embassies had unlimited right of access to us, provided one of the 'big fry' was present as a chaperon. At night, security guards slept on the sofa, on the silk-carpeted floor and in the corridor outside our rooms. During our first morning there, the US Consul General, a professional diplomat named Wollemburg, called on us. He had read Meyan's judgment. 'Congratulations,' he whispered to me when the chaperon's concentration lapsed. Annika Svahnström, the Swedish Vice-Consul, also called on us. Exquisite, attractive, fascinated by Indian art, she plainly regarded us as insane. She had read the letter we posted from Dibrugarh.

Chandra and his men had the dignified and solemn appearance of bankers, yet behaved like dons at an Oxford viva voce examination collaborating in posing random questions of no apparent relevance. ('Mr Larsson, why didn't you write to your mother when you were in Burma?') The best thing about them is that they deserted us at sunset. Then, alone with our guards, we tinkered with the air-conditioning and telephone, watched television and drank Coca-Cola.

One evening, however, they suddenly reappeared with a frail, scholarly-looking, middle-aged man in tow. 'Have you ever seen this man before?' they asked. That afternoon, just as he was clocking out of his job at a nuclear research station, Chandra's men had pounced on this unfortunate and driven him around in a car, pummelling him with bizarre questions. He did not know who they were or understand by what authority they had seized him; what he had done that was so terrible that he could not even ring his wife to advise her that he would be late for dinner; or, now, why they were so keen on my identifying him. I looked at him, wondering if perhaps he had been one of my pupils all those many years ago at the Tyndale-Biscoe School. He reciprocated my scrutiny in a sickly kind of way. Then it came to me. '*Sinha*,' I cried. 'We met in England, Mr Sinha.'

England? He had spent the previous year in England, studying at one of the laboratories in Oxford.

'You and some friends were on the 190 City Link double-decker from London Victoria to Oxford. I boarded the same coach at Marble Arch and sat upstairs on the seat across the aisle from you. Don't you remember? We struck up a conversation, and you gave me your card, saying to look you up if I ever came to Delhi. I kept your card just in case, thinking that in that event I might look you up, and these men obviously found it among my possessions. I am terribly sorry that you have been so inconvenienced. They suspect us of spying and probably think that you are our mole.'

Chandra, disappointed, took him away. 'Never entrust your calling card to strangers,' I counselled Mats after they left.

Chandra now had one remaining trump to play – to develop our films. But we, too, had a trump, kept very much in reserve; and here it is to be borne in mind what had delayed our departure for Dali all those months ago – Mats's commitment to 'see in the New Year' in Hong Kong.

Ambassador Kaul correctly advised Senator Cohen that, regardless of the merits of our detention and whoever was responsible for continuing our detention, the Ministry of Defence was blameless.

'That may be so, Your Excellency, but the internal complexities of your government are not really our concern,' replied Senator Cohen. 'You have detained our citizen. He has been tried and sentenced. He has served his time. And you have not released him. We want him released. We do not care *who* is responsible.'

'But, Senator Cohen,' protested Ambassador Kaul, 'this is a *Home* Office matter. The Minister of Home Affairs and the Minister of Defence do not always see eye to eye.'

'Twenty-nine million dollars might concentrate their minds. They might suddenly discover that they have binary vision.'

Ambassador Kaul requested Senator Cohen's help in developing a case for our release on humanitarian grounds. The request was passed to Lamontagne. He in turn passed it to Carole, who contacted my sister, who obtained my mother's history with anamnesis, chest x-rays, electrocardiogram, three sets of cardiac enzyme levels, blood count and bone marrow reports and sent them to Senator Cohen, who transmitted them to Ambassador Kaul.

'Just the ticket!' said Ambassador Kaul.

I was not aware of how fearlessly Mats had 'seen in the New Year' until Chandra developed his films. The decision was taken late one Tuesday afternoon. The films were developed on Wednesday, and that evening, Chandra had examined the prints. Mats in a funny hat, his girlfriend under his arm. Mats with his girlfriend again, laughing hilariously. Mats with his girlfriend, arm-in-arm. Mats with his girlfriend, embracing. Mats with his girlfriend on the Star Ferry. Mats with his girlfriend on the Peak train. Mats with his girlfriend under the War Memorial, like newly-weds on their honeymoon. Mats's friend, Dany, had taken these pictures. Mats with his girlfriend ... *Mats* had taken *these* pictures.

Thursday morning's visit was qualitatively different from all the others. Chandra came to our suite alone and later than usual. We sat down together on one of the sofas. He said nothing for a very long time and seemed almost pensive. I had made a deal with him that my films would be developed only if Mats's pictures disclosed something needing clarification and was anxious to know his decision. Eventually, I broke the silence. 'Mr Chandra, this investigation has gone on for a *very* long time,' I said. 'We have already endured the equivalent of 71 days of interrogation. Not even serial killers in our countries are subjected to this much scrutiny. What is your opinion? You are a *cognoscente* of these dark processes. Can you see any light at the end of the tunnel?'

Mats's uninhibited record of 'seeing in the New Year' had made a powerful impression on him. He gazed into space and said, 'Mr Tucker, I think we are barking up wrong tree.'

That day and the next passed without anything happening. Came Saturday. We had now been at Arunachal Pradesh Bhavan for more than a week. Still nothing happened. Then, about dusk, as one of our guards was praying through a sequence of beads in a corner of the room and Mats and I, reconciled to another night in captivity, were lying on our beds staring up at the ceiling, a man dressed in the leather garments of a motorcycle courier strode into the room and nonchalantly told us to pack our things. We were leaving for the airport.

Wollemburg, Svahnström and Rennie Smith came to see us off. We did not tell them what all the fuss had really been about because we did not know ourselves. I surmised that the Indian government thought that we had seen something that, if disclosed, could prove embarrassing and left it at that. Rennie Smith stayed with us until we left the Departures Lounge, then rang Carole and informed her that we had been released.

The Moscow-bound Ilyushin IL-62M was full. I sat with my *nhtu*, *nhpye* and bamboo staff like Neptune risen from the sea between big, square-shouldered Russians, and, four rows behind me, between other Russians, was Mats. Neither they nor we showed any disposition to speak. Next day, as Mats was about to board his onward flight to Stockholm, he said, 'Until the next time that we walk across Kachinland,' and we concluded majestically with a 'completion of final stage' handshake. However, we were both too sleepy, too numb, too dazed by the pace and intensity of all that had happened to register that we were really parting.

As soon as Carole learned from Rennie Smith that we had been released she rang around to inform our friends. 'I must tell Michael Brock not to bother about the testimonial I requested for Shelby's credibility bundle,' she said to Kit Molloy, who had been my roommate at Oxford. Michael had tutored us in Constitutional History. Kit replied: 'You should ask him to compose an *undated* testimonial and save it for the next time Shelby's in trouble.'

I reached Heathrow about an hour before midnight on the Fourth of July as the night shift was about to take over at HM Immigration and Customs and Excise. Carole was nowhere in evidence in the Arrivals foyer. She had taken a nap and overslept. I kept looking around for her and for our guards.

Epilogue

It is scarcely surprising that Mats and I quarrelled often and sometimes violently. I was older than his parents and, for that reason alone, suspect. I had never smoked and was sanctimonious about alcohol, whereas tobacco and alcohol for him were innocent, almost natural pleasures. The discussion of topics that interested me, such as the KIO's aims and strategy, seemed to him presumptuous and unmanly. After deflecting him from his rugby ambitions, I treated him as though he were a parasite. Ten years have passed since we parted. I would like to think that he harbours no enduring grudges. In any event, I hope that I have communicated to the reader something of his remarkable courage.

Did we exaggerate the dangers? Were we paranoid? (Drugs do cross that border, and why shouldn't we have known more than we did? It is entirely plausible that we should have been privy to secrets that the Indian government wanted to protect.) In those moments of uncertainty and fear (it seemed to us that we were in the same predicament as the young Amish boy in *The Witness* whose life was forfeit because he had observed a gang murder), Mats was superb. He had never met anyone as cynical as, for example, Khan. ('If you are tired of my questions, Mr Larsson, then take your rest, and I will come back in ten or fifteen days when you have fully rested.') But neither Khan nor anyone else was going to get from him what he was determined not to divulge. Even the resourceful Major Banhot admitted that he was 'a tough nut to crack'. We talked a lot about what we would do after our release. In the end, he scrapped his plans to meet Dany in Queensland and returned to Sweden, from where he sent me a letter of sympathy about my mother's cancer and heart attack. He is now very happily partnered with a pretty primary school teacher, the immensely proud father of a little girl named Moa Matsdotter and training to teach wood and metal craft, design and English.

Soon after Meyan sent us to Delhi, he succeeded Arun Goyal as Deputy Commissioner of Changlang District. But his widow wrote to me three years later that he 'left for heavenly abode'. He died of kidney failure associated with cancer of the bowel.

My own postmortem began in my Deux Chevaux on the drive back to Oxford from Heathrow. ('Didn't you receive the letter I gave to a Lisu to post for me from Vijayanagar? What was the first definite news that you had that we were alive? How did Boudin [an Indologist produced by Lamontagne] know that we would be kept until after the [Indian general] election if we weren't released at once?') A month or so passed before the reality came home to me that I was free. Even then a touch of fantasy still clung to routine activities like visiting my allotment and familiar possessions like the mud-caked tools in my shed there. Our internment in India, which lasted as long as our trek across Kachinland, was nevertheless a coda to it, and, as the months passed and the memory of our internment receded, Burma returned to centre stage.

Much has changed since 13 January 1989 when we were intercepted in the forest south of the Nam Long and diverted to Möng Ko. On 12 March, the day after we arrived at KIA Second Brigade headquarters, CPB Kokang and Wa rebels seized control of Möng Ko. On 16 April, when we were taken into custody in Miau, the CPB's Wa Twelfth Brigade mutinied and seized the CPB's GHQ at Panghsang. In May, about the time that we were mooting the escape plan proposed by those Nagas in Changlang, its 768 and 815 Brigades mutinied. Some of the mutineers went back to their villages, while others reached an accommodation with Rangoon, thus ending the CPB's role in the civil war. The SSPP split into two factions, only a rump of about 1000 troops under Sai Lek remaining loyal to the NDF.

'Your ideology is divorced from reality,' fulminated the Voice of the People in delivering judgement on its former masters. 'The path that you have chosen is divorced from reality. The people no longer accept your narrow racial policy and the leadership provided by a small clique of people.' But, as so often with political dogmas, this is too simple. The Wa, Kokang, Akha and Lahu hill farmers who supplied most of the CPB's soldiers resented the constraints imposed on poppy cultivation by its Burman politburo; the mutineers' leaders exploited this discontent for their own ends; and Rangoon in turn used them for its ends. In any event, following the CPB's collapse, all the groups into which it disintegrated and other insurgent groups formerly dependent on it for weapons concluded truces with Rangoon that condone not only poppy cultivation but heroin refineries as well.[1]

As the CPB had controlled almost all the border between the Shan State and China and comprised 15,000–20,000 well-armed men, its collapse released vast numbers of Burma Army soldiers for redeployment. Thereafter, hypothetically invincible toll-gates controlled by the Karens and Mons along the Thai border — Mae Tha Waw, Klerday, Mae Tari, Maw Po Kay, Mellah, Phalu, Walle, Tibobo, Kawmoorah and Three Pagodas Pass — fell to the

---

1. Between 1963 and 1973 Rangoon fostered *ka kwe yei* (literally 'you are defending'), military alliances cum business partnerships with drug barons, of whom Lo-Hsing Han, Moh Heng and Chan Shee-fu (alias Khun Sa) were the most notorious. Following the CPB's disintegration, the SLORC revived this policy, only the partnerships thenceforth were called *pyithu sit* or people's militias, the territories they administered, 'government special zones', and their commanders, 'government special policemen'. *Pyithu sit* trafficking in narcotics with the SLORC's encouragement and assistance now include the Burma National Democratic Alliance Army or Brave Nationalist Democratic Alliance (Wa, Kokang, Palaung, Kachin and Shan – approximately 2000 men under arms formed on 14 March 1989); the Myanmar National Solidarity Party or Burma Democracy Solidarity Party or Burma National United Party, ultimately the United Wa State Army (Wa – 12,000–15,000, 8 May 1989); the *Noom Suk Harn* or Young Brave Warriors (predominantly Shan – 1000, 15 May 1989), since merged with the Eastern Shan National Democratic Alliance (Akha, Lahu and Shan – 1,000, late 1989); the Shan State Army (Shan – 2000, 24 September 1989); the National Democratic Army, later the New Democratic Force (Ting Ying and Zalum's Kachins operating in the CPB's former 101 Military District – 400–2000, 15 December 1989); the Kachin Defence Army (Kachin – 900, 11 January 1991); the Pao National Organization (Pao – 500, 18 February 1991); the Palaung State Liberation Army (Palaung – 800, 21 April, 1991); and the Shan State Nationalities People's Liberation Organization (Shan – 700, 9 October 1994). See Lintner, 1990a: 39–53 and Appendix II; Lintner, 1994: 292–9; *Far Eastern Economic Review*, 28 June 1990: 20 ff., and 20 February 1992: 23 ff.; Smith, 1991: 374–81; and *Burma Alert*, vol. 5, no. 12, December 1994.

Burma Army (with Thai Army complicity in several instances). On 27 January 1995, the Burma Army took Manerplaw, headquarters of the KNU, the NDF, the DAB and the National Coalition Government of the Union of Burma (NCGUB).[2]

As the insurgents' position on the ground weakened, the SLORC's confidence in its power strengthened; hence its response to its landslide defeat (10 seats to 392) in the May 1990 election – *it locked up the victors*. The community of nations was outraged, but international business carried on regardless. Between 1988 and 1993, 28 American firms invested $287 million in Burma; 80 Thai firms, $270 million; 11 South Korean firms, $149 million; 34 Japanese firms, $101 million.[3] Texaco, Nippon Oil, Royal Dutch, Amoco, Unocal, Kirkland, Premier, BHP, Clyde, Idemitsu and Total targeted Burma's rich oil and gas deposits. Thai, Singaporean and Hong Kong Chinese boats trawled for fish and prawn in the opalescent waters of the Gulf of Martaban. Thai loggers turned their chain saws on the trees of the Karen Hills (having already denuded northern Thailand of its once magnificent teak forests), while Chinese parastatals began exploiting the 'liberated' rain forests of Kachinland. Trade across the land borders was now encouraged, and opium production soared to 8000 times its 1948 levels. Agitation in the streets of Burma's cities died, and the voices of protest there, muted by more arrests, diminished to a whisper.

Three weeks after my release from detention I joined Ray in Washington. We lunched with Tony Lopez, an Andover classmate who had enlisted the President's help in obtaining our release. Then we called on Bill Cohen. He listened thoughtfully and summoned his intelligence aide, who listened thoughtfully and said, 'Webster ought to hear this.' But the CIA's Director was preoccupied with the assassination of an American newspaper correspondent in Lebanon; and thus it came about that I briefed his aides, the Directors of the Southeast Asia, Counterterrorism and Narcotics desks at the National Security Council. They conceded

---

2. Formed by opposition parliamentary candidates denied the right to take the seats won by them in the 1990 election. Its declared purpose is to serve as a caretaker entity pending the transfer of power to Daw Aung San Suu Kyi's National League for Democracy (NLD). It is led by her cousin, Sein Win.
3. *Burma Alert*, vol. 5, no. 3, March 1994.

that the Burmese Civil War and the heroin trade might be linked but rejected my contention that the Burma Army was a main player in the trade. There was no *constituency* for action on Burma, they said depressingly.

Thereafter, I threw myself into the hurly-burly of political activism, writing to senators, congressional representatives and MPs and urging others to write to them demanding an end to the atrocities and drug trafficking. I gave 'look at Burma' lectures. I attended rallies and meetings organized to arouse public scrutiny. I acted *pro bono* for the NCGUB and arranged meetings with executives of oil companies to raise funds for the NCGUB. I contributed to the work of preparing the draft of a proposed new Constitution for Burma. For the first time in my life I even participated in 'demos' – and was ostracized by those already prominent in the cause, who wanted nothing to do with me. Indeed, the more I tried to contribute, the more my efforts were resented. One celebrated idealist, whose help I sought in preparing for my trip to Washington, said, 'Mr Tucker, you went to Kachinland just to show off, and you have caused a lot of people a lot of trouble.' Another veteran campaigner warned the audience at one of my lectures that I was 'unreliable'. Another floated the rumour that 'the NCGUB's lawyer' was 'receiving kickbacks from oil companies'. My little venture into political activism did not discourage me. It merely reinforced what was already implicit in the Bible's teaching about original sin. Displacing the Rangoon junta with a popular government would not, of itself, resolve all Burma's divisions.[4]

Nevertheless, the Burmese people deserve better than the forced porterage, use as human minesweepers, incineration of their

---

4. For various rivalries that bedevilled the democracy movement in central Burma and its supporters elsewhere, see 'Chronological Guide to the Burmese Civil War' and compare Daw Aung San Suu Kyi's interview on 14 February 1994 with *New York Times* journalist Philip Shenon, as reported in *Burma Alert*, vol. 5, no. 2. '[We] must stop squabbling. ... We must be united if we want to get democracy. It's not going to do us any good if people keep condemning each other.' On 5–7 June 1993, 25 Burmese groups from the USA and Canada and 34 individual Burmese participated in a 'US–Burma Strategy Meeting' in Washington. They shared a common aim, to end the civil war in Burma, free political prisoners, respect human rights, institute consensus government, end the drugs trade. But their number and diversity reflected an ominous inability to form a united front.

villages and crops, slaughter of their livestock, or lopping off their ears, strapping to trees or burial up to their necks to die on suspicion of withholding information about the 'insurgents', and rape and killing of mothers that have been the almost daily concomitants of a civil war that has gone on now for 50 years and cannot be won militarily. President Clinton has written to Daw Aung San Suu Kyi: 'History is on the side of freedom throughout the world and I remain confident that your cause will prevail.' However, I very much doubt that his encouraging words will offer much comfort to those hillfolk subjected to the kind of indignities reported to the KIO in October 1989.

> There were constant sounds of gunfire as soldiers went after those porters who, unable to bear the suffering any further, decided to take a chance at escaping into the jungles. Over 100 dead bodies of recaptured and executed porters were displayed along the roadside as examples. As we reached halfway up the rocky mountain, a pregnant woman gave birth. A Burma Army sergeant had said before the delivery, 'If it is a baby boy we will be victorious, but if it is a girl, we will be defeated!' He became enraged when the baby turned out to be a girl, and he told the woman [that] she was useless and loaded her with munitions and forced her to move immediately, even before the afterbirth was delivered. The child was stillborn because of the stress. In addition, the sergeant yanked the dead child from where it was lying, still attached to the mother by the umbilical cord, and smashed the dead child and flung it away into the jungles.[5]

---

5. Since Mats and I trekked across the Kachin Hills, the junta has spent approximately $2.4 billion on armaments procured from China alone and nearly doubled the size of its army (the UN Human Development Agency reported in 1994 that it was spending 222 times as much on 'defense' as on education and health), and nothing suggests that its declared intention to relinquish power is anything but a charade. Its opponents have urged the United Nations to enforce a trade embargo on Burma and unseat the junta in the General Assembly. I would go further and confer *de jure* recognition on the NLD and move the Security Council for authority to intervene militarily in Burma. Standard authorities on the law of recognition such as Brierly and Lauterpacht do not

In 1990 I returned to Burma to compare the Karen National Liberation Army's *modus operandi* with that of the KIA and accompanied a KNLA unit that had been assigned a task in an area adjacent to the Burma Army's forward positions. We came upon the smouldering timbers of a torched village and a child whose mother had been shot. Two months after he lost his mother, my mother died – in her sleep with a smile on her face, after dancing and proud of the contribution that her final illness had made to our release. I was 55. He was five. Half a century of a mother's love is no minor loss, but to killers and killed alike it is just another mindless casualty of the civil war in Burma.

Near this lad's village was a river. I bathed in it, as I had bathed so often in the icy rivers of *Wunpawng Mungdan*, and an awful depression assailed me. Would I ever go back?

Would I ever go back?

Seng Hpung had spoken to me of his hopes for his people once peace was restored. The Kachins hungered for education, he said – but the education they receive in their forests, I knew, instructs them in values far more important than anything we receive from our schools. After the war was over, Seng Hpung said, they would have all the wonderful things that Brigadier Bowerman and Colonel Ford had told them could be theirs if they helped the British and Americans expel the Japanese from Burma; that Commissioner Stevenson had offered them at Manhkring if they opted for a protectorate under Britain instead of throwing in their lot with the Burmans; that Aung San had promised them at Panglong – the full panoply of Modern Life.

---

address the case presented by the 1990 election, where an autocratic regime has unsuccessfully tested its legitimacy, and the case for military intervention seems compelling. Burma now accounts for 60 per cent of all the heroin produced in the world, and almost everyone who has looked at this issue accepts that the engine driving this poisonous industry is its civil war. It follows that all major powers, including the countries on whose cooperation military intervention would depend, share a common interest in ending the civil war. Military intervention would cost less and prove more effective than the methods currently used in the 'war on drugs': interdicting and imprisoning traffickers, combatting crime arising from addiction, rehabilitating addicts, treating the diseases attendant on drug use, to which must be added the loss of human resources owing to addiction. See Bray, 1995: 11; and 'Chronological Guide to the Burmese Civil War'.

Seng Hpung and I had discussed this dream often in our trek across his beautiful land, and my lack of enthusiasm always puzzled him. My prayer now is that the Prince of Peace will return peace to his beautiful land of clean rivers and wood fires, and that, whatever the Modern World holds out to the Kachins, may they remain just as they were when Mats and I were privileged to share for a short while the hard lives of that band of brave little men who looked after us so selflessly.

An Appreciation

by Dr Stephen Morse

Having spent my childhood and adolescent years among the Jinghpaws, Rawang and Lisu, and having worked closely with other Kachin tribes all of my life, I can attest to the difficulties that Shelby Tucker and Mats Larsson encountered in their trek across northern Burma. Indeed, to one familiar with the dangers inherent in such an enterprise, their story almost defies belief. A 53-year-old American teams up with a 22-year-old Swede, whom he has met on a train and known for less than an hour, with the aim of trekking across one of the most inaccessible and least explored areas on earth, in a country which, everyone recognizes, is ruled by a military autocracy and which has been engaged in a vicious civil war for nearly half a century. Their first task is to reach the Burma border. They elect to cross a 250-mile sector of China that was then completely forbidden to foreigners. Their next task is to evade the police and militias posted along both sides of the border and cross some 600 miles of tangled mountainous jungle while avoiding capture by the Burma Army. Then they have to elude the police and militias posted along the Indian border and negotiate a route through an 80-mile-long, leech-infested sector of India that is also closed to foreigners. Finally, and possibly the most difficult of all their tasks, they have to pick their way through a tangle of Indian legal and administrative procedures. The story might have ended tragically almost at any moment, as they strode without knowledge of the language, the people or the terrain into dangers greater and more complex than they had bargained for. Nevertheless, whether we see them as naïve adventurers or reckless interlopers, they took on bravely and imaginatively every challenge presented by this wild enterprise – and, in the process, have helped us better to understand the Burmese Civil War and the role that the Kachins have played in it.

I can also attest to the paranoia and suspicion that confronted them once they reached India. In 1971, I visited Vijayanagar to explore in secret talks with the authorities there the possibility of leaving Burma by the same route that they travelled 18 years later. The Indian authorities counselled me to accept their protection immediately – because India was 'about to go to war with Pakistan' and, they warned me, 'the situation could change at any moment'. So, trustingly and without returning to Burma to consult my family, I presented myself to the Assam Rifles. Their commander, pretending that one of his patrols had captured me, promptly handed me over to the district officer. For the next six weeks they kept me in a bungalow under the ever vigilant eyes of soldiers armed with automatic rifles, interrogating me without remission, all the while assuring me that they were in contact with the US Embassy on my behalf. At one point an official tanked up on government-issue rum threatened to eliminate me if I did not disclose my true identity and mission. It would be done in such a way, he said, that no one would ever learn what had happened. I suddenly realized that they had contacted no one and that no one knew of my predicament.

Like Shelby and Mats, I reached an accommodation with my guards. One evening as I sat on the veranda of my bungalow strumming a borrowed guitar, one of them ordered me to dance. I replied by inviting them to dance, and two of the younger soldiers laid down their guns and began to do the twist, while the others clapped and stamped in rhythm. Every evening from then on they asked me to play the guitar and sing for them. Although they were under orders to shoot me if necessary to prevent my escape, my tough-guys image of them faded: the universal language of song and dance had melted the frozen barriers separating us. Shelby and Mats resorted to stealing and hiding their guards' clothes. ('It was a little game by which we paid tribute to our common predicament.') Like them, I considered a plan of escape – but elected instead to go on a hunger strike, which eventually secured my release.

I first heard of Shelby and Mats when Brang Seng, the late Chairman of the KIO, handed me a freshly deciphered message from KIO GHQ at Pajau Bum informing us that Colonel Seng Hpung's column had reached First Brigade headquarters at Lakawng Bum. It referred to two *shan hpraw* (white skins) with the column. The Chief of Staff of the KIA, General Zau Mai, had imposed a news blackout on their presence in the column for security reasons. The column was on a highly sensitive mission. Who were these men and what was their role in that mission? Soon we were getting enquiries from journalists and others, for only one other Caucasian, Bertil Lintner, had ventured into the Kachin Hills since the missionaries were expelled in 1965.

We discussed at length the pros and cons of this bizarre development and its implications. Nothing could be done until the column surfaced and communications were established again. Investigation disclosed that these strangers were not mercenaries but merely adventurers whom the KIA had assisted in a curious ambition of walking across Burma. Nevertheless, the discussions were very heated. One aide suggested keeping them at Second Brigade headquarters for two years. Another wanted to return them to China. Our duties to our guests, they argued, did not extend to encompassing the destruction of plans carefully worked out for the higher interest of the Kachin cause. Talk like this greatly disconcerted some of us. It brought back to me in particular the painful memory of my predicament in Vijayanagar. We kept reminding the Chairman of his open invitation to visit Kachinland and his promise to provide security and freedom to travel anywhere for anyone who took up the offer. We pointed out that the KIO's credibility was at stake.

KIO credibility was at stake in more ways than one. Shelby and Mats had stumbled unwittingly into a major KIA initiative in the west to enhance already mounting pressures on Rangoon to address through negotiations the fundamental causes of the civil war: the denial of political equality with the Burmans promised to the minority peoples of Burma at the Panglong Conference of 1947 and contempt for the minorities' traditions and human rights. Brang Seng likened Rangoon to a stubborn mule that required someone pulling it from the front, someone shouting at it from the side and someone beating it from the rear to move it along. Soon after Shelby and Mats's adventure, the KIA attacked and captured Pangsau and Namyung near the Indian border. Alas, the Burma Army counterattacked ferociously with new weapons and aircraft recently obtained from China and the KIA was forced to relinquish its gains. More young men on both sides of the conflict were sacrificed for yet another transitory change of battle lines.

No one championed the case for an amicable resolution of the war more insistently than Brang Seng. After he died, his successor, General Zau Mai, continued his policy. He now factored into the assessment of the cost of continuing the military option the disintegration of the KIA's former battle ally, the CPB, which had freed vast numbers of Burma Army forces previously opposing it for redeployment against the remaining opposition. Moreover, China was making it increasingly plain to everyone that it wanted no further strife along its borders. The differences with Rangoon were not unbridgeable, as the opposition had already abandoned its first goal of independent ethnic states in favour of accepting genuinely autonomous states within the Union of Burma. However, the many cruelties inflicted on the minorities by the Burma Army were too embittering, distrust of Rangoon was too deep, and the KIO's allies spurned its repeated attempts at winning them over to this approach. So, finally, in 1994, the KIO concluded a separate truce with Rangoon.

Affecting its decision was an understanding that the truce was only one stage in a process that would lead to Rangoon's negotiating with *all* of the opposition a comprehensive peace agreement offering genuine and significant political change. Rangoon's failure to act on this understanding is fraught with danger. On the opposition's side, it strengthens the position of those who reject any accommodation with Rangoon and argue that the current accommodation should be abandoned, while on Rangoon's side, it encourages the illusion that the junta can dominate the ethnic minorities through 'divide and rule' tactics. The KIA and most of its former allies retain their arms and have repeatedly declared that they will not surrender them until their mission to their people is fulfilled. Sooner or later the civil war will erupt again if their concerns are not met.

Meanwhile, the trade in narcotics, second only to war as Burma's leading industry and the scourge of mankind everywhere, flourishes under the joint-venture arrangements between Rangoon and the groups controlling the trade. Two days after entering Burma, Shelby and Mats found themselves in a place ringed by opium poppies blooming on all the surrounding hills. Seven years on, Möng Ko is a cluster of heroin factories.

Shelby and Mats trekked through forests abounding in teak and other hardwoods and teeming with animals – the Kachinland that my grandparents and parents knew and that I knew as a child. This magnificent forest is fast disappearing, especially east of the Mali Hka bordering on China. The Hukawng Valley, that great basin supplied by the watershed streams of the Kumawng and Patkai ranges, is less vulnerable, but recent jade mining and oil exploration activities threaten nature's balance there as well. Species of wildlife unique to this beautiful green land are hunted and trapped and their tusks, bones and skins sold on to the vast and voracious markets for traditional medicines in China.

The two men who undertook this adventure were profoundly affected by what they experienced, as is evident in page after page of Shelby's narrative. They offer no excuse for what they did. None is needed. The trek itself is sufficient justification. They accepted a challenge and in their bargain with fate learned something about themselves that is deeply and intensely personal. They have provided us with an example of the wonderfully indomitable human spirit. And they have given us a great adventure story, a discerning account of current conditions in Burma and a rare look at the Kachin people, who, together with all the peoples of Burma, deserve to live in freedom, especially freedom from fear.

Philadelphia
4 July 1998

Cartographer's Note

by John C. Bartholomew[1]

'North Burma is an excellent example of a country which is surveyed but not explored,' wrote F. Kingdon Ward in his book, *Modern Exploration*.[2] Kingdon Ward, botanist and explorer, made several expeditions into Tibet and the Kachin Hills. Ronald Kaulback accompanied him on an expedition through Mishmi country into Tibet in 1933,[3] and my uncle, L. St Clair Bartholomew, who travelled with Kingdon Ward in 1937, joined Kaulback in 1938–39 through the then (and still) little explored part of the Kachin Hills known as 'the Triangle'. This last adventure was cut short by the outbreak of the Second World War,[4] and no formal account of it was ever published. You may imagine my delight, then, when I learned of Shelby's trek across the Triangle half a century later.

The Royal Scottish Geographical Society invited Shelby to present a series of lectures about his trip, and I attended the first of these, which he gave in Edinburgh in March 1991. Many remarkable slides illustrated it. The only maps used to chart the route were copies of the *National*

---

1. FRSE, FRGS, FRSGS, President of the Royal Scottish Geographical Society (1987–93: his grandfather initiated the founding of the RSGS in 1884); President, British Cartographic Society (1970–71); Vice-President, International Cartographic Association (1970–82), member of the Permanent Committee on Geographical Names (since 1955), sixth generation and Editorial Director (1960–84) of the eponymous Edinburgh firm of mapmakers, John Bartholomew & Son Ltd – without whose help I would have not understood my own notes of my route across Kachinland (author).
2. London: Jonathan Cape, 1945.
3. *Tibetan Trek* (London: Hodder & Stoughton, 1934).
4. *Geographical Journal*, vol. 96, no. 2 (London: Royal Geographical Society, 1940), p. 82.

Geographic Map of China (1:6M), *Nelles Tourist Map of Burma* (1:1.5M), a map of Kachin State and Sagaing Division traced from a school textbook (1:1.9M), another small-scale map extracted from Eugene Morse's *Exodus from a Hidden Valley* and two sketch maps of crossing Burma Army communication lines (the Myitkyina–Chiphwe and Myitkyina–Putao roads) drawn by Captain Awng Hkawng. Having deviated from his first plan of commencing his trek from Thailand, India or Bangladesh, Shelby was obliged to scrap the large-scale *Survey of India* 'one-inch' and 'quarter-inch' sheets he had brought with him from England. He had to rely on the *National Geographic* and *Nelles* maps, which were of very limited use, the latter in particular owing to its generalized representation of relief by hill-shading, inadequate river network, and use of Burmese rather than Jinghpaw names for natural features. Much of the route as presented in his address to the Society, therefore, was raw conjecture, and when he confessed to me the difficulties he was experiencing in defining it more precisely, I offered my help.

The choice of maps to use in this enterprise fell on the *Survey of India* series. While modern air charts of the Kachin Hills revised from aerial photography and satellite imagery, such as the 1:500,000 *Tactical Pilotage Chart H–10C* (1990), had improved our picture of the northeast border, they had not enhanced the precision and detail of those parts of the Kachin Hills of concern to us exhibited in the older, ground survey maps. Allowance had to be made for changes that had occurred since survey, of course. Routes shown in the series had been abandoned, a good example being the route between Putao and Sadiya via the Chaukan Pass and the Noa Dihing — in use at the turn of the century but already obsolete in 1942, when 200–250 refugees fled from the Japanese invasion by that route. (Many of the refugees died in the effort — 15 of a party of 42 Sikhs; three out of four of the survivors required medical attention on reaching the Dapha Hka; and none would have survived had not a rescue party organized by the Assam Tea Planters Association met them there.)[5] Villages shown on the *Survey of India* sheets, moreover, had ceased to exist, as John Masters learned to his cost in 1944,[6] while others, owing to the ambulatory slash-and-burn agricultural practice common to all of Burma's hill peoples, had altered location. Nevertheless, these older maps, comprising seven 'one-inch' sheets (1:63,360), each covering a quarter-degree square (published in 1913–14); 16 'half-inch' sheets (1:126,720), each covering a half-degree square (published in 1922–30); and eight

---

5. Geoffrey Tyson, *Forgotten Frontier* (Calcutta: W. H. Targett & Co., 1945), pp. 99–143
6. *Road Past Mandalay* (London: Michael Joseph, 1961), p. 227.

'quarter-inch' sheets (1:253,440), each covering a degree square (published in 1926–40), were the best available to us.

In due course we got down to work, breaking the first ground in almost continuous session lasting several days at Shelby's house in Oxford. Those sectors travelled by petrol tankers and jeeps – 'the Burma Road' from Kunming to the Burmese border at Wanding, Möng Ko–Pajau Bum and Miau–Changlang (Tirap) – presented little difficulty, as the locations of the roads and towns featured in his itinerary had not changed and were well documented. The map in *Exodus from a Hidden Valley*, which showed the route he had taken over the Tawang Hka–Tarung Hka watershed to 'Rice Field Camp', and a sketch map of his route from Pinawng Zup over the Patkai Stephen Morse provided also simplified the tasks those sectors presented. The other sectors travelled by foot and elephant, however, presented a different order of challenge altogether.

We plotted the route chronologically according to Shelby's itinerary, sector by sector. We began by assuming that the courses of rivers crossed or tracked – the Nam Long (Möng Ko Hka), Nam Tabet (Tabak Hka), N'myen Hka, Nmai Hka, Jing Ma Hka, Tara Hka, Mali Hka, Daru Hka, Supsa Hka, Tanai Hka, Tawang Hka, Tarung Hka, Noa Dihing – had altered little since survey. We then located places – Wanding, Ruili, Möng Ko, Pajau Bum, Hpundu, Lakawng Bum and Daru Hkyet – whose locations we could be certain had not changed. We then identified villages – Hkai-lekko, Ting Rawng, Lahkra Kawng, Ga Pra – whose locations probably had not changed. Still, the limited numbers of villages identified were widely spaced. How to link them?

Bernard Ferguson writes in *The Wild Green Earth*:[7]

> If you put a map into the hands of the average man, and ask him to describe in three sentences the country it portrays, he will say something like this: 'Well, it's hilly. There's a high mountain in the right-hand bottom corner, and a river just to the left of it with a big town and a bridge. And there's a railway running right across from left to right.'

Closer inspection reveals more: the country's tilt or direction of its drainage; lines demarcating watersheds or ridges; hence, the wider scheme of its river systems. These are the primary features on which its system of communications depends. Close contouring of forested hill areas allows 3-D visualization of the terrain, and we already know that tracks, both animal and human, tend to prefer ridges (where the forest thins) and to

7. London: Collins, 1946, pp. 149–50.

follow (not transect) the grain of the country. We know, too, that shortcuts to destinations, the locations of towns and villages and security considerations can also affect the course of a route. So, armed with these principles of map interpretation and route conjecture, we turned to Shelby's diaries (transcribed in some 700 pages of single-space computer printout). Each day's march was there described in meticulous detail. In addition to the names of places and features gleaned from his KIA escort (campsites were named at his whim) were precise times of departure and arrival, minutes spent walking, minutes spent resting and the directions of the march. What his diaries omitted (for example, directions of flow of streams), he retrieved from memory. We would decide upon a plausible route and, working with highlighting pens in different colours, I would sketch that hypothesis tentatively onto the sector sheet. We then compared it with the details in the diaries and made necessary changes. A probable route began to take shape; but sometimes, at the very point of a resolution, we would have to scrap our previous conjectures and start afresh, because map, diary and route conjecture principles perversely refused to cooperate. Not until everything fitted and our posited route was the only possible route would we pronounce ourselves satisfied with that sector and move on to the next. Finally, all that remained in this interesting exercise of rediscovery was for me to replot the route at reduced scale based on the wartime 1:500,000 *Survey of India HIND 5002* air navigation sheets, NG 47 NW and SW (1944).

Chronological Guide to the Burmese Civil War[1]

1813–26[2] First Baptist missionaries arrive in Burma. Burmans invade Assam twice, claim part of Bengal and dispatch a large army to Arakan, igniting the First Anglo–Burmese War, which concludes with the Treaty of Yandabo ceding Arakan and Tenasserim to the British.

1830–43 Karens, hitherto enslaved by Burmans, begin converting to Christianity.

1852–53 The Second Anglo–Burmese War concludes with British annexation of Lower Burma.

1872–81 Roman Catholic and Baptist missionaries begin evangelizing the Kachins.

1875 British compel King Mindon to recognize independence of Western Karenni.

1885–1 January 1886 Third Anglo–Burmese War concludes with British annexation of Upper Burma. Burma will be administered separately as 'Burma Proper', or 'Ministerial Burma' (most of the Arakan, central Burma, Karen Hills and Tenasserim) and the 'Frontier', 'Scheduled' or 'Excluded Areas' (Karenni, Shan states and the northern hills).

1886–1915 'Pacification' campaigns oblige Shan, Kachin and Chin leaders to accept *sanad*s as Crown protectorates.

---

1. For narrative and more rounded and authoritative accounts, see especially Smith, 1991, and Lintner, 1994.
2. The years 1813–26 are arbitrarily chosen. The ethnic and religious differences underpinning the Burmese Civil War antedated British conquest of Burma by many centuries.

1892–1940 Burma opens to the outside world. The rural economy grows steadily more dependent on (mainly Indian) moneylenders, and increasing numbers of deracinated peasants drift into the cities. Preferment is shown to minorities in army and police recruitment, and Burmans resent non-Burmans now making most of the important decisions affecting their lives. Alien religions are spreading among them, English displacing Burmese as the language of the elite, and Western newspapers and books are corrupting their youth. This inversion of the 'natural' order, they sense, would not have been possible but for the treasonable collaboration of their former subjects (of whom many are Christians and Muslims) with their British masters.

1906 The Young Men's Buddhist Association is founded. Fusing Buddhist messianic notions with Western egalitarian concerns, it will play a prominent part in the Resistance Movement.

1917–19 Westminster accepts self-government as ultimate aim for India, but the Montague–Chelmsford Report notes that 'the desire for elective institutions has not developed' in Burma, and that 'Burma is not India'; the Burmese are 'another race in another stage of political development.'

1919–21 U Ottama organizes nationalist societies, is arrested and imprisoned for sedition. University students protest against educational measures designed to perpetuate a privileged elite, and the first student strike spreads throughout Burma Proper.

1923 Burma gets first elected assembly, but most powers are reserved to Governor.

1930–32 Saya San incites defiance with claims that tattoos and magic shirts will repel bullets. Karens are prominent in suppressing the rebellion, exacerbating Burman–Karen antagonisms.

1930–40 Other Burman nationalist organizations, such as the *Dobama Asiayone* (Our Burma Association), the *Sinyetha* (Poor Man's) *Parti* (founded by Ba Maw) and the *Myochit* (Nationalist) *Parti* (founder: U Saw), proliferate. The younger leaders, such as Nu and Aung San, are Rangoon University students. They address each other as *thakin* (master) as a snub to their foreign rulers.

1936–37 Nu and Aung San catapult to national fame when Rangoon University, under pressure of a strike, withdraws threats to expel them. Burma is separated from India, and Burma Proper becomes a diarchy with a cabinet responsible to the Governor and a parliament with reserved seats for specified minorities elected by popular franchise. As the Governor can veto any administrative or legislative act, the more radical agitators dismiss these measures as diversionary. The minorities oppose them because 'home rule' and 'democratic' government imply a reversion to Burman hegemony and an undermining of the aristocratic basis of their rulers' authority.

1938 This is the 'year of the auspicious number revolution' (1300 in the Burmese era). Countrywide strikes include an 11-month oil fields stoppage. Ba Maw founds the *Dahma Tat*, U Saw the *Galon Tat*, 'both [private armies] ... partaking of the character of the contemporary Black Shirts in Britain' (Donnison).

1939 The CPB is founded. Aung San is its first General Secretary.

1940–41 Aung San and the rest of the 'Thirty Comrades' slip out of the country and contact the Japanese, who train them and send them to Thailand to recruit other Burmans to fight for the BIA.

1942–43 Japanese occupy Burma. Fanatical nationalists, criminals and other undesirables join BIA and kill Imperial Army stragglers and civilians with suspected British sympathies, especially Karens. Ethnic war erupts. Japanese reorganize BIA and rename it Burma Defence Army.

1943 Japanese grant 'independence' to Burma under *Adipati* (President) Baw Maw and rename its forces the Burma National Army (BNA). Aung San is Minister of Defence.

1944 Communists and Socialists secretly unite in what will be known as the AFPFL or League.

1945 BNA turns on Japanese, now in full retreat. HMG decides to use Aung San rather than execute him for war crimes. Labour Party wins Britain's general election and adopts White Paper charting plan for Burma's independence protecting the hill peoples and the Karennis' treaty rights. Aung San agrees to integrate his PBF, as it is now called, into a new Burma Army of four Burman, two Karen, two Chin and two Kachin battalions. But 3500 PBF soldiers do not enlist and form instead the People's Volunteer Organization (PVO), a private army loyal to Aung San.

1946 Aung San affects cooperation with HMG while inciting mass rallies demanding immediate independence. HMG diminishes its control by demobilizing its forces, ordering Indian Army units not to intercede in Resistance Movement activities, and merging loyal Burma Army units with PBF of doubtful loyalty. HMG abandons the White Paper (despite warnings that overriding the minorities' fears will lead to civil war). AFPFL-controlled trade unions incite police, civil servant and oilfield worker strikes. A new Governor appoints Aung San as his Deputy Chairman (Prime Minister) and five other AFPFL nominees to his Executive Council, and strikes end. The League expels Communists after they accuse it of 'collaboration' and demands that the Frontier Areas be incorporated into Burma Proper. Westminster ignores a delegation of Karen lawyers who petition for separate independence.

27 January 1947 Attlee–Aung San Agreement effectively abandons HMG's wartime promises to minorities. It provides for a Frontier Areas Commission of Enquiry (FACE) to determine their wishes; for an elected Constituent Assembly to settle a future constitution; and specifies that independence is to be 'as soon as possible'.

5 February 1947 KNU is founded.

12 February 1947 Panglong Agreement signed. Shans, Kachins and Chins agree to join Burma Proper in seeking early independence; Frontier Areas are to be subject to 'full autonomy in internal administration'; Shans may secede after ten years.

April 1947 KNU and communists boycott election; League wins large majority in Constituent Assembly.

May 1947 FACE recommends federal union. Armed rebellion flares in Arakan. Aung San responds with vague promises of local statehood but insists on interim need to preserve unity. KNU begins organizing the militias that will become the KNDO.

19 July 1947 Martyrs Day. Burman rivals murder Aung San and six other ministers. Nu becomes AFPFL leader and First Minister.

September 1947 AFPFL toadies accept the Constitution on the Karens' and Karennis' behalf, and Karen Rifles battalions begin haemorrhaging weapons to KNDO.

4 January 1948, 0420 hours Independence.

28 March 1948 CPB rebels and, within a year, numbers 15,000 partisans. Nu tries to stall rebels by announcing 'leftist unity' programme, while Ne Win recruits and trains *Sitwundan* (Burman regional militias). Union Military Police (UMP) murder prominent Karenni nationalist, and insurrection sweeps Karenni. Ethnic units of Burma Army in Shan State defect to KNDO. KNDO, MNDO and Karen UMP units seize Thaton and Moulmein. *Sitwundan* order them to disarm. Grenades hurled into Karen churches during Christmas services.

1949 Attacks on Karens continue. Karen commander-in-chief, Karen air force commander and two Karen cabinet ministers resign. Ne Win takes command of Burma Army. Karens rebel and soon are joined by Paos, Karennis, Mons, and a Kachin Rifles battalion under Naw Seng. They soon control most of Burma. Socialists and PVOs resign from government and press for peace negotiations. Widespread strikes further weaken the government. HMG and Delhi reinforce Burma Army, and a Burma Army Gurkha unit, a scratch force of *Sitwundan*, PVOs loyal to the government and Burman irregulars repel a KNDO attack on Rangoon. The tide turns.

Constantly changing alliances and military expedients characterize the next 41 years. The most recurrent issues among the main players are:

Within the government

- Allocation of authority between centre and regions, Burmans and other ethnic groups, and protection of minority rights.
- More versus less central management of the economy.
- Governance by parliamentary democracy or military autocracy.
- Alliances with drug warlord private armies.
- Whether to negotiate with the rebels.
- Relations with China.

Within the CPB

- Armed struggle or the 'evolutionary path to socialism' (tactical alliances with legal opposition and front organizations such as 'peace' movements and trade unions).
- Using persuasion or intimidation to enlist popular support.
- Collectivization or land redistribution.
- Leninism (seizing cities first and expanding from there) versus 'Mao-tse Tung Thought' (seizing rural areas, thereby encircling cities).
- CPB 'vanguard' paramountcy or collaboration with opposition parties on equal terms.

Within the ethnic insurgencies

- Contesting control of territories or agreed demarcation lines and cooperation with CPB.
- Whether to submit to CPB leadership in return for arms.
- Marxist–Leninist–Stalinist–Maoist or British models in political and military organization.

Affecting all the players

- Whether to exploit, condone or prohibit the drugs trade.
- Communal rivalries.
- Personality cults.

❑ Personal greed, ambition, opportunism, suspicion and jealousy.

1949–61 Creeping Burmanization in minority areas under Burma Army control confirms separatists' predictions. Government, school and university posts are reserved for Burmans; Buddhist clergy receive special privileges; Army is increasingly Burmanized; Aung San's Panglong 'kyat for kyat' promise of infrastructure investment parity is ignored.

1950–61 Kuomintang remnants flee into Kengtung State and, assisted by the CIA, gradually assert a monopoly over the opium trade.

1951 CPB stays operations to help Rangoon drive Kuomintang from Burma.

1952–53 Combined KNU/Kuomintang units attack government positions. Kuomintang repatriates some troops to Taiwan after UN orders it to leave Burma.

1954 Burma Army opens major offensives against Karens, Kuomintang and *mujahid*.

1955 Opposition parties combine in National United Front (NUF) and blame government for continuing the war.

1956 NUF wins 36.9 per cent of vote and 48 seats in general election.

1957 KNPP founded.

1958 Nu offers rebels 'arms for peace' amnesty. Nai Shwe Kyin rejects offer and founds NMSP. Shans found *Noom Suk Harn* (Brave Young Warriors). League splits into majority 'Cleans' under Nu, who form coalition with NUF, and 'Stables' under Ba Swe and Kyaw Nyein. NUF presses for peace talks. Government concedes principle of separate Arakan and Mon states. Chins demand their own state. Fighting erupts between rival factions. Nu averts a formal coup by transferring power to the 'Caretaker Government' (Ne Win).

1958–60 Apprehending Union's disintegration, Caretaker Government arrests and deports NUF supporters, denies Shans' right to secede, purchases *saohpa*s' hereditary powers, and amends Constitution to end their reserved seats in Parliament.

1959 Karens, Karennis, Mons, Chins and Communists unite in a military alliance.

1960–61 Uprisings flare across Shan State.

1960 Sao Shwe Thaike and others found Federal Movement to promote constitutional changes relegating 'Burma' to a Burman-majority state with powers not greater than other ethnic states. General election returns Nu to power on pledges to create Arakan and Mon states and to establish Buddhism as state religion.

1961 Following combined Burma Army and PLA attack, the Kuomintang evacuates nearly half its 12,000 men from Burma. KIO is founded. Rebels now include Communists, Karens, Karennis, Shans, Mons, Lahus, Was, Paos, Palaungs, Chins, Nagas, Rakhines, *mujahid* and Kachins.

1962–64 Nu invites Federal Movement leaders to meet him in Rangoon to discuss concessions. Army arrests Nu, his cabinet and minorities' representatives; abrogates Constitution; abolishes Supreme Court; appoints soldiers to run state governments and civil service; and vests plenary executive, legislative and judicial powers in Ne Win. He issues manifestos defining Buddhist, centrist, socialist and Burman principles by which he proposes to rule; creates BSPP and a pervasive body of informers; outlaws other parties; detains political leaders refusing to join the BSPP; suppresses student demonstrations; blows up Rangoon University Students Union building; closes Rangoon University; nationalizes banks, major commercial houses and industrial groups; seizes control of commodities trade; bans new private industry; purges civil service; closes or nationalizes newspapers and magazines and bans new ones; restricts travel abroad; rescinds powers reserved to the states under 1947 Constitution; replaces missionaries with Burmans, nationalizes their schools and hospitals and expels them for alleged sympathies with insurgents; discontinues higher level English-medium schools and forms alliances with narcotics groups, arming and assisting them in their trafficking in return for their support. Growing Shan insurgency consolidates behind SSA, led by Shwe Thaike's widow. Hundreds of thousands of Indians and Chinese flee Burma, and shortages develop in staples such as rice and cooking oil.

1965–69 Mao's 'Great Proletarian Cultural Revolution' sends slogan-chanting ethnic Chinese onto streets. Many are arrested, others attacked and killed. Chinese shops are looted; the Chinese Teachers' Federation building is burned down; the seal is torn from China's embassy; an embassy official is stabbed to death, the New China News Agency's correspondent expelled. Peking Radio denounces Ne Win as a 'reactionary' and the BSPP as 'sham socialism'. CPB summarily executes many of its leaders; Chairman Than Tun (Aung San's brother-in-law) and his politbureau order further purges. Bo Mya begins building the KNLA and a KNU purged of CPB sympathizers. War over control of opium trade breaks out between Kuomintang and Shan warlord armies.

1968–75 Burma Army begins Four Cuts campaigns to sever rebel recruiting, intelligence, victualling and financing links to the people.

Crops and villages are torched, people relocated into fortified compounds. Central Burma is cleared of rebels, but PLA regulars and Chinese Red Guards leading a force of 'national revolutionary minorities' (Was, Kokangs, Kachins, Palaungs, Shans, Lahus and Akhas) invade and occupy a large part of northern Shan State. CPB encroachment into KIO and Shan territory and the zealotry of Cultural Revolution trigger fighting between CPB, KIO and Shans. Burma Army supports KIO.

1969–70 Nu slips out of Burma, establishes 'government in exile' and forms army that builds string of bases along Thai–Burma border in alliance with KNU and NMSP.

1971 Fighting erupts between SSA and KIO.

1972–73 International criticism of drug trafficking forces Rangoon to abandon Kokang, Shan and Wa warlord armies, which realign themselves with SSA.

1974–88 Annual opium yield increases twentyfold. Burma Air Force uses US-supplied aircraft, pilot training and herbicides to spray enemy crops.

1974 New Constitution confirms powers already vested in Ne Win. Limited autonomy guaranteed to ethnic states by 1947 Constitution is withdrawn, and rights protecting minority languages, customs and cultures are subject to their not being used 'to the detriment of national solidarity and socialist social order'. Riots erupt over Army's attempt to bury U Thant inconspicuously. Martial law declared; universities and colleges closed.

1975 CPB agrees a defence pact with SSA. KIO's three top leaders assassinated.

1976 Karens, Karennis, Kayans, Mons, Shans, Palaungs, Paos and Rakhines, soon to be joined by Kachins, Was, Lahus and Chins, form NDF. KIO and CPB end hostilities, demarcate operational areas and agree to cooperate militarily. Brigadier Kyaw Zaw, former Burma Army hero, broadcasts over the CPB's *Voice of the People of Burma* that Aung San had once considered sacking Ne Win and denounces Ne Win as 'morally depraved'.

1978 Fighting erupts within KNPP between pro- and anti-Communist factions.

1980 Government announces general amnesty. More than 2000 rebels surrender.

1980–81 KIO states it will accept autonomy instead of independence. Nevertheless, peace negotiations with Rangoon fail owing to Ne Win's refusal to countenance any political concession save 'rehabilitation' and on his insistence that such a constitutional change would require a referendum. Rangoon and CPB also talk – but only for two days, when Rangoon demands peremptorily that CPB dissolve itself.

1981 China stops aiding CPB.

1982–83 Rangoon bans from the civil service and political office all minorities who have settled in Burma since 1824. Wa National Organization founded and joins NDF.

1984–88 Four Cuts operation in Karen Hills halves excise taxes collected by KNU on cross-border trade.

1985 Khun Sa and Moh Heng's forces merge as MTA.

1986 NDF settles for autonomy and agrees to cooperate militarily with CPB; but Bo Mya denounces pact and CPB as arrogant drug traffickers.

1987 Rangoon invalidates Kt. 75, Kt. 35 and Kt. 25 notes and replaces them with Kt. 90 and Kt. 45 notes (Ne Win believes that 9 is an auspicious number). Enraged students storm onto streets and begin smashing government property.

1988–98 Burma Army increases from 180,000–215,000 to 320,000–350,000 men.

12–18 March 1988 Tanks roar into Rangoon, and tear gas canisters disperse crowds.

June–July 1988 More demonstrations; now, however, there is open dissent within the Army. Aung San Suu Kyi (Aung San's daughter) accuses Ne Win of destroying the country ('the country is poor while one individual is rich').

23 July 1988 Ne Win makes valedictory address ('When the Army shoots, it shoots to kill') and resigns.

26–27 July 1988 Riot police commander General Sein Lwin takes over.

August 1988 10,000 demonstrators march through Rangoon and bury effigies of Ne Win and Sein Lwin in coffins decorated with demonetized banknotes. Monks report that the Buddha's image at Sula Pagoda has changed shape and that an image in the sky above the Shwe Dagon Pagoda is standing on its head.

8 August 1988 A general strike begins. Mass demonstrations engulf country as Burmans, ethnic minorities, Buddhists, Muslims, farmers, moneylenders, rightists, leftists, old and young find common cause in multiparty democracy. Regime responds by killing hundreds and arresting

thousands; demonstrators retaliate with Molotov cocktails, swords, spears, knives, poisoned darts and slingshot propelled bicycle spokes.

12 August 1988 Sein Lwin resigns.

19 August 1988 Maung Maung (Ne Win's biographer) takes over, lifts martial law and promises referendum on whether Burma should be a single party or multiparty state.

26 August 1988 Aung San Suu Kyi addresses half a million people.

September 1988 Nine of the surviving 11 Thirty Comrades declare support for uprising, and soldiers and policemen begin fraternizing with demonstrators. Nu proclaims a provisional government and promises a general election within a month. Maung Maung promises elections within three months and a civilian commission to prepare for them.

18–19 September 1988 Generals styling themselves the State Law and Order Restoration Council (SLORC) seize power, abolish 1974 Constitution and counter demonstrations with a massacre. Soldiers who had mutinied rush into holy orders, and student activists join colleagues undergoing training at the borders.

22 September 1988 Aung San Suu Kyi appeals for help ('I would like every country in the world to recognize the fact that the people of Burma are being shot down for no reason at all'). SLORC replaces BSPP with National Unity Party and (to split the opposition) lifts ban on rival parties. Of 234 that register, the most important is Aung San Suu Kyi's NLD, whose aim is 'to secure the highest degree of autonomy consonant with the inherent rights of the minorities and the well-being of the Union'.

October 1988 The strike collapses.

November 1988 Students training at the borders found ABSDF and unite with most of NDF and various Burman, Muslim, Buddhist and expatriate groups in DAB.

1989 SLORC announces general election for May 1990. Kokangs and Was mutiny, and CPB disintegrates. SLORC renames country, replacing ethnically neutral English *Burma* with controversial Burmese *Myanmar*. Aung San Suu Kyi accuses Ne Win of teaching soldiers to kill their own people and exhorts Army to resist 'iniquitous laws'. She and many of her supporters are arrested. Two Wa groups unite as United Wa State Army. Other ex-CPB forces are now warlord-led government militias; heroin refineries proliferate. SLORC sets general election for Sunday 27 May 1990 (fourth Sunday, fifth month: 4 + 5 = 9).

1889–90 SLORC relocates one million 'squatters' to improve its electoral prospects.

1990 3000 monks protest in Mandalay. SLORC wins only 10 of 485 seats contested and 25 per cent of votes cast in 27 May general election; NLD wins 392 seats and 60 per cent of vote, and its ethnic allies most of the remaining seats and 15 per cent of vote. SLORC states it will not transfer power until a new constitution ensuring strong and stable government is adopted and claims that the election was to a constituent assembly, not a parliament. It issues Decree No. 1/90 predicating its authority on international and UN recognition and defining a sixfold procedure for transferring power: (1) a National Convention to decide guidelines for a new constitution (2) Burma Army approval of guidelines (3) draft of the new constitution prepared by the National Convention (4) revised draft prepared by an elected People's Assembly (5) Burma Army approval of revised draft (6) approval of constitution by plebiscite. Huge crowds turn out on anniversary of '8888' massacre to offer alms to monks (signifying dispatch of mass prayers for victims' reincarnated souls). Soldiers spray them with bullets; stories spread of left breasts of marble Buddhas swelling with indignation. Most of NLD's leaders still at large and 40 of its MPs-elect arrested for claiming right to form a government. Monks are required to join a union after they turn down their begging bowls to soldiers. Aung San Suu Kyi's first cousin, Sein Win, and seven other MPs-elect flee to KNU GHQ and form NCGUB.

1991 KIO outlaws opium and heroin in areas under its control. A $400 million arms procurement does not effect Burma's reported foreign exchange reserves, indicating use of fenced drugs trade money. European Parliament brands SLORC as illegal, condemns its atrocities, demands Aung San Suu Kyi's release, and urges member countries to establish relations with NCGUB. Aung San Suu Kyi awarded Nobel Peace Prize.

1991–99 UN General Assembly adopts annual resolutions to condemn human rights abuse in Burma and urge implementation of 1990 election.

1992 Scores of thousands of Karenni villagers are resettled and replaced by landless Burmans conscripted to work mines at Mawchi. Doyen of Western scholars on modern Burma, Josef Silverstein, calls for unseating SLORC at UN and recognizing NCGUB instead.

1993 NCGUB's finance minister assassinated; another member of its cabinet vanishes. SLORC offers one-on-one peace talks. NDF signals readiness to talk collectively, but NMSP, under pressure from Thailand, enters separate negotiations. Opium production in Burma reaches 2575 metric tonnes (an 8000 per cent increase since 1948).

1994 KIO and SLORC agree truce: KIO keeps its arms and areas it controls. (CPB's collapse has enabled Burma Army to redeploy; it now has 40 battalions in Kachin State.) Aung San Suu Kyi calls National Convention a farce. ('It makes no sense at all, because if people are ... just there to nod their heads, there's nothing.') Eight ethnic groups in ceasefire mode form Peace and Democratic Front and demand release of Aung San Suu Kyi and swifter progress towards NLD government; 300 Buddhists defect from KNLA, enabling Burma Army to seize positions vital to defence of Manerplaw (the KNLA's GHQ).

1995 Burma Army takes Manerplaw. NMSP agrees ceasefire.

1996 MTA surrenders; 50,000 Shan villagers are moved to SLORC-controlled areas. Burma Army arrests 242 MPs-elect, relocates 20,000 Karennis and masses troops along Thai border for new offensive against KNLA. SLORC mob attacks cars carrying Aung San Suu Kyi and her colleagues.

1997 14 ethnic groups reject National Convention as a ruse to perpetuate military dictatorship and pledge to work with NLD for genuine federal union. Burma Army (about 100,000 men) opens offensive against KNLA's Fourth Brigade (about 2500 men); 15,000 Karens flee to Thailand (joining 90,000 Karen refugees already there). Democratic Karen Buddhist Army (KNLA mutineers) attacks refugee camps. Burma joins ASEAN.

September 1997 NLD announces it will convene parliament; then appoints committee to exercise the mandate of the 251 MPs-elect remaining from the 485 elected. Shwe Thaike's son states that the most effective pressure on SPDC would be to withdraw its UN credentials.

15 November 1997 SLORC dismisses 14 of its ministers, arrests three for taking kickbacks and commissions, and changes its name to State Peace and Development Council (SPDC).

10 December 1997 Fiftieth anniversary of Human Rights Day. Aung San Suu Kyi states: 'If [the NLD] don't have the support of the Burmese people, why is it necessary to put our people in jail?' SSA leader Yod Suk blames Rangoon's unrelenting oppression of ethnic nationalities for continued opium cultivation. NLD files suit in Burma High Court, alleging unlawful arrest and false imprisonment of its members.

4 January 1998 Golden Jubilee of Independence. SPDC Chairman Than Shwe declares: 'We must be vigilant against various wily schemes of some neo-colonialists ... [and] build the three strengths of the Union – political power, economic power and national defence power.'

1999 KNU leader Bo Mya claims Burma Army is conducting a campaign of systematic terror and predicts a further flood of refugees to Thailand. Reports of growing dissent within army's ranks, desertions and sacking of four regional commanders in Rangoon area.

Bibliography

Books

Anderson, John (1876) *Mandalay to Momien: a narrative of the two Expeditions to Western China of 1868 and 1875 under Colonel E. B. Sladen and Colonel H. Browne* (London: Macmillan)

Aung San (1974) *Burma's Challenge* (Rangoon: Aung Gyi, 3rd edn)

Aung San Suu Kyi (1995) *Freedom from Fear* (London: Penguin, 2nd edn)
(1991) *Aung San of Burma: A Biographical Portrait by his Daughter* (St Lucia: University of Queensland Press, 1984; Edinburgh: Kiscadale, 2nd edn)

Aye Saung (1989) *Burman in the Back Row* (Hong Kong: Asia 2000)

Bowen, John (1978) *Undercover in the Jungle* (London: William Kimber)

Boucaud, André and Louis (1985) *Birmanie-Sur la piste des Seigneurs de la Guerre* (Paris: L'Harmattan)

Cady, John Frank (1958) *A History of Modern Burma* (Ithaca, NY: Cornell University Press)

Carey, Bertram Sausmarez and Henry Newman Tuck (1896) *The Chin Hills: A History of the People, our Dealings with them, their Customs and Manners, and a Gazetteer of their Country* (Rangoon: Superintendent of Government Printing and Stationery Office)

Carey, Peter (ed.) (1997) *Burma: The Challenge of Change in a Divided Society* (London: Macmillan)

Carrapiett, William James Sherlock (1929) *The Kachin Tribes of Burma* (Rangoon: Superintendent of Government Printing and Stationery Office)

Clifford, Francis (1979) *Desperate Journey* (London: Hodder & Stoughton)

Crosthwaite, Charles Haukes Todd (1912) *The Pacification of Burma* (London: Frank Cass) reprint 1968

Cruickshank, Charles (1983) *SOE in the Far East* (Oxford: Oxford University Press)
Davies, Henry Rodolph (1909) *Yün-nan: The Link between India and the Yangtze* (Cambridge: Cambridge University Press)
Denyer, Charles Henry (1927) *Dawn on the Kachin Hills* (London: Bible Churchmen's Missionary Society)
Donnison, Frank Siegfried Vernon (1970) *Burma* (London: Ernest Benn/New York: Praeger)
Dun, Smith (1980) *Memoirs of the Four-Foot Colonel* (Ithaca, NY: Cornell University Southeast Asia Program, Data Paper No. 113)
Dunlop, Richard (1979) *Behind Japanese Lines: With the OSS in Burma* (New York: Rand McNally)
Enriquez, Colin Metcalf (1923) *A Burmese Arcady* (London: Seeley Service)
(1933) *The Races of Burma* (New Delhi: Government of India, Manager of Publications, 2nd edn)
Fellowes-Gordon, Ian (1957) *Amiable Assassins* (London: Robert Hale)
(1971) *The Battle for Naw Seng's Kingdom* (London: Leo Cooper); reprinted 1972 as *The Magic War* (New York: Scribners)
Fergusson, Bernard (1945) *Beyond the Chindwin* (London: Collins)
(1956) *The Wild Green Earth* (London: Collins)
Fischer, Edward (1980) *Mission in Burma: The Columban Fathers' Forty-three Years in Kachin Country* (New York: Seabury Press)
Fletcher, James S. (1997) *Secret War in Burma* (published by author, 169 Wilhelmia Drive, Austell, GA 30001–6903, USA)
Gardiner, Ritchie (1942) *Diary of a Journey from Sumprabum to Margherita by the Chaukkan Pass, May–July, 1942* (manuscript)
Gilhoedes, Charles (1922) *The Kachins: Religion and Customs* (Calcutta: Catholic Orphan Press/London: Kegan Paul) reprinted in 1961 and 1995 (New Delhi: Mittal)
Hackmann, Heinrich Friedrick (1905) *Von Omi bis Bhamo: Wanderungen an den Grenzen von China, Tibet und Birma* (Halle: Gebauer-Schwetschke)
Hall, Daniel George Edward (1960) *Burma* (London: Hutchinson, 3rd edn)
Hanson, Ola (1913) *The Kachins: Their Customs and Traditions* (Rangoon: American Baptist Mission Press)
Harvey, Godfrey Eric (1925) *History of Burma: From the Earliest Times to 10 March 1824, The Beginning of the English Conquest* (London: Frank Cass) reprint 1967
Hertz, Henry Felix (1902) *A Practical Handbook of the Kachin or Chingpaw Language* (Rangoon: Superintendent of Government Printing and Stationery Office) revised and enlarged edn 1917, reprint 1954

Hertz, William Axel (1912) 'The Myitkyina District', *Burma Gazetteer*, vol. A (Rangoon: Superintendent of Government Printing and Stationery Office) reprint 1960
Hilsman, Roger (1990) *American Guerrilla* (McClean, VA: Brassey's)
Htin Aung (1948) *Burmese Folk Tales* (Calcutta: Oxford University Press)
(1976) *Folk tales of Burma* (New Delhi: Oxford University Press)
Kaulback, Ronald (1939) *Salween* (London: Hodder & Stoughton)
Kingdon-Ward, Frank (1921) *In Farthest Burma* (London: Seeley Service)
(1924) *From China to Hkamti Long* (London: Edward Arnold)
(1930) *Plant Hunting on the Edge of the World* (London: Gollanz)
(1949) *Burma's Icy Mountains* (London: Jonathan Cape)
(1956) *Return to the Irrawaddy* (London: Andrew Melrose)
Lace, John Henry (1922) *List of Trees, Shrubs, Herbs and Principal Climbers, Etc.* (Rangoon: Superintendent of Government Printing and Stationery Office) 2nd edn revised and enlarged by Alexander Rodger in 1922 and 3rd edn revised and enlarged by Gordon H. Hundley and Chit Ko Ko in 1961
Leach, Edmund Ronald (1954) *Political Systems of Highland Burma* (London: G. Bell)
Lintner, Bertil (1989) *Outrage: Burma's Struggle for Democracy* (Hong Kong: Review Publishing)
(1990a) *The Rise and Fall of the Communist Party of Burma (CPB)* (Ithaca, NY: Cornell University Southeast Asia Program)
(1990b) *Land of Jade* (Edinburgh: Kiscadale)
(1990c) *Aung San Suu Kyi and Burma's Unfinished Renaissance* (Clayton, Victoria: Monash University Centre of Southeast Asian Studies/Edinburgh: Kiscadale)
(1994) *Burma in Revolt: Opium and Insurgency Since 1948* (Boulder, CO: Westview Press)
(1999) *The Kachin: Lords of Burma's Northern Frontier* (Chiang Mai: Teak House Publications)
Lowis, Cecil Champain (1919) *The Tribes of Burma* (Rangoon: Superintendent of Government Printing and Stationery Office), Ethnographical Survey of India, Burma, No. 4
Lunt, James (1986) *The Retreat from Burma* (London: Collins)
Margary, Augustus Raymond (1876) *The journey of Augustus Raymond Margary, from Shanghae to Bhamo and back to Manwyne* (London: Macmillan). Originally published (1875) as *Notes of a Journey from Hankow to Ta-li Fu* (Shanghai: F. & C. Walsh)
Masters, John (1961) *The Road Past Mandalay* (London: Michael Joseph)
Maung Maung, Dr (1956) *Burma in the Family of Nations* (Amsterdam: Djambatan)
(1959) *Burma's Constitution* (The Hague: Martinus Nijhoff)

(1962) *A Trial in Burma: The Assassination of Aung San* (The Hague: Martinus Nijhoff)

(ed.) (1962) *Aung San of Burma* (The Hague: Martinus Nijhoff for Yale University Press Southeast Asia Studies)

(1969) *Burma and General Ne Win* (Rangoon: Religious Affairs Department Press/London: Asia Publishing House)

(1974) *To a Soldier Son* (Rangoon: Sarpay Beikman Press)

Maung Maung, Dr U (1980) *From Sangha to Laity: Nationalist Movements of Burma 1920–1940* (New Delhi: Manohar for Australian Nat. Univ.)

(1989) *Burmese National Movements 1940–1948* (Edinburgh: Kiscadale)

Maung Maung Pye (1951) *Burma in the Crucible* (Rangoon: Khittaya)

McCoy, Alfred William (1972) *The Politics of Heroin in Southeast Asia* (New York: Harper & Row)

(1991) *The Politics of Heroin: CIA Complicity in the Global Drug Trade* (New York: Lawrence Hill)

McEnery, John (1990) *Epilogue in Burma 1945–48* (Tunbridge Wells: Spellmount)

McLeish, Alexander (1928) *Christian Progress in Burma* (Rangoon: American Baptist Mission Press) reprinted 1929 (London: World Dominion Press)

(1942) *Burma: Christian Progress to the Invasion, War-Time Survey Series*, no. 4 (London: World Dominion Press)

McMahon, Alexander Ruxton (1876) *The Karens of the Golden Chersonese* (London: Harrison)

Mirante, Edith (1993) *Burmese Looking Glass* (New York: Grove Press)

Morrison, Ian (1946) *Grandfather Longlegs* (London: Faber & Faber)

Morse, Eugene (1974) *Exodus to a Hidden Valley* (New York: Readers Digest Press; London: Collins, 1975)

Morse, Gertrude (1998) *The Dogs May Bark: But the Caravan Moves On* (Joplin, MO: College Press, ed. Helen Morse)

Ni Ni Myint (1983) *Burma's Struggle Against British Imperialism 1885–1895* (Rangoon: The Universities Press)

Nu, U (1954) *Burma under the Japanese* (London: Macmillan) translated by J. S. Furnivall

(1975) *Saturday's Son* (New Haven, CT: Yale University Press) translated by Law Yone

O'Brien, Harriet (1991) *Forgotten Land* (London: Michael Joseph)

O'Brien, Terence (1987) *The Moonlight War* (London: Collins)

Ogburn, Charlton Jr (1956) *The Marauders* (New York: Harper)

Owen, Frank (1946) *The Campaign in Burma* (London: Central Office of Information, prepared for South-East Asia Command)

Peacock, Edgar Henry (1933) *A Game Book for Burma and Adjoining Territories* (London: Witherby)
Peacock, Geraldine (1958) *The Life of a Jungle Walla: Reminiscenses in the Life of Lieutenant-Colonel E. H. Peacock* (Ilfracombe, England: Arthur H. Stockwell)
Pe Kin (1994) *Pinlon: An Inside Story* (Rangoon: Guardian Press)
Phayre, Arthur Purves (1883) *History of Burma* (London: Trübner)
Renard, Ronald Duane (1996) *The Burmese Connection: Illegal Drugs and the Making of the Golden Triangle* (Boulder, CO and London: Lynne Rienner)
Saimong Mangrai (1965) *The Shan States and the British Annexation* (Ithaca, NY: Cornell University Southeast Asia Program, Data Paper No. 57)
San Crombie Po (1928) *Burma and the Karens* (London: Elliot Stock)
Sargent, Inge (1994) *Twilight over Burma* (Honolulu: University of Hawaii Press)
Scott, James George, assisted by John Percival Hardiman (1900–01) *Gazetteer of Upper Burma and the Shan States* (Rangoon: Superintendent of Government and Printing and Stationery Office)
(1912) *Burma: A Handbook of Practical Information* (London: O'Connor)
(1924) *Burma: From the Earliest Times to the Present Day* (New York: Knopf)
Seagrave, Gordon Stifler (1943) *Burma Surgeon* (New York: Norton; London: Gollanz, 1944)
(1946) *Burma Surgeon Returns* (London: Gollanz)
(1957) *My Hospital in the Hills* (London: Robert Hale)
Seagrave, Sterling (1985) *The Soong Dynasty* (London: Sidgwick & Jackson)
Shakespear, Leslie Waterfield (1914) *History of Upper Assam, Upper Burma, and Northeastern Frontier* (London: Macmillan)
Silverstein, Joseph (1977) *Burma: Military Rule and the Politics of Stagnation* (Ithaca, NY: Cornell University Press)
(1980) *Burmese Politics: The Dilemma of National Unity* (New Brunswick, NJ: Rutgers University Press)
(ed.) (1989) *Independent Burma at Forty Years: Six Assessments* (Ithaca, NY: Cornell University Southeast Asia Program)
(1993) *The Political Legacy of Aung San* (Ithaca, NY: Cornell University Southeast Asia Program, Data Paper No. 11, revised edn)
Sladden, Edward Bosc (1870) *Official Narrative of the Expedition to Explore the Trade Routes to China via Bhamo, Selections from the Records of the Government of India, Foreign Department no. 79* (Calcutta: Office of Superintendent of Government Printing)
Slim, William Joseph (1956) *Defeat into Victory* (London: Cassell)

Smeaton, Donald MacKenzie (1887) *The Loyal Karens of Burma* (London: Kegan Paul)
Smith, Donald Eugene (1965) *Religion and Politics in Burma* (Princeton, NJ: Princeton University Press)
Smith, Martin (1991) *Burma: Insurgency and the Politics of Ethnicity* (London: Zed Books)
(1994) *Ethnic Groups in Burma* (London: Anti-Slavery International)
Steinberg, David (1982) *Burma: A Socialist Nation of Southeast Asia* (Boulder, CO: Westview Press)
Stevenson, Henry Noel Cochrane (1944) *The Hill Peoples of Burma* (London and Rangoon: Longmans Green)
Symes, Lieutenant-Colonel Michael (1795) *An Account of an Embassy to the Kingdom of Ava in the Year 1795* (Edinburgh: Constable) abridged edn prepared by D. G. E. Hall, 1955 (London: Allen & Unwin)
Taylor, Robert (1987) *The State in Burma* (London: Hurst)
Tegenfeldt, Herman Gustaf (1974) *A Century of Growth: The Kachin Baptist Church of Burma* (South Pasadena, CA: William Carey)
Tinker, Hugh (1957) *The Union of Burma: A Study of the First Years of Independence* (London: Oxford University Press)
(ed.) (1984) *Burma: The Struggle for Independence 1944–1948* (London: HM Stationery Office)
Trager, Frank Newton (1966) *Burma: From Kingdom to Republic* (New York: Praeger/London: Pall Mall)
Trager, Helen Gibson (1966) *Burma through Alien Eyes: Missionary Views of the Burmese in the Nineteenth Century* (Bombay: Asian Publishing House)
Toke Gale (1974) *Burmese Timber Elephant* (Rangoon: Trade Corporation 9)
Tysson, Geoffrey (1945) *Forgotten Frontier* (Calcutta: W. H. Targett)
US Army Center of Military History (1945) *Merrill's Marauders* (Washington: US Government Printing Office)
Williams, Clement (1868) *Through Burma to Western China* (Edinburgh: Blackwood)
Williams, James Howard (1950) *Elephant Bill* (London: Rupert Hart-Davis)
Winnington, Alan (1959) *The Slaves of the Cool Mountains* (Berlin: Seven Seas Books)
Woodman, Dorothy (1962) *The Making of Burma* (London: Cresset)
Yang Li (Jackie Yang) (1977) *The House of Yang: Guardians of an Unknown Frontier* (Sydney: Bookpress)
Yawnghwe, Chao Tzang (1987) *The Shan of Burma: Memoirs of a Shan Exile* (Singapore: Institute of Southeast Asian Studies)

Bibliography

Papers and Articles

Amnesty International (1988) 'Burma-Extrajudicial Execution and Torture of Members of Ethnic Minorities' (London)

(1989) 'Prisoners of Conscience in Myanmar: A Chronicle of Developments since September 1988' (New York)

Asia Watch (1989) 'Killing its own People: Asia Watch condemns Burma's Death March of Prisoners and Crackdown against Opposition' (New York)

Bray, John (1995) 'Burma: The Politics of Constructive Engagement' (London, Royal Institute of International Affairs) Discussion Paper 58

Burma Affairs Bulletin (bi-monthly periodical published until April 1991 by Committee for the Restoration of Democracy in Burma, United Kingdom, thereafter until December 1994 as *Burma Affairs Monitor* edited by Nyunt Aung, 11 Shire Place, Swaffield Road, Earlsfield, London SW18 3BP)

Burma Alert (monthly periodical published until May 1997 by the Associates to Develop Democratic Burma, c/o Harn Yawnghwe, RR 4, Shawville, Quebec JOX 2YO, Canada)

Burma Debate (monthly periodical published by Open Society Institute, PO Box 19126, Washington, DC)

Dawn News Bulletin (bi-weekly periodical published by All Burma Students' Democratic Front, PO Box 1352, Bangkok 10500)

Fletcher, James S. (1984) 'Jingpaw Rangers', *Military History Review* (Sacramento, CA) vol. 1, no. 5, pp. 30–9

(1985) 'The Capture of Myitkyina — Part I', *Military History Review* (Sacramento, CA) vol. 2, no. 1, pp. 18–23

(1985) 'The Capture of Myitkyina — Part II', *Military History Review* (Sacramento, CA) vol. 2, no. 2, pp. 8–12

Frontier Areas Committee of Enquiry (1947) *Report* [presented to British Government, 24 April 1947] (London: HM Stationery Office/Rangoon: Superintendent of Government Printing and Stationery Office)

George, Edward Claudius Scotney (1892) 'Memorandum on the Kachins on our Frontier, Census of India, 1891', *Burma*, vol. IX, Appendix A, pp. x–xxxviii (Rangoon: Superintendent of Government Printing and Stationery Office)

Leyden, John (1984) 'Note by John Leyden on the Panglong Conference, (1947)', Item no 294 in Hugh Tinker (ed.) *Burma: The Struggle for Independence 1944–1948* (London: HM Stationery Office)

MacGregor, Charles Reginald (1887) 'Journey of the Expedition under Colonel Woodthorpe, R.E., from Upper Assam to the Irawadi, and return over the Patkoi Range', *Proceedings of the Royal Geographical Society* (London) vol. 9, pp. 19–42

Matthews, Bruce (1994) 'Religious Minorities in Myanmar: Hints of the Shadow' (unpublished paper submitted to Burma Studies Group, Northern Illinois University, 7 October)

Mirante, Edith (1987) 'Destroying Humanity: Report of a Survey on Human Rights Abuse in Frontier Areas of Burma, 1986–1987' (privately published by the author, 0104 S.W. Lane Street, Portland, Oregon 97201, USA)

(ed.) (1989) 'Burma in Search of Peace', *Cultural Survival Quarterly* (Cambridge, MA) vol. 13, no. 4

Morse, Stephen (1988) 'US Policy and Narcotics Eradication Strategy in Burma' (mimeograph, Chiang Mai)

Pritchard, B. E. A. (1914) 'A Journey from Myitkyina to Sadiya via the N'Mai Hka and Hkamti Long', *Geographical Journal*, (London) vol. 43, pp. 521–35

Sandeman, J. E. (1887) 'The River Irawady and its Sources', *Proceedings of the Royal Geographical Society* (London) vol. 4, pp. 257–73

Sladen, Edward Bosc (1871) 'Expedition from Burma, via the Irrawaddy and Bhamo, to Southwestern China', *Journal of the Royal Geographical Society* (London) vol. 41, pp. 257–81

US Committee for Refugees (1990) 'The War is Growing Worse and Worse: Refugees and Displaced Persons on the Thai-Burmese Border' (Washington: US Government Printing Office)

US General Accounting Office (1989) 'Drug Control: Enforcement Efforts in Burma Not Effective' (Washington: US Government Printing Office)

US State Department (1989/90) 'Report on Human Rights' (Washington: US Government Printing Office)

U Thaung (1990) 'Army's Accumulation of Economic Power in Burma: 1950–1990', paper presented to Burma Seminar, Washington, DC, October (author's address, 1976 SW 67th Terrace, Pompano Beach, FL 33068, USA)

Walker, James Thomas (1892) 'Expeditions among the Kachin Tribes of the North East Frontier of Upper Burma compiled by General J. J. Walker from the reports of Lieutenant Eliot, Assistant Commissioner', *Proceedings of the Royal Geographical Society* (London) vol. 14, pp. 161–73

Note to the Author from Ronald Kaulback

During the war in Burma, the Americans had their equivalent to our SOE [Special Operations Executive] in the OSS (Office of Strategic Services – a cover name), which operated against the Japanese in an area of the Kachin Hills. The overall commander of the Kachin OSS was a Colonel Eifler, an excellent and unconventional officer, who had been a Chicago cop before the war, I was told.

Very early in 1945, one of his young officers in the field sent him a radio message to the effect that several of the Kachin headmen had been particularly helpful, and what could he do to show gratitude in a fitting manner. At that period, the US Army was careful to insert punctuation into its radio signals, as 'prd' (for 'period', full stop), 'cma' (comma) and so on. Colonel Eifler replied, 'Award clothes cma money etc prd', and thought no more about it until, a little later, he flew in to visit this same young officer in one of the very light planes the British called Proctors. I cannot now recall what the US name was. Sitting around their bowl of rice that evening, the YO said: 'Say, Colonel, about those awards. I've awarded clothes and money – and I've awarded the CMA, 22 of them; but what in hell *is* the CMA?' 'Oh!' said Eifler, fixing the YO with his most turtle-like gaze. 'And what did you *say* it was?' 'Well, Colonel, I *said* it was the Citation for Military Assistance.' 'Oh, you did,' replied Eifler. 'It may interest you to know that you have awarded 22 commas! But,' he continued, 'I have never let my officers down yet, and, from this moment, the CMA is born.'

The next day, when he flew back to his headquarters, he called in his executive officers and told them: 'Boys, you will now design the Citation for Military Assistance – and you better make it good!' And make it good they certainly did. It was a noble medal, about two inches in diameter, of heavy silver. On the obverse was the Burmese Peacock, in high relief, and, on the reverse, what I remember as a wreath of wheat stalks, but were probably rice plants, with an inscription in the middle, again in relief, reading 'Citation for Military Assistance. Awarded by the Government of the United States of America to Magwi La' — or whomever it might have been. The medal hung from the neck on a ribbon of green and gold with little silver peacocks on it. Not unnaturally this glorious gong was highly popular in the OSS and quite a number of them were issued.

When the Japanese took Burma in 1942, the Burma Rifles (of which a fair proportion was from the hill tribes) was disbanded. Some of the men made their way to India and served for the rest of the war with the Indian Army, while others returned to their villages, where they served with the OSS or the SOE, as the case might be. Of these, quite a few received the CMA. When the Japanese surrendered, the Burma Rifles were reinstituted, and all ex-riflemen who could be traced were ordered to report to one of several recruiting centres in order to be signed on. There they were drawn up in line to have their names and numbers taken. Some of these men were wearing war ribbons, while others had CMAs in all their beauty dangling over their solar plexi, at which the recruiting officers ordered, 'Not uniform. Take those off!' This caused something of an uproar, those with the CMA complaining bitterly that their fellow tribesmen, who happened to have served outside Burma, were allowed to wear their ribbons, while those who had done their bit with the OSS were stripped of their decorations. This was a baffler for the wretched officers, who told the Kachins they had better wear their CMAs as a temporary measure, while they put the problem up to Army. Army took one look at 'Awarded by the Government of the United States of America', said, 'This is political' and hastily shuffled it on to the Government of Burma. This was not really working as yet, for which they were grateful, and so it passed to the Government of India. These gentlemen realized that they had no direct dealings with the USA, and sent it to Whitehall without delay, where the Foreign Office took a very grave view of a foreign power issuing decorations to British subjects without prior reference to HM Government and instructed the Ambassador in Washington to make severe representations to the Secretary of State.

And that, unfortunately, is almost the end of my story. England and America must have come to some amicable agreement, in that there was no diplomatic rupture about then as I recall; but the important point, as to whether the CMA was permitted to be worn in uniform, remains unknown to me. When I left Rangoon that political battle was still undecided, and my last connection (if one can call it such) was when I paid a farewell visit to Colonel Eifler, sitting gloomily ruminating at his desk. I said, 'Goodbye,' and then added, 'Oh, and how's the CMA coming along?' That gingered him. He sat bolt upright. 'Kee-*rist*' he positively snarled. 'To think that a couple of supposedly intelligent governments could make such a fuss over a bunch of commas.'

Early in 1945, when I was OC Tac headquarters Force 136 at 14th Army headquarters (then in Meiktila), Force 136 had some 15,000 Karens fighting for them in the Karen Hills as guerrillas under British officers. At this time, the Japanese were making a big effort to stamp out these guerrillas and were destroying crops and villages and slaughtering the women, children and old men wherever they could. The Karens said that they were prepared to put up with all their sacrifice and would continue to fight for the British as loyally as ever; but what was going to happen to them after the war was over; that the Burmese were already saying that they would get their independence and would possess the whole country from Victoria Point to Putao and, if that were so, then it would be essential for the Karens to make peace now or face possible destruction later. The Burmese, of course, were fully supporting the Japanese at this time. I was in no position to answer the Karens, so I referred the question to the headquarters of Force 136 in Calcutta, who referred it, in their turn, to the Supreme Allied Commander South East Asia (Admiral Lord Mountbatten). The reply was as clear as daylight – that under no circumstances would the Karens be handed over to the Burmese after the war. I passed that on to the Karens, who continued to fight with us as courageously as ever until the war ended. And then the British handed them over to the Burmese.

8 February 1991

Index

Adehdi, 241–2, 246–8, 298
Adeu Guide, 251–3, 256–61, 266
Adeu Hkasher, 249, 251–61, 266
Adeu Hunter, 249–50, 252–4, 259–61, 266
Adeu Nephew, 251, 253–5, 260–1, 266
Adi, 209, 213–15, 217–22, 235, 237, 239, 243–4
Afoi, 249–51, 253
Ahom, 68, 82–5
Akha(s), 34, 46, 233, 331, 353
Alaunghpaya, 42n
Alex, 105, 109, 112, 122, 145, 148–9, 196, 235, 240; *see also* La Awng
Alexander the Great, 139
All Burma Students Democratic Front (ABSDF), 71, 72n, 80–2, 285, 355
American Baptist Mission, 127
American Baptist Missionary High School, 88, 95
Amnesty International, 81
Amoco, 332
Amoy, 37
Andover, 310, 332
Anglicans, 95
Anna, 216–18, 221
Anti-Fascist People's Freedom League (AFPFL), 39–41, 348–9
Arab League, 310
Arabs, 56, 168
Arakan, 34, 41, 346, 349, 351–2
Aris, Michael, 271–2
Arora, Kum Archana, 281, 302, 307
Arunachal Pradesh, 239, 259, 263, 274, 306–7, 312–13, 318–19, 322–3
Arunachal Pradesh Bhavan, 324, 327
Asoka, 137, 139, 145
Assam/Assamese, 68, 83, 85, 238, 267, 283, 294, 306–7, 309–10, 319, 321, 324, 343, 346
Assam Rifles, 241, 246–7, 338
Ata, 216–18, 224, 236, 240, 243–4
Ati, 216–18, 221, 235, 238–9, 242–5, 247
Attlee, Clement, 40, 349
Aung Gyi, General, 29, 48, 50–1, 60, 288
Aung San, Thakin, 37, 39–40, 42, 74, 79, 90, 135, 167–8, 262, 266, 334–5, 347–9, 351–5
Aung San Suu Kyi, Daw, 37n, 271n, 332n, 333n, 334, 354–7

Aura Yang, 132
Ava, 99, 151
Awng Hkawng, Captain, 103–5, 108, 111, 117–19, 121–2, 124, 126, 129, 131, 134, 136, 138, 141–2, 144–8, 150, 161, 163, 170, 172, 176–7, 185–6, 188, 189, 193, 195, 197, 199, 204, 206–8, 211, 213–17, 220–3, 225, 234–7, 239–40, 243–4, 246, 343
Awng Lawt, 199, 204–5, 211
Awng Seng La, Sergeant, 71, 73, 284
Azi (or Szi), 67–8, 70, 111, 113–14, 178

Ba Maw, 347–8
Ba Swe, 351
Bahadur, Prem, 299–301, 304, 314, 323
Bahadur, Som, 261–4, 267–8
Balezino, 5
Ban Huai Dua, 7
Ban Sap Mea Sant, 7
Ban Tha Pu Deang, 7
Banerji, Ranjit and Sara, 309–10
Bangkok, 7, 13, 53, 288
Bangladesh, 7, 343
Banhot, Major, 283–6, 294, 329
Banzai, 19, 23, 48
Baoshan, 12, 14, 16, 267
Barabinsk Steppe, 5
Bassein, 99
Bawlake, 7
Benares, 264
Bengal Eastern Frontier Regulation (1873), 279, 318, 321
Berlin, 2, 279
Bhamo, 93, 95, 99, 100–1, 173, 200
Bhamo District, 43, 90
Bhatia, Prem, 311
Bhattacharjee, A. K., 273, 276–8, 318
BHP, 332
Bhutta, 311
Bi Hka, 206
Binuzu, 198, 228, 230, 236, 240; *see also* Pinawng Zup
Blasius, Father, 38
Bo Mya, 352, 354, 358
Bodawpaya, 42n
Bode, Ann and Paul, 313
Bogalay, 99
Bogotá, 3
Bombay Burmah Trading Corporation, 36
Bora, Mr, 279–80, 289, 315–16
Boudin, 330
Bowerman, Brigadier, 335
Boyce-Morton, Captain, 108n
Brahmaputra, 67, 323
Brang Seng, 87–8, 91, 95, 339–40
Brang Seng, Janan, 102
Brang Shawng, 183
Brang Wa, 168–9, 170–1, 173
Brave Nationalist Democratic Alliance, 61n, 331n
Brock, Michael, 328
Bruce, James, 77
Bum Lang Bum, 182
Bum Nen Bum, 182
Bum Noi Hka, 186, 189
Bum San Yang, 140, 147
Bumpa Bum, 237
Burma Army, 1, 11–12, 19, 24, 26, 30, 42, 47, 55–7, 72, 76–7, 80–2, 87, 89–90, 92–6, 103–4, 106, 108, 115–17, 119–22, 124–6, 128–32, 136–7, 139, 143, 145–6, 148, 150, 156, 159, 164, 164, 170–1, 176, 179, 181–3, 197–9, 206–7, 229, 232–3, 236, 241, 247, 253, 262, 273, 285, 331–5, 337, 340, 343,

348–9, 350–4, 356–8; *see also* *Tatmadaw*
Burma Frontier Force, 78, 127
Burma Independence Army (BIA), 37–9, 74, 348
Burma National Army, 39, 90, 266, 348
Burma Nullah, 265
Burma Railway, 100
Burma Regiment, 43, 56, 95
Burma Rifles, 90, 368
Burma Socialist Programme Party (BSPP), 42, 101, 199, 352, 355
Burmah Oil, 36
Burmah Ruby Mines Company, 36
Burmah Trading Corporation, 36
Burnes, Alexander, 5
Burney, Major Henry, 151
Bush, President George, 305

Calcutta, 23, 290, 302, 308–9, 369
Columban Fathers, 95, 101, 152
Camp End-of-Toil, 125, 131
Camp Four Papayas, 213
Camp Mound of Blessings, 246, 248–9, 251, 257, 266
Canton, 8–9, 113, 269
Capo, the, 297–9, 303, 323
Caretaker Government, 351
Carey, Peter, 271
Castro, 82–5, 97, 294
Central Intelligence Agency (CIA), 1, 56–7, 87, 307, 316, 319, 332, 351
Cha Huo, 59
Chan Shee-fu, 55n, 331n; *see also under* Khun Sa
Chandra, 324–7
Chandra Bose, Subhas, 266
Chang, 11, 14, 16–19, 31
Changlang, 11, 273, 277–8, 280, 289, 292, 295–6, 305, 307–8, 312, 315, 318, 323, 330, 344
Chaukan Pass, 77, 228, 244, 343
Chefang, 62
Chiang Kai-shek, 78, 101n
Chiang Mai, 7, 233
Chin(s), 34, 40, 42, 58, 67, 94, 168, 207, 262, 346, 348–9, 351–3
Chin Hills, 7, 195
Chin National Front (CNF), 73n, 262
China, 1, 3, 8–11, 19, 23, 27, 29, 31, 44, 49, 56, 59, 66–7, 77, 80, 86, 90, 104, 106, 112, 114, 117, 148, 187, 195, 227–8, 241, 267–72, 274–6, 281, 288, 290–1, 293, 298, 311, 319–20, 331, 337, 339–41, 350, 352, 354
Chindit(s), 78, 204
Chindwin River, 33, 195, 197
Upper Chindwin, 77, 185; *see also under* Tanai Hka
Chinquapin Hill, 230–2, 242
Chiphwe, 117, 120, 131–2, 163, 343
Church of Christ, 101, 241
Chyahkyi Hting Nan, Sergeant, 164–5
Chyanya Hka, 139
Circuit House, 268, 278, 290, 300–1, 302
Cleans, 41, 351
Cleveland, 313
Clinton, President, 58n, 334
Clyde, 332
Co-Prosperity Sphere, 39
Cohen, Bill, 316, 318, 326, 332
Cohen, Chris, 316
Collins, Major, 168–71
Cologne, 3
Communist Party of Burma (CPB), 28–30, 37, 44, 44, 46–7, 49–54, 60–1, 75, 87, 89–91, 94, 270–1,

287–90, 320, 330–1, 340, 348–55, 357
Communist Party of China (CPC), 290
Congress Party, 137, 202, 318
Conolly, Arthur, 5
Cooke, Alistair, 228
Cultural Revolution, 48, 352–3

Dahma Tat, 348
Dai, 10–13, 15; *see also* Shan(s)
Dali, 10–11, 15, 22, 30, 77, 111, 247, 264, 273–4, 331
Danang, 277
Dany, 6, 8–9, 53, 327, 329
Darawalla, 311
Darawng Hka, 143
Daru Bum, 182, 189
Daru Hka, 181, 185–6, 189, 344
Daru Pass, 185
Das Guptaji, Shri, 254
Datong, 6
Dau Gyung, 122, 153, 176, 191, 209, 211
Dauje, 201–2
Davies, Major, 35, 127
Dawn Calm, 268, 273–4, 276
Dehra Dun, 79
Dei Kau Reng, 83
Delhi, 34, 50, 82, 85, 157, 238, 277–8, 280, 290, 292, 294–6, 307–8, 311–12, 314, 316, 318, 321, 326, 330, 350
  New Delhi, 322–4
Democratic Alliance of Burma (DAB), 73, 332, 355
Democratic Karen Buddhist Army, 357
Deng Xiaoping, 29
Deori, Sub-Inspector, 278, 282
Dewan, 264, 266, 274
Dibrugarh, 264, 268, 277, 295–7, 323, 325
Djakarta, 3
Dobama Asiayone, 36, 347
Doctrine of the Elders, 41
Dole, Senator, 312
Drug Enforcement Agency (DEA), 54, 87, 93, 95
Drummond, Andrew, 55n
Du Kaba, 103, 129, 133–4, 155, 186, 191, 202, 206, 213, 247
Dulengs, 67n

East India Company, 36, 56
Eastern Shan National Democratic Alliance, 331n
Eastland, Senator, 313
Empty Valley, 236
Ethiopia, 3
Everest, 31, 33, 282

Farrell, J. G., 157n
Farrell, Jo, 157, 273n
Federal Movement, 351–2
Fellowes-Gordon, Ian, 78, 179
Fleming, Peter, 33, 76
Fletcher, Colonel James, 76, 179
Ford, Colonel, 335
Foreign Missions Society, 101
Fort Harrison, 173
Fort Hertz, 173
Fort Morton, 108n, 173
Four Cuts, 43, 89–90, 352, 354
Frontier Areas, 34, 40, 74, 349
Frontier Areas Commission of Enquiry (FACE), 349

Ga Hkyeng, 66
Ga Pra, 183, 185, 344
Galon Tat, 348
Gam Seng, 189, 190, 194
Gandhi, Indira, 311
Gandhi, Mohandas Karamchand (Mahatmaji), 202, 266

Gandhigram, 257, 260–1, 318; *see also* Sherdi
Gang Dau Yang, 138–9
Gap Dup Hka, 206, 208–9, 211
Gaspar, Father, 38
Gauhati, 277, 307, 323
Gauris (Jinghpaws), 67n
Gaw Nam Yang, 133, 136
Gaw Nan, 196, 203
Geis, George, 100, 127
General Council of Burmese Associations, 36
Genghis Khan, 116, 145
Gentry, Nancy, 310
Geu Sadi, 246, 259–61
Geucherdi Lo, 255–6
Geudi, 246
Ginsberg, Allen, 135
Gogoi, Mr, 280, 282
Golden Triangle, 6, 7, 54, 56, 157, 178, 271
Gondar, 77
Goyal, Arun, 302, 307, 330
Great Wall of China, 6, 269
Gulfport, 313
Gupta, Mr, 294–5, 297–9
Gurkha, 30, 127, 165n, 182, 192, 355
Gyung Zang, *Salang Kaba*, 154, 163

Halliburton, Richard, 76
Hanson, Ola, 66–7, 67n, 68n, 70, 72–3, 100–2, 160
Haynes, Consul, 302–3, 308, 310, 312
Helms, Senator Jesse, 58n
Hertz, Henry Felix, 66
Hidden Valley, 217, 228, 230, 232–4, 240–1, 245, 297
Hilary, Sir Edmund, 31, 282
Hka Htu, 174
Hka Khyens, 99; *see also* Kachin(s)
Hka Mai Yang, 180–2
Hka Taw, 212
Hkagaran, 186
Hkahku(s), 69, 143, 158, 169, 171, 173
Hkai-lekko, 25–6, 257, 344
Hkalue, 247, 249
Hkamaw Hka, 204, 212n
Hkamti, 281
Hkamti Long, 68, 95, 101, 173, 198, 227–30, 233, 244
Hkasher, 247–9
'Hkaw Ying, Private, 103, 125, 128, 136, 181, 207, 211
Hkawn Shawng, 200–1
Hkrang Ku Majoi, 187
Hkyen Naw, 105, 133n, 191; *see also under* Philip
Ho Mön, 55n
Homalin, 195
Hong Kong, 9, 124, 227, 269–70, 326, 332
Hpa Kan, 156
Hpau Jung Roi, 43
Hpau Yan Gam, Sergeant, 71
Hpauwung Tanggun, 199, 204–5, 208–9
Hpauwung Yaw Htung, Lieutenant, 199, 205
Hpauyu family, 175
Hpaw Lam Hpya Bum, 139, 141–2; *see also under* Slaughtered Wild Ox, Mount
Hpundu, 108–9, 113, 344
Hpung Gan Yang, 142–3
Hput Daw Mare, 182
Htiyi Hka, 146
Hubbard, John, 308, 313
Hukawng River, 198, 203, 283
Hukawng Valley, 68–9, 77–8, 95, 194–5, 198, 203–5, 209, 283–4, 341

Huxley, Elspeth, 114

Idemitsu, 332
Imphal, 78
India, 1, 3, 6–7, 9, 11, 17, 51–2, 54, 56, 63, 65–6, 77–9, 84–6, 102, 138–41, 145, 195, 198, 202, 211, 213, 217, 235, 240, 246, 250–2, 255, 265–6, 271–2, 275, 279–81, 285–7, 291–3, 297–8, 304, 306–11, 318–22, 324, 330, 337–8, 343, 347, 368
India House, 311
Indian Army, 79, 84, 262, 265, 267, 283, 286, 348, 368
Insein, 44
Irrawaddy Flotilla Company, 36
Irrawaddy Delta, 38
Irrawaddy River, 33, 47, 67–8, 92, 100, 111, 115, 131, 151, 195

Janbai Bum, 200
Japan/Japanese, 4, 37–9, 56, 74, 76, 78–9, 80n, 89, 101, 124, 152, 156, 165, 179, 195, 243, 266, 273, 332, 335, 343, 348, 367–9
Japanese Army, 39
Jaraimpur, 260, 267
Jasens, 69
Java, 56
Jellicoe, Robin, 165n, 179
Jim's Peace Café, 10, 12
Jing Ma Hka, 144, 146, 203, 344
Jing Ma Yang, 144–5, 149
Jinghpaw, 25, 28, 66–70, 87, 97, 99–100, 102, 107, 115, 118–19, 124, 128–9, 134–5, 142–3, 147, 153, 164, 174–5, 180, 193, 195, 203, 205–7, 227, 231, 250, 253, 264, 337, 343
John, 105, 107, 109, 112, 116–17, 133–5, 145, 148–9, 169, 183, 197–7, 235, 240, 249–52 *see also under* Tu Lum
Juba, 3
Jubeli Yang, 132 137, 138
Jum Yang, 119, 121, 133, 144

Ka Le Pass, 129–30
Kabul, 5
Kachin(s), 28, 34–5, 39–41, 43, 56–9, 65–71, 73–9, 81, 86–8, 90–3, 95–6, 98–102, 104–6, 109–11, 114, 122, 124, 130, 132–3, 136, 139, 142–4, 146, 148, 151, 153, 155, 158–60, 165, 167–8, 171–4, 179, 182, 186–9, 190–2, 195, 201, 203–4, 207, 214, 222, 225, 241, 255, 261–2, 266, 273, 276, 284–5, 290, 304, 335–6, 337–9, 341, 346, 348–9, 352–3, 367–8
Kachin Baptist Church, 100, 105, 132
Kachin Baptist High School, 76
Kachin Defence Army, 331n
Kachin District, 100
Kachin Hills, 1, 43, 46, 61n, 95, 151, 153, 167, 167n, 173, 200n, 285, 334n, 342–3, 367
Kachin Independence Army (KIA), 28, 31, 43, 46, 53–4, 61, 64, 70–2, 75–7, 79–80, 82, 87–92, 96–7, 102–3, 105–7, 111–13, 119, 121, 124, 130–3, 135, 138–9, 143, 148–50, 154–6, 161, 164, 166, 170, 175, 182, 183, 186, 188, 196, 201, 216, 236, 240–1, 243, 247–9, 257, 271–2, 283–6, 290, 296–7, 301, 304–5, 330, 335, 339–40, 345
Kachin Independence Organization (KIO), 28, 43, 46, 49, 53, 55, 57–62, 64, 70–3, 76–7, 82, 86–7, 89–92, 94, 95–6, 101–2,

120, 139–40, 170, 196, 205, 329, 334, 339–40, 352–3, 356–7
Kachin Rangers, *56*, *165*
Kachin Rifles, 41, 61, 79, 89, 165–8, 349
Kachin State, 72, 88–9, 91, 93, 144, 167, 343, 357
Kachin University Students Association, 88
Kachin Youth Culture and Literature Uplift Organization, 88
Kachinland, 11, 31, 46, 66, 72–3, 75–6, 79, 92, 95–101, 116, 151, 154, 160, 167–8, 193, 196, 199, 205, 225, 231, 241, 273, 283, 301, 328, 330, 332–3, 339, 341; *see also Wunpawng Mungdan*
Kadaingti, 38
Kajihtu, 95, 152
Kalewa, 195
Kalimpong, 293
Kam Htoi, Lieutenant-Colonel, 72
Kanapa Village, 43
Kanau Kana Bum, 182
Kanmachyi Hka, 251
Kanpur, 324
Karen(s), 34, 38–42, 45, 57–8, 67, 74, 79, 88, 91, 94, 98, 101, 168, 331, 346–9, 351–3, 357, 369–70
Karen Hills, 37, 332, 346, 354, 369
Karen National Defence Organization (KNDO), 41, 349–50
Karen National Liberation Army (KNLA), 335, 352, 357
Karen National Union (KNU), 73n, 332, 349, 351–4, 356, 358
Karen Rifles, 41, 349
Karenni(s), 34, 40, 42, 57–8, 88, 94, 346, 348–9, 351–3, 356–7
Karenni National Organization (KNO), 41
Karenni National Peoples' Party, 88
Karenni National Progressive Party (KNPP), 73n, 351, 353
Kasu, 111
Katihar, 324
Kaul, P. K., 316, 318, 326
Kawmoorah, 331
Kawthoolei (Karenland), 41
Kayah, 40n, 42
Keane, Michael, 157
Kengtung, 1, 35, 351
Khamti, 297
Khan, Mr, 286–7, 289–94, 329
Khonsa, 291
Khrushchev, Nikita, 5
Khun Sa, 52, 55–6, 94, 354; *see also under* Chan Shee-fu
Kincaid, Eugenio, 99, 102
Kindrin Hka, 250, 251–2, 266
Kirkland, 332
Klerday, 331
Knapp-Fisher, Peter, 157
Ko River, 58; *see also under* Nam Ko
Kokangs, 34, 46, 58, 330–1, 353, 355
Kol Liang, Colonel, 27–9
Konshua, 26–7, 47
Kra Isthmus, 3
Kumawng *shagawng*, 171, 182–3, 185, 193, 195–6, 200, 212, 341
Kumhtat Gam, Major, 154–6, 158–69, 163–4, 183
Kunming, 251, 344
Kuomintang, 48, 56–7, 351–2
Kutkai, 57, 79, 94, 200, 288
Kyaw Nyein, 351
Kyaw Nyunt, 29, 50, 52, 60–5, 70
Kyaw Zaw, 353

Kyi Myint, General, 29–31, 46–56, 58–61, 156, 287

La Awng, 105; *see also under* Alex
La Nan, Captain, 147–8
La Ring, Reverend, 98–9, 101–2
La Roi, 198, 201, 203, 210
Labangs, 69
Lahkra Kawng, 181, 183, 344
Lahpai, 68–9, 174–5, 200
Lahpai Zau Awng, 166–8, 173
Lahtaw, 69, 174–5
Lahu(s), 34, 46, 57, 58, 67, 233, 331, 352–3
Lahu National Organization (LNO), 73n
Lakawng Bum, 149, 154, 155, 171, 176, 182, 339, 344
Lama, 282–3, 289, 290, 293–4
Lamontagne, Ray, 310, 316, 326, 330
Lamun-Lisu, 207
Lamung, 175
Landour Mission Language School, 254
Laos, 3, 56, 57n
Larsson, Berit, 155, 270–2, 303, 309, 312, 323
Larsson, Mats, 2, 6, 8–9, 13, 15–18, 20–3, 25, 31–3, 45, 49, 51–4, 57, 59–60, 63–5, 72, 75–7, 82, 85, 95, 97, 100–1, 103, 106–10, 112, 115, 117–18, 120, 124–5, 128–9, 131–2, 134–5, 137–9, 144–50, 155, 158–62, 163–4, 166, 168–70, 172, 177–8, 181–2, 184–6, 189–94, 196, 201, 210–11, 213, 235, 238, 241, 243, 246–8, 250, 253–6, 258–1, 261, 264–7, 269–71, 274, 276–7, 280, 283, 290, 293, 296, 298, 300–1, 304, 310, 312, 314–17, 320, 326–30, 336, 337–41; *see also under* Clear Second Son
Lashi(s), 67–8, 70, 174, 207
Lashio, 23–5, 79
Latut Shawng, Major, 154, 161, 163–4
Lawk Hpyu, 115
Lawrence, T. E., 76
Leach, E. R., 1, 68, 71n
Leary, Timothy, 135
Ledo, 246, 277
Lhasa, 293
Likhapani, 277
Lintner, Bertil, 29n, 31–2, 61n, 72–3, 77, 156, 160, 165, 199, 200n, 205, 271–3, 304, 339
Lisa's, 10, 13
Lisu, 67–8, 70, 115, 118, 121, 123, 124, 154, 174, 187, 198, 207–9, 213–14, 216–17, 221, 223–34, 236–40, 243–51, 253–62, 264, 281, 285, 291, 297–8, 330, 337
Liu Shaoqi, 29
Livingstone, David, 3
Lo-Hsing Han, 331n
Lohpa Bum, 241
Loi Dau, 94
Loije, 107
Loingu Bum, 129–30, 138
Long River, 58; *see also* Nam Long
Longchuan River, 17–19
Longling, 16, 17
Lopez, Tony, 332
Lott, Senator, 312–13
Lung Ga Hka, 125
Lung Hpraw Yang, 106–7, 115
Lyon, Albert, 99

Ma Ding Yaw, 187
Macau, 9
McCoy, Alfred, 56

Machiavelli, Niccolò, 202
Maclean, Fitzroy, 76
Madai Hpraw Nga, 69
Mae Hong Son, 7
Mae Sariang, 7
Mae Tari, 331
Mae Tha Waw, 331
Maji, 200–1
Majoi Shingra Bum, 67
Malang, 129
Mali Hka, 67–8, 78, 86, 131, 154, 156, 161, 163, 171, 173–6, 341, 344
Mali-Hkrang Walawng, 182
Mamio, Inspector, 274–5, 277, 289
Man Guo, 19, 21–3, 27
Man Hpang, 94
Man Je, 95
Man Win, 117, 121, 129
Manau Mam-htu, 187
Mandalay, 7, 23, 57, 135, 195, 220, 270, 356
Manerplaw, 94, 332, 357
Mangshi, 12, 14–18, 48, 59, 62
Manhkring Conference, 167–8, 168, 335
Mansai, C. P., 278, 289–90, 296, 300, 303–5, 323
Maran(s), 68–9, 174–5, 200
Maran Naw, Private, 103, 124, 142, 182, 185, 213, 215, 217, 220–2, 239, 243
Margherita, 277, 290, 295, 300
Marip(s), 69, 174–5
Martaban, Gulf of, 332
Maru(s), 67–70, 174
Masters, John, 204, 343
Matsihku Bum, 237
Matsdotter, Moa, 330
Maung Maung, 355
Maw Po Kay, 331
Mawlaik, 195
Maymyo, 79
Mazup Yang, 145
Mej, 299–301, 304, 314, 323
Mekong, 3, 46, 54
  Upper Mekong, 227
Mellah, 331
Meng Hai, 61
Merrill's Marauders, 56, 78
Metemma, 3
Meugahpi, 252, 259
Meyan, Narayan S., 280–2, 289–91, 295–6, 298–300, 302–8, 313–18, 323, 325, 330
Miau, 238, 241, 246–8, 251, 259–60, 262, 264, 267–8, 274, 277, 307, 318, 320–1, 330, 344
Midi, 246, 249, 253
Mimo, 111, 124, 134, 145, 174, 190–1
Mindon, King, 346
Mirante, Edith, 74n
Mishmi, 274, 281, 342
Mississippi, 140, 204, 313
Mizo, Zaua, 262–3
Mizo National Front, 262
Mizos, 262, 294, 320
Model Brigade, 89, 170
Mogaung, 173
Mogaung District, 66
Mogaung River, 68
Moh Heng, 55n, 73n, 331n, 354
Mohnyin, 82
Moi River, 58
Molloy, Kit, 328
Mon National Defence Organization (MNDO), 41, 349
Möng Bo, 24–7, 48
Möng Fang, 91
Möng Hsat, 57
Möng Ko, 19, 27–8, 45, 47–8, 51, 53–4, 57–8, 61, 70, 75, 80,

86–7, 92, 95, 104, 144, 156, 270, 285, 288–9, 330, 341, 344
Möng Leng, 46
Möng Nye, 94
Möng Pa Liao, 57
Möng Tai Army (MTA), 52, 55n, 73n, 94, 354, 357
Möng Ya, 90
Möng Yu, 23–4
Mongolia, 67, 324
Mongol(s), 75, 145
Monkey Tree Hill, 242
Mon(s), 34, 40–2, 57–8, 67, 94, 331, 349, 351–3
Montague–Chelmsford Report, 347
Monywa, 7
Morrison, Ann, 313
Morrison, Ian, 37
Morse, Betty, 229, 232–3
Morse, Bobby, 227, 234
Morse, Camille, 227
Morse, David, 227, 230–1, 233
Morse, Deedee, 227
Morse, Drema Esther, 226–7, 231, 233
Morse, Eugene, 227, 230, 233–4, 343
Morse, Genevieve, 227, 230
Morse, Gertrude, 226–7, 233–4, 241, 253
Morse, Helen, 227, 231, 233, 253
Morse, Jeannette, 227, 253
Morse, Jesse, 231–3
Morse, Joni, 227, 229, 232–3, 250
Morse, LaVerne, 227
Morse, Lucy, 227
Morse, Margaret, 227
Morse, Marilyn, 237, 233, 253
Morse, Robert, 227–30, 232–3, 242–3, 250–1
Morse, Ron, 227
Morse, Russell, 226–7, 230, 233–4, 241, 251, 253
Morse, Sam, 227
Morse, Stephen, 101, 227, 233, 250, 344
Morse, Tom, 227
Morse family, 95, 101, 225, 228–30, 232–3, 236, 241–3, 250
Moscow, 3, 8, 41, 274, 328
Moulmein, 41, 349
Moynihan, Senator, 312
Muhpa Lo, 251–3, 255
Muivah, Thuingaleng, 284n
mujahid, 349, 352
Muladi, 226–7, 231, 238
Mung Hkum Yang, 121–2
Munga Zup, 111–12
Mukerji, Dr, 267–8
Murphy, Dervla, 273
Mussoorie, 254
Myanmar National Solidarity Party, 331n
Myaungmya, 38
Myitkyina, 39, 69, 76, 78, 81, 87–8, 93, 95, 100, 115, 117, 142, 155, 164–5, 169, 173, 177, 188, 220, 343
Myochit Parti, 347

N Chyaw Tang, Major, 78–80, 87, 96–8, 102, 127, 165, 173, 206n, 243
N Myen Hka, 119
N'Gawk Sinwa, Captain, 154, 163
N'Gum La, 166–7, 169, 171–2, 183
N'krawn Hka, 130
N'Lam Awng, 143, 146, 148, 155, 164
N'rawng Kawng, 164–5, 171
N'wan Hka, 122, 123, 177
Naga Hills, 195, 283
Naga National Council (NNC), 284n
Nagaland, 31, 199, 272, 284, 310

Nagas, 31, 34–5, 58, 67, 69, 77, 195, 205, 232, 247, 278, 281, 283–6, 294, 301, 304–5, 320, 330, 352
Nam Hkam, 28, 101, 186
Nam Hkam Pa, 93
Nam Hkam Shweli Valley Baptist High School, 88, 95
Nam Ko, 47, 62
Nam Long, 18–19, 29, 47, 57, 330, 344; *see also* Long River
Nam Tabet, 111, 344; *see also under* Tabak Hka
Namhpakka, 23–4, 57
Namlang River, 227
Namyung, 198, 232–3, 237–8, 241, 250–1, 340
Nanding He, 46
Nath, Mr, 294–5, 297–9
National Coalition Government for the Union of Burma (NCGUB), 332–3, 356
National Democratic Army/New Democratic Force, 331n
National Democratic Front (NDF), 73, 91, 94, 262, 330, 332, 353–6
National League for Democracy (NLD), 37n, 332n, 334n, 355–7
National Security Council (NSC), 55, 58, 94, 332
National Socialist Council of Nagaland (NSCN), 206n, 284
National United Front (NUF), 351
National United Party, 355
National Unity Front of Arakan (NUFA), 73n
Naw Lawn, 105; *see also* Paul
Naw Seng, 61, 79, 90, 349
Ne Win, General, 28, 41–2, 44–5, 51, 74, 80–1, 88–9, 93, 101, 105, 135, 167–8, 199, 202, 225, 228, 349, 351–5
Nehru, Pandit Jawaharlal, 84, 202, 275, 281
Nepal, 302
New Delhi, *see under* Delhi
New Mon State Party (NMSP), 73n, 351, 356–7
Ngalung Ga, 246
Ngaw La Bum, 182
Ngaw Yi Bum, 182
Nhku, 190
Nhkum(s), 69, 174–5
Nicholas II, 5
Nippon Oil, 332
Nixon, Richard, 6
Nizhneudinsk, 5
Nlum Zau Awng, 143
Nmai Hka, 67–8, 86, 103, 131, 132, 138, 140, 344
Noa Dihing, 67, 244, 257–9, 267, 298, 343–4
Noah, 244–7, 291, 294, 297
Noom Suk Harn, 331n, 351
North Thailand Christian Mission, 233
Northeast Command, 61
Northern Bureau, 27, 29, 31–2, 48–51, 61n, 75, 270–1, 287–8
Northern Kachin Levies, 56, 78
Nu Jiang, 12, 14–15, 17, 31 *see also* Salween, River
Nullabor, 3
Nung(s), 67n, 68, 174, 207

Oxford, 2–3, 8, 139, 224, 271, 325–6, 328, 330, 344

Padaung(s), 34, 41
Pajau Bum, 53, 71–2, 75, 77, 82–3, 86–7, 95, 97–8, 103, 114, 127, 138–9, 155–6, 171–3, 186, 196, 205, 242, 271, 285, 323, 339, 344

Palaung(s), 19n, 28, 34, 58–9, 66, 91, 331n, 352–3
Palaung State Liberation Party (PSLP), 73n, 331n
Palaw, 74
Pan Lawng Yang Mare, 174, 175, 182
Pang Sau Yang, 150–1
Panghsang, 46, 51, 53, 330
Panglong, 40–2, 74, 79, 88, 91, 144, 167–8, 262, 335, 339, 349, 351
Pao(s), 34, 41–3, 67, 94, 284n, 331n, 349, 352–3
Pao National Organization (PNO), 73n, 331n
Papun, 38
Pascagoula, 313
Pascal, Father, 38
Pass Christian, 313
Patkai range, 58, 67, 195, 244, 246, 251, 257–8, 278, 295, 341, 344
Patna River, 324
Patrick Henderson & Company, 36
Patriotic Burmese Forces (PBF), 39, 41, 348
Paul, 105, 108–9, 111, 117, 122, 124, 133–4, 145, 148, 149, 171, 177, 182–3, 195, 210, 226, 235, 243, 247, 249; *see also* Naw Lawn
Pegu Yomas, 29
Peking, 3, 6, 8, 15, 296, 352
Pelletreau, Bob, 310
People's Army, 27, 31–2, 46, 51–2, 257, 286, 320
People's Liberation Army (PLA), 22, 24, 26, 57, 86, 352–3
People's Volunteer Organization (PVO), 348–50
Perm, 5
Peshus, 34
Peter, 105, 111, 113, 117, 143, 154, 174; *see also under* Wana Yaw Htung
Phalu, 331
Philip, 105, 113, 117–18, 122–6, 133–4, 136, 142, 145–7, 149, 153, 172, 177–87, 190–5, 200–1, 203–4, 208–10, 235, 247, 249; *see also under* Hkyen Naw
Phizo, Angami Zapu, 284
Pinawng Hka, 240
Pinawng Zup, 198, 206, 209, 216–17, 228, 238–41, 285, 291, 296, 344
Ponna, 7
Pradip, 300, 303–4
Premier, 332
Public Works Department (PWD), 258–61, 263, 264, 267, 318
Pum Pan, 153
Putao, 163, 177, 186, 208, 226, 229, 231–2, 237–8, 241, 250
Pyang Hka, 153–4

Queensland, 329

Rajput, 264
Rakhine(s), 34, 41–2, 58, 91, 94, 284n, 352–3
Rangoon, 7, 23–4, 35n, 36–7, 41, 49, 55n, 57, 72, 73n, 74, 79–81, 90–5, 120, 135, 156, 165n, 220, 226, 270–1, 285, 288, 320, 330–1, 333, 339–41, 350–4, 357–8
Rangoon University, 29, 37, 42, 88, 347, 352
Ravi, Inspector, 274–6
Rawang(s), 67–9, 174, 207, 227, 232–3, 297, 337
Reagan, President, 113
Red Army, 72

Red Cross, 47
Red Guards, 29, 48, 56, 353
Roberts, William Henry, 99–100
Rohingyas, 34, 41
Roosevelt, Franklin, 78n
Rowland, Geoffrey, 203
Royal Dutch, 332
Ruili, 16–19, 63, 344

Saboi Mare, 154
Sadi, 250
Sadiya, 68, 243
Sadodi, 246
Sadon, 173
Sadon District, 43
Sai Lek, 30, 53, 56, 289, 330
Salons, 34
Salween District, 38
Salween River, 15n, 33, 46–7, 53, 58, 67–8, 94; *see also* Nu Jiang
Upper Salween, 227
Sama hills, 75, 173
Sama Pa, 108, 111
San Awng, Sergeant, 53, 103, 122, 124–5, 128, 131, 136, 142, 144–5, 150–1, 153, 155, 161, 175, 178, 180, 186, 194, 200–1, 206, 257, 249
San Yu, General, 163
Sanjay, 303–4
Sao Shwe Thaike, 88, 351
Sapru, Colonel, 276, 283
Sara Kahtawng, 204
Sasans, 67n
Saur, Chaunday, 262–3, 266–7
Saya San, 36, 347
Scott, Ian, 35n, 179
Seagrave, Dr Gordon, 28, 101
Seagrave, Sterling, 101n
Seagrim, Major Hugh, 37
Second World War, 56, 76, 89, 153, 168, 202, 277, 342
Sein Lwin, 45, 354–5
Sein Win, 356
Seng Hpung, 27–31, 33, 45–6, 53–5, 57–8, 60–2, 64–5, 86–7, 93, 103–4, 106–13, 115, 117–40, 142–7, 150, 153, 155–6, 158–61, 163, 165–6, 169–82, 184, 186, 189–94, 196, 199–202, 205–6, 209–13, 227, 237–40, 242–3, 245–8, 266, 335–6, 339
Seng Leng Bum, 129, 138
Sethi, R. B, 321
Sha It Yang, 103, 105–6, 112
Shadip, 68, 105
Shalawt Kawng, 116–18
Shameen Island, 110
Shan State, 28, 40–1, 56–7, 69, 94, 101, 331, 349, 351, 353
Shan State Army (SSA), 53, 56, 331n, 352–3, 357
Shan State Nationalities People's Liberation Organization, 331n
Shan State Progress Party (SSPP), 30, 46, 53, 73n, 91, 330
Shan(s), 10, 19–20, 28, 30, 34, 40–2, 47, 58–9, 63, 66, 68–9, 77, 79, 83, 89, 111, 129, 143–4, 146, 168, 187n, 197, 262, 297, 346, 349, 351–3, 357; *see also* Dai
Shan United Army, 55n
Shan United Revolutionary Army, 55n
Shang Ngaw *shagawng*, 149
Shar'ya (Nizhni Novgorod), 4
Sharaw Kawng, 107
Sharaw Kawng Nleng, 176
Sharma, Lieutenant, 274–7
Shatnga Bum, 182
Shau Kawng, 153
Shelton, Dr Albert, 227
Sherdi, 239, 246–7, 252, 257–9, 261; *see also under* Gandhigram
Shing Rai Ga, 176

Shingra dynasty, 69
Shiransam Bum, 238
Shwegu Plain, 89
Shweli River, 28, 47, 58, 62
Siba, Prince, 84
Siberia, 3, 6, 274
Sibsagar, 84
Sikiani, Sub-Inspector, 279, 282
Sikkim, 293
Siliguri, 324
Silverstein, Professor Josef, 33n, 36, 356
Simalaik, 44
Sin Wa, Captain, 176–9, 189
Sin Wa Nawng, Sama *Duwa*, 135, 167, 173
Singapore, 23, 332
Singh, Devi, 264–6, 268
Singh, Harinder Prasad, 300
Singhpo, 281
Sinha, Major, 283, 294, 325
Sinkiang, 33
Sinlum, 107
Sinlumkaba, 173
Sinyetha Parti, 36, 347
Sittang River, 33
Sitwundan, 349–50
Slaughtered Wild Ox, Mount, 139, 141–2; *see also under* Hpaw Lam Hpya Bum
Smith, Rennie, 312–13, 327–8
Soviet Union, 3
Srinagar, 276
Stables, 351
Stanley, Henry, 3
State Department, 3, 92, 94, 302, 310, 312
State Law and Order Restoration Committee (SLORC), 58n, 331n, 332, 355–7
State Peace and Development Council (SPDC), 357
Steel Brothers, 36
Steere, Bishop, 3
Stevenson, Commissioner Henry Noel, 74, 167–8, 335, 364
Stilwell, General, 78
Stoddart, Charles, 5
Strawberry Hill, 230
Sumpawng Yaw, 207
Sumprabum, 171, 173, 199
Supsa Hka, 185, 190, 193–4, 344
Sut Awng, 161
Sut Awng Yang, 194, 203
Sut Lut Gam, Captain First Son of, 70, 96
Suu Aung, 50, 52, 59
Svahnström, Annika, 325, 327
Sverdlovsk (Ekaterinburg), 5
Sweden, 6, 72, 100n, 160, 265, 296, 329
Szechuan, 67

Tabak Hka, 111–12, 115, 344; *see also* Nam Tabet
Tabyi Hka, 212, 214
Tachilek, 1
Tai, 66
Tai Revolutionary Council, 55n
Tanai Hka, 185, 194–6, 203, 283, 344; *see also* Upper Chindwin
Tanai Len Mare, 204, 207
Tara Hka, 149, 152–3, 344
Tara Yang, 156
Tartar(s), 8, 145
Tarung Hka, 195, 198, 233, 238–40, 246, 396, 344
Tarung, 198, 216
Tatmadaw, 42–3; *see also* Burma Army
Taungdut, 195
Taunggyi, 88
Tawang Hka, 124, 195, 206, 208, 215, 217, 220–1, 228, 236–8, 243, 264, 296, 344